FAIR DIVISION AND COLLECTIVE WELFARE

FAIR DIVISION AND COLLECTIVE WELFARE

Hervé Moulin

The MIT Press
Cambridge, Massachusetts
London, England

First MIT Press paperback edition, 2004

© 2003 Massachusetts Institute of Technology

This book was set in Times Roman by Interactive Composition Corporation and was printed and bound in United States of America.

Library of Congress Cataloging-in-Publication Data

Moulin, Hervé.
   Fair division and collective welfare / Hervé Moulin.
     p.   cm.
   Includes bibliographical references and index.
   ISBN 978-0-262-13423-1 (hc. : alk. paper)—978-0-262-63311-6 (pb. : alk. paper)
    1. Welfare economics. 2. Equality—Economic aspects. 3. Income distribution. 4. Wealth—Moral and ethical aspects. 5. Distributive justice. I. Title.

HB846 .M68   2003
330.12′6—dc21   2002075387

10 9 8 7 6 5 4 3

Contents

1 Microeconomic Foundations

1.1 Fairness: Equal and Unequal Treatment

Justice is blind, and fairness requires anonymous rules of arbitration. "Equals should be treated equally, and unequals unequally, in proportion to relevant similarities and differences" (*Nicomachean Ethics*). Aristotle's celebrated maxim, in its modern rendition, is the first step toward the formal definition of distributive fairness.

Equal treatment of equals is a clear-cut principle, an axiom in the terminology of this book, and the minimal test of fairness throughout the book: if two persons have identical characteristics in all dimensions relevant to the allocation problem at hand, they should receive the same treatment—the same share of goods, of decision power, or of whatever is being distributed. *Unequal treatment of unequals,* on the contrary, is a vague principle open to many interpretations.

Four elementary ideas are at the heart of most nontechnical discussions of distributive justice. They organize neatly our thinking about conflictual interpretations of fairness. The four ideas are *exogenous rights, compensation, reward,* and *fitness;* I discuss them briefly below in that order. A more detailed discussion is the subject of section 2.1.

Equal treatment of equals is the archetypal example of an exogeneous right. Consider the democratic principle "one person, one vote," expressing the basic requirement that voting procedures must not be biased in favor of particular electors, and implemented by the simple device of anonymous ballots (I can't tell who casts which ballot; hence I can't give more weight to the vote of a particular citizen).

One could argue that certain differences among voters are entirely relevant to the way that we should evaluate their votes. At one extreme, we find *conscientious* citizens who collect information about the issues at hand and discuss them with other citizens; at the other extreme, the *whimsical* citizens use their voting right arbitrarily, for spurious reasons or no reason at all, and refuse to make any effort toward gaining some understanding of the issues. Surely the difference between conscientious and whimsical voters affect the normative "value" of their respective ballots, a fact that the "one person, one vote" principle refuses to acknowledge. The exogeneous right to an equal vote is a normative postulate that suffers very few exceptions (insanity, certain criminal records). Other times saw other postulates: medieval religious assemblies typically gave more weight to the vote of their more senior members, and voting rights were commonly linked to wealth throughout the nineteenth century.

When differences in individual characteristics are deemed relevant to fairness, the two ideas of compensation and reward come into play. In order to meet their needs of some essential commodities, such as the regular intake of some vitamins, adequate shelter and clothing—some of us need more resources than others—and the compensation principle justifies this inequality in order to restore equality (or at least, diminish inequality) of the shares of the essential commodity in question. Those of us who cannot metabolize a key vitamin from their food deserve a free supply in pills, those who lost their home to a natural disaster deserve assistance, those who did not receive adequate basic education deserve a tuition waiver, and so on. The common feature in these instances of compensation is to justify unequal shares of certain resources for the sake of equalizing the shares of a higher-order commodity.

We reward an employee for her contribution to the profit of the firm, an athlete for his contribution to the success of the team, an investor for the risk he took in financing the project. In each case a larger share of the pie is justified by a larger responsibility in making the pie. Symmetrically I must bear a share of joint costs commensurate to my own impact on these costs: businesses sharing a parking lot find it fair to split its maintenance cost in proportion to the traffic that each business generates.

To illustrate the tensions among the three principles above, consider the division of the parent's estate between siblings. Compensation suggests to give more to the poorest sibling, who needs more the extra cash. The devoted child who took care of the parents' business deserves to be rewarded by a bigger share. Finally, strict equality of the shares, no matter what, is a popular and haggle-free division method according to exogenous rights.[1]

The last commonsense principle of distributive justice, fitness, is the most subtle of the four, and the most fertile ground for microeconomic analysis. Fitness says to give the resources to whomever makes the best use of it: the flute to the flutist, the books to the avid reader, the voting right to the wiser among us, and so on. The difficulty is the interpretation of the "best" usage. If Ann can play popular melodies on the flute that most everybody enjoys, whereas Bob can play esoteric atonal music that a small minority loves intensely, who should get the instrument? The interpretation of the "wise" voters, or the "best" reader is equally fuzzy. In microeconomic language the problem is to make intercomparison of individual welfares, and deal with trade-offs such as the mild pleasure of many when Ann is playing versus the intense aesthetic emotions of a few when Bob does.

The subject of this book is the contribution of modern microeconomic thinking to distributive justice. I submit that this approach is the only conceptual framework to date in which not only fitness (as just described) but also compensation and reward can be analyzed with mathematical rigor.

The main building block is the concept of individual welfare, modeled first with the help of a utility function transforming physical resources into utility, and more generally, some resources devoid of ethical content into a higher-order resource, which is the object

---

1. Giving more to the more loving child who took care of his parents' needs is also an exogeneous right, inasmuch as the loving care is unrelated to the value of the estate.

of our normative judgment. Thus compensation amounts to the equalization of individual utilities and the maximization of their sum is the interpretation of fitness known as classical utilitarianism: chapters 2 and 3.

A more versatile modeling of welfare is as an ordinal preference relation, describing individual choices but pointedly avoiding the cardinal statement conveyed by the measurement of utility: chapters 4, 6, and 7.

The collective welfare approach remains the most influential application of economic analysis to distributive justice. It offers the first entirely rigorous definition of fitness as Pareto optimality, and operational definitions of fairness by means of collective utility functions—in the cardinal version—and of social welfare orderings—in the ordinal version. It is the subject of chapters 2, 3, and 4, and its methodological premises are reviewed in the next two sections.

If the collective welfare approach yields a systematic interpretation of the fitness and compensation principles, it gives no basis to discuss either reward or exogenous rights such as private or common ownership of resources. In the last fifty years microeconomic theory has made significant progress toward understanding these two pervasive principles. The two most important discoveries are the formula called the Shapley value (chapters 5 and 6) and the test of no envy (chapters 6 and 7): they offer, respectively, an interpretation of the reward principle in the context of production, and of fair division of resources under common ownership.

In sections 1.4 and 1.5, I introduce the microeconomic background in which these two concepts are born, namely the management of externalities by private agreements (free trade under private ownership) or public contracts (normative principles of equity). Then in section 1.6, I describe the organization of the book and review the contents of its successive chapters. Section 1.7 concludes with an introduction to the literature.

1.2   Collective Welfare: Cardinal

The postulate of rational choice for individual decision-making is the central assumption of microeconomic analysis. It posits that individual choices consist in maximizing a given preference relation (a complete and transitive binary relation over the feasible choices) representing the welfare of the agent in question. Outside economics, this postulate is not universally accepted, and neither is its prerequisite of methodological individualism.

Methodological individualism is the intellectual construction on which the political philosophy known as liberalism is founded. The central postulate is that we can draw a clear line between the self and the world: on the one hand, the human subjects, each one endowed with values, preferences, experiences, beliefs, and so on, and on the other hand, the material resources of the world, natural and technological. Each individual person is an irreducible atom of the social body, and the public authority can no more alter individual values than the chemist can alter the inner structure of the atoms. Individuals act on the world by consuming or transforming its resources, and by interacting with other individuals (to influence their values and beliefs as well as their actions). The collective authority merely affects the appropriation of the resources of the world (how and by whom are these resources transformed, consumed?) and the interpersonal interactions (who can do what to whom?); it has no tools to influence individual values.

The most sophisticated model of methodological individualism is microeconomic analysis. The physical description of the world is captured by a set of *feasible states of the world* (each state specifies who consumes what resources, who works and for how long, etc.). The values of an individual agent (or citizen) are described by her *welfare,* measuring the degree to which a certain state of the world fulfills her values. And finally, the *rights* of an agent specify which actions are open to her (physically feasible and legally permitted), how these actions influence the state of the world, and in particular, how they interact with other agent's actions. Examples include private ownership (under which all voluntary trades are feasible) and political rights (specifying how each citizen can influence public policy).

Given the feasible states of the world and each citizen endowed with her welfare and her rights, the liberal social order results from the interaction of free wills. Each citizen pursues her own good by her own means; in other words, she chooses her actions (within the limits of her rights) in order to maximize her own welfare. When every citizen acts in this way, the eventual state of the world results from the balance of these individual powers and is called the equilibrium outcome. The only role of the collective authority is to enforce the free exercise of individual rights without influencing in any way the individual choices or the resulting state of the world.

There are two sides to distributive justice in the microeconomic world: Is the distribution of rights fair? Is the outcome of the game fair? Procedural justice addresses the former question, endstate justice addresses the latter.

The collective welfare approach focuses on endstate justice exclusively, by assuming that the decision power lies entirely in the hands of a judge, a benevolent dictator, who must propose a fair and principled compromise taking into account the conflicting interests and unequal characteristics of the participants. This is a convenient stylized description of the public authority, or of the decision-making process of an ad hoc committee. A full-fledged analysis encompassing the procedural and endstate aspects of distributive justice is currently out of our analytical reach, even for a question as basic as the design of a simple voting rule. In this book the discussion of procedural justice within the collective welfare model reduces to a few remarks about the incentives consequences of various collective utility functions in chapter 3, and the brief discussion of strategic voting in chapter 4 (see section 4.3). Procedural justice in fair division receives more attention; see chapter 6, in particular, section 6.4, and chapter 7, sections 7.1 to 7.3.

Thanks to the elimination of individual rights, the welfarist approach to distributive justice provides systematic methods to resolve the conflict between individual welfares. It does not endow the feasible states of the world with any normative content, regards them merely as means toward the satisfaction of individual values. This point of view distinguishes the welfarist methodology from the fair division problems of chapters 5, 6, and 7. There the production and allocation of physical resources play a key role in the definition of fairness.[2]

The concept of individual welfare can be modeled in two ways: as a *cardinal* utility function or an *ordinal* preference relation. These two models partition the welfarist approach in two branches of comparable importance.

Cardinal welfare is measured by a number, called the utility level, and the utility levels of different agents are comparable. The following statement is meaningful: "eating this cookie makes my utility increase (or decrease!) more than your utility would increase if you eat the cookie in question." In this context the interpretation of the sum of individual utilities as an index of collective fitness makes good sense. Imagine that we must allocate scarce medical resources among a given set of critically ill patients (e.g., that blood for transfusion is in short supply and must be rationed). If we can estimate, for each patient, the probability of recovery as a function of the amount of blood he receives, a sensible rule is to distribute the blood so as to maximize the sum of these probabilities, namely the expected total number of recoveries.[3] In other words, we take the probability of recovery as a proxy for utility, follow Bentham's *classical utilitarian* imperative, and so we maximize the sum total of individual utilities.

The more general tool of a *collective utility function* aggregates (by means of a mechanical formula) a profile of individual cardinal utilities into an index of collective utility. This operation is naively anthropomorphic if we try to interpret collective utility as a measure of the "welfare" of the group, or that of its benevolent dictator. However, as a mere technique for selecting a reasonable compromise, it is strikingly effective and easily applicable.

Collective utility functions are well suited to explore the trade-offs between the principles of compensation and fitness. Maximizing the classical utilitarian sum of individual utilities often results in "sacrificing" some individuals: if a majority of the roommates want to watch only sports on the only TV set, the minority who wishes to catch the news will never have its way under the utilitarian rule. Thus this particular collective utility function is orthogonal to the concern for compensation: in the TV example, the latter would require the roommates to tune in the news some of the time.

---

2. For instance, the Shapley value is computed directly from the cost or production function.

3. This is indeed a common approach to deal with the medical triage problem. See section 2.2.

By contrast, the *egalitarian* utility function is the embodiment of compensation in the welfarist model. This function is computed as the smallest individual utility; hence its maximization leads the benevolent dictator to implement a tiny utility increase for the worst-off member of the group, even if this implies a huge loss for many well-to-do agents. In the TV example the egalitarian judge awards equal time shares to the sport and news channels regardless of the relative support of the two programs, which is surely an unreasonable solution when the minority is small enough.

Chapter 3 describes a rich family of collective utility functions, ranging continuously from the classical utilitarian to the egalitarian one. The *Nash* collective utility function stands out as a remarkable member of this family: it computes the collective utility as the *product* of individual utilities. It strikes an appealing compromise between the two polar methods: in the TV example, it splits viewing time between the two channels in proportion to the number of their supporters.[4]

1.3   Collective Welfare: Ordinal

The core of the cardinal welfarist model is the feasibility of objective interpersonal comparisons of utility. This is not plausible when choices are governed by subjective tastes and values instead of an objective index related to health, nutrition, or any other primary human need. In the TV example, individual tastes for sports versus news are taken as given and radical: those who like sports never show any interest in news (and vice versa); any amount of time spent watching sports, however small, is better than any amount spent on news. Moreover taking "viewing time" as a proxy for utility amounts to ignore the variations in the intensity of feelings among the roommates, from the sports fanatic to the nearly indifferent. Measuring subjective feelings as an outside observer is, for all practical purposes, impossible. If we ask the agents themselves to help us in this assessment (by asking them to fill out a questionnaire), we can expect gross strategic manipulations, which is especially difficult in the TV example.

The objective measurement of utility is not only practically hard to impossible, it is also a logical contradiction of methodological individualism. A fully "objective" notion of welfare is alienated from the "subject" individual; hence it denies the pluralism of individual values, and defeats the purpose of methodological individualism. Paraphrasing Sen, classical utilitarianism views the individuals as petrol tanks among whom we must distribute the gasoline of the world.

---

4. See example 3.6.

There is a private, inviolable sphere around each of us that cannot be captured by an objective measurement, that cannot even be apprehended by an outside observer, where the self is defined independently of any social construction. In this sphere are produced some components of our personality of great relevance to social interactions—some of our value systems, such as our philosophical and political convictions, our religious beliefs, as well as our body, our psychological disposition to happiness—see next point—and much more. The point is that the public authority should not be allowed to control, or even monitor, these components of our own welfare: even the staunchest welfarist must concede this kernel of inviolable rights. The hope of an objective measurement of welfare is as unrealistic as that of comparing by a common index two different value systems, two outlooks on life. Bentham's sum of pleasures and pains is nonsensical (on stilts!) because my pain and your pain are incommensurable.

The last objection to the interpersonal comparison of welfares is a moral one. It is the strongest of the three.

An important element of personal responsibility is our ability to transform resources into welfare (our good or bad nature, our optimism or pessimism, etc.). Ignoring this important factor, the welfarist allocating resources in order to equalize welfare penalizes those agents who scale down their expectations to their lot.

The story of Tiny Tim, physically challenged and poor, yet fiercely happy is a case in point. Tim will be denied a larger share of resources on account of his good nature, of his ability to generate much welfare from an objectively poor endowment of personal characteristics. The blasé John, on the other hand, is a wealthy spoiled brat with natural talents that he does not enjoy using, and expensive tastes; he gets thoroughly depressed if he cannot drink champagne. Because his depression is real, does John deserve extra cash to buy an adequate supply of Dom Perignon? Similarly, in a political election, paying attention to the intensity of feelings over the various candidates would amount to giving more weight to the opinion of a fanatic than a cool-headed citizen.

Is there a future for welfarism in a world where many—most—factors relevant to welfare escape the eye of, or should not be assessed by, the benevolent dictator? The answer is yes, provided that we replace utilities by *choice*. The *ordinal welfare* of an agent is d*efined* as the set of his choices. If we extract from individual welfares only the choice component (i.e., the underlying ordinal preferences), then we will be unable, by construction, to make any interpersonal comparisons of the levels of welfare; our social decisions will reflect equitable compromises between conflicting preferences/opinions, without any invasion of the private spheres where actual welfare (enjoyment, happiness) is produced.

Under the rational choice postulate, the choices of an agent maximize a certain *preference relation* over the potential outcomes (states of the world). In other words, this relation is a ranking of all outcomes from best to worst (indifferences are permitted) and from any feasible set of outcomes (the actual choice set); our agent picks the highest ones according to the ranking. An increase in his ordinal welfare means a switch to an outcome higher up on this relation, no more, no less. In particular, unlike a utility level, the notion of ordinal welfare is not logically separable from the physical states of the world under consideration.

All models of fair division in chapters 5, 6, and 7 are built upon ordinal preference relations. The common denominator of collective welfare in these models is the central notion of *Pareto optimality,* also called *efficiency.* An outcome x is Pareto inferior to another outcome y if every concerned agent views y as at least as desirable as x, and at least one of them views y as strictly more desirable than x. In other words, y stands at least as high as x in every agent's ranking (preference relation) and strictly higher for at least one agent. An outcome is *Pareto optimal* if it is Pareto inferior to no feasible outcome.

Pareto optimality is the single most important tool of normative economic analysis. Its desirability is undisputed. In the endstate version of distributive justice, it is the one requirement that cannot be dispensed with. Not so under procedural justice, where the informational context of the "procedure" may push the equilibrium outcome away from the Pareto frontier (the set of efficient outcomes).

Under ordinal preferences the welfarist program of anthropomorphic aggregation is alive and kicking. The tool is the aggregation of a profile of preference relations into a collective preference relation—just as in the cardinal world we aggregate a profile of individual utilities into a collective utility. The aggregation operator is called a *social welfare function,* and this concept is the object of chapter 4.

Because preference relations can only be defined within an explicit set of feasible outcomes, the aggregation method amounts to a decision process very much like voting, where the input (the ballot box) consists of a list of preference relations over the outcomes (candidates), and the output is to elect one particular outcome. The two objects, voting rules and social welfare functions, are so closely related that the two most important aggregation methods are directly adapted from two voting rules introduced more than two centuries ago by Condorcet and Borda.

Borda's proposal is to elicit from each voter a complete ranking of all candidates, and to record a score of 0 for the last ranked candidate, 1 for the next to last candidate, 2 for the next lowest one, and so forth. The total score awarded by all voters determines the winner. Condorcet's proposal elicits the same information but uses it to compute the majority relation: for any two candidates a, b it only records who wins the largest support when only these two are competing. The Condorcet winner is the candidate (if any) who wins all such pairwise contests.

The two rules above offer quite different interpretations of collective welfare. The majority relation compares any two candidates without taking into account their relative rankings with other candidates (a property known as *independence of irrelevant alternatives*). This ensures that the procedure is immune to strategic misreporting of one's preferences whenever the majority relation has no cycle. However, cyclical majorities do appear for some configurations of individual preferences, and this pattern is unavoidable for any minimally fair aggregation method under independence of irrelevant alternatives (Arrow's theorem).

Borda's scoring rule, on the other hand, is robust to the decentralization of the decision process among subsets of voters. It delivers a social ranking of the candidate that is not plagued by any cycle.

1.4   Externalities and Fair Division

In the welfarist world, the physical resources of the world are fuel for welfare and are pointedly devoid of any ethical content. The allocation of vitamins among medical patients is methodologically identical to that of good wines or subsidies for college education among siblings, or cocaine among drug dealers. Voting to choose the president for millions of citizens is conceptually identical to the choice of the wallpaper among a handful of office mates.

In real life, the physical characteristics of the resources we consume strongly influence our definition of the "fair" production and distribution of these resources. The economic concept of *externalities*, and the related notions of private and public goods, provide important insights into this complicated interaction.

Risky choices are an example of externalities: if I am hurt in an accident because I do not wear my seat belt, my welfare loss is the greatest, but part of the cost of treating me is ultimately borne by my fellow citizens. Therefore my decision to buckle up or not affects more than my own welfare. Polluting activities, the exploitation of exhaustible resources (fish in the sea), create externalities too: the more I fish, the more costly it is for others to capture a certain amount of fish.

A commodity is a *private good* if its consumption by one agent generates no externalities on other agents. Thus a fruit is a private good, whereas a cigarette consumed in a public place is not. A commodity is a (pure) *public good* if it must be consumed identically by all agents in a given community (the economic terminology speaks of consumption without exclusion and without rivalry). Thus the legal system, the police, as well as a radio broadcast (when everybody owns a receiver) are pure public goods. On the other hand, a road system entails partial rivalry (congestion occurs when the number of users is large enough) and possibly exclusion (if only cars with odd plate numbers are allowed to move on a certain day). Fishing in the sea involves a private good as input (fishing effort) and a private good as output (the catch) but partial rivalry—as well as no exclusion—on the *return* of output to input.

A central tenet of economic analysis is that competitive markets work well for the exchange and production of private commodities but do not work well when the consumption or production of these goods entails externalities (e.g., when some of them are public goods). "Working well" means to achieve an efficient (Pareto optimal) utilization of the resources, through the decentralized selfish behavior of the agents, as captured by Adam Smith's invisible hand paradigm.

The microeconomic models developed in chapters 5, 6, and 7 illustrate these two dual propositions of economic wisdom, and show their relevance to the fair division problems. Chapters 5 and 6 focus on the management of a commons, the oldest and simplest story where production externalities hinder efficiency if access to the commons is not regulated. Chapter 7 considers the efficient distribution of pure private goods by the invisible hand. I review the latter first.

Start from a distribution of the property rights over the private goods where every market participant is "small," in the sense that nobody owns a large fraction of the total endowment in the economy; the distribution of property rights is otherwise arbitrary. Then the strategic equilibrium of voluntary, mutually advantageous trades is Pareto optimal and decentralized by a competitive price signal, namely a price for every traded commodity. Each agent receives the price list and requests the net trade (i.e., what quantity of each good he wants to buy or to sell), maximizing his preference ordering given the budget constraint imposed by the prices. The sum of all net trades cancels out; hence it is feasible to meet the demand of every participant in the market.

The price list is the same for every agent, and all competitive net trades are worth zero at these prices. Every agent can afford everyone else's net trade, and the net trade one chooses is the best for her preferences. Therefore she prefers her net trade to everyone else's, and this is the sense in which competitive trade is fair. Whether or not we agree that the initial distribution of property rights is fair, the move from this inefficient initial allocation to the competitive one is fair in the sense just described.

Now consider the problem of dividing a common property, namely a pile of private goods on which all agents have identical rights (think of siblings splitting an estate). Transforming common property into equal shares of private property is unquestionably fair. On the other hand, the allocation of equal shares of all goods to all participants is inefficient, if differences in individual preferences allow for mutually advantageous trades. But the competitive allocation resulting from the initial distribution of equal shares is surely efficient. Moreover it is fair in the sense of the no-envy test: no agent i would prefer to receive agents j''s competitive lot rather than her own competitive lot. This follows, as above, from the fact that everyone chooses optimally from a common budget set (equivalently they can choose the same net trades and the initial lot is the same).

Chapter 7 examines the fair division method just described called the *competitive equilibrium with equal incomes*. The endstate of this solution is just because of no envy. The solution is also the strategic equilibrium of a just procedure, namely the trading game from equal endowments.

We observe in chapter 7 the deep technical link between the competitive equilibrium with equal incomes and the optimum of the Nash collective utility function. We further compare it with another solution of straightforward egalitarian inspiration, called the *egalitarian equivalent* solution.

We turn to the complex issue of fair division under production externalities, where we encounter a fundamental contribution of normative microeconomics originating in cooperative game theory. In the very simple models of the commons in chapters 5 and 6, a given technology is the common property of a set of users, and the problem is to exploit the technology fairly and efficiently. The first difficulty comes from the fact that individual actions (input contributions or output demands) are not aggregated additively by the technology: the marginal return of input or the marginal cost of output is not constant. Therefore we cannot easily separate the impact of a particular user's actions. This issue is at the heart of the reward principle (section 1.1) and is the subject of chapter 5, where efficiency considerations are mostly absent.

The Shapley value is a systematic formula used to divide a joint cost or a jointly produced output. It offers a reasonable definition and computation of the share of cost or surplus for which a user of the commons is deemed responsible. A simple example shows why this question requires a genuinely new interpretation of the reward principle.

This four-story building has one apartment on each of the second, third, and fourth floors; the three apartments are otherwise identical. The manager of the building wishes to split fairly the cost of running an elevator to the three apartments. The cost of an elevator serving only the second floor is $5,000. That of an elevator serving the second and third floors is $10,000. An elevator serving all floors would cost $40,000 because reaching the fourth floor requires structural changes to the building that could be avoided if the elevator shaft ends at the third floor. It has been decided to have the elevator serve all four floors.

The point of this example is that simple cost shares based on equality or proportionality contradict our intuition about individual responsibilities in total cost, as required by the reward principle.

Clearly apartment 4 (on the fourth floor) should be charged more than apartments 2 and 3, but how much more? Charging each apartment in proportion to the service (= number of floors transported) would give shares $1/6$, $2/6$, and $3/6$ respectively to apartments 2, 3, and 4: apartment 2 ends up paying $6,667 and apartment 3 pays $13,333, which is grossly unfair because each one of apartments 2 and 3 pays more than the full cost of an elevator stopping at its own floor.

A more reasonable set of shares would be based on the *stand-alone costs*. Here 5K, 10K, and 40K are the respective stand-alone costs of the three apartments. Dividing 40K in proportion to these costs yields:

apartment 2: $\dfrac{5}{5 + 10 + 40}\, 40,000 = \$6,636$

apartment 3: $\dfrac{10}{5 + 10 + 40}\, 40,000 = \$7,273$

apartment 4: $\dfrac{40}{5 + 10 + 40}\, 40,000 = \$29,091$

Apartments 2 and 3 are still subsidizing unfairly apartment 4 because their joint share is $909 higher than the cost of an elevator stopping at the third floor!

The Shapley value in this example simply splits the cost of each segment of the elevator (from floor 1 to 2, 2 to 3, and 3 to 4) among the users of that segment. Thus the first segment is split three ways, the second is split equally between apartments 3 and 4, the third is charged to apartment 4 alone:

apartment 2: $\dfrac{1}{3}\, 5,000 = \$1,667$

apartment 3: $\dfrac{1}{3}\, 5,000 + \dfrac{1}{2}\, 5,000 = \$4,167$

apartment 4: $\dfrac{1}{3}\, 5,000 + \dfrac{1}{2}\, 5,000 + 30,000 = \$34,167$

In general, the Shapley value assigned to each agent is her expected marginal cost (or surplus) when agents are randomly ordered with uniform probability on all orderings. This formula has strong normative foundations, expressed in a handful of different axiomatizations discovered after Shapley's initial characterization half a century ago. Two of these axiomatizations are discussed in chapter 5.

The applications of the Shapley value are remarkably versatile, as the examples in chapters 5 and 6 demonstrate abundantly. It is the most important contribution of game theory to distributive justice.

In chapter 6 the fairness (reward) and efficiency issues are addressed jointly in a simple model of the commons with variable returns, where all agents may consume at most one indivisible unit of identical output (service), and they only differ with respect to their willingness to pay for the service. Free access to the commons means that each agent decides to "buy" service or not and total cost is equally divided between all buyers. The strategic equilibrium of this natural procedure may, however, be severely inefficient: this difficulty is known as the *tragedy of the commons*.

Because individual preferences (willingness to pay) vary, efficient use of the commons commands to serve the agents with the largest willingness to pay, up to the "marginal" agent whose willingness to pay barely exceeds the marginal cost of production. Other agents are not served, and must be fairly compensated. We compare three competing interpretations of fairness.

The first one is the no-envy test, whereby the "efficient" agents pay the marginal cost of service and the balance (revenue collected at that price minus total cost of production) is divided equally among all agents, efficient and inefficient alike. The corresponding solution is the competitive equilibrium with equal incomes discussed above.

The second solution is defined by the property that any agent's share of surplus (for an efficient agent: willingness to pay for service minus his payment; for an inefficient agent: a positive or negative cash transfer) is the same *as if* everyone was offered the service at a common *virtual price*.

The third solution considers the joint surplus generated by any subset (coalition) of agents *standing alone* to use the technology, and applies the *Shapley value* of this cooperative game.

Each one of these three solutions is subtle in its own way, and proposes a different interpretation of what common property of a technology could mean when there are production externalities (variable returns). We also study the implementation of the three solutions by appropriate procedures.

1.5   Private versus Public Contracts

Libertarian political philosophy offers a simple solution to deal with the externalities just discussed. Assume that the property rights over the existing resources—consumption goods as well as means of production—are clearly defined and entirely distributed among the economic agents. The libertarian postulate (formulated most clearly by Coase) predicts that the interested parties will spontaneously enter private contracts to reallocate the property rights to their mutual advantage.

Say that Ann lives upstream and has the right to pollute the river, thus harming Bob who lives downstream. The opportunity for private recontracting hinges upon the comparison of the cost x to Bob of Ann's polluting activities and the cost y to Ann of refraining from polluting. If x is larger than y, then an offer by Bob to buy Ann's pollution rights at a price between y and x is attractive to both parties, and the postulate says that they will somehow agree on a price—that is, reach an agreement on the division of the surplus $(x - y)$. If, on the other hand, y is larger than x, then it is efficient that Ann continues to pollute, and the status quo will prevail because Bob cannot make an offer that would appeal to both parties. Therefore an efficient utilization of the resources will result regardless of the initial distribution of property rights.

A *private contract* is a mutually advantageous deal: every party is better off when the contract is implemented, therefore signing the contract is the consequence of rational behavior. The contract is explained from no other principle than the pursuit of one's own selfish welfare by all the parties: no social value judgment enters the description of this transaction, and no coercive device is needed to enforce compliance with the terms of the agreement. In other words, the contract is free of value: either party can revoke it if it is advantageous to do so, and the price they agree upon, for instance, is not grounded on any fairness principle: it is simply the equilibrium result of selfish bargaining.

Public contracts are designed by a party of disinterested rational actors, under the veil of ignorance, in the name of compelling arguments of justice—in practice, by a small number of experts, judges, or "founding fathers" who agree on the best organization of a certain institution of concern to all members of society. As explained below, the allocation methods and collective decision rules studied in this book are all examples of public contracts expressed in the microeconomic language and yet broadly applicable. They are miniature social contracts.

Public contracts require a normative justification, must be explained from first principles of rationality and justice, and administered by a central agency, whereas private contracts have no ethical content. Private contracts result from the balance of power between the agents qua players, and from a decentralized, spontaneous process of interaction that requires no social evaluation.

The libertarian credo dismisses public contracts as unwarranted and detrimental to efficiency, as they place constraints on private initiatives to invent beneficial private contracts. In the libertarian world the only interference of the public authority in the lives of private citizens is to enforce their private property rights, which is a "minimal" definition of the role of the state.

Thus the kind of principled discussion of distributive justice that is the object of this book has no place in the libertarian world. The normative/axiomatic approach is built upon a more balanced interpretation of the liberal political philosophy that recognizes the need for public contracts alongside private ones.

The Achilles heel of the libertarian view is to ignore the huge costs, practical and psychological, of direct, value-free bargaining. Exclusive reliance on private contracting to resolve countless externalities and conflicts of opinion—generated by the apparently limitless division of labor in industrialized societies—is plainly utopian.

The transaction cost of reaching an agreement rises more than linearly with the number of parties involved, in any measure of the amount of interpersonal communications implied by collective negotiation. Think of the unanimous consent required in jury decisions: a single stubborn juror can "block" the entire process. The European union will grow soon to more than two dozen members, and must consequently drop its rule of unanimous consent on most issues. When we choose a rule of universal concern (a bill), we must rely on voting rules to achieve a compromise between conflicting opinions. Passing bills by majority voting is a prima facie liberal institution, yet it is not equivalent, by any stretch of the imagination, to a private contract signed by all citizens: it forces coercively an outcome that certain citizens find detestable.

Thus a contract binding a large community requires coercive intervention of the public authority. The latter is acceptable to all (most) members of the community only if it is justified by a "reason," a general anonymous principle. This is precisely what public contracts are about.

Even transactions on a very small scale are often resolved more effectively by public contracts than by private ones. Consider the division of assets during a divorce. Many couples find it emotionally difficult to reach a reasonable settlement without the help of some guidelines on the division process, such as, provision for child support. These guidelines (whether or not enforceable in a court of law) embody the impersonal principles of fairness of a public contract. The situation is similar in most fair division issues involving a specific type of transaction: sharecropping, profit sharing between an artist and her agent, a publisher and its authors, bankruptcy settlements. A customary division rule is a focal principle of justice that all parties can easily adopt; whether or not this principle is legally enforceable influences how often the parties comply with its recommendation, but the principle remains an instance of a public contract between a very small number of parties.

1.6   Organization and Overview of the Book

In this book I propose a handful of fundamental public contracts, formulated in microeconomic language, as methods for allocating certain resources or rules for reaching a compromise between conflicting opinions. These rules and methods include the equal sacrifice taxation schemes (chapter 2), collective utility functions (chapter 3), voting by majority à la Condorcet or by scoring à la Borda (chapter 4), the Shapley value (chapters 5 and 6), the competitive equilibrium with equal incomes (chapters 6 and 7). They are simple tools for social engineering, and their normative justification is provided by a series of *axioms*.

A full-fledged discussion of the axiomatizations relevant to the rules and methods just listed is beyond the scope of this introductory text. However, the book describes informally some of the main axioms and the corresponding key axiomatic characterization results or impossibility theorems. Specifically, section 3.2 states the central result of cardinal welfarism, namely the characterization of additively separable collective utility functions. Section 4.6 describes Arrow's impossibility theorem, the seminal result of ordinal welfarism, and its key axiom of independence of irrelevant alternatives. The two most important axiomatizations of the Shapley value are the subject of section 5.5. An axiomatic comparison of the three efficient methods for managing the commons is provided in section 6.6. Section 7.6 compares similarly our two methods for the fair division of heterogeneous commodities, the competitive equilibrium with equal incomes and the egalitarian equivalent solution.

Only two axioms qualify as universal within the confines of this book: they are the basic symmetry property equal treatment of equals, and efficiency/Pareto optimality. All other axioms are used to inform the differences among competing allocation methods. Examples include choices among utilitarian, egalitarian, and Nash collective utility functions in chapter 3, between Condorcet and Borda voting methods in chapter 4, or between the competitive equilibrium with equal incomes and the egalitarian equivalent solution in chapters 6 and 7.

The book is self-contained, yet a familiarity with microeconomic thinking and/or mathematics modeling will make the reader's task easier. It is best suited for advanced undergraduates, in particular, those who have been exposed to intermediate microeconomics, or first-year master or graduate students.

Each chapter, starting with chapter 2, is organized as a sequence of intuitive examples, intertwined with more general discussions in which the mathematical arguments, if any, are elementary. It contains one technically challenging section evoking the relevant axiomatic results (as explained above). Each chapter offers about a dozen detailed exercises, some of them simple numerical examples, others developing some formal properties alluded to earlier in the chapter. It ends with a short introduction to the relevant literature.

The sequence of chapters corresponds to a partly subjective list of the most influential normative models of resource allocation.

In chapter 2 the resources in question are just a sum of money or of any other desirable homogeneous commodity, and the relevant individual characteristics are a single number. Examples of application include rationing an overdemanded commodity, designing a tax schedule, or sharing the benefit from a joint investment. The three basic division methods are simple proportionality of shares to claims, equalization of shares, and equalization of losses (= claims − shares). Depending on the normative interpretation of the resources and of individual characteristics, these methods translate the compensation or the reward principle into an operational formula, exactly as Aristotle had suggested in the first place.

The cardinal welfarist model is the subject of chapter 3. The physical resources generate individual welfare measured by a cardinal index of utility, but the physical allocation process is devoid of normative content. Consequently all relevant information is contained in the utility profiles (specifying the cardinal utility of each concerned agent) achievable by a feasible allocation of the underlying (unspecified) resources. A collective utility function provides an interpretation of the compensation principle compatible with efficiency fitness (Pareto optimality; see section 1.3). Three such functions stand out of the axiomatic discussion, namely the *classical utilitarian* sum of individual utilities, the *egalitarian* minimum of individual utilities, and the *Nash* product of individual utilities.

Chapter 4 is devoted to the ordinal welfarist model, in which individual welfare is described by a preference relation and collective welfare is computed by an aggregation method called a social welfare function. As explained in section 1.3, the two leading aggregation methods are the majority relation proposed by Condorcet, and the scoring method advocated by Borda. The celebrated impossibility result due to Arrow states that no social welfare function can yield rational collective preferences at every profile of individual preferences (as Borda's method does but Condorcet's does not) and base the collective opinion between two outcomes solely on the profile of individual opinions between these two outcomes (as Condorcet's, but not Borda's, method does). The two general principles at play in chapter 4 are fitness and (equal) exogenous rights.

The microeconomic problems of fair division discussed in chapters 5, 6, and 7 have been already presented in section 1.4. Recall that the Shapley value, defined in chapter 5, is a mathematical formula cutting the Gordian knot of widespread production externalities, and that it is applicable to a wide array of fair division problems. Its focus is on the reward principle, when a given production process intertwines the inputs of different agents in a complex interaction from which each individual contribution cannot be easily separated (e.g., the impact of the various inputs is not additive). The question is to give every participant in the production effort his or her fair share of the resulting output; alternatively each participant demands a different output share, and we seek to divide fairly the total cost of production.

In chapter 5 we also introduce the stand-alone test, another equity property for the allocation of joint costs or joint surplus. When the test is applied to individual participants, it is never violated by the Shapley value, but in its stronger form, known as the stand-alone core property, it may rule out the Shapley value altogether.

The model of chapter 6 is a simple and familiar example of production externalities often called the problem of the commons. The three solutions defined and compared there are reviewed at the end of section 1.4. They are three different interpretations of the reward principle when a common property technology is used efficiently. Note that chapter 6 stands out in this book for its more demanding technical level, as well as for the originality of the material discussed there. The less technical reader may choose to skip it.

Chapter 7 starts with a brief review of competitive trade under private ownership, and of its relation with the core of the cooperative game of free trade. We show, in particular, that the competitive trade may break down when production exhibits nondecreasing returns to scale, and the same applies to the core stability of free trade.

The second half of chapter 7 deals with the fair and efficient division of a "pie" in the common ownership regime, where a pie means a list of divisible private commodities.

Common ownership, here as in the production model of chapter 6, is no more and no less than the vague principle of equal property rights. An *envy-free* division of the pie is a resting point of the interpersonal comparison of individual shares (as opposed to individual welfares) in the following sense: no one strictly prefers the share received by another participant to her own share. The combination of no envy and of efficiency-fitness (Pareto optimality) leads to the fair division method called competitive equilibrium with equal incomes (section 1.4). To find this solution, we must discover a list of prices, one for each commodity, such that when each participant spends a fair share of the total worth of the pie at those prices, the aggregate demand equals precisely the contents of the pie.

An alternative solution is the egalitarian-equivalent division method, whereby each participant receives a share that he/she views as equivalent to a common fraction of the pie. The numerous examples and the axiomatic discussion in section 7.6 reveal that our two methods (competitive with equal incomes and egalitarian equivalent) are two versatile and plausible normative interpretations of fair division.

The brief chapter 8 provides, for each of chapters 2 to 7, a formal, mathematical definition of the relevant concepts and a precise statement (without proof) of the results alluded to in the course of the successive chapters. Thus chapters 8 serves as a glossary of the technical material underpinning the less formal discussion in the successive examples and exercises.

1.7   Introduction to the Literature

The material covered in this book has deep roots in the economic and political philosophy literature.

The central concept of collective welfare, in its cardinal or ordinal form, is a famously general and far-reaching intellectual construction more than two centuries old. In its cardinal form, it provides the backbone of the political philosophy known as utilitarianism, starting with Bentham and John Stuart Mill; it also delivers practical tools for conflict resolution such as the Nash solution to the bargaining problem. In the ordinal form, the aggregation of individual preferences is an abstract model of democratic elections formalizing the political concept of the "will of the majority."

The systematic discussion of collective welfare, and the contrast between the cardinal and ordinal models (sections 1.2 and 1.3), was the central theme of the "new welfare economics," summarized in the classic Samuelson (1948) book. The seminal axiomatic contribution bear on classical utilitarianism (Harsanyi 1955) and on the aggregation of ordinal preferences (Arrow 1951). The analysis of cardinal collective utilities and ordinal social choice functions was developed mainly throughout the 1960s and 1970s. The organizing principle is the informational content of welfare, and the related axioms of measurement invariance, discussed in sections 3.2 to 3.4. The classic reference is Sen (1971); more recent surveys include Moulin (1988, chs 1 and 2) and Bossert and Weymark (1996).

The theme of externalities is as old as economic analysis, but the modern concepts discussed in section 1.4 are approximately fifty years old: Shapley invented the "value" in 1953 and the concept of no envy is generally credited to Foley (1967). Further references are given at the end of chapters 5, 6, and 7.

The concepts of private and public contracts sketched in section 1.5 allude to the central debate of contemporary political philosophy, pitting the liberalism against the social contract traditions. The libertarian position is spelled out most clearly by Hayek (1976), Buchanan and Tullock (1962), and Nozick (1974). In my view, this position inspires the extremely influential formal work on repeated games (Aumann 1987) and the spontaneous evolution of cooperation (Axelrod 1984; Binmore 1994). This view is developed in Moulin (2001b).

Rawls's 1971 book, *A Theory of Justice,* inspired a striking revival of the social contract tradition, and in particular of its egalitarian variant. Kolm's 1972 book, *Justice et equité,* offers the first formal presentation of the egalitarian collective utility. The egalitarian position was subsequently articulated both as a philosophical statement, Dworkin (1981), Sen (1985), and Cohen (1995), and as an axiomatic model of economic theory: Roemer (1996, 1999) and Fleurbaey (1996).

2 Fair Distribution

2.1 Four Principles of Distributive Justice

In this chapter and the next, a *benevolent dictator* representing the public authority seeks a reasonable compromise between the conflicting interests of the parties involved in a given problem of distribution. Reasonable means "for a reason," and the axioms are the formal expression of such reasons. The manager of a firm, the parents in a family, and the judge in a litigation are all acting as benevolent dictators.[1]

Recall Aristotle's maxim, sometime called the formal principle of distributive justice: "Equals should be treated equally, and unequals unequally, in proportion to the relevant similarities and differences." The term "proportion" should not be taken too literally here; the interesting point is to draw our attention to the "relevant" similarities and differences.

Four principles guide the definition of "relevance," and are not exclusive of one another. They are *compensation, reward, exogenous rights,* and *fitness.* The canonical story[2] is that of a flute that must be given to one of four children. The first child has much fewer toys than the other three, hence should get the flute by the compensation principle. The second child worked hard at cleaning and fixing it, so he should get it as a reward. The third child's father owns the flute (although the father does not care for it), so he has the right to claim it. The fourth child is a flutist, so the flute must go to him because all enjoy the music (fitness argument).

Compensation, reward, and exogenous rights belong squarely to the principles of fairness. As explained below, fitness is related to fairness as well as to welfare.

Compensation and Ex post Equality

Certain differences in individual characteristics are involuntary, morally unjustified, and affect the distribution of a *higher-order* characteristic that we deem to equalize. This justifies unequal shares of resources in order to compensate for the involuntary difference in the primary characteristic and achieve equality of the higher-order characteristic.

Nutritional *needs* differ for infants, pregnant women, and adult males, and hence call for different shares of food. The ill *needs* medical care to become *as* healthy as a "normal" person. The handicapped *needs* more resources to enjoy certain "primary" goods, such as transportation or access to public facilities. A socioeconomic disadvantage calls for more educational resources to restore equal access to the job market. Economic needs are the central justification of the macroeconomic redistributive policies, taking the form of tax breaks, welfare support, and medical aid programs.

---

1. The discussion of cost- and surplus-sharing in chapter 5 takes place in the benevolent dictator context.
2. The story goes back to Plato.

Formally, the compensation principle is implemented by defining an index v_i representing the level of the higher-order characteristic enjoyed by agent i, and a function u_i transforming her share of resources y_i into her index $v_i = u_i(y_i)$. For instance, v_i is the level of satisfaction of i's nutritional needs (with $v_i = 1$ and $v_i = 0$ representing full satisfaction and starvation, respectively) and y_i is the amount of food she eats (where for simplicity food is measured along a unidimensional scale, e.g., calories). Thus a pregnant woman i and an elderly male j who eat the same amount of food y are not nourished equally, $u_i(y) < u_j(y)$, or equivalently, it takes more food to bring i at the same level of nourishment than j, $u_i(y_i) = u_j(y_j) \Rightarrow y_i > y_j$. The other examples are similar: if v_i is the level of health, and y_i the amount of medical care devoted to agent i, a healthy person i needs no care at all $u_i(0) = 1$, and the amount of care y_j it takes to restore j's health measures the seriousness of his condition. The definition of the function u_i is "objective," and agent i bears no responsibility in its shape. This feature is essential to the benevolent dictator interpretation.

Equality ex post can be applied to many other indexes than the satisfaction of basic needs. Handicaps in a horse race restore equal chances of winning by an unequal distribution of weight, tax breaks to certain businesses restore their compensation, travel subsidies for conference participants restore equality of the cost of attending, and so on.

Reward

Differences in individual characteristics are morally relevant when they are viewed as voluntary and agents are held responsible for them. They justify unequal treatment.

Past sacrifices justify a larger share of resources today (veterans). Past wrongdoings justify a lesser share: reckless drivers should pay more for insurance, no free healthcare for the substance abuser, no organ transplant for the criminal. Past hardships to my ancestors justify, vicariously, a compensation transfer today: affirmative action.

Merit by extraordinary achievement calls for reward: prizes to a creator, an athlete, a peacemaker, and other outstanding individuals.

A central question of political philosophy is the fair reward of individual productive contributions: the familiar Lockean argument entitles me to the fruit of my own labor, but this hardly leads to a precise division rule except when the production of output from the labor input unambiguously separates the contributions of the various workers. Separating the fruit of my labor from that of your labor is easy only when your labor creates no externality on mine, and vice versa. If we are fishing in the same lake, cutting wood from the same forest, or sharing any other kind of exhaustible resources, this separation is no longer possible hence the fair reward of one's labor is not a straightforward concept. The same difficulty arises when sharing joint costs or the surplus generated by the cooperation of actors with different input contributions: some bring capital, some bring technical skills, and so on. This question is the subject of chapter 5; it is also discussed in this chapter (e.g., example 2.4).

Exogenous Rights

Certain principles guiding the allocation of resources are entirely *exogenous* to the consumption of these resources and to the responsibility of the consumers in their production. Such is the right of private property in the flute story: the point is that ownership is independent from the consumption of the flute (and the related questions who needs it?, who deserves it?, who will make the best use of it?).

A paramount instance of exogenous rights is the fairness principle of equality in the allocation of certain basic rights such as political rights, the freedom of speech and of religion, or access to education. My right to vote and to be eligible for office equals yours, despite the fact that I don't care to vote or to run for office, or that I will use my vote irrationally or wastefully, such as by voting according to the phases of the moon. My right to education is not related to my IQ, nor to the admirable deeds I perform when I am not in school.

Equal exogenous rights correspond to *equality ex ante,* in the sense that we have an equal claim to the resources (be they the ability to vote and the weight of one's vote, the duty to be drafted, the right to police protection, the access to a public beach, etc.) regardless of the way they affect our welfare and that of others. This stands in sharp contrast with equality ex post suggested by the compensation principle.

Examples of unequal exogenous rights are numerous and important as well. Beside private ownership (see above), there is also the difference in status brought about by social standing or by seniority. When the beneficiaries of the distribution are institutions or represent groups of agents, the inequality in their exogenous rights is commonplace: shareholders in a publicly traded firm, or political parties with different size of representation in the parliament, should have unequal shares of decision power; creditors in the American bankruptcy law are prioritized, with the federal government coming first followed by the trustees, and the shareholders come last; and so on.

Fitness

Resources must go to whomever makes the best use of them, flutes to the best flutist, the child to his true mother (Solomon), the book in Japanese to whomever can read Japanese, the cake to the glutton, and so on.

Thus *fitness* justifies unequal allocation of the resources independently of needs, merit, or rights. Formally, fitness can be expressed in two conceptually different ways, *sum-fitness* and *efficiency-fitness*.

The concept of sum-fitness relies on the notion of utility, namely the measurement of the higher-order characteristic that is relevant to the particular distributive justice problem at hand. Going back to the discussion of the compensation principle above, the central object is the function transforming resources into utility. If we distribute medical care among a group of patients, the index v_i represents the health level of patient i and $v_i = u_i(y_i)$ is the function telling us what health level is achieved by what level of care. If we distribute food, v_i is i's level of nourishment (satisfaction of nutritional needs) and y_i her share of food. If we divide a cake, v_i is the degree of "pleasure" accruing to i when he eats the share y_i.

Sum-fitness allocates resources so as to maximize total utility of the concerned agents. Sum-fitness is a fairness principle, however unsettling and radical its recommendations may be at times. The critical comparison of sum-fitness—maximizing the sum $\sum_i u_i$ of individual utilities—and of compensation—equalizing u_i across all agents—accounts for a familiar trade-off of distributive justice.

Consider the flute example. The only use of the flute is to play music and music can be heard by everyone. Say that the utility of child i has two components: the objective quality a_i of the music being played, and the pleasure b he derives from playing the instrument (the same for every child). With n being the number of children, total utility when the flute is given to child i is $n \cdot a_i + b$, where a_i measures how well i plays the flute. Here sum-fitness unambiguously recommends giving the flute to the most talented flutist. The compensation principle, on the other hand, would sometime time-share, allowing the children to take turn playing the flute.[3]

In section 2.5 we compare sum-fitness and compensation in a simple model of fair division: often their recommendations differ sharply, yet at a deeper level of analysis the two principles can be viewed as two faces of the same coin.

The more general concept of efficiency-fitness (or simply efficiency, or Pareto optimality) is the central normative requirement of collective rationality; section 1.3. Efficiency-fitness is developed in chapter 3, and it plays a leading role in the subsequent chapters.

Efficiency-fitness typically imposes much looser constraints than sum-fitness on the allocation of resources. For instance, in the simple models of this chapter,[4] efficiency-fitness is automatically satisfied. In the general welfarist approach of chapter 3, efficiency-fitness is compatible with sum-fitness—also called classical utilitarianism—with compensation—in the form of the egalitarian collective utility function—and with many other compromises between these two extremes.

---

3. If each child plays $1/n$th of the time, each will enjoy the utility $b/n + Ea$, where Ea is the average skill of the children. For some values of b and a_i, $b/n + Ea > \max_i a_i$ so that time-sharing improves upon the utility of all agents but one (the best flutist) and yields a more egalitarian distribution of net utilities.

4. Here the resources are "one-dimensional," meaning that, a given amount of a single divisible commodity is distributed.

We now discuss some examples, contrasting the four principles of distributive justice.

Example 2.1 Lifeboat   Consider the allocation of a single indivisible "good": each agent can either have it or not. The benevolent dictator must choose, under some constraints, who will get it and who will not. The paradigmatic example is access to the lifeboat when the ship is sinking: the lifeboat is too small to accommodate everyone. Other dramatic examples include medical triage—who will receive medical attention, in a war or a natural disaster—the allocation of organs for transplant, and immigration policies.

We start by the genuine lifeboat story, where seats in the boat must be rationed. The simplest version of exogenous rights is strict equality: we draw lots to pick who should be sacrificed. Alternatively, exogenous rights amount to an exogenous priority ranking: keep the good citizen (respected scientist, politician, or whatever, provided that his skills are not useful in these circumstances) and throw out the bad one (criminal). Compensation suggests letting the "strong" men take their chance by swimming, whereas the "weak" women and children stay on the boat, thus equalizing ex post chances of survival. The reward viewpoint would dispose of the one who causes the ship to sink. Finally fitness commands to keep on board the crew (for their navigation skills) or the women and children (for the sake of future humankind: the child has more potential for welfare than the old; the women can bear children).

Another example is food rationing in a besieged town. Compensation says to give more food to the sick and the children; fitness favors those who fight in defense of the town, whereas reward favors those who risked their lives to get the supplies; finally exogenous rights enforces either strict equality of rations or make the size of one's ration depend on social status.

In medical triage, compensation gives priority to the most severely wounded, reward gives priority to the bravest soldiers, exogenous rights enforces strict equality or priority according to rank in the hierarchy, and fitness maximizes the expected number or recoveries (where recovery refers to the ability to fight) implying that one badly wounded soldier who needs intensive care is sacrificed in favor of several soldiers to whom recovery can be guaranteed with few medical resources.[5] An alternative interpretation is priority according to rank (a general is more important to victory than a private). A variant is medical triage where, after an earthquake, fitness gives priority to doctors and engineers who produce the most social value under the circumstances; reward is not relevant, unless we want to punish looters.

In the allocation of organs for transplant, compensation gives priority to whose who can survive the shortest time or whose life is most difficult without a new organ; reward gives

---

5. Later in example 2.7 we have a model of medical triage where the decision is not simply "in" or "out" but the quantity of medical resources allocated to each wounded soldier.

priority according to seniority on the waiting list (first come, first served); exogenous rights enforces strict equality of chances (lottery) or priority according to social status, or wealth (if the donation of the wealthy patient does not increase the availability or organs); fitness maximizes medical fitness, namely chances of success of transplant.

In the next three examples, the decision does not bring life or death. But the problem is formally equivalent in the sense that we must decide who is "in" and who is "out."

In immigration policy, compensation admits political or economic refugees; exogenous rights is blind equality (lottery) or priority based on an ethnic, religious, or racial characteristic (e.g., Germany, Israel); reward gives priority to those with a *record* of "good deeds" for the country in question (even if they will retire after immigration, and be a net burden to their host) such as investments and political support; fitness gives priority to those with an *expectation* of good deeds, with useful skills, with a commitment to invest, and the like, or priority to those whose relatives have already immigrated.

In admission to colleges, compensation gives priority to applicants with disadvantageous socioeconomic background; exogenous rights give equal right to admission (often the rule in European universities—France, Netherlands—where rationing can take the form of a lottery); unequal exogenous rights include quotas favoring minority students (regardless of their own circumstances), children of alumni, or citizens of foreign countries; reward gives priority to the student's academic record as it reflects *past* efforts and achievements; fitness also uses the academic record but as a signal correlated to *future* success in the college itself (note the analogy with the previous example).

In tickets for an overdemanded musical performance or sporting event, compensation gives priority to out-of-town residents or to applicants who have not been attending any of the previous events; for exogenous rights a lottery is faultlessly egalitarian, or alternatively, priority to politicians, honor students in the local high school, or to any group whose distinctive characteristic bears no relation to the event; reward gives priority to sponsors of the orchestra or team; fitness favors musicians or music teachers, or athletes.

Example 2.2 Queuing and Auction   Two common methods used to ration seats in concert halls but also in planes and in private clubs are queuing and auction. Queuing (with a real waiting cost) rewards effort and effort is correlated to benefit from the good in question; therefore it meets the sum-fitness criterion better than a lottery because seats will go to their most eager consumers. On the other hand, queuing is an inefficient use of time. Auctioning the goods is in one sense the best system from the fitness angle because the goods go to those who value them most without any waste of resources; hence total utility is maximized. This argument is rigorous only if all agents are of comparable wealth: the most eager opera fan will be denied access if she is short of cash. Thus auctioning is unpalatable because it favors the rich (think of the right to buy off conscription), a criterion orthogonal to merit (reward) and to fitness. Only if agents have comparable wealth, will auctioning maximize sum-fitness *and* efficiency-fitness. Yet the common practice of bumping passengers off a plane by auction shows that wealth differences are not always viewed as an ethical obstacle to the fairness of the auctioning method. The choice to be bumped is voluntary, which makes the method more acceptable than if the airline was auctioning the right to *stay* on the plane (with the proceeds being redistributed to passengers who are bumped).

Example 2.3 Political Rights   Plato (in the *Republic*) invoked the fitness argument when proposing to place philosophers at the reins of government. As recently as one hundred years ago, inequalities in voting rights (or eligibility to a political office) based on wealth, land ownership, or literacy were more common than the universal suffrage (and eligibility to office) that has become the modern norm. The moral basis of these unequal voting rights was a combination of fitness (uneducated and/or poor citizens cannot form a reasonable opinion) and reward (the wealthier I am, the higher my contribution to the commonwealth, hence the higher my stake in the decisions being taken). Both arguments have been swept aside to leave room for the strict exogenous equality of individual political rights, an inalienable component of membership in the political community. The age limit and the denial of voting rights to the insane are two fitness arguments still in place. Denial of rights to criminals is a reward argument.

In many voting bodies, equality of voting rights is not warranted: members of the European union, and shareholders in a board meeting, are given unequal voting weights because they represent unequal population sizes or capital investment. An interesting and important question is the just distribution of weights. Simple proportionality does not work because a small agent may end up with no influence whatsoever on the decision process, and we must rely on other normative principles.[6]

2.2   A Simple Model of Fair Distribution

The model discussed in this and the next two sections is the simplest formal model of distributive justice. There is a given amount t of a commodity to be divided among a given set of agents, and each agent i is endowed with a claim x_i. The commodity can be a "good" (valuable resource) or a "bad" (a cost to be shared, e.g., a tax burden): if the former, we call x_i the demand of agent i; if the latter, we speak of his liability.

The problem is that t, the available resource, differs from the total sum x of claims: $t \neq x_N = \sum_i x_i$. If there is equality, we simply meet each agent's demand, or assign his liability to each agent.

---

6. The most popular method is an application of the Shapley value.

We distinguish the cases where t is smaller or larger than x_N: we speak of a *deficit*, of a rationing situation, in the former case, of *excess* in the latter case. The most frequent case is when the commodity is a good and the resource t falls short of x_N. One example is rationing an overdemanded good, as in rationing prescription drugs: x_i is the quantity prescribed to agent i and t is the pharmacist's supply. Two other examples are bankruptcy (x_i is the bankrupt firm's debt to creditor i, t is its liquidation value; see below) and inheritance (x_i is agent i's deed and t the value of the estate).

The case with a "good" commodity and resources in excess of the claim is illustrated in example 2.4 about a joint venture: x_i is agent i's opportunity cost of joining the venture (in our story, we speak of stand-alone salaries) and t its total revenue. Of course, both cases $t > x_N$ (excess) and $t < x_N$ (deficit) are possible here.

The case where the commodity is a bad is no less interesting. The design of a taxation schedule (section 2.4) is a key example: x_i is agent i's taxable income and t total tax to be levied.[7] Other examples discussed below include a fund-raising story and the distribution of chores. In the fund-raising story, x_i is agent i's pledge and t is the amount that must be raised; thus both cases of an excess $t > x_N$ or a deficit $t < x_N$ are plausible. In the distribution of chores, x_i is the amount for which i is responsible and t is the actual workload.

Throughout the rest of chapter 2 we assume equal exogenous rights, namely the differences in their claims is the only reason to give different shares to the agents. In particular, two agents with identical claims must receive the same share. Also fitness plays no role, with the exception of the model in section 2.5.[8] As either every agent wants more of the good or every agent wants less of the bad, efficiency-fitness is automatically satisfied. Moreover we identify an agent's share with her welfare; therefore sum-fitness has no bite either. Thus our discussion bears on the principles of compensation and reward.

Example 2.4a Joint Venture: Excess   Teresa is a pianist and David is a violinist. They work as a full-time duo. Before the duo was formed, Teresa was earning \$50K a year as a teacher and solo artist, and David \$100K as the first violinist of a symphony orchestra. After one year of performing together, the net revenue of their duo is \$210,000. What is a fair split of this revenue?

The key to the example is the interpretation of the cooperation technology.

One viewpoint is that the stand-alone salaries are relevant to the cooperative process, and agents are held responsible for them. The presumption is that the input of each instrument is to some extent separable in the final product; it makes sense to take stand-alone salaries as a

---

7. In section 2.4 we consider a dual interpretation where $x_N - t$ is the tax and t is the net salary mass; the taxation problem becomes an instance of dividing an overdemanded good.

8. Here we model explicitly a utility function transforming a share of resources into welfare. This gives the sum-fitness property some bite.

proxy for the value of their respective contributions, and to divide profit in the corresponding proportions. To make this interpretation more plausible, consider the case of a famous singer and her unknown accompanying pianist, so their ex ante earnings are very different.

This first solution is called the *proportional* solution, and its mathematical formulation is transparent. Teresa and David in our example receive 70K and 140K respectively. More generally, if x_i is agent's stand-alone salary and t total revenue of the joint venture, agent i's share is

$$y_i = \frac{x_i}{\sum_N x_j} t \tag{1}$$

Here is another plausible solution: taking their stand-alone salaries as the "status quo ante" outcome, the agents divide equally the surplus (in excess of the status quo) generated by their cooperative venture: in this view the difference in the voluntary characteristics (stand-alone salaries) is preserved (at 50K). Teresa and David get 80K and 130K respectively, and more generally,

$$y_i = x_i + \frac{1}{n}\left(t - \sum_N x_j\right) \tag{2}$$

This is the *equal surplus* solution that is always more (resp. less) advantageous to the agent with the smallest (resp. largest) value x_i than the proportional solution above.[9]

The third solution of interest pushes the egalitarian criterion one step further. The stand-alone salary sets a floor on an agent's share because no one should be penalized for joining the cooperative venture. Except for this constraint, the revenue is shared equally among all agents. This solution regards the individual contributions as no more separable than that of the left and right hands clapping, hence stand-alone salaries as irrelevant to the production process—if not to the division of the proceeds. In our example Teresa and David get 105K each. With a total revenue of 190K, they would get 90K and 100K respectively: as long as total revenue is below 200K, David's share stays put at 100K and Teresa gets all the surplus. When revenue is above 200K, it is split equally.

The mathematical expression of this third solution is slightly more involved. Agent i receives a common share λ or his stand-alone salary, whichever is largest: $y_i = \max\{\lambda, x_i\}$. The common share λ is computed by solving the equation

$$\sum_N \max\{\lambda, x_i\} = t \tag{3}$$

---

9. This mathematical fact is easy to check using the two formulas above; see exercise 2.5.

This solution is called the *uniform gains* solution. It is more (resp. less) advantageous to the agent with the smallest (resp. largest) value than the equal surplus solution (exercise 2.5).

Example 2.4b Joint Venture: Deficit   Now suppose that total revenue falls short of 150K, the sum of the stand-alone salaries. We must divide a *deficit* instead of a surplus. Her stand-alone salary is an upperbound on an agent's share because everyone must bear a share of the deficit.

The three solutions are easily adapted to the deficit case. The proportional solution is given by the same formula (1).

The uniform gain solution pursues the same egalitarian goal, but this time the share y_i must not exceed x_i. Each agent receives a common share λ or x_i, whichever is less: $y_i = \min\{\lambda, x_i\}$. The common share λ is the solution of the equation:

$$\sum_N \min\{\lambda, x_i\} = t \tag{4}$$

Finally the equal surplus solution becomes the *uniform losses* solution, which aims at subtracting the same amount from every stand-alone salary. Say that total revenue is 90K: the deficit 60K is shared equally between Teresa and David who end up with 20K and 70K. But if total revenue is very low, say 40K, the deficit 110K cannot be split equally lest Teresa ends up paying David from her own pocket! In other words, equalization of the losses must be adjusted to take into account the constraint $y_i \geq 0$. In the example Teresa ends up with nothing at all, and David keeps the 40K. This contradicts even the mildest version of the reward principle, as Teresa gets nothing for her work!

If the uniform losses solution is implausible in the joint venture problem, for the reasons given above, it is very convincing in other contexts, examples of which are provided below. Its mathematical expression is as follows: if the common loss is μ, agent's share y_i is $y_i = \max\{x_i - \mu, 0\}$; in other words, i's loss is the smallest of the two numbers μ and x_i. The common loss μ is the solution of the equation

$$\sum_N \max\{x_i - \mu, 0\} = t \tag{5}$$

Figure 2.1 illustrates our three solutions, proportional, uniform gains and equal surplus/ uniform losses in the case of two agents with claims x_1, x_2. The vector $x = (x_1, x_2)$ is fixed and the total t to be divided varies from 0 to infinity, generating a path for the vector of shares $y = (y_1, y_2)$.

The figure illustrates the three solutions in a deficit case (with total resources t, solutions a, b, and c) and in an excess case (t', a', b', c'). In the deficit case, agent 2 with the smallest claim of the two prefers his share under the uniform gains solution (point c) to his

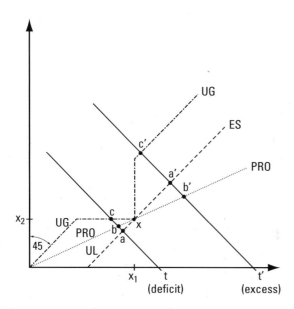

Figure 2.1
Three basic rationing/surplus-sharing methods

proportional share (point b), and the latter to his uniform losses share (point a). In the excess case, his first choice is uniform gains (c'), and his last is proportional (b'). Exercise 2.5 generalizes to an arbitrary number of agents these preferences of the agent with the largest or smallest claim.

We now discuss three examples where the three solutions appeal differently to our intuition.

First, consider *bankruptcy:* creditor i has a claim $\$x_i$ and the total liquidation value t of the firm is smaller than the sum of the debts. If our creditor have equal exogenous rights, the proportional solution is compelling. It is the legal solution as well.

An important—indeed a characteristic—feature of this solution is its robustness to the transfer of claims. If creditors i, j with claims x_i, x_j reallocate the entire claim to agent i—effectively merging the two claims in one—their total share $y_i + y_j$ is unaffected. The same is true if a creditor i splits into two creditors $i_1 + i_2$, and divides his claim x_i as $x_i = x_{i_1} + x_{i_2}$ in arbitrary shares for i_1 and i_2: the splitting operation leaves the total share of $\{i_1, i_2\}$ identical to that of i. Contrast this with the uniform gains solution, where the merging of two claims x_i, x_j in one of size $x_i + x_j$ results in either a smaller or the same share for the "merged" agent; symmetrically the splitting of one claim x_i into two subclaims x_{i1}, x_{i2}

can only increase the total share ($y_{i_1} + y_{i_2} \geq y_i$). The reverse statements (i.e., merging is advantageous and splitting is disadvantageous) hold for the uniform losses solution in the case of a deficit. See exercise 2.2.

It is not too difficult to show that the proportional solution is the only solution in the deficit problem robust with respect to the transfer of claims (exercise 2.2). Hence it is compelling in any situation where claims are akin to anonymous bonds, as is nearly the case in a bankruptcy situation (e.g., stocks are transferable), except for some creditors with special status such as the federal government.

Next, consider rationing *medical supplies*. The pharmacist has t units of a certain drug— say insulin—in stock and patient i shows a prescription for x_i units; t falls short of x_N. The uniform losses solution is appealing here: x_i represents an objective "need," and it seems fair to equalize net losses, assuming that a loss of k units of insulin below the optimal level is equally harmful to every patient. On the other hand, if the demand for the drug is not based on an objective need, say sleeping pills or diet pills, uniform gains seems most fair: it corresponds to the familiar rationing by individual coupons—the same number of coupons per person. In both cases—insulin and diet pills—the proportional solution is not especially appealing.

Third, consider a *fund-raising* situation. Donor i offers to contribute \$$x_i$ to the project in need of funding. If the actual cost t exceeds the sum of x_i, and it must be raised among these same donors, the proportional solution will unfairly penalize the most generous donor, unless we can view x_i as a proxy of his ability to pay. Equal surpluses is not appealing even if all donors are viewed as equally able—if unequally willing—to pay for the project. In this case the uniform gains solution is the most plausible of the three, charging the extra cost to the most timid donors first.

Symmetrically, suppose that the actual cost t falls short of the sum of the pledges x_i: How should we allocate rebates? Here the uniform gains is quite appealing. If the pledges are ranked as $x_1 \geq x_2 \geq x_3 \geq \ldots$, this solution gives the first ($x_1 - x_2$) dollars of rebate to donor 1, splits equally the next $2(x_2 - x_3)$ dollars of rebate between donors 1 and 2, and so on.[10] If the donors have similar ability to pay, uniform gains rewards first the most generous agents, meaning the highest contributors. On the other hand, uniform losses is not palatable for symmetric reasons as it gives an equal rebate irrespective of the size of x_i. If all agents have the same ability to pay, this rewards bad behavior; if, on the contrary, x_i is a proxy of their ability to pay, a proportional rebate is the most natural compromise.

Example 2.5   We illustrate the three solutions by a numerical example with five agents with respective claims and 20, 16, 10, 8, and 6, so the total claim is 60. The table gives the shares for five values of total resource t: $t = 20, 40, 50$ yield a deficit and $t = 80, 120$ an excess.

---

10. This algorithm is described in exercise 2.6.

Claims		20	16	10	8	6
$t = 20$	PRO shares	6.7	5.3	3.3	2.7	2
	UG shares	4	4	4	4	4
	UL shares	11.3	7.3	1.3	0	0
$t = 40$	PRO shares	13.3	10.7	6.7	5.3	4
	UG shares	8.7	8.7	8.7	8	6
	UL shares	16	12	6	4	2
$t = 50$	PRO shares	16.7	13.3	8.3	6.7	5
	UG shares	13	13	10	8	6
	UL shares	18	14	8	6	4
$t = 80$	PRO shares	26.7	21.3	13.3	10.7	8
	UG shares	20	16	14.7	14.7	14.7
	ES shares	24	20	14	12	10
$t = 120$	PRO shares	40	32	20	16	12
	UG shares	24	24	24	24	24
	ES shares	32	28	22	20	18

We turn to the issue of computing two of our three solutions, the uniform gains and uniform losses solution, of which the mathematical definitions (3), (4), and (5) are not entirely transparent. A simple algorithm to compute the uniform gains solution works as follows. Divide t in equal shares and identify agents whose claims are on the "wrong" side of t/n. If we have a deficit, this means those agents with $x_i \leq t/n$; if we have an excess, it means those with $x_i \geq t/n$. Give their claim x_i to those agents, decrease the resources accordingly, and repeat the same computation among the remaining agents, with the remaining resources.

A similar algorithm delivers the uniform losses solution in the deficit case: apply formula (2) and identify all agents who receive $y_i \leq 0$, give zero to these agents. Repeat the algorithm among the remaining agents.

In the deficit case the algorithm computing the uniform gains solution reveals that agent i's share must be at least t/n or x_i, whichever is smaller: $y_i \geq \min\{x_i, t/n\}$. Indeed, an agent who is on the wrong side of t'/n', at any stage of the algorithm where t' units remain to be shared among n' agents, receives $y_i = x_i$. Moreover the sequence of per capita shares $t/n, t'/n', t''/n''$, is nondecreasing because at each step the claims of the agents who are dropped are below the per capita share. Therefore an agent who is always on the right side of t'/n' receives no less than t/n. Exercise 2.8 elaborates on such lower bound for the uniform gains shares, and stresses that neither uniform losses nor proportional meets any nontrivial lower bound. Exercise 2.6 offers two more algorithms for computing the uniform gains and uniform losses solutions.

Our final example shows the versatility of the three basic solutions, which can be adapted to a distribution problem with indivisible units and lotteries.

Example 2.6 Scheduling A server processes one job per unit of time. User i demands x_i jobs. For every user, the earlier a job is done, the better. The server must schedule total demand $x_N = \sum_i x_i$, namely decide in what order the x_N jobs will be processed. A scheduling sequence is a list $\{i_1, i_2, \ldots, i_t, \ldots, i_{x_N}\}$, where for all t, i_t is one of the users and where user i appears exactly x_i times in the sequence. For the sake of fairness, the server randomizes the choice of the sequence $\{i_1, \ldots, i_{x_N}\}$.

The link between this scheduling problem and the rationing of an overdemanded commodity is apparent if we fix a date t and consider the number y_i of user i's jobs processed up to date t. The vector (y_i) is a division of t units among users with demand profile (x_i); it is a solution to a rationing problem where the resources come in indivisible units and their allocation is random.

The proportional solution works by filling an urn with x_N balls, where x_i balls are labeled i, then drawing balls from the urn successively and without replacement: in other words, all sequences $\{i_1, \ldots, i_{x_N}\}$, where each i appears x_i times are equiprobable. An alternative definition of proportional scheduling goes as follows: if at time t user i has z_i jobs still unserved, the $(t + 1)$th job will be given to user i with probability z_i/z_N. To see why this method corresponds to the proportional solution of the rationing problem, observe that the *expected* number of i's jobs served in the first t periods is $(x_i/x_N) \cdot t$.

Proportional scheduling has been deemed an unfair solution because a small demand x_i is swamped by a much larger demand x_j. If x_j becomes arbitrarily large, the expected share of agent i up to a fixed date t dwindles to zero (his expected waiting time until completion of all his jobs becomes arbitrarily large). The simple method known as "fair queuing" avoids this problem by giving an equal chance of receiving the first (most preferred) unit of service, irrespective of the sizes of their demands.

Specifically, fair queuing serves first one job of each user i such that $x_i \geq 1$, using an ordering of these agents selected at random, with uniform probability on all orderings; next all users i such that $x_i \geq 2$ are served a second unit in random order, and so on. In other words, the method empties a series of urns where each agent is allowed to throw at most one ball in each urn.

Figure 2.2 illustrates the method in the two agents' case, and suggests its relation to the uniform gains solution. In the first t periods, the expected number of i's jobs served is precisely given by the uniform gains shares.

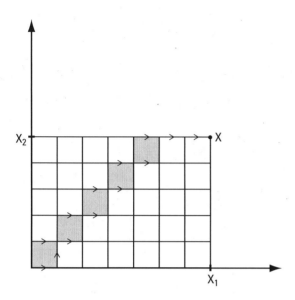

Figure 2.2
Fair queuing in example 2.6

Under fair queuing a small demand is not swamped by a large demand, as with proportional scheduling. In fact an agent's delay is unaffected when another agent with a larger demand raises his demand even further.

A related observation is the following incentive property of fair queuing. Suppose that agent i needs x_i jobs. By inflating his demand to x_i' jobs, $x_i' > x_i$, she will not affect in any way the (random) scheduling of her x_i first jobs: hence this move is not profitable (and neither is a symmetric reduction of her demand, obviously). By contrast, artificially inflating one's demand is always profitable if the proportional scheduling method is used, in the sense that the first x_i jobs (the true demand) will be served earlier.

Our third scheduling method works by simply reversing the scheduling sequence of fair queuing and for this reason is called its dual method[11] and denoted fair queuing*. This means that fair queuing* selects the sequence $\{i_1, i_2, \ldots, i_{x_N}\}$ with the same probability as fair queuing selects the sequence $\{i_{x_N}, i_{x_N-1}, \ldots, i_2, i_1\}$; see figure 2.3.

This definition is not very intuitive, but fortunately a more direct one is available: fair queuing* gives the first job to one of the agents with largest demand x_i(with equal probability among these agents if they are two or more); the $(t+1)$th job goes (with equal

_____
11. More on duality appears in the next section.

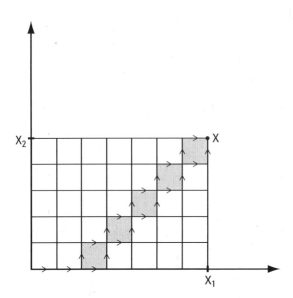

Figure 2.3
Fair queuing* in example 2.6

probability) to one of the agents with the largest remaining demand z_i after the first t periods. This algorithm is entirely similar to the algorithm provided in exercise 2.6 to compute the uniform losses solution. Hence, in particular, the expected distribution of jobs served after t periods is given by the uniform losses formula (5).

The scheduling example uncovers several properties of great relevance for the general deficit-sharing problem when the resources are divisible and shares are deterministic—formulas (1), (4), and (5). First of all it suggests a dynamic interpretation of the three basic methods, proportional, uniform gains and uniform losses in the case $t < x_N$. Think of the resources t as being distributed progressively, at a rate of 1 unit per unit of time. Uniform gains shares the incremental resources dt equally among all agents whose demand x_i is not yet met at date t. Uniform losses shares dt equally among all agents with the largest remaining demand at date t. Proportional simply shares dt in proportion to x_i at all time.

Next we check that the two properties of fair queuing discussed above apply to the uniform gains solution as well. First, consider the effect on agent 1 of raising the claim/demand of another agent, say agent 2, whose demand was larger than agent 1's in the first place. That is, we start from claim $x_1, x_2, x_3, \ldots$ with $x_1 \leq x_2$, and raise x_2 to $x_2', x_2' > x_2$, leaving all other claims and the resources t unchanged. Under the uniform gains solution, agent

1's share does not change either. To see this, consider equation (4), with solution λ before and λ' after the raise of agent 2's claim. If $\lambda \leq x_2$, then $\lambda' = \lambda$ solves (4) in both cases; hence agent 1's share $\min\{\lambda, x_1\}$ does not change. If $\lambda > x_2$, λ' is smaller than λ but cannot fall below $x_2 : \lambda' \geq x_2$ (exercise: Why?). The assumption $x_1 \leq x_2$ now implies that agent 1's share is x_1 before and after the raise. Exercise 2.3 shows that this property (known as *independence of higher claims*) is in fact characteristic of the uniform gains solution.

The second idea emerging from the discussion of example 2.5 is the immunity to a strategic misreport of one's characteristics, in this case the report of an inflated demand: under the proportional method such a report is profitable, under fair queuing/uniform gains it is not. The immunity in question is called *strategy-proofness* in microeconomic jargon; it plays a central role in chapters 4 and 6. It turns out that uniform gains is the only equitable and strategyproof division method. Exercise 2.4 explains this remarkable property.

*2.3   Contested Garment Method

Consider an inheritance or bankruptcy problem where agent i's claim x_i is the debt he holds on the bankrupt firm or a legitimate deed he received from the deceased. The liquidation value of the firm—or the actual value of the estate—is t and $t < x_N$.

Suppose that agent i holds a claim x_i and $x_i \geq t$. This means that this agent claims the entire estate. In this case the uniform gains solution does not pay attention to the *unfeasible* claim $x_i - t$. For instance, two agents i, j such that $x_i \geq t$ and $x_j \geq t$ must receive the *same* share under uniform gains, though x_i and x_j may be very different. Formally, the uniform gains solution is unchanged when we replace claim x_i by $x_i' = \min\{x_i, t\}$. This follows at once from the fact that the solution λ of equation (4) cannot exceed t (exercise: Why?). Therefore $\min\{\lambda, x_i\} = \min\{\lambda, \min\{x_i, t\}\}$, and λ is still the solution of (4) in the problem with claims x_i'.

We call the *truncation property* the fact that we can truncate any claim larger than t at the level t without affecting the distribution. Obviously neither the proportional solution nor the uniform losses have the truncation property, but we have seen that the uniform gains solution does.

A property related to truncation (the link will become clear only after we define the duality operation below) rests on the idea of *concession*. In the problem x, t, the quantity $t - x_{N\backslash i}$ represents what is left of the resources after all agents but i have received their full claim. Naturally this number may be negative or zero, but if it is positive, it is a share of the resources that agent i will necessarily receive.[12] We write $c_i = \max\{t - x_{N\backslash i}, 0\}$ and call this quantity the concession by $N\backslash i$ to agent i.

---

12. This is because $y_j \leq x_j$ for all j and $t - x_{Ni} < x_i$.

In the example 2.5 nobody gets a concession if $t = 20$ or $t = 40$. However, if $t = 50$, we have $c_1 = 10, c_2 = 6, c_i = 0$, for $i = 3, 4, 5$. We take away these concessions from the initial claims and distribute the $50 - 10 - 6 = 34$ remaining units given the profile of reduced claims $(10, 10, 10, 8, 6)$. Under the uniform losses solution we can simply compute the shares for this reduced problem, namely $(8, 8, 8, 6, 4)$ where everyone loses two units. The solution to the initial problem obtains by adding the profile of concessions, namely $(10, 6, 0, 0, 0)$.

The decomposition above does not work for the uniform gains (or proportional) solution because the uniform gains shares of the reduced problem are $(7, 7, 7, 7, 6)$, and

$$(7, 7, 7, 7, 6) + (10, 6, 0, 0, 0) \neq (13, 13, 10, 8, 6)$$

We call the *concession* property the fact that the distribution of t units can be done in two steps, first giving concession c_i to each agent i, next sharing $t - c_N$ units according to the profile of reduced claims $x_i - c_i$. We note that the uniform losses solution satisfies the concession property,[13] but neither uniform gains nor proportional does.

The *contested garment* solution to the deficit problem t, x_1, x_2 takes its name from the following passage in the Talmud: "Two people cling to a garment; the decision is that one takes as much as his grasp reaches, the other takes as much as his grasp reaches, and the rest is divided equally among them."

We interpret agent i's concession c_i as his "grasp," namely the part of the garment that the other agent is not claiming. In a two-person problem the definition of c_i is

$$c_i = \max\{t - x_j, 0\} = t - \min\{x_j, t\}, \qquad \text{where } \{i, j\} = \{1, 2\}$$

The contested garment (CG) solution gives concession c_i to agent i for $i = 1, 2$, and it divides the remaining resources $t - (c_1 + c_2)$ equally: agent i receives $c_i + (t - c_1 - c_2)/2$. Rearranging this expression with the help of the formula for c_i above, we get the *contested garment shares:*

$$y_1 = \tfrac{1}{2}(t + \min\{x_1, t\} - \min\{x_2, t\})$$
$$y_2 = \tfrac{1}{2}(t - \min\{x_1, t\} + \min\{x_2, t\}) \tag{6}$$

Recall that in example 2.4b, we had $x_T = 50K, x_D = 100K$, and $t = 90K$. Here $c_T = 0$, $c_D = 40$, and (6) gives $y_T = 25, y_D = 65$.

Unlike any of our three earlier solutions, the contested garment solution meets *both* the concession property and the truncation property. This is clear for the truncation property,

---

13. To prove this fact, observe that a solution r meets the concession property if and only if its dual r^* (defined below) meets truncation.

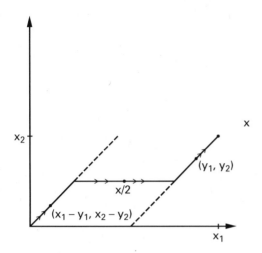

Figure 2.4
Contested garment method

since formula (6) depends only on $\min\{x_i, t\}, i = 1, 2$. It takes some work to check the concession property. Moreover the the contested garment solution is the *only* two-person solution for which both concession and truncation hold: exercise 2.9 explains this axiomatization of the contested garment.

Figure 2.4 depicts the path among which the vector of shares (y_1, y_2) given in (6) varies as the resources t vary from zero to $x_1 + x_2$. It reveals that our new solution coincides with uniform gains for small t (i.e., when $t \leq \min\{x_1, x_2\}$) and with uniform losses for large t (when $t \geq \max\{x_1, x_2\}$). These two observations follow respectively from the truncation and concession properties (exercise: Why?).

In figure 2.4 we see that the path between 0 and x is symmetric around the midpoint $x/2$. If (y_1, y_2) is on this path, so is $(x_1 - y_1, x_2 - y_2)$. In words, if the contested garment solution divides t as (y_1, y_2), it divides $x_1 + x_2 - t$ as $(x_1 - y_1, x_2 - y_2)$, meaning it also divides a *deficit* of t as (y_1, y_2)—receiving $x_1 - y_1$ is the same for agent 1 as incurring a deficit y_1.

This property is called *self-duality:* the method divides a deficit exactly as it divides a gain (so a bottle half full is really the same as a bottle half empty). The relevant concept here is the *duality* operation. Given a solution $y = r(t, x)$, where x stands for the vector (x_i) of claims, and y for the vector (y_i) of shares, the dual solution r^* is defined as follows:

$$r_i^*(t, x) = x_i - r_i(x_N - t, x)$$

Thus r^* divides t units of "gain" exactly as r divides t units of deficit. For instance, the proportional solution is self-dual because it divides gains and deficits alike in proportion to claims.

The dual of the uniform gains method is the uniform losses method, and vice versa. Taking example 2.5, let us compare uniform gains and uniform losses at $t = 20$ and $t = 40$, meaning 20 units of gains and 20 units of deficit. Agent 1 with claim 20 has a uniform losses share 11.3 at $t = 20$ and a uniform gains share $8.7 = 20 - 11.3$ at $t = 40$. Similarly he has a uniform gains share 4 at $t = 20$ and uniform losses share $16 = 20 - 4$ at $t = 40$. The same comparison applies to all agents.

The normative appeal of a self-dual method ($r = r^*$) is to eliminate the difference between a gain and a loss with respect to the individual claims. The choice of the reference point (at the full or null satisfaction of one's claim) does not matter.

In particular, if the bottle is exactly half full, $t = x_N/2$, a self-dual method gives half of his claim to every agent, $y_i = x_i/2$. The method requires one to be oblivious to the orientation of the units to be divided as gains or losses.

How can we generalize the two-person contested garment solution to an arbitrary number of agents? There are two natural ways to do so. They both preserve the truncation and concession properties, as well as self-duality. In view of truncation, whenever every agent claims the entire resources ($t \leq x_i$ for all i), the resources t are split equally just like uniform gains does. By concession, whenever the deficit can be covered by any agent ($x_N - t \leq x_i$ for all i), this deficit is split equally, as under uniform losses.[14]

The first idea to generalize contested garment is *random priority*. Taking a two-agent problem, let us suppose that the two agents toss a fair coin to decide whose claim has absolute priority over the other claim. If agent 1 wins, the shares are $y_1 = \min\{x_1, t\}$, $y_2 = t - \min\{x_1, t\}$; if agent 2 wins, the shares are $y_1' = t - \min\{x_2, t\}$; $y_2' = \min\{x_2, t\}$. The average of these two vectors is precisely the vector of shares (6). Exercise 2.10 describes the application of the random priority idea with an arbitrary number of agents.

The second generalization of the contested garment solution to any number of agents is a clever hybrid between a uniform gains solution whenever the bottle is more than half empty $-t \leq x_N/2$, and a uniform losses solution when it is more than half full $-t \geq x_N/2$. It is the subject of exercise 2.11.

---

14. Indeed, $c_i = t - x_{N\setminus i} \geq 0$; hence after distribution of c_N, agent i's remaining claim is $x_i - c_i = x_N - t$. In the reduced problem each agent has the same claim, so each gets $1/n$ of $t - c_N = (n - 1)(x_N - t)$. This in turn yields the UL shares.

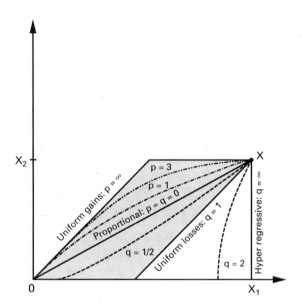

Figure 2.5
Progressive and regressive methods

*2.4   Equal Sacrifice in Taxation

In the taxation problem, x_i represents agent i's taxable income, and a given amount of tax must be divided among the n agents. We choose to write t for the total aftertax income so that $x_N - t$ is the total tax to be levied, and the share y_i is agent i's aftertax income.[15]

The simple property called *fair ranking* places some minimal equity constraints on tax shares:

$$x_i \leq x_j \Longrightarrow y_i \leq y_j \quad \text{and} \quad x_i - y_i \leq x_j - y_j \tag{7}$$

A higher taxable income warrants a higher after-tax income *as well as* a higher tax burden. In particular, equal incomes are equally taxed. In figure 2.5 the shaded area represents, in the case $n = 2$, the vectors (y_1, y_2) circumscribed by inequalities (7). Notice that the path of the uniform gains solution forms the northeastern boundary of this region, while that of the uniform losses solution forms the southwestern boundary.

---

15. The dual representation where t is total tax and y_i is i's tax share can be used just as easily.

Next consider the familiar ideas of progressivity and regressivity:

$$\text{progressivity:} \quad x_i \leq x_j \Rightarrow \frac{x_i - y_i}{x_i} \leq \frac{x_j - y_j}{x_j}$$

$$\text{regressivity:} \quad x_i \leq x_j \Rightarrow \frac{x_i - y_i}{x_i} \geq \frac{x_j - y_j}{x_j}$$

$$(8)$$

Under a progressive tax scheme, the higher the (taxable) income, the higher will be the tax rate, namely the fraction taxed away. The opposite statement holds true under a regressive scheme. Observe that the proportional solution (flat tax) is *both* progressive and regressive.

In figure 2.5 progressivity means that the vector (y_1, y_2) must be above the straight line from 0 to (x_1, x_2), and regressivity means that it must be below this line. Thus the uniform gains solution is progressive, whereas uniform losses is a regressive solution.

Uniform gains (resp. uniform losses) is in fact the most progressive (resp. the most regressive) solution among those meeting fair ranking. This is intuitively clear in figure 2.5, and exercise 2.7 gives a precise statement of these facts for an arbitrary number of agents.

The idea of equal sacrifice yields a rich family of taxation schemes that contains our three basic solutions, proportional, uniform gains, uniform losses, and much more. J. S. Mill introduced this idea first in the context of taxation: "Equality of taxation means equality of sacrifice. It means apportioning the contribution of each person towards the expenses of government, so that he shall feel neither more nor less inconvenience from his share of the payment than every other person experiences from his."

We pick an arbitrary increasing (continuous) function $z \rightarrow u(z)$ representing the conventional "utility" associated with the income z. Then the u-equal sacrifice method chooses aftertax incomes y_i so as to satisfy

$$u(x_i) - u(y_i) = u(x_j) - u(y_j) \qquad \text{for all } i, j \tag{9}$$

For a given vector of taxable incomes (x_i) and total after-tax income t, we may or may not be able to find a vector (y_i) satisfying the system above and $\sum_i y_i = t$. For instance, with the function $u(z) = \log z$ it reads $x_i/y_i = x_j/y_j$ and yields the proportional solution. On the other hand, if we set $u(z) = z$, the u-equal sacrifice method resembles the uniform losses solution but the system (9) may yield some negative shares y_i. In order to guarantee a solution meeting the constraint $y_i \geq 0$ for all i, we modify the system as follows:

$$\text{for all } i: \quad y_i > 0 \Rightarrow u(x_i) - u(y_i) = \max_j \{u(x_j) - u(y_j)\} \tag{10}$$

Only those agents who get a positive after-tax income incur the largest sacrifice. The system (10), together with $\sum_i y_i = t$, always has a unique solution (exercise: prove this claim). With $u(z) = z$ this solution is uniform losses.

An equal sacrifice method always meets half of the fair ranking property (7), namely $x_i \le x_j \Rightarrow y_i \le y_j$. The other half, $x_i \le x_j \Rightarrow x_i - y_i \le x_j - y_j$, is satisfied if and only if u is a *concave* function ($u'(z)$ nonincreasing in z).

The u-equal sacrifice method is progressive if and only if $z \cdot u'(z)$ is nonincreasing in z, namely u is more concave than the log function;[16] it is regressive if and only if $z \cdot u'(z)$ is nondecreasing in z, meaning that u is less concave than the log function.[17]

The simplest family of equal sacrifice methods comes from taking for u a power function. This allows the u-equal sacrifice method to be *scale invariant:* if we multiply all taxable incomes as well as the aftertax total income by a common factor, the corresponding aftertax incomes are also multiplied by the same factor. Thus only the relative incomes x_i/x_j and total tax ratio $(x_N - t)/x_N$ matter. Two subfamilies arise.

First consider the utility function $u(z) = -1/z^p$, where p is a positive parameter. This function is increasing, concave, and more concave than the log function. Therefore it defines a progressive taxation method. Notice that this method never gives $y_i = 0$ whenever $x_i > 0$, and guarantees equal sacrifice for all: $1/y_i^p - 1/x_i^p = 1/y_j^p - 1/x_j^p$ for all i, j; together with $y_N = t$, the system (9) has a unique solution with $y_i > 0$ for all i.

In the case $n = 2$, the path $t \to (y_1, y_2)$ is depicted in figure 2.5 for $p = 1$ and $p = 3$. Two important facts: the p-method approaches the proportional one when p goes to zero; it approaches uniform gains when p goes to infinity. Thus the positive parameter p adjusts the degree of progressivity of our methods, and the u-methods connect smoothly the proportional to the uniform gains method.

Next we consider the utility function $u(z) = z^q$, where q is a positive parameter, $0 \le q \le 1$. This function is increasing and concave, and less concave than the log function; therefore it defines a regressive taxation method. Note that the system (10) must be used, because for small values of t some agents end up with $y_i = 0$. The corresponding path $t \to (y_1, y_2)$ is depicted in figure 2.5 for $q = \frac{1}{2}$. When q goes to zero, the u-method approaches the proportional one, and it shows uniform losses when $q = 1$.

When $q > 1$, the function $u(z) = z^q$ is convex instead of concave, so the u-equal sacrifice method violates fair ranking. Indeed, (9) implies that the smaller the income x_i, the higher is the tax $x_i - y_i$. For instance, when q goes to infinity, the u-method approaches the *hyperregressive* method, taxing exclusively the poor: the tax burden $x_N - t$ is allocated first to the agent(s) with the smallest x_i; if $x_i < x_N - t$ (i.e., taxing away all of agent i's income is not enough), the method taxes the next smallest x_j, and so on. See exercises 2.7 and 2.14.

---

16. This means that we can write u as $u(z) = a(\log z)$ for all z, where a is concave and increasing.

17. In other words, we can write $u(z) = b(\log z)$, where b is convex and increasing.

2.5 Sum-Fitness and Equality

The principles of compensation and of sum-fitness come into play with interesting differences in the simple utilitarian model of resource allocation that is our subject in this section. This model is a prelude to the more general welfarist approach in the next chapter (in particular, section 3.4). It is different from but related to the model of sections 2.2 to 2.4. The benevolent dictator must share t units of resources between n agents, and each agent has his own utility function u_i to "produce" utility from resources: $u_i(y_i)$ is agent i's utility when consuming the share y_i.

The function u_i is a personalized measurement of the benefitness derived by this agent from any possible share of resources. Depending on the context, this measure may be subjective or objective. In one instance, t may be the size of a cake and $u_i(y_i)$ the subjective pleasure derived by child i from a piece of size y_i. In another, t measures some medical resource (e.g., blood or a certain drug) and $u_i(y_i)$ is patient i's objective chance of recovery (measured before treatment) if he receives the quantity y_i.

The two principles of compensation and sum-fitness (section 2.1) correspond to, respectively, the solution that equalizes individual utilities and the solution that maximizes the sum of individual utilities:

egalitarian solution: find $y_i \geq 0$ such that $u_i(y_i) = u_j(y_j)$ and $y_N = t$

(classical) utilitarian: find $y_i \geq 0$ maximizing $\sum_i u_i(y_i)$ under $y_N = t$

$$(11)$$

If the utilitarian solution is always well-defined mathematically (provided that each function u_i is increasing and continuous), the egalitarian one is not. For instance, the ranges of the functions u_1 and u_2 may not overlap. The proper formulation is that some agents may receive zero, $y_i = 0$, but only if they enjoy the largest utility level:

egalitarian* solution: find $y_i \geq 0$ such that $y_N = t$ and for all i

$$y_i > 0 \Rightarrow u_i(y_i) = \min_j u_j(y_j)$$

$$(12)$$

Whenever each function u_i is continuous and nondecreasing, this definition is unambiguous. See exercise 2.15 for the mathematical discussion of this fact.

A crucial factor influencing the comparison of the egalitarian* and (classical) utilitarian solutions is whether or not the marginal utility functions decrease, namely whether or not the functions u_i are concave. They are if consuming one more unit of resources always increases an agent's utility less than did the previous unit.

This fundamental property of utility functions plays a central role in chapters 5 and 6, as in most of economic analysis. It is quite plausible in the cake-tasting example: the first bite is always the most enjoyable! Much less so in the case of medical drugs (one pill of antibiotics won't do any good but 20 may cure you) and other commodities whose consumption must reach a certain threshold in order to have an impact.

We will discuss the utilitarian model of resources allocation first in the case where all utility functions are concave. We emphasize that the classical utilitarian and egalitarian* solutions are different and yet that at a deeper level they are identical. We will show that the three solutions discussed earlier—proportional, uniform gains, uniform losses—are simple special cases of this model.

However, if utility functions are not concave, the egalitarian* and classical utilitarian solutions are irreconcilable, and they lead to radically different conceptions of distributive justice.

Example 2.7 Common Utility and Unequal Endowments   The base utility function is u and agent i is initially endowed with x_i units of the resources. Upon receiving the share y_i of the resources, her final utility is $u_i(y_i) = u(x_i + y_i)$. One interpretation is redistribution of income: x_i is the income before the division of the subsidy t.

Assume that u is increasing and concave. A simple observation, due to Mill, is that the egalitarian* and classical utilitarian programs coincide in this case. Their recommendation is to equalize the net income $x_i + y_i$, taking into account the nonnegativity constraint on y_i. We compute the egalitarian* solution first. The system (12) gives

$$\text{for all } i: \quad y_i > 0 \Rightarrow x_i + y_i = \min_j \{x_j + y_j\} \tag{13}$$

Upon writing $z_i = x_i + y_i$ for the net income, we recognize here the uniform gains solution which allocates the resources $s = x_N + t$ (the surplus t) given the claims x_i.

The classical utilitarian solution maximizes $\sum_i u(x_i + y_i)$ under the constraints $y_i \geq 0$, $y_N = t$. Because u is a concave function, the first-order optimality conditions capture the optimal solution:

$$y_i > 0 \Rightarrow u'(x_i + y_i) = \max_j u'(x_j + y_j)$$

which is the same system as (13) because u' is decreasing.

Next we consider the case of an increasing and strictly *convex* utility function u (strictly increasing marginal utility). The egalitarian* solution is still computed as the uniform gains solution of the problem with claims x_i and resources $x_N + t$. It is entirely independent of the choice of the increasing utility function u. The classical utilitarian solution, on the other hand, allocates the entire subsidy to one agent with the largest initial endowment. In other words, the richest agent takes all!

To check this claim, consider two agents i, j such that $x_i \geq x_j$, and assume that they receive positive shares y_i, y_j. Convexity of u implies that

$$u(x_i + y_i) + u(x_j + y_j) < u(x_i + y_i + y_j) + u(x_j)$$

Hence transferring y_j to the "richer" agent i increases the sum of individual utilities, as required by classical utilitarianism. It is now a simple matter to deduce that an allocation is optimal for the classical utilitarian criterion if and only if it gives all the resources to an agent i with the largest initial endowment x_i (if there is exactly one such agent, the optimal allocation is unique).

In the context of redistribution of income, a convex utility function makes little sense. It does in the medical triage problem: if we have barely enough medicine to save two patients, it is ethically sensible to concentrate on the two most promising patients and ignore the others altogether. Another example is the distribution of subsidies among ailing firms in a regulated economy.

A difficulty of the "richest takes all" solution is its discontinuity with respect to individual characteristics. A small increase in the initial endowment x_i may result in a dramatic shift of the share y_i: it may give agent i the largest initial endowment, thus shifting all the resources onto his plate. This unpalatable feature never occurs with the classical utilitarian solution if utilities are concave, or with the egalitarian* solution for any utility functions; see exercises 2.15 and 2.16.

Example 2.8 Constant Utility Ratios   The base utility function u is strictly concave, and agent i's utility from taking a bite of cake piece y_i is $u_i(y_i) = a_i u(y_i)$. The constant factor a_i measures agent i's productivity in generating utility. Here the compensation and sum-fitness principles make two opposite recommendations.

Assume for simplicity that $u(0) = 0$. The egalitarian* solution simply equalizes net utilities

$$a_i u(y_i) = a_j u(y_j) \qquad \text{for all } i, j$$

Therefore $a_i > a_j \Rightarrow y_j > y_i$: a larger share compensates the agents with low productivity. By contrast, the classical utilitarian solution rewards productivity and gives a larger share to the agents with a larger coefficient a_i. To see this, we write the first-order optimality condition of the maximization problem:[18]

$$a_i u'(y_i) = a_j u'(y_j)$$

and the conclusion $a_i > a_j \Rightarrow y_i > y_j$ follows because u' is decreasing.

The link between the classical utilitarian and egalitarian solutions when individual utility functions are concave is apparent when we write the first-order optimality conditions of the

---

18. In order to avoid boundary solutions, let us assume, for instance, that $u'(0) = +\infty$. Then the first unit of the good is infinitely more valuable than the next one.

classical utilitarian program (11). Because each u_i is concave, these conditions completely characterize the optimal solution. They are written as follows:

for all i: $y_i > 0 \Rightarrow u'_i(y_i) = \max\limits_j u'_j(y_j)$

Hence the utilitarian solution with utilities u_i equals the egalitarian solution with utilities $-u'_i$. Symmetrically the egalitarian solution with utilities u_i equals the classical utilitarian one with utilities $U_i = \int (A - u_i)$, where the constant A is large enough to ensure $u_i(y_i) \leq A$ for all y_i.

An important property shared by the classical utilitarian solution when utilities are concave and the egalitarian* solution for any individual utilities is *resource monotonicity*: when t increases, every individual share y_i increases. The proof is the subject of exercises 2.15 and 2.16.

Given resource monotonicity, we can think of the allocation process with given utility functions u_i and varying t, as one of pouring water into individual vessels of arbitrary shapes. In figure 2.6 are depicted three such vessels connected to a common reservoir. If the height reached by the quantity y_i of water in vessel i equals $u_i(y_i)$—the width at this level being $1/u'_i(y_i)$—the law of gravity delivers the egalitarian* solution for these utility functions.

A property related to resource monotonicity is *population monotonicity*: when an agent absconds and the resources to be divided remain the same, this is good news for all remaining

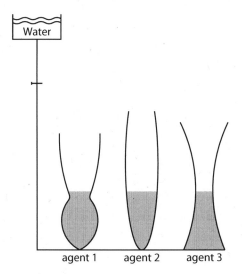

Figure 2.6
Hydraulic method

agents. This property is clear in the hydraulic representation: when agent i's vessel is shut down or destroyed, "his" water share is redistributed to all other vessels, so the level of water does not fall.

We check now that our three basic solutions, proportional, uniform gains, and uniform losses, admit a hydraulic representation. The corresponding vessels are depicted in figures 2.7 to 2.9.

In figure 2.7 the width of agent i's vessel is proportional to her claim, resulting in the proportional solution. In figures 2.8 and 2.9 the vessels are of equal width, or reduce to a tube of insignificant width. In figure 2.8 agent 4 with the largest claim x_4 receives the first $(x_4 - x_3)$ units of water; the next $2(x_3 - x_2)$ units are split equally between agents 3 and 4; the next $3(x_2 - x_1)$ units are split equally among 2, 3, and 4; all additional units are split equally among all four agents. This algorithm delivers precisely the uniform losses solution in the deficit case (see exercise 2.6), and the equal surplus solution is the excess case. We see similarly (again with the help of exercise 2.6) that the hydraulic method in figure 2.9 illustrates the uniform gains method in the deficit as well as excess cases.

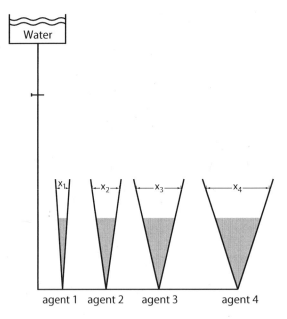

Figure 2.7
Proportional method

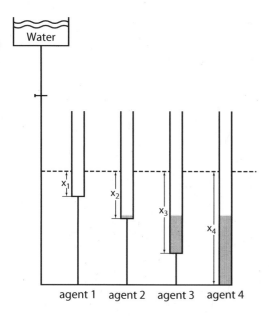

Figure 2.8
Uniform losses/equal surplus

In the hydraulic representation of the proportional solution, the height of agent i's vessel when it contains y_i units of water is $u_i(y_i) = y_i/x_i$, up to the normalization at one when the vessel contains exactly x_i units. For this choice of utilities, this solution is egalitarian* as in system (12). If we choose instead the utility functions $u_i(y_i) = Ay_i - (y_i^2/2x_i)$, where A is larger than the ratio t/x_N, the proportional solution becomes classical utilitarianism as in (11).

Computing similarly the "volume to height" function in figures 2.8 and 2.9 yields a representation of uniform losses/equal surplus and of uniform gains as egalitarian* methods in the sense of (12),[19] or classical utilitarian in the sense of (11). For instance, the uniform losses solution is classical utilitarian for $u_i(y_i) = x_i y_i - (y_i^2/2)$.

We conclude this chapter with an example where individual utilities are not concave, and the classical utilitarian solution is neither resource nor population monotonic.

---

19. The utility functions are, however, discontinuous, and this creates a minor technical difficulty.

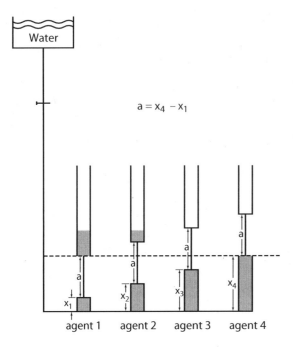

Figure 2.9
Uniform gains

Example 2.9 Failure of Resource and Population Monotonicity Two agents have the following utility functions:

$$u_1(y_1) = 2y_1, \qquad \text{all } y_1 \geq 0$$

$$u_2(y_2) = y_2 \qquad \text{for } 0 \leq y_2 \leq 10$$

$$\qquad = 4y_2 - 30 \qquad \text{for } y_2 \geq 10$$

Agent 1's marginal utility is constant and equal to 2; agent 2's is 1 up to ten units and rises to 4 afterward.

The classical utilitarian solution gives all the resources t to agent 1 or all to agent 2:

$$t < 15 \Rightarrow u_1(t) > u_2(t) \Rightarrow y_1 = t, y_2 = 0$$

$$t > 15 \Rightarrow u_2(t) > u_1(t) \Rightarrow y_1 = 0, y_2 = t$$

Notice that for $t = 15$, the solution can give t to either agent, with no possibility of compromise.

Thus an increase of the resources from $t = 10$ to $t = 20$ wipes out agent 1's share, and resource monotonicity is violated. Compare this with the egalitarian solution:

$$t \leq 15 \Rightarrow y_1 = \tfrac{1}{3}t, \; y_2 = \tfrac{2}{3}t$$

$$t \geq 15 \Rightarrow y_1 = \tfrac{2}{3}t - 5, \; y_2 = \tfrac{1}{3}t + 5$$

To check that the classical utilitarian solution is not population monotonic, fix $t = 18$ and consider a third agent with a marginal utility of 4 up to five units and zero afterward:

$$u_3(y_3) = 4y_3 \qquad \text{for } 0 \leq y_3 \leq 5$$

$$u_3(y_3) = 20 \qquad \text{for } 5 \leq y_3$$

The classical utilitarian distribution of 18 units is $y_1 = 13$, $y_2 = 0$, $y_3 = 5$. Upon dropping agent 3, the distribution becomes $y_1 = 0$, $y_2 = 18$. So that agent 1's share vanishes, in violation of population monotonicity.

2.6   Introduction to the Literature

The four principles of section 2.1 are inspired by similar taxonomies in the social psychology literature: see Deutsch (1975), Rescher (1966), and Cook and Hegtvedt (1983).

The lifeboat stories in example 2.1 are discussed by the literature on medical triage, in particular, Winslow (1982). Elster (1992) provides many examples of rationing problems, inspiring some of your examples in section 2.2 as well as in exercise 2.1. The indexes of voting power alluded to in example 2.3 are discussed extensively in two introductory books, Straffin (1980) and Felsenthal and Machover (1998).

The model of fair division developed in sections 2.2 to 2.4 appeared first in the papers by Banker (1981) and O'Neill (1982), and inspired a sizable body of axiomatic research. Recent surveys include Moulin (1988, ch. 6), Herrero and Villar (2001), and Moulin (2001a).

Aumann and Maschler (1985) focused on the contested garment method (section 2.3) and its generalization to an arbitrary number of agents (exercise 2.11). This article, together with O'Neill (1982), stresses the origin of the problem in the Talmudic literature; Rabinovitch (1973) is the historical source from which the contested garment quote is borrowed. See also exercises 2.10.

The entire section 2.4 is inspired by Young's (1988, 1990) work on equal sacrifice methods. He provides axiomatic characterizations of these methods based on the separability property known as consistency, already used by Aumann and Maschler (1985). The general characterization of consistent methods in Young (1987) is related to the hydraulic representation of deficit and surplus-sharing methods in section 2.5. Kaminski (2000) introduces this intuitive representation and explains its link with consistency. Finally the scheduling story in example 2.6 is inspired by the work on fair queuing due to Shenker (1995) and Demers et al. (1990).

Exercise 2.2 borrows ideas from Moulin (1987), and exercises 2.3 and 2.9 from Herrero and Villar (2001). Exercise 2.4 is generalized by Sprumont (1991) into a characterization of the uniform gains solution.

Exercises to Chapter 2

Exercise 2.1

In the following examples, identify the principle or principles in section 2.1 of which a given policy is an example. Find more policies and connect them similarly to the four principles.

a. For the education of which child should we spend more resources?

- The hardworking but not very gifted
- The good tempered and parent loving
- The least academically gifted
- The most academically gifted
- Equally, irrespective of gift or work

b. How to allocate scarce legal resources, namely public defenders?

- Favor defendants with the cleanest criminal record
- Favor defendants accused of the lesser crimes
- Favor defendants accused of the worst crimes
- Equalize the lawyer x hours expense on all defendants
- Minimize the total number of jail years awarded to the group of defendants
- Minimize the maximal number of jail years awarded to any one defendant

c. How to prioritize the restoration of electric power after a storm?

- Easy customers first (near to source)
- Hospitals, fire station first
- Elderly residential customers first
- Big industrial users first

- Small residential users first
- Important citizens first

Exercise 2.2 Merging and Splitting

We start with the resources t and a vector of claims (x_i), $i = 1, \ldots, n$. Both cases $t \leq x_N$ and $t \geq x_N$ are possible. We say that agents i and j merge their claims if j transfers his claim x_j to i so that the new problem has $(n-1)$ agents and agent i's claim is $x_i + x_j$. Symmetrically we say that agent i splits his claim x_i if i is replaced by two agents i_1, i_2 with claims x_{i_1}, x_{i_2} such that $x_{i_1} + x_{i_2} = x_i$, so the new problem has $(n+1)$ agents.

a. Under the proportional solution in both cases, deficit or excess, show that merging or splitting is a matter of indifference.

b. Show that under the uniform gains solution in both cases, merging is bad and splitting is good:

- After-merging share $y_i' \leq$ before-merging shares $y_i + y_j$
- After-splitting shares $y_{i_1}' + y_{i_2}' \geq$ before-splitting share y_i

c. Show that under the equal surplus solution, merging is bad and splitting is good. Show that under the uniform losses solution, merging is good and splitting is bad.

*d. For the deficit case, $t \leq x_N$, the proportional solution is characterized by the indifference to merging/splitting property.

*Exercise 2.3 Independence of Higher Claims

For a distribution problem with deficit, t, x_i, $t \leq x_N$, the property independence of higher claims (IHC) is discussed at the end of section 2.2:

for all i, j: $x_i \leq x_j \leq x_j' \Rightarrow y_i = y_i'$

where y_i and y_i' are respectively agent i's share for the initial profile of claims x_i and for the profile where x_j' replaces x_j, everything else equal.

The goal of the exercise is to show that there is only one solution satisfying equal treatment of equals and independence of higher claims, and it is uniform gains. Fix a profile of claims x_i, and label the agents in such a way that $x_1 \leq x_2 \leq \cdots \leq x_n$. Define for $k = 1, 2, \ldots, n$, $z_k = \sum_{j=1}^{k-1} x_j + (n-k+1)x_k$ so that $z_1 = nx_1 \leq z_2 \leq z_3 \leq \cdots \leq z_n = x_N$.

a. Choose t such that $0 \leq t \leq z_1$. By ETE, at the profile $x_i', x_i' = x_1$ for all i, each agent gets t/n. Show that by ETE and IHC, the same is true at the profile x_i'' where $x_1'' = x_1$,

$x_i'' = x_2$ for $i = 2, \ldots, n$. Repeat the argument to show that equal shares still prevail at profile x_i''' where $x_1''' = x_1$, $x_2''' = x_2$, $x_i''' = x_3$, for $i = 3, \ldots, n$. Conclude that a method meeting ETE and IHC coincides with uniform gains whenever $t \leq z_1$.

b. Choose t such that $z_1 \leq t \leq z_2$ and consider first the profile of claims x_i^*, $x_1^* = x_1$, $x_i^* = \frac{t - x_1}{n - 1}$ for $i = 2, \ldots, n$. Show by a similar argument that ETE and IHC force the uniform gains solution for the interval $[z_1, z_2]$. Generalize to any t, $0 \leq t \leq z_n$.

Exercise 2.4 Strategy-Proofness of the Uniform Gains Solution

a. Consider a problem with deficit, t, x_i, $t \leq x_N$, and denote the uniform gains shares by (y_i). Show that an agent's share y_i is nondecreasing in his claim: if x_i increases to x_i', everything else (t and x_j, for all $j \neq i$) equal, agent i's new share y_i' is not smaller than y_i.

Show that if y_i is strictly smaller than x_i, and x_i increases to x_i', everything else equal, agent i's share does not change: $y_i' = y_i$.

Deduce that if agent i prefers a larger share to a smaller one—provided they are both below x_i—he cannot benefit from altering (increasing or decreasing) his claim x_i.

b. Consider now a problem with excess, $t \geq x_N$. Show similarly that y_i is nondecreasing in x_i and show the following:

$$\{y_i > x_i \text{ and } x_i' < x_i\} \Rightarrow y_i = y_i'$$

Deduce that if among two shares not smaller than x_i, agent i prefers the smaller one, he cannot benefit from altering his claim x_i.

c. Under the proportional method, check that increasing one's claim is profitable in the deficit case, and that decreasing it is profitable in the excess case (preferences over shares are as in questions *a* and *b* respectively).

d. Under the uniform losses/equal surplus solution, which distortion of one's claim is profitable?

*Exercise 2.5

a. We fix a profile of claims x_i, ranking increasingly as $x_1 \leq x_2 \leq \cdots \leq x_n$. Prove that agent 1 and agent n have unambiguous preferences over the three basic methods, in the sense that the three corresponding shares are always ranked in the same way.

Denoting by $y_i(X)$ agent i's share under the method X, prove the following inequalities:

Deficit

$$y_1(UL) \leq y_1(PRO) \leq y_1(UG)$$

$$y_n(UG) \leq y_n(PRO) \leq y_n(UL)$$

Excess

$$y_1(PRO) \le y_1(ES) \le y_1(UG)$$

$$y_n(UG) \le y_n(ES) \le y_n(PRO)$$

b. Find an example of a three person deficit problem, $x_1 < x_2 < x_3, \ t < x_1 + x_2 + x_3$, such that the proportional method is the worst for agent 2:

$$y_2(PRO) < y_2(UG) \quad \text{and} \quad y_2(PRO) < y_2(UL)$$

c. For an arbitrary excess problem with an arbitrary number of agents, show that the equal surplus method cannot be the worst of the three for anyone, namely that the two inequalities

$$y_i(ES) < y_i(PRO) \quad \text{and} \quad y_i(ES) < y_i(UL)$$

are incompatible for i.

Exercise 2.6 Other Algorithms to Compute the Uniform Gains and Uniform Losses Solutions

a. Given is a problem with excess, t, x_i, $x_N \le t$, where the claims are ordered increasingly, $x_1 \le x_2 \le \cdots \le x_n$. Consider the following algorithm:

Step 1.   Increase agent 1's claims by up to $(x_2 - x_1)$ units

Step 2.   Increase agent 1, 2's claims by up to $(x_3 - x_2)$ units each

Step 3.   Increase agent 1, 2, 3's claims by up to $(x_4 - x_3)$ units each

$\vdots$

The algorithm stops when $(t - x_N)$ units have been distributed.

Show that the outcome is the uniform gains solution.

b. Given is a problem with deficit $t \le x_N$, and with the claims increasingly ordered $x_1 \le x_2 \le \cdots \le x_n$. The following algorithm reduces the individual claims, starting from the highest claims:

Step 1.   Decrease n's claim by up to $(x_n - x_{n-1})$ units

Step 2.   Decrease n and $(n - 1)$'s claim by up to $(x_{n-1} - x_{n-2})$ units each

Step 3.   Decrease n, $(n - 1)$ and $(n - 2)$'s claim by up to $(x_{n-2} - x_{n-3})$ units each

$\vdots$

We stop whenever total reduction in claims reaches $(x_N - t)$ units. At this point, each agent receives his reduced claim

Show that this algorithm delivers the uniform gains solution.

c. Given a deficit problem as in question b, consider the following algorithm:

Step 1.   Give the first $(x_n - x_{n-1})$ units to agent n

Step 2.   Split up to $2(x_{n-1} - x_{n-2})$ units equally between agents $n, n-1$

Step 3.   Split up to $3(x_{n-2} - x_{n-3})$ units equally between agents $n, n-1, n-2$

$\vdots$

The algorithm stops when t units have been distributed.

Show that the outcome is the uniform losses solution.

*Exercise 2.7

We are in the deficit case, $t \le x_N$.

a. The goal is to show formally that uniform gains is the most progressive among all methods meeting fair ranking, which is property (7) in section 2.4. We fix a list of increasing claims $x_1 \le x_2 \le \cdots \le x_n$. Let y_i^* be agent i's share under uniform gains and y_i be his share under an arbitrary method satisfying fair ranking. Prove that

$$y_1 \le y_1^* \Leftrightarrow \frac{x_1 - y_1^*}{x_1} \le \frac{x_1 - y_1}{x_1}$$

If $y_1 = y_1^*$, prove similarly that $y_2 \le y_2^*$; if $y_1 = y_1^*$ and $y_2 \le y_2^*$, prove that $y_3 \le y_3^*$; and so on. State and prove an analogue sequence of properties establishing that the uniform losses method is the most regressive among those meeting fair ranking.

b. Consider the hyperregressive solution r alluded to at the end of section 2.4; the profile of shares $y = r(t, x)$ is defined by the following property:

$$\{x_i < x_j \text{ and } y_j < x_j\} \Rightarrow y_i = 0 \qquad \text{for all } i, j$$

and by equal treatment of equals. Show that this corresponds to the definition given at the end of section 2.4. Show that this solution violates fair ranking, property (7). Show that among all solutions r of the deficit problem where $0 \le y_i \le x_i$ for all i, the solution above is the most regressive one.

c. Define similarly the hyperprogressive method, the dual of the hyperregressive one, and show that it is the most progressive of all solutions r of the deficit problem.

*Exercise 2.8 Lower Bounds, Upper Bounds

We are in the deficit case, $t < x_N$.

a. We fix t the resources, n the number of agents and x_i the claim of a certain agent i. Show that under uniform gains, agent i's share is bounded below as follows:

$$y_i \geq \min \left\{ x_i, \frac{t}{n} \right\}$$

The inequality above holds true for any choice of the variables x_j, $j \neq i$, provided $t \leq x_N$.

b. Show that under uniform losses or proportional, agent i's share can only be bounded below by zero if we do not know the variables x_j, $j \neq i$ (we only know that they satisfy $x_i + \sum_j x_j \geq t$).

c. Now we fix n, x_i and the *deficit* t^* (i.e., $t^* = x_N - t$); we do not know the variables x_j, $j \neq i$ (except that we must have $t^* \leq x_N$). Show that under uniform losses agent i's share is bounded above as follows:

$$y_i \leq \max \left\{ x_i - \frac{1}{n} t^*, 0 \right\}$$

What is the corresponding upper bound under proportional or uniform gains?

Exercise 2.9 Truncation and Concession

a. Fix a two-person solution for the deficit problems of section 2.3, satisfying equal treatment of equals, truncation, and concession. Fix a profile of claims x_1, x_2 with $x_1 \leq x_2$. For t such that $0 \leq t \leq x_1$, use T and ETE to show that t is split equally. For $x_2 \leq t \leq x_1 + x_2$ use similarly C and ETE to compute the shares. Finally compute the shares for $x_1 \leq t \leq x_2$ and conclude that our method is the contested garment solution.

b. Show that a solution satisfies truncation if and only if its dual (section 2.3) satisfies concession.

Exercise 2.10 Run to the Bank

We are in the deficit case, $t \leq x_N$. Given a rationing problem, we let the agents run to the bank, and we suppose that the ordering of their arrival is random and without bias: each ordering is equally plausible. The bank then serves the agents in the order of their arrival; the first agent receives his full claim or the entire resources, whichever is less; if there is something left after the first agent, the second one gets his full claim or all the remaining resources, whichever is less; and so on.

a. Show that for a two-person problem, "run to the bank" coincides with the contested garment method.

b. Consider the following inheritance problem, due to the Talmudic scholar Ibn Ezra:

Jacob died and his son Reuben produced a deed duly witnessed that Jacob willed to him his entire estate on his death, his son Simeon also produced a deed that his father willed to him half of the estate, Levi produced a deed giving him one-third and Judah brought forth a deed giving him one-quarter. All of them bear the same date.

Compute the division of the estate under "run to the bank."
Compare it to the divisions under proportional, uniform gains, and uniform losses.

c. In example 2.5 compute the "run to the bank" solution for the values, $t = 20, 40$, and 50.

*d. Show that run to the bank is self-dual. Show it satisfies truncation and concession (recall from exercise 2.9 that T and C are dual properties).

*e. To a problem with deficit t, x_i, we associate the following cooperative game (see chapter 5):

$$v(S) = \min\left\{ t, \sum_{i \in S} x_i \right\}$$

Show that the Shapley value of this cooperative game is precisely the "run to the bank" solution.

*Exercise 2.11 The Talmudic Solution

We are in the deficit case $t \leq x_N$. The Talmudic solution is a hybrid of the uniform gains and uniform losses solutions. The method divides $t^* = x_N/2$ in proportions to the claims x_i:

$$\text{at} \quad t^* = \frac{x_N}{2} \quad \text{we have} \quad y_i^* = \frac{x_i}{2} \quad \text{for all } i$$

Then the method follows uniform gains with *respect to the halved claims* for t, between 0 and t^*. It follows uniform losses with respect to the halved claims for t, between t^* and x_N:

$$y_i = UG\left(t; \frac{x_i}{2}, i \in N \right) \qquad\qquad \text{if } 0 \leq t \leq t^*$$

$$y_i = UL\left(t - t^*; \frac{x_i}{2}, i \in N \right) + \frac{x_i}{2} \quad \text{if } t^* \leq t \leq x_N$$

a. Check that this method is the contested garment solution when $n = 2$.

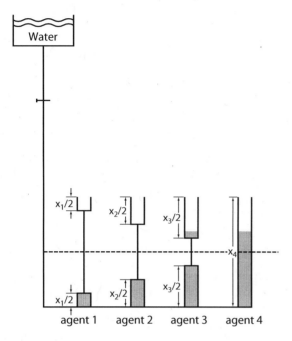

Figure 2.10
Talmudic method

b. Check its hydraulic representation on figure 2.10.

c. Compute the Talmudic solution in the numerical example of question *b* of the previous exercise.

d. Compute the Talmudic solution in example 2.5 for the three values $t = 20, 40$, and 50.

*e. Show that the Talmudic solution is self-dual. Show it satisfies truncation and concession.

Exercise 2.12

Consider a society $N = \{1, 2, 3, 4, 5, 6, 7\}$ and the method that

· Gives absolute priority to any agent in $\{1, 2\}$ over any agent in $\{3, 4, 5\}$ and absolute priority to any agent in $\{3, 4, 5\}$ over any agent in $\{6, 7\}$

· Between agents 1 and 2 is the proportional method

· Between agents 3, 4, and 5, is the uniform gains method

· Between agents 6 and 7 is the uniform losses method

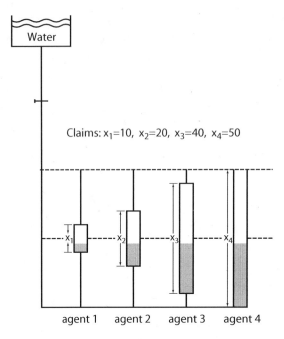

Claims: $x_1=10$, $x_2=20$, $x_3=40$, $x_4=50$

agent 1   agent 2   agent 3   agent 4

Figure 2.11
Method of exercise 2.13

a. Compute the solution it recommends in the following examples:

Agent	1	2	3	4	5	6	7	Resources
Claim	10	0	0	10	15	0	15	12 or 40
Claim	5	10	80	70	10	5	0	50 or 120
Claim	100	50	10	10	20	15	25	130 or 180 or 200

b. Give, as in section 2.5, a "hydraulic" representation of this method.

Exercise 2.13

Consider the rationing method of which the hydraulic representation is given on figure 2.11.

a. Compute the allocation it recommends for $t = 20$, $t = 50$, $t = 80$, and $t = 90$.

b. Is this method progressive? Regressive?

*c. Generalize the method to an arbitrary number of agents and give a formula to compute the shares it recommends. *Hint:* Compare it to the Talmudic method in exercise 2.11.

Exercise 2.14

We consider the equal sacrifice methods of section 2.4.

a. Show that the method where $u(z) = z^q$ for all z, converges to the proportional solution when q is positive and approaches zero. To this end, fix a problem t, x_i, with $t < x_N$ and write $y(q)$ its solution under this method. Show that the limit y of $y(q)$ as q approaches zero is the proportional solution. Show that as q goes to infinity, the limit of $y(q)$ is the hyperregressive solution defined in exercise 2.7.

b. Consider the method where $u(z) = -1/z^p$ for all z. Show that it converges to the proportional solution when p is positive and approaches zero, and to uniform gains when p becomes arbitrarily large.

c. Show that the u-method meets fair ranking (7) if and only if u is concave.

d. Show that the u-method is progressive (resp. regressive)—see (8)—if and only if $z.u'(z)$ is nonincreasing (resp. nondecreasing) in z.

*Exercise 2.15

We consider the egalitarian* solution to the problem t, u_i, defined by the system (12) in section 2.5.

a. Show that if u_i is continuous and strictly increasing, system (12) always has a unique solution. Show that if u_i is continuous and nondecreasing, the system (12) may have several solutions, but they all yield the same utilities $u_i(y_i)$.

b. Assume that u_i is strictly increasing and continuous. Show that the egalitarian* solution is *strictly* resource monotonic: $t < t' \Rightarrow y_i < y_i'$ for all i.

c. Show that the egalitarian* solution is robust to a small change in the utility functions. To this end, assume that u_i takes the form $u_i(a_i, x_i)$ where a_i is a real parameter and that u_i is continuous in the pair (a_i, x_i), as well as strictly increasing in x_i. Show that the egalitarian* solution depends continuously on a_i.

Exercise 2.16

Consider the classical utilitarian solution (11) to the allocation problem t, u_i of section 2.5.

a. Assume that each function u_i is strictly increasing and strictly convex (marginal utility u_i' is strictly increasing). Show that the utilitarian solution gives all the resources to a single agent (this generalizes the argument given in example 2.7).

b. Assume that each function u_i is strictly increasing and strictly concave. Recall from section 2.5 that the utilitarian solution coincides with the egalitarian* solution for the utilities $-u_i'$. Deduce that it is strictly resource monotonic. Show that it is robust to a small change in the utility function u_i, as in question c of exercise 2.15.

3 Cardinal Welfarism

3.1 Welfarism

The welfarist postulate states that the distribution of individual welfare across the agents/ citizens is the only legitimate yardstick along which the states of the world can be compared. In the cardinal version of welfarism,[1] individual welfare is measured by an index of *utility*, and comparisons of the utilities of two different agents are meaningful.

Welfarism is a reductionist model of distributive justice. It views an agent as a machine producing welfare/utility at a given state of the world, and compares two feasible states by means of the two utility profiles they generate. Welfarism is endstate justice at its best; that is to say, the process by which a particular utility profile is reached (e.g., the physical allocation of the resources of the world) is devoid of ethical content: it is the means toward achieving a particular profile of utilities. For instance, the criterion "no envy" discussed in chapters 6 and 7 is irrelevant to welfarism because it relies on interpersonal comparisons of individual allocations of resources.

The most basic concept of welfarism[2] is efficiency-fitness (Pareto optimality) of which we repeat the definition already given in section 1.3. Consider two feasible states of the world x and y, resulting for agent i in the utility $u_i(x)$ and $u_i(y)$ respectively. State y is Pareto superior to state x if no agent j strictly prefers state x to state y, that is to say, $u_j(x) \le u_j(y)$ for all j, and moreover at least one agent i strictly prefers state y, $u_i(x) < u_i(y)$. Thus y is Pareto superior to x if the move from x to y is by unanimous consent (in the sense that everyone agrees to a change that does not decrease his or her own utility level). A state x is *Pareto optimal* (efficient) if there is no feasible state y Pareto superior to x. Thus, if the current state is x, we cannot generate a consensus to move to another state y (except in the case where everyone enjoys the same utility level in both states).

The task of cardinal welfarism is to pick, among the feasible utility profiles (lists of one utility level per agent), one of the Pareto optimal ones. In many specific allocation problems, the Pareto optimality property has much bite, in the sense that it eliminates many if not most feasible allocations of the resources. Examples 3.2, 3.3, 3.8, and 3.9. On the other hand, in the fair division problems of section 2.5, all feasible allocations are Pareto optimal because there is a single commodity and everyone prefers a bigger share to a smaller one. The only way to increase agents i's utility is to give him more resources, which in turn decreases the utility of another agent. The same property (all feasible allocations are Pareto optimal) holds true in examples 3.1, 3.4, 3.5, and 3.6.

---

1. The ordinal version of welfarism is called social choice; it is the subject of chapter 4.
2. Be it in its cardinal or ordinal version.

A general fact is that the property of efficiency/Pareto optimality is orthogonal to distributive concerns. Typically the allocation where all of the available resources are used to the benefit of a single agent meets the criterion, although it is the most unfair of all distributive systems.

The task of the welfarist benevolent dictator is to compare normatively any two utility profiles (u_i), (u_i') and decide which one is best. The key idea is to insist that this comparison should follow the rationality principles of individual decision-making, namely *completeness* and *transitivity*.[3] Completeness says that any two profiles can always be compared: either (u_i) is preferred to (u_i'), denoted $(u_i) \succ (u_i')$, or the reverse preference $(u_i') \succ (u_i)$ holds, or they are declared indifferent $(u_i) \sim (u_i')$. Transitivity means that $(u_i) \succsim (u_i')$—that profile (u_i) is preferred or indifferent to profile (u_i')—and $(u_i') \succsim (u_i'')$ imply $(u_i) \succsim (u_i'')$.

The preference relation is called a *social welfare ordering*, and the definition and comparison of various social welfare orderings is the object of cardinal welfarism. The two most prominent instances of social welfare orderings are the *classical utilitarian*, namely $(u_i) \succsim (u_i')$, if and only if $\sum_i u_i \geq \sum_i u_i'$, and the *egalitarian one*, namely $(u_i) \succ (u_i')$ if and only if, upon reordering the profile by increasing coordinates as (u_i^*) and $(u_i^{*'})$, the former is lexicographically superior to the latter. The former expresses the sumfitness principle in the welfarist world, whereas the latter conveys the compensation principle. A variety of social welfare orderings in between those two are introduced in the subsequent sections.

Before we start the general discussion of social welfare orderings in section 3.2, it is important to recall that we focus exclusively on the "micro" version of welfarism, and pay only lip service to its "macro" interpretation still an influential idea in contemporary political philosophy. We look at microallocation problems, involving a small number of commodities and where utility is tailored to the problem at hand. For instance, in the problem of locating a facility (examples 3.4 and 3.8), utility measures the (negative of the) distance between the agent in question and the facility. In example 3.11 the issue is to distribute fruits from which our agents metabolize vitamins, and utility is measured by the quantity of such vitamins. And so it goes on. Thus the context dictates the interpretation of utility and, in turn, influences the choice of the social welfare ordering (see the distinction between tastes and needs in the examples just mentioned). The central assumption that individual utilities can be objectively measured and compared across different agents can be more or less convincing. The distance from an agents' home to the facility (examples 3.4, 3.5, and 3.8) is an objective fact, as is, to a large extent, the amount of a certain vitamin or drug he needs to be healthy. But his taste for a certain piece of cake, or for art, cannot be measured along a common scale.

---

3. A general discussion of the rationality of choice for a single decision-maker is in section 4.1.

The microwelfarist viewpoint separates the allocation problem at stake from the rest of our agent's characteristics. It assumes that the level of my utility from the allocation I receive in the microproblem can be measured independently from the rest of my characteristics. Moreover the utility of those agents not concerned by the microallocation problem should not matter either. This crucial property of *separability* is expressed axiomatically in the next section and is the basis of the additive representation discussed there.

From this axiomatic analysis, three paramount social welfare orderings emerge. In addition to the classical utilitarian collective utility function and the egalitarian social welfare ordering already mentioned, the Nash collective utility function is simply the product of individual utilities. From the theoretical discussion of section 3.2, as well as the examples of sections 3.4 and 3.5, the Nash collective utility function emerges as a sensible compromise between the egalitarian and classical utilitarian ones. The nontechnical reader is urged to skip section 3.2 and go directly to the examples listed from section 3.3 on.

In contrast to microwelfarism, macrowelfarism is an encompassing approach to social justice, where utilities measure the overall level of happiness of a given agent/citizen (the sum of his pleasures and pains, in Bentham's words), so that the choice of a social welfare ordering amounts to an entire program of social justice.

Recall from section 1.3 the two main objections to macrowelfarism. An objective grasp of individual welfare defeats the purpose of methodological individualism. And ignoring individual responsibility in the formation of one's own welfare is morally untenable.

A popular macrowelfarist method to take into account agent's responsibility in the formation of their own welfare is to use proxy commodities (called *primary goods* by Rawls) as surrogate measurement of individual welfare. The idea is that our ability or inability to lead full and satisfying lives, to achieve high or low levels of welfare, is determined by our share of certain fundamental goods: food, shelter, health, self-respect, love, education, wealth, job, and so on. The catalog of these goods is the common denominator of human nature. The actual distribution of these primary goods tells us all that we can hope to learn about actual welfares; hence it can be used as a surrogate measurement of the distribution of welfare. If the trick of primary goods, due to Rawls, succeeds in maintaining a private sphere around each person, while offering an objective index of (access to) welfare, it pushes the difficulty back without eliminating it. The choice of a method to aggregate my holdings of primary goods into a summary "index" is tantamount (although in a less obvious way) to imposing a common value system upon all individual citizens: it imposes the same trade-offs among primary goods on all citizens. Yet an important component of my value system is my own trade-off between health and wealth (e.g., I may choose a physically dangerous, well-paid job) or between education and leisure, and so on.

*3.2   Additive Collective Utility Functions

In this section we describe the most important axiomatic results of the cardinal theory of welfarism. We state a handful of axiomatic requirements pertaining to collective rationality or fairness. Then we deduce the small family of collective utility functions (and social welfare orderings) satisfying these requirements. In this family three key social welfare orderings stand out: the classical utilitarian and Nash collective utility functions and the leximin social welfare ordering.

Two basic requirements of a social welfare ordering $\succeq$, beside the property of completeness and transitivity already mentioned, are *monotonicity* and *symmetry*. The social welfare ordering $\succeq$ is monotonic in utility u_i if an increase in agent i's utility, ceteris paribus, increases social welfare. That is, if two utility profiles $u = (u_j)$ and $u' = (u'_j)$ are such that $u_j = u'_j$ for all j, $j \neq i$, and $u_i > u'_i$, then $u \succ u'$; that is, the social welfare ordering prefers the former profile to the latter. Monotonicity has much to do with Pareto optimality: a monotonic social welfare ordering is compatible with the Pareto relation[4] in the sense that if u is Pareto superior to v, then $u \succ v$. In particular, the maximal elements of a monotonic social welfare ordering, over any feasible set of utility profiles, are Pareto optimal.

The social welfare ordering $\succeq$ is symmetric if it does not pay attention to the identity of the agents, only to their utility level. If the utility profile u obtains from v simply by permuting the index of the agents in arbitrary fashion, as (7, 2, 8, 2, 4, 4, 2) obtains from (4, 8, 4, 2, 7, 2, 2), the social welfare ordering views these two profiles as equivalent: $u \sim v$. Symmetry is equal treatment of equals, namely the basic fairness axiom discussed in section 1.1: agents can only be discriminated on the basis of their utilities, not of any other exogenous factors.

Most social welfare orderings of importance[5] are represented by a *collective utility function,* namely a real-valued function $W(u_1, u_2, \ldots, u_n)$ with the utility profile for argument and the level of collective utility for value. The function W represents the social welfare ordering $\succsim$ if $u \succsim u'$ is logically equivalent to $W(u) \geq W(u')$. The monotonicity and symmetry properties of $\succsim$ translate into the properties with the same name, for W: W is strictly monotonic in each of the variables u_i and a symmetric function of the profile.

The next property is the key argument of welfarist rationality. It says that we can ignore the unconcerned agents when choosing between two particular utility profiles u and u'. That is, if agent j receives the same utility in both profiles, $u_j = u'_j$, his utility level has no influence on the comparison of u and u'. Formally, we denote by $(u_i \mid^j a)$ the utility vector identical to (u_i) except that the jth coordinate has been replaced by a. Then the property

---

4. This relation is transitive but not complete; therefore it is not a social welfare ordering.

5. The leximin social welfare ordering is a notable exception, discussed in the next section.

independence of unconcerned agents reads as follows:

$$(u_i \mid^j a) \succsim (u_i' \mid^j a) \; \Leftrightarrow \; (u_i \mid^j b) \succsim (u_i' \mid^j b) \qquad \text{for all } u, u', j, a, \text{ and } b \tag{1}$$

This means that an agent who has no vested interest in the choice between u and u'—because his utility is the same in both profiles—can be ignored.

If property (1) fails, the choice between two particular states of the world will depend on the utility of some agents who are truly indifferent between these two states. This runs counter to the intuition of endstate justice. Absent the property, the set of agents whose utilities can influence the social welfare ordering (whether or not they are personally affected by the subsequent decisions) must be defined precisely for any microproblem of distributive justice. By contrast, under independence of unconcerned agents, microjustice works very well with a loose, encompassing set of potentially concerned agents. The property guarantees that the social welfare ordering (and the associated collective utility function) focuses exclusively on those agents whose utility is affected by the decisions to be made.

The collective utility function W is called *additive* if there is an increasing function g of one real variable such that

$$W(u) = \sum_i g(u_i) \qquad \text{for all } u \tag{2}$$

It should be clear that the social welfare ordering represented by an additive collective utility function meets property (1). If we restrict attention to continuous[6] social welfare orderings, the following converse property holds. If the continuous ordering $\succsim$ is independent of unconcerned agents, then it is represented by an additive collective utility (2). This important theorem gives a convenient representation of a rich family of social welfare orderings.

We introduce two additional properties of the collective utility (2), that limit the choice of the function g. The first property is one of fairness, and expresses an aversion for "pure" inequality. It is called the *Pigou-Dalton transfer principle*. Say that $u_1 < u_2$ at profile u and consider a transfer of utility from agent 2 to agent 1 where u_1' and u_2', the utilities after the transfer, are such that

$$u_1 < u_1', u_2' < u_2 \quad \text{and} \quad u_1' + u_2' = u_1 + u_2$$

Thus total utility to agents 1 and 2 is preserved, and the inequality gap is reduced (note that it could be reversed: $u_2' < u_1'$ is possible). We say that the move from u to u' (where $u_j = u_j'$ for $j \geq 3$) reduces the inequality between agents 1 and 2. The Pigou-Dalton transfer

---

6. The social welfare ordering $\succsim$ is continuous for all u, the sets $\{v \mid v \succsim u\}$ and $\{v \mid u \succsim v\}$, called respectively the upper and lower contour sets of u, are topologically closed.

principle requires that the social welfare ordering increases (or at least, does not decrease) in a move reducing the inequality between any two agents.

Applying this principle to the additive collective utility (2) we find that

$$\{u_1 < u'_1, u'_2 < u_2 \text{ and } u_1 + u_2 = u'_1 + u'_2\} \Rightarrow \{g(u_1) + g(u_2) \le g(u'_1) + g(u'_2)\}$$

which is equivalent to the concavity of the function g, namely its derivative is nonincreasing.

The next property is one of invariance. It is called *independence of common scale* (ICS). The property requires us to restrict attention to positive utilities, a feature that is automatically satisfied in most of our examples where the zero of utilities corresponds to the minimal feasible level; see examples 3.1, 3.2, and 3.5. The ICS property states that a simultaneous rescaling of every individual utility function does not affect the underlying social welfare ordering; it yields the same binary comparisons of utility profiles:

$$u \succsim u' \Leftrightarrow \lambda u \succsim \lambda u' \tag{3}$$

where the two profiles u, u' as well as the scaling constant λ are positive and otherwise arbitrary. For instance, if utilities represent money = willingness to pay (as in chapter 5), it does not matter if we compare cents, dozens of dollars, or thousands of dollars: the order of magnitude of the utility levels under comparison does not matter.

For an additive collective utility taking the form (2), the ICS property holds true only for a very specific family of power functions. To see this, apply (3) to the function (2), which yields

$$\sum_i (g(u_i) - g(u'_i)) \ge 0 \Leftrightarrow \sum_i (g(\lambda u_i) - g(\lambda u'_i)) \ge 0$$

It can further be shown that the only (increasing, continuous) functions g satisfying this property are (up to a multiplicative constant) of exactly three types:

$g(z) = z^p$ for a positive p

$g(z) = \log(z)$

$g(z) = -z^{-q}$ for a positive q

The corresponding collective utility W take the form

$$W_p(u) = \sum_i u_i^p, \quad \text{with } p > 0 \text{ and fixed}$$

$$W_0(u) = \sum_i \log u_i \tag{4}$$

$$W^q(u) = -\sum_i \frac{1}{u_i^q} \quad \text{with } q > 0 \text{ and fixed}$$

The family (4) has many interesting features. First, the particular collective utility function $\sum_i \log u_i$ is the limit of the other two families when p or q, respectively, approach zero.[7] It is called the *Nash collective utility* function, and is usually written in the equivalent multiplicative form $W_N(u) = \Pi_i u_i$. Of course, the function W_N is not additively decomposed as in (2), but it represents the same social welfare ordering $\succsim$ as the additive collective utility W_0.

Another collective utility function of interest within the family (4) is the classical utilitarian $W_1(u) = \sum_i u_i$, corresponding to $p = 1$. It embodies the idea of sum-fitness, and its implications are discussed in a variety of examples in the subsequent sections.

Finally we examine the impact of the Pigou-Dalton transfer principle on the family of utility functions (4). Consider the quadratic $W_2(u) = \sum_i u_i^2$. Far from seeking to reduce inequality, this collective utility function is actively promoting it. For instance, the following mathematical fact

$$u_1^2 + u_2^2 < (u_1 + u_2)^2 + (0)^2$$

implies that under W_2, transferring all the utility to one agent is desirable. Such a preference runs counter to the basic distributive fairness conveyed by the Pigou-Dalton principle.

As noted earlier, an additive collective utility (2) meets the Pigou-Dalton principle if and only if g is a concave function. Within the family (4), this eliminates all the functions W_p with $1 < p < +\infty$ and only those.

We are ready to sum up the results of our axiomatic discussion. Starting with a continuous collective utility function W representing the social welfare ordering $\succsim$, we imposed successively three requirements: independence of unconcerned individuals (1), independence of common scale (3), and the Pigou-Dalton transfer principle. Together, these properties leave us with a one-dimensional family of collective utility functions, namely

$$W_p(u) = \sum u_i^p, 0 < p \le 1$$
$$W_0(u) = \sum_i \log u_i \tag{5}$$
$$W^q(u) = -\sum_i u_i^{-q}, 0 < q < +\infty$$

Notice the striking similarity of the formula above with the family of equal sacrifice methods presented in section 2.4.

---

7. To see this, use the approximation $z^p = e^{p \log z} \simeq 1 + p \log z$, valid when p is close to zero.

Although it is defined in three pieces, the family (5) is actually continuous in the sense that W_0 is the limit of W_p and of W^q as p or q goes to zero. Two outstanding elements are the classical utilitarian W_1 and the Nash utility function W_0 (often written in multiplicative form as W_N). The third remarkable point of the family is the limit of (the social welfare ordering represented by) W^q as q goes to infinity: this is the important leximin social welfare ordering, defined and illustrated in the next section.

The three social orderings, classical utilitarian, Nash, and leximin are the three most important objects of cardinal welfarism. They are systematically compared in sections 3.4 and 3.5.

3.3   Egalitarianism and the Leximin Social Welfare Ordering

We focus in this section on the welfarist formulation of the compensation principle as the equalization of individual utilities. Full equalization is often impossible within the set of feasible outcomes—as in examples 3.1, 3.2, 3.4, and 3.5; in other cases it is feasible but incompatible with Pareto optimality—see example 3.3. The leximin social welfare ordering then selects the most egalitarian among the Pareto optimal utility distributions.

Example 3.1 Pure Lifeboat Problem   As in example 2.1, some but not all agents can be allowed on the boat, and the arbitrator must choose which subset will be saved. She can pick from a given list of subsets. Suppose that five agents are labeled $\{1, 2, 3, 4, 5\}$ and that the feasible subsets are

$\{1, 2\}\{1, 3\}\{1, 4\}\{2, 3, 5\}\{3, 4, 5\}\{2, 4, 5\}$

Thus agents 1 and 5 cannot both be in the lifeboat; we can have one of agents 2, 3, or 4 along with 1, or two of these three along with 5.

A less dramatic story is the purchase of a software program that will be available to our five agents: there are six programs to choose from, and each program is only compatible with the machines of a certain subset of agents. Or we must choose the musical background in the office space occupied by our five agents; they are six programs to choose from and a given agent likes certain programs and dislikes others: only agents 1 and 2 like the first program, and so on.[8] Note that each one of the six feasible outcomes is Pareto optimal: there is no unanimous agreement to dismiss any one of the six outcomes.

Suppose first that for each agent the utility of staying on the boat is 10 and that of swimming is 1. Then the classical utilitarian utility recommends choosing one (any one) of

8. In example 3.1 the arbitrator must choose one of the six subsets, with no possibility of compromise by randomization or timesharing. The latter is the subject of example 3.6b. See also exercise 3.6b, question c.

the three largest subsets (each one with three agents). The egalitarian arbitrator makes the same choice, based on comparing the increasing profile of utilities from lowest to highest. If a two-person subset stays on the boat, this profile is $(1, 1, 1, 10, 10)$ and if a three-person subset stays, it is $(1, 1, 10, 10, 10)$ which is lexicographically superior because the third ranked utility level is higher in the latter profile.

The point of the example is much sharper when we assume that the individual utility for being among the chosen ones varies across agents—such as in the radio program interpretation, some agents are more partial to "good" versus "bad" music than others:

Agent	1	2	3	4	5
Utility for good outcome	10	6	6	5	3
For bad outcome	0	1	1	1	0

Now the classical utilitarian arbitrator prefers to choose $\{1, 2\}$ or $\{1, 3\}$, for a total utility of 16, over any other subset; the second best is $\{2, 4, 5\}$ yielding total utility 15. His ranking of the six outcomes is as follows:

$$\{1, 2\} \sim \{1, 3\} \succ \{1, 4\} \sim \{2, 3, 5\} \succ \{2, 4, 5\} \sim \{3, 4, 5\}$$

The egalitarian arbitrator, by contrast, prefers any three-person subset over any two-person one; his ranking is as follows:

		$\{2, 3, 5\}$	with	utility	profile	$(0, 1, 3, 6, 6)$
$\{2, 4, 5\}$	$\sim$	$\{3, 4, 5\}$	with	utility	profile	$(0, 1, 3, 5, 6)$
$\{1, 2\}$	$\sim$	$\{1, 3\}$	with	utility	profile	$(0, 1, 1, 6, 10)$
		$\{1, 4\}$	with	utility	profile	$(0, 1, 1, 5, 10)$

Exercise 3.1 contrasts the classical utilitarian and egalitarian choices in example 3.1 for arbitrary utility functions.

Example 3.2 Fair Division with Identical Preference We must divide six indivisible objects among three agents, and each lot must contain two objects. Individual preferences over the different lots are identical: given any two lots, everyone agrees on which one is the better lot, or everyone is indifferent between the two lots.

The leximin social welfare ordering compares all feasible allocations, and does not require one to attach a common cardinal utility to each lot. For instance, assume that the common ordering of the fifteen lots from the objects a, b, c, d, e, and f is as follows:

$$\{a, b\} > \{b, f\} \sim \{b, e\} > \{c, d\} > \{a, c\} > \{d, e\} \sim \{b, c\} > \{c, f\} > \{a, d\} > \{a, e\}$$
$$\sim \{c, e\} \sim \{e, f\} > \{b, d\} \sim \{a, f\} \sim \{d, f\}$$

There are fifteen ways to split the six objects in three lots of two objects, and the leximin ordering allows us to compare all fifteen. For instance, $\{a, b\}\{c, d\}\{e, f\}$ is ranked above $\{a, f\}\{d, e\}\{b, c\}$, because in the latter, one lot yields the worst welfare, whereas *all* lots yield a higher welfare in the former. Next compare $\{a, e\}\{b, f\}\{c, d\}$ and $\{a, d\}\{b, f\}\{c, e\}$: both yield the same lowest welfare level (at $\{a, e\}$ and $\{a, d\}$ respectively); the latter gives this level to two agents and the former to only one agent: therefore the former division is better. Here the leximin social welfare ordering picks $\{a, c\}\{b, f\}\{d, e\}$ as the unambiguous best split, followed by $\{a, b\}\{c, f\}\{d, e\}$: the lowest welfare level is for whomever gets $\{d, e\}$ in the former, and for whomever gets $\{c, f\}$ in the latter, and $\{c, f\}$ is worse. The fact that one agent gets the absolute best lot $\{a, b\}$ in the latter split is unimportant.

We give now the general definition of the leximin social welfare ordering, also called the egalitarian social welfare ordering, and sometimes "practical egalitarianism." Given two feasible utility profiles u and u', we rearrange them first in increasing order, from the lowest to the highest utility, and denote the new profiles u^* and $u'^* : u_1^* \leq u_2^* \leq \cdots \leq u_n^*$ and $u_1'^* \leq u_2'^* \leq \cdots \leq u_n'^*$. The leximin social welfare ordering compares u^* and u'^* lexicographically. Thus $u \succ u'$ holds if $u_1^* \succ u_1'^*$ ($u_1'^* \succ u_1^*$ implies similarly that $u' \succ u$): if the lowest utility is higher in one profile than in the other, this is enough to declare it a better profile. If $u_1^* = u_1'^*$, the leximin ordering compares the second lowest utilities u_2^* and $u_2'^*$; if they differ, the profile with the higher one is preferred. Thus $\{u_2^* = u_1'^*$ and $u_2^* > u_2'^*\}$ implies that $u \succ u'$. And so on: if the k lowest utility levels coincide in both profiles ($u_1^* = u_1'^*$ for $i = 1, \ldots, k$) and the $(k + 1)$ lowest differ, the latter determines the preferred profile.

The mathematical definition of the leximin ordering is slightly more involved than that of any additive collective utility in the family (5). In fact this ordering cannot be represented by *any* collective utility function. On the other hand, leximin belongs to the family (5) in a limit sense: as q goes to infinity, the social welfare ordering represented by the collective utility function W^q converges to the leximin one. Moreover the leximin ordering is independent of unconcerned individuals, independent of the common scale of utility and satisfies the Pigou-Dalton transfer principle.[9]

In many examples, such as examples 3.3 and 3.4, finding the maximum of the leximin ordering reduces to maximizing the first component $u_1^* = \min_i u_i$ of the utility profile rearranged in increasing order. In such cases we are simply maximizing the egalitarian collective utility function $W_e(u) = \min_i u_i$, meaning that we maximize the utility of the

---

9. Exercise 3.12 states formally the limit property and discusses these properties of the leximin.

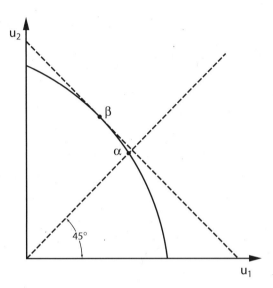

Figure 3.1
No equality/efficiency trade-off

worst-off individual. Of course W_e is not a proper representation of the leximin ordering, because $u \succsim u'$ implies that $W_e(u) \geq W_e(u')$, but the converse implication does not hold.

Example 3.3 The Equality/Efficiency Trade-off with Two Agents   Consider the feasible utility sets in figures 3.1 and 3.2. We do not specify from what allocation problem these utility profiles come from. Under the welfarist postulate (section 3.1) this does not matter.

In figure 3.1 there is a fully egalitarian and efficient utility profile α. This profile is the unique maximizer of the egalitarian collective utility W_e, hence the leximin optimum as well. There is no conflict between equality and efficiency.

In figure 3.2, by contrast, the profile α is the highest feasible equal utility one, but it is not efficient: both agents enjoy a higher utility at profile α^* that maximizes the egalitarian utility W_e (and the leximin ordering). Here we have a trade-off between equality and efficiency. The egalitarian collective utility function justifies the inequality at α^* to augment the utility of the worst off agent.

The configurations in figures 3.3 and 3.4 are similar with an equality/efficiency trade-off in the latter (successfully resolved by the maximum of W_e) but not in the former.

We conclude this section with a crucial—indeed a characteristic—property of the leximin ordering. Recall that in example 3.2 all we need to define the egalitarian division in lots is the ability to rank any two lots. More generally, consider two utility profiles u and u'.

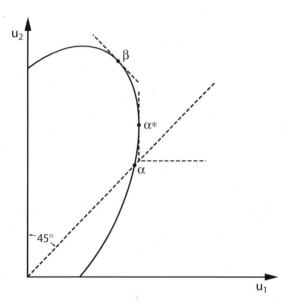

Figure 3.2
Equality/efficiency trade-off

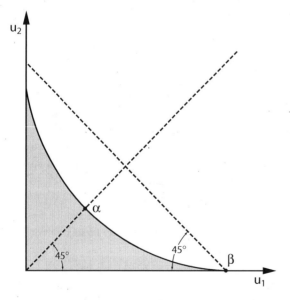

Figure 3.3
No equality/efficiency trade-off

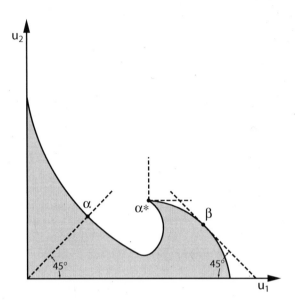

Figure 3.4
Equality/efficiency trade-off

Suppose that for any one of the n^2 pairs $u_i, u'_j, i, j = 1, \ldots, n$, we know their relative ranking, meaning that we know which one of $u_i > u'_j, u_i < u'_j$, or $u_i = u'_j$ holds. This is enough to deduce the ranking of u versus u' in the leximin ordering. For instance, let us take four agents and the following pattern:

	u'_1	u'_2	u'_3	u'_4
u_1	>	<	>	<
u_2	<	<	=	<
u_3	>	>	>	>
u_4	=	<	>	<

where an entry > reads: the row u_i is greater than the column u'_j.
From this pattern we deduce the rankings of u_i, u'_j:

$$u_2 = u'_3 < u_4 = u'_1 < u_1 < u'_4 < u'_2 < u_3$$

Hence

$$u^*_1 = u'^*_1, u^*_2 = u'^*_2 \quad \text{and} \quad u^*_3 = u_1 < u'^*_3 = u_4$$

We conclude that u' is preferred to u by the leximin ordering.

The invariance property underlying the example above is that the leximin ordering is preserved under a common arbitrary (in particular, nonlinear) rescaling of the utilities. Thus the comparison of u versus u' is the same as that of $v = (u_i^2)$ versus $v' = (u_i'^2)$, or of $(e^{u_i + \sqrt{u_i}})$ versus $(e^{u_i' + \sqrt{u_i'}})$, and so on. This property is called *independence of the common utility pace*.

Leximin is not the only social welfare ordering independent of the common utility pace. But it is the only one that also respects the Pigou-Dalton transfer principle.[10] This remarkable characterization result explains why this social welfare ordering occupies such a central place in cardinal welfarism.

In the next two sections, we compare systematically the three basic social orderings—leximin, classical utilitarian, and Nash—and explain along the way the axiomatic characterizations of the latter two.

3.4 Comparing Classical Utilitarianism, Nash, and Leximin

In section 3.2 we identified three outstanding welfarist solutions as the classical utilitarian and Nash collective utility functions, and the leximin social welfare ordering. We now compare them in a series of examples, where we stress their relation to the compensation and sum-fitness principles. Thus this section and the next pursue a discussion initiated in section 2.5, by testing our three welfarist solutions in more general problems of resource allocations.

The central tension between the classical utilitarian and egalitarian welfarist objectives was already uncovered in section 2.5. They are advocating different kinds of sacrifices. Under the former, the welfare of a single agent may be sacrificed for the sake of improving total welfare (the slavery of the talented—example 3.9—is a striking case in point). Under the latter, large amounts of joint welfare may be forfeited in order to improve the lot of the worst off individual (e.g., examples 3.4 and 3.6).

Example 3.4. Location of a Facility   A desirable facility (examples are given below) must be located somewhere in the interval [0, 1], representing a "linear" city. Each agent i lives at a specific location x_i in [0, 1]; if the facility is located at y, agent i's *dis*utility is the distance $|y - x_i|$. The agents are spread arbitrarily along the interval [0, 1], and the problem is to find a fair compromise location.

The egalitarian solution is the easiest to compute. Suppose that there are some agents living at 0 and some living at 1. Then the egalitarian collective disutility function W_e equals

---

10. Exercise 3.12 offers more discussion of these two facts.

$\frac{1}{2}$ when the facility is located at $y_e = \frac{1}{2}$. For any other location y, the distance from y to 0 or to 1 is larger than $\frac{1}{2}$. Thus the unique egalitarian optimum is the *midpoint* of the range of our agents.

Classical utilitarianism chooses the *median* of the distribution of agents, namely the point y_u such that at most half of the agents live strictly to the left of y_u and at most half of them live strictly to its right. To see why this is so, observe that a move of ε to the right of y_u increases by ε the disutility of at least one-half of the agents (i.e., those located at y_u or to its left) while reducing by ε that of at most one-half. A similar argument shows that a move to the left cannot reduce the sum total of individual disutilities.[11]

The interpretation of the facility has much to do with the choice between the two solutions. If the facility is a swimming pool, or an information booth, then the utilitarian choice is more appealing because it minimizes overall transportation costs, and we accept to sacrifice the isolated rural resident: disutility is interpreted as distaste and the isolated agents have chosen freely to be so. On the other hand, if the facility meets a basic need, such as a post office or a police station, the egalitarian compromise has more appeal, because equal access to the facility is tantamount to meeting this need equally. Some cases are more ambiguous: if we are locating a fire station, the goals of equal access and of maximizing the expected return (i.e., the expected reduction of property losses) are both valid, but they pull us toward the midpoint and the median respectively.

The Nash collective utility function is not easy to use in this example because the natural zero of individual utilities is when the facility is located precisely where the agent in question lives, say x_i: then we set $u_i(y) = -|y - x_i|$ if the facility is located at y. The Nash utility is not defined when some utilities are negative; therefore we must adjust the zero of each agent so as to ensure she gets nonnegative utility for any choice of y. One way to do so is to set the zero of an agent's utility where the distance from his location to the facility is 1:

$$u_i^1(y) = 1 - |y - x_i|$$

Another way is to set agent i's zero where y is as far as can be from his location, namely at $y = 0$ if $x_i \geq \frac{1}{2}$ and at $y = 1$ if $x_i \leq \frac{1}{2}$. This yields the following utility:

$$u_i^2(y) = x_i - |y - x_i| \quad \text{if } i \text{ is such that } x_i \geq \frac{1}{2}$$

$$u_j^2(y) = 1 - x_j - |y - x_j| \quad \text{if } j \text{ is such that } x_j \leq \frac{1}{2}$$

---

11. In section 4.3 we give an alternative interpretation of the median location y as the Condorcet winner outcome: for any other location y, more than half of the citizens prefer y_u to y.

Clearly, the choice of one or the other of the two normalizations is of great consequence on the optimal location for the Nash collective utility.[12]

The great advantage of the classical utilitarian utility is to be *independent of individual zeros of utilities*. If we replace utility $u_i = -|y - x_i|$ by u_i^1 or u_i^2 above for any number of agents, the optimal utilitarian location remains the median of the distribution and the preference ranking between any two locations does not change. This independence property uniquely characterizes the classical utilitarian among all collective utility functions.[13]

Notice that the egalitarian location remains at $y_e = \frac{1}{2}$ with all utility functions normalized as u_i^1, or all as u_i^2 (exercise: Why?), but this is not a general feature. For instance, if no one lives near the location 0, the optimal egalitarian location under u_i^1 moves above $\frac{1}{2}$ but remains at $\frac{1}{2}$ under u_i^2.

Example 3.5 Location of a Noxious Facility Now the facility is a toxic waste disposal, a jail, or any other operation from which everyone wants to live as far away as possible. The distance from x_i, where agent i lives, to the facility at y measures her *utility*, instead of her *dis*utility in the previous example.

If the agents are spread all over the interval [0, 1], the egalitarian collective utility is zero everywhere: $W_e(y) = 0$ for all y because there is always someone living at y. The leximin social welfare ordering, on the other hand, wants to locate the noxious facility at a point where the *density* of agents is lowest. If there are several such points, it breaks ties in favor of a location where the second derivative of the density is lowest (exercise: Why?).

The utilitarian collective utility $W_1(y)$ is now minimal at the median y_u and maximal at one of the two endpoints 0 or 1.[14] Thus it is enough to compare $W_1(0)$ and $W_1(1)$. Denoting by $f(x)\,dx$ the population density at x, we compute

$$W_1(0) < W_1(1) \Leftrightarrow \int_0^1 x f(x)\,dx < \int_0^1 (1-x) f(x)\,dx$$

$$\Leftrightarrow Ex = \int_0^1 x f(x)\,dx < \tfrac{1}{2}$$

We conclude that the utilitarian location is the endpoint farthest away from the mean location Ef.

---

12. And in each case this optimum is neither easy to compute nor to interpret.

13. Even those that are not independent of unconcerned agents (see section 3.2).

14. Each utility function is convex in the variable y. Therefore so is W_1; a convex function reaches its maximum over an interval at one of the endpoints.

We turn to a simple, yet important model where the problem is to pick a fair compromise between several pure public goods. The model brings to the fore the contrasting distributive policies of our three basic collective utility functions.

Example 3.6a Time-Sharing   The n agents work in a common space (e.g., fitness room) where the radio must be turned on one of five available stations (one of them may be the "off" station). As their tastes differ greatly, they ask the manager to share the time fairly between the five stations.

Each agent likes some stations, and dislike some; if we set her utility at 0 or 1 for a station she dislikes or likes, respectively, we have a pure lifeboat problem as in example 3.1. The difference is that we allow mixing between the five decisions: the manager chooses a list of timeshares $x_k, k = 1, \ldots, 5$ such that $x_k \geq 0$ and $x_1 + x_2 + \cdots + x_5 = 1$.

In this example we assume a simple preference pattern that makes it easy to compute and contrast the solution chosen by our three basic collective utility functions. Each agent likes exactly one station and dislikes the other four, with corresponding utilities at 1 and 0. There are n_k fans of station k, with $n_1 + \cdots + n_5 = n$.

The classical utilitarian manager chooses the "tyranny of the majority": the station with the largest support is on all the time (and if there are several such stations, any mixing between them is optimal as well). The egalitarian manager does exactly the opposite, namely it pays not attention to the size of support and plays each station $\frac{1}{5}$th of the time (provided that each station has at least one fan) so that everyone is happy 20 percent of the time.

The Nash collective utility picks an appealing compromise between the two extremist solutions above. The relative sizes of n_k matter *and* everyone is guaranteed some share of her favorite station. The optimal times shares x_k for the Nash utility maximize $\sum_k n_k \log x_k$ under the constraint $\sum_k x_k = 1$; therefore $x_k^* = n_k/n$, namely the time share of each station is proportional to the number of its fans. This can be interpreted as random dictatorship: each agent gets to choose the station he likes for $1/n$th of the time.

The proportional time shares make good sense in the radio-sharing story, because we interpret utilities as subjective tastes for one type of music or the other. Alternative interpretations of utilities yield a very different intuition.

Consider a pure lifeboat decision, where we must choose, literally, whom to save: say five boats are about to sink, and we can only help one of them. Who would hesitate to give all his help to the most populated boat, as utilitarianism recommends? Flipping a fair coin to decide which boat to help allows the rescuer to give an equal chance of survival to every person, but our claim is that he won't and that utilitarianism is compelling here.

In some other contexts utilities may measure the satisfaction of a need: our agents are away from home, and the radio broadcasts news from their hometown station. They come from five different towns and station k gives news from town k only. Now the egalitarian solution makes a lot of sense!

Example 3.6b Time-Sharing   Five agents share a radio as in example 3.6a, and the preferences of three of them (agents 3, 4, and 5) are somewhat flexible, in the sense that they
like two of the five stations according to the following pattern:

		Station				
		a	b	c	d	e
	1	1	0	0	0	0
	2	0	1	0	0	0
Agent	3	0	0	1	1	0
	4	0	0	0	1	1
	5	0	0	1	0	1

The utilitarian manager shares the time between the three stations c, d, and e but never
plays stations a or b. The egalitarian manager selects $x_a = x_b = \frac{2}{7}$, $x_c = x_d = x_e = \frac{1}{7}$, so
that everyone listens to a program he or she likes 28.6 percent of the time. The utilitarian
solution is too harsh on agents 1, 2, while the egalitarian solution appears too soft on
these two agents: agents 3, 4, 5 should be somewhat rewarded for the flexibility of their
preferences.

The Nash collective utility function recommends a sensible compromise between utilitarianism and egalitarianism: it plays each station with equal probability $\frac{1}{5}$. To check this, we
note that outcomes a, b play a symmetrical role, hence are allocated the same time share x;
similarly each one of c, d, and e receives the same time share y. The Nash maximization
problem is now

maximize $x^2(2y)^3$ under $x, y \geq 0, 2x + 3y = 1$

A straightforward computation gives the optimal solution $x^* = y^* = \frac{1}{5}$.

To conclude this section, we illustrate the great advantage of the Nash collective utility
function in the variant of example 3.6a where individual utilities for listening to the "right"
kind of music differ across agents: a supporter i of station k enjoys utility u_i if k is on and
0 otherwise. Both the classical utilitarian and egalitarian collective utility functions pay a
great deal of attention to the relative intensities of these utilities. For instance, the egalitarian
arbitrator computes for each k the smallest individual utility a_k among the fans of station k
and allocates to k a time share proportional $1/a_k$ (exercise: prove this claim). And classical
utilitarianism may end up broadcasting exclusively a station with a handful of very vocal
supporters.

The Nash utility function, by contrast, is *independent of individual scale of utilities*. In
our example, this means that the intensity u_i of agent i's musical pleasure is irrelevant to the

choice of a fair time-sharing. Indeed, for a profile of time shares $(x_1, \ldots, x_5)$ the collective utility W_N is computed as follows:

$$W_N = \sum_{k=1}^{5} \sum_{i \in N_k} \log(u_i.x_k)$$

$$= \left(\sum_i \log u_i \right) + \sum_{k=1}^{5} n_k \log x_k$$

where N_k is the set of k fans. The maximization of this collective utility is independent of the numbers u_i; hence the Nash arbitrator still recommends giving station k a time share proportional to n_k.

Independence of individual scales of utilities eliminates the possibility of influencing the arbitrator's choice by distorting the intensity of one's utility for good music. If the arbitrator is classical utilitarian, it is clearly to agent's i advantage to increase u_i (which may make his favorite station look best); if he is egalitarian, it is advantageous to decrease u_i (exercise: prove these claims). The Nash collective utility function is immune to both kinds of distortions, which is a considerable advantage in a context where utility measures subjective tastes. Notice that the profitability of increasing one's utility scale under classical utilitarianism (resp. to decrease it under egalitarianism) is fully general (not limited to our simple example): exercise 3.14 explains this important property. Similarly, under an egalitarian or a Nash arbitrator, it is always profitable to increase one's zero of utility.

The Nash collective utility function is uniquely characterized among all collective utility functions,[15] by the property independence of individual scales. Thus each of the three basic social welfare orderings is characterized by a specific independence property: the independence of common utility pace picks the leximin social welfare ordering,[16] and the independence of individual zeros captures the classical utilitarian collective utility.[17]

3.5 Failures of Monotonicity

Some paradoxical features of welfarism affect our three basic collective utility functions. The main issue is how the optimal solution reacts when the resources of the economy change and was already discussed in section 2.5. There we noticed that the property may fail under classical utilitarianism if some individual utility functions are not concave in the

---

15. Even those that fail independence of unconcerned agents.

16. See the discussion at the end of section 3.3.

17. As discussed after example 3.4.

amount of resources. Below we give examples displaying the same failure with concave utility functions both for the classical utilitarian and Nash arbitrators.

For the egalitarian solution, resource monotonicity is always satisfied if the optimal allocation gives equal utilities to all agents—namely if there is no equality/efficiency trade-off (example 3.3). This important fact is obvious: if my utility and yours remain equal whenever an arbitrary parameter affecting the allocation of resources changes, we will both benefit or we will both suffer from the change, or we will both be unaffected. Shocks do not break the egalitarian harmony.

However, practical egalitarianism (i.e., maximization of the leximin ordering) may lead to the paradoxical feature. An elementary example involves indivisible goods.

Ann, Bob, and Chris want to play tennis, but they do not have enough racquets (balls and courts are not scarce). Ann enjoys playing against the wall as much as against Bob or Chris. Bob and Chris hate to play the wall and only enjoy playing against each other or against Ann. If only one racquet is available, the leximin ordering tells us to give it to Ann (indeed, this is the only efficient allocation of the resources). If two racquets are available, the egalitarian solution is an equitable time-sharing arrangement where the three pairs take turns on the court and everyone plays $\frac{2}{3}$ of the time: thus Ann is worse off after the resource increase.

Our next fair division example has divisible goods and concave utility functions, therefore no equality/efficiency trade-off. Thus the egalitarian optimum has equal utilities for both agents, and resource monotonicity is automatically verified. On the other hand, maximizing the Nash or classical utilitarian collective utility leads to monotonicity failures.

Example 3.7 Dividing Complementary Goods   Jones and Smith both use a different mix of two goods labeled A and B. To produce one unit of utility, Jones needs one unit of A for two of B while Smith needs two units of A for one of B.

Jones: $u_1(a_1, b_1) = \min\{2a_1, b_1\}$

Smith: $u_2(a_2, b_2) = \min\{a_2, 2b_2\}$

A "serious" example is the mix of labor and capital to produce a certain service: good A is labor and good B a certain machine, both measured in hours; Jones's technology is less labor intensive than Smith's. A "frivolous" one involves a cocktail of two liquors that they mix in different proportions.

Suppose first that 12 units of each good are available. The set of feasible utility profiles is depicted on figure 3.5a. Any collective utility function that does not like inequality (i.e., meeting the Pigou-Dalton transfer principle in section 3.2) chooses the equal utility profile $(u_1, u_2) = (8, 8)$ coming from the allocation $(a_1, b_1) = (4, 8)$, $(a_2, b_2) = (8, 4)$.

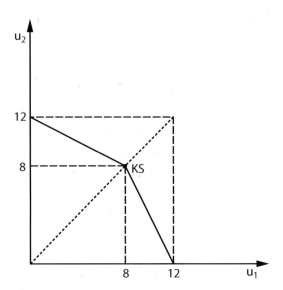

Figure 3.5a
Feasible utility profiles in example 3.7

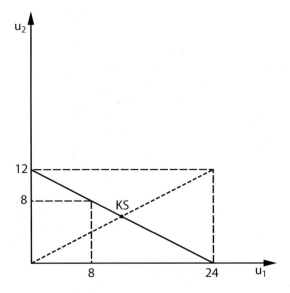

Figure 3.5b
Modified feasible utility set

Next suppose that 12 more units of good B are available, for a total of 12 units of A and 24 units of B. The new feasible set of utility profiles is depicted on figure 3.5b: it has increased to the triangle of all pairs (u_1, u_2) such that $u_1 + 2u_2 = 24$ and $u_i \geq 0$: for any $x, 0 \leq x \leq 12$, the utility profile $(u_1, u_2) = (24 - 2x, x)$ comes from $(a_1, b_1) = (12 - x, 24 - 2x)$, $(a_2, b_2) = (x, 2x)$. The egalitarian arbitrator still picks the utility profile $(8, 8)$: the additional resources are simply discarded. The classical utilitarian solution gives all the resources to agent 1 so that $(u_1, u_2) = (24, 0)$. Agent 2's utility loss is less severe under the Nash solution: the corresponding optimal utility profile is $(u_1, u_2) = (12, 6)$, namely the solution of the following problem:

$$\max \log u_1 + \log u_2 \quad \text{under constraint} \quad u_1 + 2u_2 = 24, u_i \geq 0,$$

$$i = 1, 2$$

The failure of resource monotonicity in the example above is generalized in example 7.12 to many more solutions than the two above.

We give now a pure public good example where both the egalitarian and utilitarian solutions fail resource monotonicity.

Example 3.8 Location of a Facility (continued)   In this variant of example 3.4, the road network is depicted on figure 3.6. The agents live on the roads AB, BC, CD, and DE where

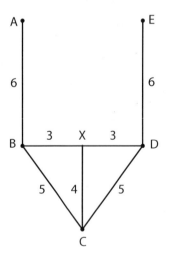

Figure 3.6
Road network in example 3.8

their density is constant and equal to one. Nobody lives on *BX*, *XC*, and *XD*. As before, the distance of the facility to one's location is the disutility (negative of utility).

Suppose first that the facility can only be located wherever the agents live (thus the inner roads *BX*, *XC*, and *XD* are not feasible locations). Then by the symmetry of our problem, the egalitarian and the classical utilitarian collective utilities are maximized at *C*. Actually *C* is the optimal location for *any* collective utility function, by virtue of symmetry and monotonicity (exercise: prove this claim).

Now suppose every point of the road network is a feasible location of the facility. This is unambiguously an increase of the available resources. The optimal location for the egalitarian collective utility is now at *X*, from where the distance to any agent is at most 9 miles, whereas with the facility at *C*, agents living at *A* or *F* are 11 miles away. Thus the agents living at *C* and near *C* see their utility decrease as the resources improve.[18]

The optimal location for the classical utilitarian is also *X* (exercise: Why?). Therefore resource monotonicity fails for this solution as well.

Our last paradoxical example is a famous one. It shows the utilitarian and Nash solutions penalizing the more productive agent in a distinctly unpalatable fashion.

Example 3.9 Slavery of the Talented   In this simple production economy, two agents can use their labor to produce corn, at a constant productivity s_i, $i = 1, 2$: one unit of agent i's labor produces s_i units of corn. Agents consume corn and leisure, and these two goods are perfect complements: if agent i consumes z_i units of corn and y_i of leisure, her final utility is $\min\{z_i, y_i\}$. Finally each agent can split 20 hours of time between x_i units of labor and y_i of leisure: $x_i + y_i = 20$.

Consider first the benchmark case where both agents are equally productive at $s_1 = s_2 = 1$. The efficient production plan treating the two agents equally (i.e., respecting the symmetry of the problem) is the "decentralized" outcome where each agent keeps the corn he produces; hence $x_i = y_i = z_i = 10$, $i = 1, 2$, and each agent gets 10 utils, $u_i = 10$. The egalitarian, Nash, or any collective utility function that is strictly averse to inequality[19] picks this allocation uniquely. The utilitarian function is an exception, as it is indifferent to inequality.[20]

Next suppose that agent 1's productivity raises to $s_1' = 2$, while agent 2's productivity remains $s_2 = 1$. Efficiency commands to give agent i exactly the same amount of leisure

---

18. Those living no more than 4 miles away from *C*.

19. That is to say, a collective utility that increases from a Pigou-Dalton transfer (section 3.2).

20. Here all efficient allocations maximize the utilitarian function. These allocations are parametrized by the amount of labor $x_1 = \lambda$ supplied by agent 1, an arbitrary number between 0 and 20. Then $u_1 = y_1 = z_1 = 20 - \lambda$, $x_2 = 20 - \lambda$, $u_2 = y_2 = z_2 = \lambda$.

and of corn, i.e., $z_i = 20 - x_i$. The feasibility constraint is now

$$20 - x_1 + 20 - x_2 = 2x_1 + x_2 \Leftrightarrow 3x_1 + 2x_2 = 40, \qquad x_1, x_2 \geq 0$$

Under the egalitarian collective utility, the increase in agent 1's talent benefits both agents equally, who end up with $u_1 = u_2 = 12$ utils. The corresponding allocation is $x_i = 8$, $u_i = z_i = y_i = 12$, $i = 1, 2$: both agents work less hard and 4 units of the corn produced by agent 1 are transferred to agent 2.

Under the classical utilitarian and the Nash solutions, the fate of agent 1 is less enviable. Say that agent i works x_i hours, $i = 1, 2$, so that total output is $z = 2x_1 + x_2$. Efficiency commands to give exactly $z_i = 20 - x_i$ units of corn to agent i. Thus the classical utilitarian solution maximizes $(20 - x_1) + (20 - x_2)$ under the above feasibility constraint.

The optimal solution is $x_1^* = 13.3$, $x_2^* = 0$, resulting in the allocation $u_1 = z_1 = y_1 = 6.7$, $u_2 = z_2 = y_2 = 20$. This is slavery because the talented agent 1 works 33 percent harder and consumes 33 percent less than before acquiring his special talent. He is also frustrated to see agent 2 reap all the benefits and get a "free ride," whereas he (agent 1) experiences a sharp decrease in his utility!

The utilitarian argument is that one more unit of leisure for agent 2 has a lower opportunity cost, in terms of lost production, than one unit for agent 1, and this argument holds until agent 2 is totally exonerated from work.

The Nash collective utility function yields a milder slavery of the talented, but slavery nevertheless. The Nash arbitrator solves the program

$$\max \log(20 - x_1) + \log(20 - x_2) \qquad \text{under } 3x_1 + 2x_2 = 40$$

The solution is $x_1^0 = 10$, $x_2^0 = 5$ hence the allocation $u_1 = z_1 = y_1 = 10$, $u_2 = z_2 = y_2 = 15$. Here agent 1 does not suffer anymore from his productivity boost, but he does not benefit either; all the benefit goes to the untalented agent who ends up working less hard and consuming more corn (and leisure) than the talented one.

In section 6.2 we propose a different solution of the above production problem based on the Lockean theory of entitlements rather than welfarism. This solution rules out any externality in productivity; hence it eliminates slavery entirely.

3.6   Bargaining Compromise

The bargaining compromise places bounds on individual utilities that depend on the physical outcomes of the allocation problem; thus it moves a step away from the strict postulate of welfarism (section 3.1).

Example 3.10 Priorities   Ann, Bob, and Charles work in the same company. Each needs a computer repair job, and their respective repair jobs are not equally long: Ann's repair can be done in 1 hour; Bob's takes 4 hours, and Charles's takes 5 hours.

There is a single repairman in the company. Since an agent must stay idle until the completion of his or her repair, the total waiting time until the repair is completed measures his or her disutility.

The classical utilitarian solution minimizes total waiting time, and this is achieved by serving the shortest repair job first. So the respective disutilities are

Ann: 1,   *Bob*: 5,   *Charles*: 10

Total disutility is 16, and it is a simple matter to check that any other ordering of the jobs yields a larger total waiting time. This is hard on Charles, especially so if we reduce the difference between Bob's and Charles' repair jobs. If Charles's job is one minute longer, he still has to wait 4 hours more.

If the only available choices are the six deterministic orderings of Ann, Bob, and Charles, the leximin ordering selects the same ordering Ann $<$ Bob $<$ Charles, as the reader can easily verify. However, in this example we allow randomization over the six orderings in order to achieve equitable compromises where two agents with nearly identical characteristics (job length) have nearly identical expected waiting times.

Classical utilitarianism refuses to compromise, because the ordering above uniquely minimizes total waiting time. The contrast with the egalitarian solution could not be sharper, as the latter gives to each participant precisely the same expected disutility. Note that the smallest waiting time u that can be guaranteed to all three participants is $u = 7.1$,[21] which obtains for instance by randomizing as follows over three different schedulings of the three jobs:

Scheduling	u_A	u_B	u_C	Probability
B, A, C	5	4	10	0.4
A, C, B	1	10	6	0.1
C, B, A	10	9	5	0.5
	7.1	7.1	7.1	Expected utility

Now we see that Ann, whose job is shortest by far, is served first only 10 percent of the time, whereas Bob is first 40 percent of the time and Charles 50 percent.[22] The solution ignores the differences between the delay externalities caused by jobs of different length.

---

21. To check this, observe that for *any* scheduling of the three jobs, the utility of the three agents satisfy $u_A + 4u_B + 5u_C = 71$. This observation is generalized in exercise 3.10.

22. Note that the probability of agent i being served first is proportional to the length of her job. This is a general property: see exercise 3.10.

The bargaining compromise here equalizes "priorities" instead of utilities: each agent has an equal right to be served first, or second, or third. If we randomize over all six orderings, with equal probability to each ordering, the expected waiting time of our three agents are

$$u_A = \frac{1}{3}1 + \frac{1}{6}5 + \frac{1}{6}6 + \frac{1}{3}10 = 5.5$$

$$u_B = \frac{1}{3}4 + \frac{1}{6}5 + \frac{1}{6}9 + \frac{1}{3}10 = 7$$

$$u_C = \frac{1}{3}5 + \frac{1}{6}6 + \frac{1}{6}9 + \frac{1}{3}10 = 7.5$$

This outcome is an egalitarian compromise in the following *relative* sense: everyone ends up half-way between his or her worst wait (i.e., 10) and his or her best wait (i.e., 1 for Ann, 4 for Bob, 5 for Charles). These two bounds of the best and worst wait are very natural, but their meaning goes beyond the mere description of welfare: they depend on the set of feasible outcomes in the particular allocation problem.

The choice of the zero and/or the scale of individual utilities is crucial whenever a social welfare ordering picks the solution: with the exception of the classical utilitarian (independent of individual zeros but not scales) and the Nash collective utility function (independent of individual scales but not zero), all other social welfare orderings depend on both the individual zeros and scales.

The bargaining version of welfarism incorporates an objective definition of the zero of individual utilities, which corresponds to the worst outcome deemed acceptable from the point of view of a certain agent. In some cases this outcome is interpreted as the *disagreement* outcome because each agent has the strategic option to "walk away" from the arbitration table, so the arbitrator must take the corresponding utility as a hard lower bound. In other cases, like examples 3.10 and 3.11, zero utility simply comes from the worst feasible outcome in the allocation problem; hence we call it the *minimal utility*.

The bargaining approach then applies a scale invariant solution to the zero normalized problem, which in turns ensures that the solution is independent of both individual zeros and scales of utilities.

The two prominent bargaining methods are the Nash bargaining and Kalai-Smorodinsky solutions introduced in our next example.

Example 3.11   Ann and Bob represent two companies selling related yet different products, and share a retail outlet. They can set up the outlet in three different modes denoted $a, b,$

and c that bring the following volumes of sales (in thousands of dollars):

	a	b	c
Ann	60	50	30
Bob	80	110	150

(6)

Both managers are only interested in maximizing the volume of their own sales (which may not be the same thing as maximizing profit) and accounting rules prohibit any cash transfers. Thus the only tool for compromises is time-sharing among the three modes: over a yearly season, they can mix them in arbitrary proportions such that x, y, z such that $x + y + z = 1$.

Applying any one of our three basic welfarist solutions to the raw utilities given in (6) make little sense. For instance, the egalitarian collective utility picks outcome a where Ann's utility is highest. But the fact that Ann's business always yields a smaller volume of sales should not matter: the issue is to find a compromise between three feasible outcomes over which the agents have opposite preferences; the relative size of Ann's business to Bob's business is irrelevant.

Total utility in classical utilitarian fashion—maximal at c—is similarly irrelevant. We wish to define a fair compromise that depends neither on the scale nor on the zero of both individual utilities.

For minimal utility of either player, we pick the lowest feasible volume of sales: 30K for Ann and 80K for Bob. Indeed, this level is guaranteed even by conceding to the other agent his or her favorite outcome. This yields the new utility table:

	a	b	c
Ann	30	20	0
Bob	0	30	70

(7)

The idea of a random ordering, successful in example 3.10, suggests letting Ann and Bob each have their way 50 percent of the time: this means that $x = z = \frac{1}{2}$, outcomes a and c each with a timeshare $\frac{1}{2}$. But the resulting normalized utilized vector is (15, 35), whereas the outcome $y' = 0.8$, $z' = 0.2$ (b or c with respective timeshares 0.8 and 0.2) yields the utilities (16, 38), and hence is Pareto superior.

It turns out that any combination of a and c is Pareto inferior to some combination of a and b, or of b and c: this is apparent on figure 3.7, where compromises of a and c produce the utility vectors in the segment AC.

There are now two simple ways to select the shares x, y, z without taking into account the scales of individual utilities. The first one is to maximize the Nash collective utility function:

$$\max \log(30x + 20y) + \log(30y + 70z) \tag{8}$$

$$\text{under} \quad x + y + z = 1, x, y, z \geq 0$$

The second way is the Kalai-Smorodinsky solution, equalizing the *relative* utility gains, namely the ratio of the actual gain to the maximum feasible gain. In this example the maximal feasible gains are 30 and 70 for Ann and Bob respectively. Therefore the KS solution selects the shares x, y, z so as to

$$\text{maximize} \quad \frac{30x + 20y}{30} = \frac{30y + 70z}{70} \tag{9}$$

$$\text{under} \quad x + y + z = 1, x, y, z \geq 0$$

The resolution of programs (8) and (9) is greatly simplified by taking a look at the feasible utility set of the normalized utilities (7). Figure 3.7 reveals that the efficient compromises among a, b, and c involve either a and b only ($z = 0$: interval AB) or b and c only ($x = 0$: interval BC). On each one of these two intervals, there is only one degree of freedom, so the resolution of programs (8) and (9) becomes easy.

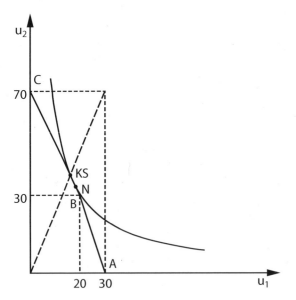

Figure 3.7
Bargaining solutions in example 3.11

Consider first the interval AB, corresponding to $z = 0$ and to the utility vectors $(10x + 20, 30 - 30x)$ for $0 \le x \le 1$. We see that equation (9) is impossible, namely

$$\frac{10x + 20}{30} = \frac{30 - 30x}{70} \Rightarrow x = -\frac{5}{16}$$

Therefore the KS solution lies on BC, corresponding to $x = 0, z = 1 - y$:

$$\frac{20y}{30} = \frac{70 - 40y}{70} \Rightarrow y = \frac{21}{26}, z = \frac{5}{26}$$

We turn to the resolution of program (8). We know that its optimal solution lies either on AB or on BC. We check that B is the solution of (8) on AB, but on BC we can do better, namely maximize $\log(20y) + \log(30y + 70(1 - y))$ under $0 \le y \le 1 \Rightarrow y = \frac{7}{8}$, hence

Nash solution: $y = \dfrac{7}{8}, z = \dfrac{1}{8} \Rightarrow u_1 = 17.5, u_2 = 35$

KS solution: $y = \dfrac{21}{26}, z = \dfrac{5}{26} \Rightarrow u_1 = 16.1, u_2 = 37.7$

where the utilities are normalized as in (7).

Note that both solutions are Pareto superior to the random dictator outcome $a/2 + c/2$, with associated utilities $(15, 35)$. This is a general property, discussed below, of our two bargaining solutions.

We give now the general definition of the Nash and Kalai-Smorodinsky bargaining solutions. The data are a set U of feasible utility profiles and a distinguished minimal utility profile u^0. See figure 3.8 where an important feature is the fact that the set U is convex.[23] We set the zero of agent i's utility at u_i^0: figure 3.9.

The Nash bargaining solution maximizes the Nash utility under this normalization of individual zeros, namely $\Pi_i(u_i - u_i^0)$. Of course the maximization bears exclusively on those utility profiles in U such that $u_i \ge u_i^0$ for all i.

Next we compute the maximal utility level $u_i^{\max}$ that agent i can achieve whenever other agents receive at least their minimal disagreement utility: that is to say, $u_i^{\max}$ solves the program max u_i over all $u \in U$ such that $u \ge u^0$. The quantity $\delta_i = u_i^{\max} - u_i^0$ is the maximal feasible gain of agent i above and beyond his minimal utility. The KS solution equalizes the relative gains (fraction of maximal feasible gains) of all agents. It is the unique

---

23. It contains the segment joining any two of its points.

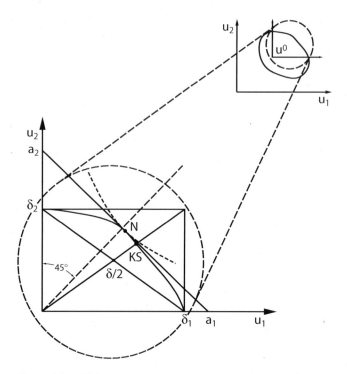

Figures 3.8 and 3.9
Nash and KS solutions

utility profile u such that

u is efficient and $\dfrac{u_i - u_i^0}{\delta_i} = \dfrac{u_j - u_j^0}{\delta_j}$ for all i, j.

Figure 3.9 shows the geometry of this construction in a two-agent example: draw first the utopian utility profile δ where each agent gets δ_i; the KS solution is at the intersection of the efficiency frontier of U with the line from the zero profile to the utopian profile.

The geometric characterization of the Nash solution is an interesting first-order condition, namely a property of the line tangent to the efficiency frontier of U at the Nash point N. Writing a_i for the intersection of this line with the u_i axis, N is simply the midpoint of $a_1 a_2$, as shown on figure 3.9.[24]

---

24. Note that this property implies that the tangent line is orthogonal to the vector (u_2, u_1): hence if (du_1, du_2) is a small variation of u at N along the efficiency frontier, we have $u_2 du_1 + u_1 du_2 = 0$, which is the first-order condition for the maximization of $u_1 u_2$.

Both the Nash and the KS solutions are independent of the individual scales of utilities. We know this to be true for the Nash utility function, hence for the outcome maximizing this function over U. As for the KS solution, we note that the ratios $(u_i - u_i^0)/\delta_i$ are invariant under a rescaling of utility u_i (because both numerator and denominator are multiplied by the same rescaling factor), which proves the point.

Another appealing feature shared by the Nash and KS solutions is to guarantee for agent i his minimal utility *plus* $1/n$th of his maximal feasible gain δ_i:

$$u_i \geq u_i^0 + \frac{1}{n}\left(u_i^{\max} - u_i^0\right) \tag{10}$$

In other words, we draw an agent at random (with uniform probability) and give him the entire feasible surplus while other agents merely get their minimal utility. The resulting expected utility is a lower bound of what every agent receives under the Nash or the KS solution. The proof of this claim in the two-agent case is clear on figure 3.9.[25]

Our last example emphasizes a property of the KS solution that sets it apart from the Nash bargaining solution, and from any solution maximizing a collective utility function after normalizing individual zeros in some objective fashion. The KS solution depends on the entire shape of the feasible set U: the solution is not independent of irrelevant utility profiles, meaning utility profiles that are "far" from the equitable compromise.

Example 3.12 Vitamins A bottle containing 10 grams of vitamin X and 10 grams of vitamin Y must be shared by Ann and Bob, who both need to increase their level of zygum, a certain compound that can only be metabolized from vitamin X or vitamin Y. The zero utility outcome is that no one gets any vitamin: the agents hold no claim on any of the resources, which are entirely under the control of the benevolent dictator.

We learn first that both Ann and Bob metabolize 1 unit of zygum from 1 gram of vitamin X or Y. Thus the utility (quantity of zygum) they derive from the allocation (x_i, y_i) is $u_i = x_i + y_i$. By the symmetry of the problem, the only fair utility profile is $(u_1, u_2) = (10, 10)$ (10 grams of vitamins per agent).

Now further testing reveals that Bob's metabolism is only half as efficient at producing zygum from vitamin Y than originally thought. From the allocation (x_2, y_2), Bob derives $u_2 = x_2 + (y_2/2)$. Ann's metabolism, on the other hand, still gives her $u_1 = x_1 + y_1$. The efficient allocation of vitamins now precludes giving positive amounts of vitamin Y to Bob *and* of vitamin X to Ann (for they would be able to find a mutually advantageous swap).

---

25. Note that U contains both points $(0, \delta_2)$ and $(\delta_1, 0)$. Therefore, because U is convex, it contains their midpoint $\delta/2$. The KS solution lies on the segment $[0, \delta]$ beyond $\delta/2$, which proves (10). Next we check $a_i \geq \delta_i$, again by the convexity of U: therefore the Nash solution $(a_1/2, a_2/2)$ in Pareto superior to $(\delta_1/2, \delta_2/2)$, establishing (10).

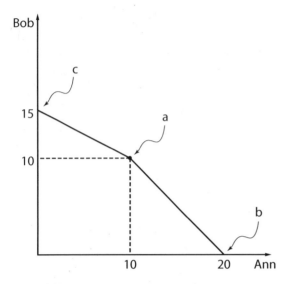

Figure 3.10
Feasible utility set in example 3.12

The efficiency frontier depicted on figure 3.10 comes from *either* giving all 10 grams of vitamin Y to Ann (segment ab) or giving all 10 grams of vitamin X to Bob (segment ac).

The point is that the utility profile $(10, 10)$ is still feasible (all the vitamin X to Bob, all the vitamin Y to Ann), and that Bob's decrease in productivity only eliminates certain utility profiles such as $(0, 20)$ that were unfair in the first place. Any social welfare ordering called $(10, 10)$ optimal in the former problem still calls it optimal in the latter problem. This includes the Nash collective utility, the leximin social ordering, and any social welfare ordering that strictly improves under a Pigou-Dalton transfer.

The KS solution takes a different viewpoint. In the first problem it picks $u = (10, 10)$ but in the second it recommends $u' = (11.4, 8.6)$. To see this, check that the maximal feasible utilities are $\delta'_1 = 20$, $\delta'_2 = 15$; therefore equality of relative benefits means $u'_1/20 = u'_2/15$. An efficient allocation with associated utility vector on ab (figure 3.10) takes the form

Ann: $x_1 = z$, $y_1 = 10 \Rightarrow u'_1 = 10 + z$

Bob: $x_2 = 10 - z$, $y_2 = 0 \Rightarrow u'_2 = 10 - z$

thus equality of relative benefits yields $z = 1.43$, and the announced utility vector.

The decrease of Bob's maximal utility weakens his position, even though it relates to the "irrelevant" allocations where he would get a higher utility than Ann does. The KS solution is even less a welfarist solution than the Nash solution because it takes into account not only an exogenous notion of minimal utility, but also the corresponding maximal feasible surplus of each participant.

In the "vitamin" interpretation of our example, the KS solution is not very appealing. It is, however, plausible if utility represents subjective tastes instead of needs. Think of the division of ten free meals in restaurant X and ten free meals in restaurant Y. Say that restaurant Y is strictly nonsmoking, whereas restaurant X has a smoking section. Bob is a smoker who enjoys one meal where he can smoke as much as two where he can't. Is it unfair to give Ann ten meals at Y and one meal at X, whereas Bob gets nine meals at X? After all, meals at Y are to Bob a low-quality commodity, so he cannot object to Ann getting a larger number of such meals than he gets of "good" meals. This kind of argument takes us directly into the discussion of fair division with respect to heterogeneous preferences and to the no-envy property, the subject of chapter 7.

In chapter 7 we stress the systematic connection between the two bargaining solutions, Nash and KS, and the two central fair division methods, known respectively as the competitive allocation with equal incomes and the egalitarian-equivalent solution. See, in particular, examples 7.12 and 7.10, which are related to examples 3.7 and 3.12.

3.7   Introduction to the Literature

Rawls (1971, 1988) introduced the notion of primary goods; its critique as briefly discussed in section 3.1 is well articulated by Roemer (1996); see also Sen (1985).

The central result for section 3.2 is the representation of a separable social welfare orderings by additive collective utilities, also known as the Debreu-Gorman theorem; see Debreu (1960) and Gorman (1968). A systematic treatment is in Blackorby et al. (1978). The further role of invariance axioms and of the Pigou-Dalton transfer principle was developed through the seventies and is nicely summarized by Sen (1977) and Roberts (1980a, b).

The egalitarian collective utility appeared first in Kolm (1972), and the leximin preordering was axiomatized by d'Aspremont and Gevers (1977); see section 3.3. The problem of example 3.2 is the subject of Brams and Fishburn (2000).

The informal comparison of the leximin, Nash, and classical utilitarian solutions in section 3.4 is inspired by chapters 1, 2, and 3 in Moulin (1988), which provides a systematic formal presentation of the material in sections 3.2 to 3.6.

Example 3.4 on the location of a facility is related to the central model of party competition—Black (1958), whereby the "facility" is the political platform submitted to the voters whose ideal platforms are spread over the left-right spectrum represented by an interval. See the discussion of voting over single-peaked preferences in section 4.3.

Resource monotonicity plays an important role in this book; in addition to section 3.5, the concept is discussed in sections 2.5, 6.6, and 7.6. The idea appeared first in axiomatic bargaining, where it yields a simple characterization of the egalitarian solution; see Kalai (1977). A more systematic discussion of this idea in axiomatic bargaining is in Thomson (1999). Its application to resource allocation problems are reviewed in Roemer (1996) and Moulin (1995).

The two classic bargaining solutions of section 3.6 were first axiomatized by Nash (1953) and Kalai and Smorodinsky (1975). Several surveys on axiomatic bargaining are now available: Roth (1979), Peters (1992), and Thomson (1999).

Example 3.12 is inspired by Yaari and Bar-Hillel (1984), who conducted stimulating experiments on fairness in resource allocation. The slavery of the talented—example 3.8— is due to Mirrlees (1974).

Exercises to Chapter 3

Exercise 3.1 Variant of Example 3.1

We have five agents and the six feasible subsets are the same as in example 3.1.

a. Assume that the utility of agent i being saved is u_i, and zero otherwise, with $u_i > 0$. Show that the leximin ordering always picks one of the three subsets with three agents.

b. Assume from now on that the utility of being saved is u_i, and v_i otherwise, with $u_i > v_i > 0$. Show that $u_i, v_i, i = 1, \ldots, 5$ can be chosen so that $\{1, 2\}$ is the unique optimal choice of the leximin ordering.

c. Find some values of u_i, v_i such that the egalitarian arbitrator ranks all three subsets of size two above those of size three, whereas the classical utilitarian arbitrator does just the opposite.

Exercise 3.2 Fair Division with Identical Preferences

We have 3 gold coins, 5 silver coins, and 8 bronze ones. As in example 3.1, all agents have identical preferences over lots. We assume that a gold coin is worth two silver ones, or three bronze ones. Thus we measure the common utility for a lot by adding 6 utils for a gold coin, 3 utils for a silver one, and 2 utils for a bronze one. In particular, total utility is 49, irrespective of the number n of agents among whom the sixteen coins must be divided.

Given n, call "n-equal division" a division of p into n integers a_i such that any two integers a_i, a_j differ by at most 1. For instance, with $n = 5$, an equal division of 49 is (10, 9, 10, 10, 10) but (10, 9, 9, 11, 10) is not.

Clearly, an n-equal division of p exists for all n and all p, and is unique up to permuting the a_i.

a. Suppose that the 16 coins can be divided in n lots such that the corresponding profile of utilities is a n-equal division of 49. Show that these allocations, and only these, maximize the leximin social welfare ordering.

b. Show that for $n = 2, 3, 4, 5, 6, 8, 9$, the 16 coins can be divided in lots in such a way that the corresponding utility profile is a n-equal division of 49. Show that this is not possible for any other choice of n.

c. Find the division of the 16 coins selected by the egalitarian arbitrator for $n = 7$ and for $n = 10$.

Exercise 3.3 Cake Division with Altruism

One unit of cake is to be distributed between Ann and Bob. The utility of each agent has two components:

The "selfish" utility increase derived from one's own consumption and measured by a function $u(x_i)$ where x_i is one's own share.

The "selfish" utility of the *other agent*.

These two components are combined in some proportion, and the proportion measures the degree of altruism of each agent. Specifically, we denote by a and b the shares of Ann and Bob, and we write their utility for a division (a, b) of the cake as follows:

Ann: $u(a) + \lambda_A u(b)$

Bob: $u(b) + \lambda_B u(a)$

Here λ_A is Ann's "degree of altruism," $0 \leq \lambda_A \leq 1$, and the interpretation of λ_B is similar. We assume that the common function u (measuring utility increase from own consumption) is increasing and concave.

The goal of the exercise is to assume that Ann is more altruistic than Bob, namely $\lambda_A > \lambda_B$, and to find out if she receives a bigger share, smaller share, or equal share of the cake:

- If the utilitarian collective utility is maximized
- If the egalitarian collective utility is maximized
- If the Nash collective utility is maximized

Answer first in the two following examples, then with maximal generality, namely without specifying u, λ_A, or λ_B:

Example 1: $\lambda_A = \frac{1}{3}, \lambda_B = \frac{1}{4}, u(x) = x$

Example 2: $\lambda_A = \frac{1}{3}, \lambda_B = \frac{1}{4}, u(x) = \sqrt{x}$

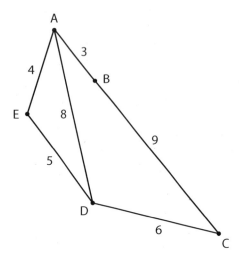

Figure 3.11
Road network for exercise 3.4a

Exercise 3.4 Location of a Facility on a Network with Loops

a. Consider the road network of figure 3.11, where each dot represents an agent (five agents in total), and numbers represent distances in miles. As in example 3.8, the distance between two points is that of the shortest path on the network connecting them. Disutility is the distance between one's location and that of the facility. The facility can be located anywhere on the road network.

Where will the classical utilitarian arbitrator locate a desirable facility? *Hint:* Check first that the utilitarian optimum must be at one of the five points where an agent resides.

What about the egalitarian arbitrator?

b. Consider the road network of figure 3.12. Two agents live at B, three live at C, and four at D (9 agents in total). There is no direct road between B and C. Find the optimum locations for the egalitarian and the classical utilitarian arbitrators.

c. Suppose now that the dotted line between B and C in figure 3.12 is a new road of length 8. Answer the same questions as in b. Which agents benefit and which are hurt by the increase in the resources?

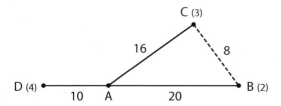

Figure 3.12
Road network for exercise 3.4b

*Exercise 3.5 Location of a Noxious Facility

a. Consider a variant of example 3.5 where the densities of the agents over the interval $[0, 1]$ are as follows:

Density 2 on $\left[0, \frac{1}{3}\right]$
Density 1 on $\left[\frac{1}{2}, \frac{2}{3}\right]$ and on $\left[\frac{3}{4}, 1\right]$
Density 0 on $\left]\frac{1}{3}, \frac{1}{2}\right[$ and on $\left]\frac{2}{3}, \frac{3}{4}\right[$

Show that the location selected by the classical utilitarian is $y_u = 1$. Show that the egalitarian arbitrator selects $y_e = 5/12$.

b. Next consider the following densities:

Density 2 on $\left[0, \frac{1}{3}\right]$
Density 1 on $\left[\frac{1}{2}, \frac{2}{3}\right]$
Density 3 on $\left[\frac{5}{6}, 1\right]$
Density 0 on $\left]\frac{1}{3}, \frac{1}{2}\right[$ and on $\left]\frac{2}{3}, \frac{5}{6}\right[$

Find the locations selected by the classical utilitarian, egalitarian (leximin), and Nash arbitrators.

c. Consider the road network of question a in exercise 3.4 depicted in figure 3.11. Show that the classical utilitarian locates the noxious facility on the road CD, one mile away from C. Show that the egalitarian selects the midpoint between B and C.

d. Consider the road network of questions b and c in exercise 3.4 depicted on figure 3.12. Show that the egalitarian arbitrator picks the same location for both networks (with or without the direct road BC). Show that the utilitarian arbitrator selects B in the network of questions b, and the location 2 miles away from B on BC in the network of question c.

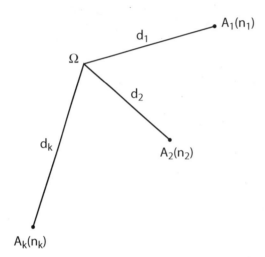

Figure 3.13
Road network for exercise 3.6

*Exercise 3.6 Location on a Star-Tree

The road network depicted on figure 3.13 is a "star-tree." The outer node A_k is connected to the center O by a direct route of length d_k, and there is no other road going through A_k. For concreteness, assume ten nodes $A_1, \ldots, A_{10}$. There are n_k agents living at A_k, and no one lives anywhere else. So $n = n_1 + \cdots + n_{10}$ is the total number of agents.

a. In this question the facility is a "good" one, as in example 3.4 and exercise 3.4. Show that the optimal egalitarian location is the midpoint between the two outer nodes A_i, A_j farthest away from the center (i.e., d_i and d_j are the two largest distances). Check that this location is unambiguous, even if there are several possible choices for A_i, A_j.

   Show that the unique classical utilitarian optimum is at the center if no outer location contains more than one-half of the agents: $n_k < n/2$ for $k = 1, \ldots, 10$. What happens in the remaining case?

b. Now the facility is noxious, as in example 3.5 and exercise 3.5. Show that the egalitarian optimum is the midpoint between the outernode farthest away from the center and the one closest to the center. That is, if $d_{i^*} = \max_i d_i$ and $d_{j^*} = \min_i d_i$, the midpoint of $A_{i^*} A_{j^*}$ maximizes the egalitarian collective utility. Can we use the leximin ordering to break ties?

Show that the optimal locations for the classical utilitarian are all the nodes A_{k^*} maximizing the product $(n - n_k)d_k$. Comment on the trade-off leading the choice of the utilitarian arbitrator.

Exercise 3.7 *Time-Sharing* The exercise proposes variants of examples 3.6a and 3.6b.

a. Consider example 3.6a. Compute the optimal time-sharing for the collective utility functions $W_p, 0 < p \leq 1$ and $W^q, 0 < q$, as is defined by (5) in section 3.2. Check that when p or q go to zero (resp. q goes to infinity), the solution converges toward the Nash (resp. the egalitarian) optimum.

b. In the following four examples we have one agent per row and three decisions. The arbitrator can mix between the three decisions. Find the classical utilitarian, egalitarian, and Nash solutions:

	a	b	c
Ann	1	1	0
Bob	0	0	1
Chris	0	1	0
Dave	1	0	0

	a	b	c
Ann	1	0	0
Bob	0	1	0
Chris	0	1	1
Dave	1	1	0

	a	b	c
Ann	1	0	1
Bob	0	1	0
Chris	1	0	0
Dave	0	1	1

	a	b	c
Ann	1	0	0
Bob	1	1	0
Chris	1	0	1
Dave	0	1	1

Hint: For the first and fourth example, use the symmetry between two of the three decisions; for the fourth example, the egalitarian collective utility is not enough, and you must invoke the leximin ordering.

c. Now we have four types of agents and three decisions a, b, c. The total number of agents is $n = 2m + 2p$.

	a	b	c
m	1	0	0
m	0	1	0
p	1	0	1
p	0	1	1

Find the three usual solutions, distinguishing the cases $p \geq m$ and $p < m$.

d. We have here four decisions and four agents:

	a	b	c	d
Ann	1	0	1	1
Bob	1	1	0	0
Chris	0	0	1	0
Dave	0	1	0	1

Compute the egalitarian and Nash solutions.

e. Consider example 3.1 where we have six deterministic choices and five agents. Each choice corresponds to a subset of agents who receive a utility of one, so that the six choices are

$$a = \{1, 2\}, b = \{1, 3\}, c = \{1, 4\}, d = \{2, 4, 5\}, e = \{2, 3, 5\}, f = \{3, 4, 5\}$$

Find the time-sharing recommended by the three usual solutions.

Exercise 3.8 Slavery of the Talented

This is a variant of example 3.9 where the only difference is the common utility function of the two agents: $u_i(z_i, y_i) = \sqrt{z_i y_i}$.

a. Assume that $s_1 = 2, s_2 = 1$. Show that if an allocation is efficient and z_i, y_i, x_i are all positive, we must have

$$z_1 = 2y_1, \quad z_2 = y_2, \quad 2y_1 + y_2 = 30, \quad 5 \le y_1 \le 15, \ 0 \le y_2 \le 20$$

b. Show that the utilitarian solution is full slavery of the talented: when productivities are $s_1 = 2, s_2 = 1$, agent 1 works full time and consumes no corn.

c. Show that there is no failure of monotonicity under the Nash solution: both agents benefit when agent 1's productivity increases from 1 to 2; yet agent 1's gain is smaller than agent 2's.

d. Compare the two solutions above with the egalitarian solution.

Exercise 3.9 Bargaining Compromises

We consider three variants of example 3.11. Compute in each case the Nash and KS bargaining solutions

a.

	a	b	c
Ann	70	50	20
Bob	80	90	110

As in example 3.11 we normalize utilities at the worst utility between a, b, and c:

	a	b	c
Ann	40	20	10
Bob	20	30	70

b. Two agents and four outcomes. Minimal utility is at outcome a (thus the data are "pre-normalized"):

	a	b	c	d
Ann	0	1	5	6
Bob	0	11	6	3

c. Variant of question b: with have two agents with utility identical to Ann's, and three with utility identical to Bob's.

Exercise 3.10 Generalization of Example 3.10

The job of agent i requires a_i units of time, and we assume that $a_1 < a_2 < \cdots < a_n$. Disutility is total waiting time until completion of one's job.

a. Assume that the server must choose a deterministic priority ordering. Show that it chooses the ordering $\{1, 2, \ldots, n\}$ under any social welfare ordering (monotonic and symmetric).

b. Now the server can mix over all $n!$ orderings σ of $\{1, 2, \ldots, n\}$, with arbitrary probability $\pi_\sigma \geq 0$, $\sum_\sigma \pi_\sigma = 1$. Show that the utilitarian server chooses the ordering $\{1, 2, \ldots, n\}$ with probability 1, as in question a.

c. Show that for the profile of utilities u^σ resulting from an ordering σ of $\{1, 2, \ldots, n\}$, the sum $\sum a_i u_i^\sigma$ is independent of σ. Deduce that any convex combination of the profiles π^σ is a Pareto optimal and feasible utility profile.

d. Compute the expected utility profile when the priority ordering σ is selected at random with uniform probability on all orderings σ. Check that it is the Kalai-Smorodinsky solution if the maximal disutility (minimal utility) is $a_N = \sum_j a_j$ for every agent, and agent $i's$ minimal disutility is a_i.

e. Consider the n orderings σ^k, $k = 1, \ldots, n$, obtained by successive applications of the circular permutation $i \rightarrow i + 1$.

$$\sigma^1 = \{1, 2, \ldots, n\}; \quad \sigma^2 = \{2, 3, \ldots, n-1, 1\}; \ldots; \sigma^k = \{k, k+1, \ldots, k-1\}; \ldots$$

Check that if we choose the priority ordering σ^k with probability a_k/a_N, for $k = 1, \ldots, n$, the resulting utility profile is egalitarian.

Exercise 3.11 Sharing One Commodity

a. We must divide \$100 between two agents with the following utilities for money:

$$u_1(x) = \sqrt{x}, \ u_2(x) = 2\sqrt{x} \qquad .$$

Compute the classical utilitarian, egalitarian, Nash, and KS solutions (for the latter two, take the minimal utility to be zero).

b. Answer the same questions with the utility functions:

$$u_1(x) = x^{2/3}; \quad u_2(x) = x^{1/3}$$

c. Answer the same questions with the utility functions:

$$u_1(x) = x; \quad u_2(x) = \frac{100x}{100 + x}$$

d. What happens in the problems of questions a, b, and c when the cash prize increases? Which agent gets a bigger share of the increment according to what solution?

*Exercise 3.12 Leximin and Leximax

Given a utility profile $u = (u_i)$ in $\mathbf{R}^n$, we denote by u^* (resp. $^*u$) the vector obtained by rearranging the coordinates of u increasingly (resp. decreasingly). The leximin ordering compares two profiles u, v by comparing u^* and v^* for the lexicographic ordering:

$$u \succeq v \overset{\text{def}}{\Longleftrightarrow} \{u_1^* > v_1^*\} \quad \text{or} \quad \{u_1^* = v_1^* \text{ and } u_2^* > v_2^*\}$$

$$\text{or} \quad \{u_1^* = v_1^*, u_2^* = v_2^* \text{ and } u_3^* > v_3^*\} \ldots$$

$$\text{or} \quad \{u^* = v^*\}.$$

The leximax ordering compares u and v as the lexicographic ordering compares $^*u$ and $^*v$.

a. Show that both orderings, leximin and leximax, are independent of unconcerned agents (property 1).

b. Show that they are both independent of the common utility pace (discussed at the end of section 3.3).

c. Show that leximin meets, but leximax fails—the Pigou-Dalton transfer principle.

d. Show that leximin is the limit as q goes to infinity of the social welfare ordering W^q defined in (4). Show that leximax is the limit of W_p (also defined in 4) as p goes to infinity. The convergence statement is defined as follows. Suppose that the two profiles u, v in $\mathbf{R}^n$ are such that $W^q(u) \geq W^q(v)$ for all q large enough. Then $u \succsim v$ for the leximin ordering.

The other convergence is defined similarly.

*Exercise 3.13 Independence of Common Zero of Utilities

Consider the family of collective utility functions:

$$V_p(u) = \sum_i e^{pu_i} \quad \text{for some fixed} \quad p, p > 0$$

$$V^q(u) = -\sum_i e^{-qu_i} \quad \text{for some fixed} \quad q, q > 0$$

a. Show that each collective utility function V_p and V^q is independent of unconcerned agents. Show that it is independent of the common zero of utilities, a property similar to (3) bearing on a simultaneous shift of all individual zeros of utilities.

b. What is the limit of the social welfare ordering V_p (resp. V^q) as p (resp. q) goes to infinity? As p (resp. q) goes to zero?

*Exercise 3.14 Distortion of Individual Zeros and Scales

a. Consider the binary choice between the two four-person utility profiles

$$u(a) = (1, 4, 4, 0), \quad u(b) = (0, 4, 4, 2)$$

The arbitrator uses the leximin ordering to select a or b with no possibility of mixing. Now agent 1 inflates the scale of his utility by a factor of 3, so his new utility is $u'_1(a) = 3$; $u'_1(b) = 0$. Show that this distortion is profitable even if it is a lie (agent 1's true utility remains u_1).

Next suppose that the arbitrator can mix a and b, and still is an ardent egalitarian. Show that the (untrue) distortion by agent 1 ends up hurting him.

b. From now on we restrict attention to strictly positive individual utilities. We fix a social welfare ordering $\succsim$ and define the property: "increasing strategically the scale of one's utility can't hurt." For all profile u, all agent i, and all $\lambda, \lambda > 1$, we write $u' = (u \mid^i \lambda u_i)$ for the profile $u'_j = u_j$ if $j \neq i$ and $u'_i = \lambda u_i$.

The property above is now defined:

for all i, $\lambda > 1$, u and v: $\{v \succ u$ and $u' \succ v'\} \Rightarrow \{u_i > v_i\}$

Interpret this definition and explain its name. We say "increasing one's scale is profitable" if, in addition to the property above, we have

for all i, and all u, v: $\{v \succ u$ and $u_i > v_i\} \Rightarrow \exists \lambda > 1 : (u \mid^i \lambda u_i) \succ (v \mid^i \lambda v_i)$

Consider the collective utility W_p, $p > 0$ defined in (4). Show that increasing one's scale is profitable for W_p, hence for its limit as well, the leximax social ordering (defined in exercise 3.12). What about W_0, namely the Nash collective utility?

Define similarly the properties "decreasing one's scale cannot hurt" and "decreasing one's scale is profitable." Show that for the collective utility W^q, $q > 0$, in (4), decreasing one's scale is profitable. Therefore the same holds true for its limit, the leximin social welfare ordering.

c. We still assume strictly positive utilities only. We define "increasing the zero of one's utility can't hurt":

for all i, $\lambda > 0$, u and v: $\{v \succ u\}$ and $(u \mid^i u_i - \lambda) \succ (v \mid^i v_i - \lambda) \Rightarrow \{u_i > v_i\}$

Consider an additive collective utility W as in (2). Show that its ordering meets the above property if and only if g is concave. Show that decreasing one's zero cannot hurt if and only if g is convex.

Deduce that increasing one's zero can't hurt if we are using the collective utility W^q in (4) or W_p for $0 \leq p \leq 1$. In particular, this holds true for the leximin social welfare ordering.

4 Voting and Social Choice

4.1 Ordinal Welfarism

As discussed in section 1.3, ordinal welfarism pursues the welfarist program in those situations where the cardinal measurement of individual welfares is either unfeasible, unreliable, or ethically untenable.

Consider voting among several candidates competing for a certain political office. Who would think of measuring the relative impact of electing Jones or Smith on the individual welfare of each and every citizen? Say that Ann favors Jones and Bob favors Smith. It is typically impossible to decide whether Ann's utility gain from having Jones in office rather than Smith is larger than Bob's gain from having Smith rather than Jones. Such an evaluation would require that each voter forms expectations about all decisions influenced by the election of Jones or Smith and computes his or her expected utility. The complexity of these computations destroys the plausibility of the cardinal utility model: electors simply do not perform elaborate computations of cardinal welfare, and even the task of ranking all candidates from best to worst is challenging, given limited information about the consequences of the election.

In most real life elections, in the large or in the small, voters are not asked to express more than an "ordinal" opinion, namely a preference ordering (which may or may not allow for indifferences) of the names on the ballot. There is more to this restriction than the practicality and simplicity of an ordinal message.

Recall from section 3.1 the strong ethical objections to the interpersonal comparison of cardinal welfares. If the outcome of the election depends on the intensity of the voters' feelings and emotions about the candidates, a minority of fanatics will influence the outcome more than the quiet majority; worse yet, a subset of voters *faking* fanaticism are more influential than the honest, truth-telling voters.

The central postulate of ordinal welfarism is that individual welfare is entirely captured by a preference ordering of the possible outcomes, also called states of the world. This ordering is a binary relation R of the set A of possible outcomes (A is often called the choice set). The relation xRy reads "x is at least as good as y," or "welfare at x is not below welfare at y." The relation R is assumed to be *complete* and *transitive*. Completeness of R means that all pairs x, y in A can be compared: at least one of xRy and yRx holds. If xRy but not yRx, we say that x is strictly preferred to y and write xPy; if xRy and yRx, we say that the choice between x and y is a matter of indifference (or, abusing language, that x and y are "indifferent") and we write xIy. Transitivity of R means that xRy and yRz imply xRz. In particular, strict preferences are transitive (xPy and yPz imply xPz), and so are indifferences (xIy and yIz imply xIz).

The preference relation R expresses the opinion, tastes, or values of a certain agent over the outcomes in A, and it pointedly avoids any statement about the intensity of these preferences. The empirical basis of R is the *choice* between outcomes: if an agent with preferences R is presented with a choice between two states of the world x and y, she will choose x if xPy and y if yPx. If presented with a choice over a subset $\{x, y, z, \ldots\}$ of outcomes, she will pick one of the outcomes ranked highest in R, namely a^* such that a^*Rx, a^*Ry, a^*Rz, and so on.

The choices made by a given agent over the various subsets of outcomes that she may be presented with, are entirely determined by her preference relation R. Conversely, if we observe a series of choices, we may or may not be able to identify an underlying preference relation *rationalizing* these choices, in the sense that the observed choices are the highest ranked for R among the feasible choices. For instance, imagine that Ann has been presented with three successive pairs $\{x, y\}$, $\{y, z\}$, and her choices are as follows: choose x from $\{x, y\}$, choose y from $\{y, z\}$, or choose z from $\{x, z\}$. If the preference relation R rationalizes these choices, it must have xPy because x was unambiguously chosen from x, y (Ann could say "both choices are okay" but not choose to do so), and similarly we must have yPz and zPx, in contradiction of the transitivity of R. Another configuration ruling out the existence of R is

choose x from $\{x, y\}$

$$\tag{1}$$

choose y from $\{x, y, z\}$

Here the first choice reveals xPy, but the second implies yPx, yPz, in contradiction of the definitions of P.

In the configuration (1) the peculiarity of the observed choices is illustrated by the following classic air travel story. The flight attendant asks this passenger if he will have fish or chicken for his meal, and his answer is "fish." A minute later he comes back announcing that the pasta meal is still available, and would he like to change his mind? Yes, says the passenger, in that case I will have chicken.

The choices over all conceivable feasible subsets of outcomes are said to be *rational* (or rationalizable) if there exists a preference relation R such that for any feasible subset B of outcomes, the outcomes (or outcomes) $S(B)$ selected from B are precisely the highest ranked outcomes in B according to R : xPy if x is in $S(B)$ and y is not in $S(B)$; xIx' if x and x' are both in $S(B)$. The formal theory of rational choice explores in great detail what restrictions on the various choices over the various subsets guarantee that these choices can be rationalized by a preference relation.

The identification of welfare with preferences, and of preferences with choice, is an intellectual construction at the center of modern economic thinking. We will refer to this construction as the ordinal approach. It eschews heroic assumptions about cardinal measurement of utility, and offers a testable empirical basis for the construction of individual preferences, namely the actual choices made by the agents. Social choice theory adapts the welfarist program—namely the definition of just compromises between the conflicting goals of maximizing different individual welfares—to the ordinal approach.

The concept of Pareto optimality, already central in chapter 3, is clearly an ordinal concept. Outcome y is Pareto superior to outcome x if $y R_j x$ for all agent j and $y P_i x$ for at least one agent i: everyone is at least as satisfied with y as with x and at least one agent is strictly better off with y.

The main new feature of the ordinal context is that individual welfare can no longer be separated from the set A of outcomes to which it applies: the binary relation R bears on A and cannot be defined in a vacuum. Contrast this with the cardinal approach, where we can compare utility levels $u_1, u'_1, u_2, u'_2, \ldots$ without specifying the outcomes from which these utilities are derived. Therefore, in the ordinal world, collective decision-making can only be defined if we specify the set A of feasible outcomes (states of the world), and for each agent i a preference relation R_i on A. The focus is on the distribution of decision power, namely how the configuration of these relations R_i—called the profile of preferences—affects the choice of an outcome in A, or affects the collective preference relation on A—in the cases of voting and preference aggregation, respectively—as explained below.

We define now the two central models of social choice theory. A *voting* problem specifies the set A of outcomes, the set N of agents, and a profile of preferences; the problem is to "elect" an outcome a in A from these data. A systematic solution of this problem (a rule for selecting an outcome from any profile of preferences) is a pure example of a public contract in the sense of section 1.5. Key to the discussion starting in the next section is the knowledge of which subsets T of N "control" the choice of a in the sense that if all voters in T have a as their first choice, a will be elected. For instance, under majority voting, any coalition T containing strictly more agents than N/T controls the outcome of the election.

The voting model has two complementary interpretations, normative and strategic. In the normative one, the benevolent dictator discovers the profile of preferences R_i and enforces the compromise outcome deemed just by the voting method. Alternatively, the preference relation R_i is private information to agent i and a voting rule is a decentralized decision process enforced by the public authority. Every voter reports a preference relation $\tilde{R}_i$ to the central agency, who takes these messages on face value to compute the winning outcome. As the agency has no way to determine whether the reported preference relation $\tilde{R}_i$ is indeed the true relation R_i, each agent is free to report a nontruthful relation if this serves his or her interest better than reporting the truth. Thus, in the second interpretation of the voting model, the issue is strategic voting, and how the central agency can avoid misreporting.

The second model of social choice theory is the *preference aggregation* problem. Here we associate to a preference profile a collective preference. Much as in chapter 3 a collective utility function associates a cardinal index to any profile of cardinal utilities; the aggregation method computes an ordinal preference relation from any profile of preference relations. The anthropomorphic bias is the same in both cases, but the new ordinal model is technically more involved.

We are given, as in the voting model, the outcome set A, agent set N, and a profile of preferences, but we are now looking for a collective preference R on A, one that will order all outcomes instead of selecting just one "best" outcome. The two problems are closely related, and under the axiom independence of irrelevant alternatives (section 4.6), they are formally equivalent.

The voting and preference aggregation problems are truly the most general microeconomic models of collective decision-making because they make no restrictive assumption, neither on the set A of outcomes or on the admissible preference profiles of the agents. Therefore these models encompass, in principle, all resource allocation problems from chapter 5 onward. On the other hand, the extreme generality of the model leads to two severe impossibility results, namely Arrow's theorem about preference aggregation (section 4.6), and Gibbard-Satterthwaite's theorem about strategic voting (briefly discussed at the end of section 4.4). More palatable results obtain when the domain of individual preferences is suitably restricted, and two important examples of such restrictions are discussed in sections 4.4 and 4.5.

4.2 Condorcet versus Borda

The two most important ideas of voting theory originated more than 200 years ago, in the work of two French philosophers and mathematicians, Jean-Antoine the marquis de Condorcet and Jean-Charles de Borda. Both articulated a critique of plurality voting and proposed a (different) remedy. Their two methods are defined and illustrated in the examples below.

Plurality voting is, then as today, the most widely used voting method, of unrivaled simplicity. Each voter chooses one of the competing candidates, and the candidate with the largest support wins. Thus a voter only needs to designate his or her most preferred candidate.[1] Electors do not need to spell out a complete preference relation ordering all candidates, and the rule is at once transparent and easy to implement. German tribes elected their new chief by raising contenders on a shield, around which their supporters gathered: a simple head count and a couple of strong shields, is all the hardware they needed.

Condorcet and Borda agreed that plurality voting is seriously flawed, because it reflects only the distribution of the "top" candidates and fails to take into account the entire preference relation of the voters. It I vote for an extremist candidate who stands no chance of

---

1. Barring strategic manipulations, which cannot be ignored among "sophisticated" voters.

being elected, my ballot will play no role in the "real" contest between the two centrist candidates. Both the Condorcet and the Borda voting rule offer a (different) remedy to this difficulty.

The next three examples are borrowed from Borda's and Condorcet's essays on voting.

Example 4.1. Where Condorcet and Borda Agree   Borda proposes the following example with 21 voters and three candidates (or outcomes) a, b, c. The voters are split in three groups of respective sizes 6, 7, and 8, and all voters within a given group have identical preferences:

$$
\begin{array}{rccc}
\text{Number of voters:} & 6 & 7 & 8 \\
\text{Top:} & b & c & a \\
: & c & b & b \\
\text{Bottom:} & a & a & c
\end{array}
\tag{2}
$$

In the table above a preference relation is represented as a column, with the top candidate outcome ranked first and the bottom one ranked last. Note that a voter is never indifferent between two outcomes.

Plurality voting elects a in this profile, yet b is a more convincing compromise. Borda's and Condorcet's argument is that b is just below a in 8 ballots, but a is either just below or two positions below b in 13 ballots.

Borda proposes to tally the score of a candidate x by counting 2 points for each voter for whom x is the best candidate, 1 point for each voter who ranks x as second and 0 point for each voter ranking x last. Thus the Borda scores in example (2) are

$$\text{score}\,(a) = 8 \times 2 = 16$$

$$\text{score}\,(b) = 6 \times 2 + 15 \times 1 = 27$$

$$\text{score}\,(c) = 7 \times 2 + 6 \times 1 = 20$$

Now b has the highest Borda score hence is elected, whereas the plurality winner a has the lowest Borda score.

Condorcet's argument in support of the election of b is different. Suppose that the vote reduces to a duel between a and b (ignoring c altogether): then b wins by 13 votes against 8; similarly a duel between b and c has b winning 14 to 7, and finally c wins the a versus c duel by 13 to 8. Thus the *majority relation* R^m that records the winner of each duel x, y as "x is preferred to y by a majority of voters," is as follows:

$$b P^m c \quad b P^m a \quad c P^m a$$

We call b, the top outcome of the majority relation, the *Condorcet winner,* whereas a is the Condorcet *loser,* namely the bottom outcome of the majority relation.

In the second preference profile, 60 voters must decide among four candidates:

Number of voters:	23	19	18
Top:	a	b	c
	d	d	d
	b	a	a
Bottom:	c	c	b

The plurality winner is a but d is a more equitable compromise when the entire profile is taken into account.

Borda scores are computed by giving 3 points for each first place, 2 points for each second place, 1 point for each third place, and no point for each fourth place:

score $(d) = 120 >$ score $(a) = 106 >$ score $(b) = 80 >$ score $(c) = 54$

As in example (2), the majority relation yields the same ordering of the candidates as the Borda scores:

$$d P^m a \ (37/23); \quad d P^m b \ (41/19); \quad d P^m c \ (42/18)$$

$$a P^m b \ (41/19); \quad a P^m c \ (42/18)$$

$$b P^m c \ (42/18)$$

In our next example, the majority relation and the Borda scores make different recommendations, and this divergence reveals some important structural features of these two methods.

Example 4.2 Where Condorcet and Borda Disagree   The profile has 26 voters and three candidates:

Number of voters:	15	11	
	a	b	
	b	c	(3)
	c	a	

The plurality winner is a, and it is the Condorcet winner as well: a wins by 15 to 11 both duels against b and c. Borda's objection is that the eleven "minority" voters (supporters of b) dislike a more than the fifteen majority voters (supporters of a) dislike b. Indeed, a is the worst outcome for 42 percent of the voters, whereas b is always the first or second choice. This is reflected in their respective Borda scores:

score $(b) = 15 + 2 \times 11 = 37 >$ score $(a) = 2 \times 15 = 30 >$ score $(c) = 11$

Notice that Borda's argument relies on the conventional choice of points for first, second, and third place, which plays the role of a cardinal utility, albeit a mechanical one, unrelated to the real intensity of feelings of our voters for these three candidates (the voting rule prevents them from reporting any such intensity). Plurality voting is the voting method where first place gives one point and any other ranking gives no point.

The general family of *scoring methods* include Borda's and the plurality methods as special cases. Say that p candidates are competing. A scoring method is defined by the choice of a sequence of scores $s_1, s_2, \ldots, s_p$: a candidate x scores s_k points for each voter who ranks x in the kth place; the candidate or candidates with the highest total score wins. Naturally the scores decrease with respect to ranks, $s_1 \geq s_2 \geq \cdots \geq s_p$ and moreover $s_1 > s_p$, lest all candidates receive the same score irrespective of rank. Plurality corresponds to the scores $s_1 = 1, s_k = 0$ for $k = 2, \ldots, p$ and Borda to the scores $s_k = p - k$ for $k = 1, \ldots, p$. Another method of interest is *antiplurality,* for which $s_k = 1$ for $k = 1, \ldots, p-1$ and $s_p = 0$. In other words the antiplurality winner is the candidate who is least often regarded as the worst.

In example 4.2, depending on the choice of the scores, either a or b is elected[2]—but never c, whose score is always smaller than that of b, irrespective of the choice of s_1, s_2, s_3. This flexibility contrasts with the inflexible message of the Condorcet approach: a must be elected because the "will of the majority" is to prefer a to b and a to c. The fact that a is ranked last by the minority voters, whereas b is second best for all majority voters, is irrelevant to the majority relation. This is precisely the reason why the Borda method prefers b to a. Here Borda's method takes into account the entire preference profile but Condorcet's does not. We abstain at this point to make a normative judgment about this difference, which is at the heart of the axiom independence of irrelevant alternatives (IIA) discussed in section 4.6.

In our third example, slightly adapted from one of Condorcet's examples, the contrast between the Condorcet approach and the scoring approach (irrespective of the choice of scores) is especially clear.

Example 4.3 Condorcet against Scoring Methods   There are 81 voters and three candidates, with the following preferences:

Number of voters:	30	3	25	14	9	
	a	a	b	b	c	
	b	c	a	c	a	(4)
	c	b	c	a	b	

---

2. For instance, $s_1 = 4, s_2 = 1, s_3 = 0$, makes a the winner with a score of 60 against 59 for b.

Candidate b is the plurality and the Borda winner in this profile. In fact, b wins for *any* choice of scores for first, second, and third place. To check this, we assume without loss of generality that these scores are 1, s, and 0, respectively, with $0 \leq s \leq 1$ (thus $s = 0$ is plurality and $s = \frac{1}{2}$ is the Borda method). Compute

$$\text{score } (b) = 39 + 30s > \text{score } (a) = 33 + 34s > \text{score } (c) = 9 + 17s$$

By contrast, the Condorcet winner is a because $a P^m b$ by 42/39 and $a P^m c$ by 58/23.

Notice that outcome c fares badly in both approaches. However, for the scoring methods the relative position of c with respect to b and a matters enormously: b wins essentially because c is much more often between b and a when b is first choice (this happens for 14 voters) than between a and b when a is first choice (happening only for 3 voters). On the other hand, a is a Condorcet winner, whether or not we take into account the irrelevant outcome c, or any other sure loser. This is, again, the IIA property alluded to above. It is a very strong argument in favor of the election of a in this example, and in support of the majority relation in general.

The most serious critique of the Condorcet approach is the observation, due to Condorcet himself, that the majority relation may cycle, meaning that it may fail the transitivity property (section 4.1). If the cycle involves the best outcomes of the majority relation, no Condorcet winner exists.

The simplest profiles of preferences exhibiting such cycles involve three outcomes a, b, c and only three different preference relations:

$$
\begin{array}{cccc}
\text{Number of voters:} & n_1 & n_2 & n_3 \\
 & a & c & b \\
 & b & a & c \\
 & c & b & a
\end{array}
\tag{5}
$$

If the sum of any two among the three numbers $n_i, i = 1, 2, 3$, is greater than the third, the majority relation has the following cycle:

$$n_1 + n_2 > n_3 \Rightarrow a P^m b$$

$$n_1 + n_3 > n_2 \Rightarrow b P^m c$$

$$n_2 + n_3 > n_1 \Rightarrow c P^m a$$

and there is no Condorcet winner. Condorcet was keenly aware of this problem and proposed to break the cycle at his weakest link, namely to ignore the majority preference supported by the smallest majority.

For instance, suppose that $n_1 = 18, n_2 = 20$, and $n_3 = 10$. Then the link bP^mc is the weakest because b versus c yields a $28/20$ split versus $38/10$ for aP^mb and $30/18$ for cP^ma. Thus Condorcet suggests to elect c at this profile. Compare with the Borda method, electing a because score $(a) = 56 >$ score $(c) = 50 >$ score $(b) = 38$. In this example the election of either a or b is plausible.

Our last example uncovers a serious defect of any voting method electing the Condorcet winner whenever there is one, no matter how this method chooses to break the cycles of the majority relation when there is no Condorcet winner. To fix ideas, we assume as above that a cycle is broken at its weakest link, but the example can be adapted to any cycle-breaking rule.

Example 4.4 The Reunion Paradox   We consider two disjoint groups of voters, with respectively 34 and 35 members, who vote over the same three candidates a, b, c. The first group contains left-handed voters, and the second one right-handed voters:

Number of left-handed voters:	10	6	6	12
	a	b	b	c
	b	a	c	a
	c	c	a	b

Number of right-handed voters:	18	17
	a	c
	c	a
	b	b

Candidate a is the majority winner among right-handed voters. Among left-handed voters, the majority relation has a cycle, $aP^mbP^mcP^ma$, of which the weakest link is cP^ma (by $18/16$ versus $22/12$ for the other two links); therefore we remove this link and elect a.

As a wins both among left-handed and among right-handed voters, we would expect—even request—that a be still declared the winner among the overall population of 69 voters. Yet c is the Condorcet winner there: cP^ma by $35/34$ and cP^mb by $47/22$!

The example above reveals a troubling paradoxical feature of the Condorcet approach. The paradox does not occur if a is a "real" Condorcet winner among left-handed and among right-handed electors, namely if for any other candidate x, a majority of lefties prefer a to x and a majority of righties do too: the union of these two majorities makes a majority in the grand population. Thus the paradox is a direct consequence of cycles in the majority relation.

Notice that any scoring method is immune to the reunion paradox. In the example a is the Borda winner in each subgroup and in the grand population. It is a simple exercise to check that for any system of scores, if two disjoint subsets of voters elect the same candidate a from the same pool of candidates, then a is still elected by the reunion of all the voters.

A related problem is the no-show paradox: at certain profiles of preferences, certain agents are better off staying home rather than participating in the election and casting a truthful ballot. This paradox affects all voting methods choosing the Condorcet winner when there is one, and none of the scoring methods.

4.3   Voting over Resource Allocation

In the discussion of the Condorcet and Borda voting methods, the set A of candidates/ outcomes is typically small, and voters may be endowed with arbitrary preferences over A. This is the correct modeling assumption when we speak about a political election, where the ability to report any ranking of the candidates is a basic individual right. However, when the issue on the ballot concerns the allocation of resources, some important restrictions on individual preferences come into play. The examples discussed below include voting time shares (example 4.5), over the location of a facility (example 4.6) and over tax- or surplus-sharing methods (examples 4.7 and 4.8). We find that majority voting works brilliantly in several of these problems (sections 4.4 and 4.5) but produces systematic cycling in others (example 4.5).

On the other hand, scoring methods are hopelessly impractical in all of these models because the set A of outcomes is large, and typically modeled as an infinite set, such as an interval of real numbers (example 4.6) or the simplex of an euclidean space (example 4.5). For instance, assume $A = [0, 1]$: a scoring method associates to an ordinal preference relation on A a scoring function representing the relation in question like a utility function. There are many different ways to define this representation,[3] and no natural way to select any of the scoring methods.

Another serious difficulty limiting the application of scoring methods in resource allocation problems comes from the IIA property: it is explained in the discussion following example 4.6.

In our next example, the issue is to divide a homogeneous private good when each voter cares only about his or her share. The commodity is a time share in example 4.5; it could be interpreted as money when the voters decide on a distribution of tax shares, or on the allocation of a surplus. The central feature is the pervasive cycling of the majority relation.

Example 4.5 Voting over Time Shares: Example 3.6a Continued   We can choose any mixture $(x_1, \ldots, x_5)$ of the five radio stations, where x_i represents the time share of

---

3. One way is to pick a positive measure m on $[0, 1]$ and define the score $s(x) = m(P(x))$, where $P(x)$ is the set of outcomes y in A such that $x \succsim y$.

station i, and $\sum_1^5 x_i = 1$. The agents use majority voting to decide on the distribution of time shares.

The set of agents N is partitioned into five disjoint groups of one-minded fans: the agents in N_i like station i and no other station. We write n_i for the cardinality of N_i so that $\sum_1^5 n_i = n$. If one of the five subgroups N_i contains a majority of voters—$n_i > n/2$— then playing their station all the time—meaning $x_i = 1$—is the Condorcet winner (and the plurality winner as well). On the other hand, if none of the five coalitions forms an absolute majority, $n_i < n/2$ for $i = 1, \ldots, 5$, then the majority relation is strongly cyclic and there is no Condorcet winner.

Consider an arbitrary distribution of time shares $x_1, \ldots, x_5$. Suppose that station 1 receives a positive share $x_1 > 0$. The coalition of all agents who do not like station 1 can "gang up" on the n_1 supporters of this station and give a positive piece of the spoil to each one of the four other stations. In other words, consider the following vector of timeshares $y_1, \ldots, y_5$:

$$y_1 = 0, \quad y_i = x_i + \tfrac{1}{4}x_1, \qquad \text{for } i = 2, 3, 4, 5$$

Every supporter of station $i, i = 2, \ldots, 5$, strictly prefers the distribution y over x. Our assumption $n_1 < n/2$ means that $\sum_2^5 n_i > n/2$; that is to say, a majority of voters prefer y over x so that x can't be a Condorcet winner. But, for *any* distribution x of time shares, some station i receives a positive share, and the argument above shows that taking away the share x_i to distribute it among all other stations is a move from which a majority of voters benefit. Hence there is no Condorcet winner.

The example illustrates a strategic situation known as "destructive competition," that often emerges when relatively small coalitions can inflict severe negative externalities upon the complementary coalition. Examples of destructive competition involving production and exchange of private goods are discussed in section 7.3. There as here, the issue is a failure of the logic of private contracting. Every distribution of time shares among the five coalitions is threatened by a private contract of at most four coalitions joining to deprive the remaining coalition of any benefit whatsoever. The cycles of the majority relation correspond to the never ending process of these majority "coups." Instability and unpredictability of the eventual outcome is a consequence of the excessive power awarded to any majority of the voters. A solution to destructive competition in the voting context is to reduce the power of coalitions, for instance, by requiring a qualified majority (a larger support) to overturn a given outcome.

In example 4.5, to fix ideas, assume that $n = 100$ and $n_1 = 40, n_2 = 25, n_3 = 15, n_4 = 12, n_5 = 8$. We require a qualified majority of Q or more to overturn any given allocation. If $51 \le Q \le 60$, destructive competition reigns, exactly as before, because any reunion of four out of the five homogeneous subgroups reaches the quota Q. If $61 \leq Q \leq 75$, the coalition $N_2 \cup N_3 \cup N_4 \cup N_5$ no longer passes the quota Q, so these agents can't get together to "steal" the time share x_1. On the other hand, the four other coalitions made of four of the five subgroups reaches Q; therefore the argument in example 4.5 shows that a distribution x where $x_i > 0$ for one of $i = 2, 3, 4, 5$ will be outvoted when the union of N_j, for all $j \neq i$, forms. In turn this establishes that the only stable allocation of time shares is $x_1 = 1$, $x_i = 0$ for $i = 2, 3, 4, 5$! The homogeneous group N_1 holds veto power and uses it to extract the entire surplus. The strategic logic here is core stability (as in sections 7.1 through 7.3).

Next consider the case $76 \leq Q \leq 85$. Now we need some voters in N_1 and some voters in N_2 to form a coalition of size Q or more; therefore both N_1 and N_2 have veto power. As a result the corestable outcomes are all distributions x of time shares such that $x_1 + x_2 = 1$, $x_i = 0$ for $i = 3, 4, 5$. A similar argument shows that all distributions x such that $x_1 + x_2 + x_3 = 1$, and only those, are corestable when $86 \leq Q \leq 88$. Finally when the quota reaches 93, the core stability property loses all bite, and any distribution x, $\sum_1^5 x_i = 1$, is stable.

4.4 Single-Peaked Preferences

The domain of preferences discussed in this section guarantees the transitivity of the majority relation, in turn making the Condorcet approach to voting unambiguously successful.

Example 4.6 Location of a Facility (Example 3.4 Continued)   As in example 3.4 the voters live in a linear city represented as the interval $[0, 1]$. A voter living at x, $0 \leq x \leq 1$, wishes that the facility be located as close as possible to x, and her utility when the facility is at y is the negative of the distance between x and y, $u_i(y) = -|y - x_i|$. The distribution of our voters along $[0, 1]$ is represented by a cumulative function F, where $F(z)$ is the proportion of voters living on $[0, x]$, and $1 - F(z)$ is the proportion of those living on $[z, 1]$.

We assume, for simplicity, that there is a large number of voters spread continuously between 0 and 1 so that the function F increases continuously from $F(0) = 0$ to $F(1) = 1$. In other words, the proportion of agents living at a given point z is always zero.[4]

The median of the distribution F is this point y^* such that $F(y^*) = \frac{1}{2}$, meaning that half of the population lives to the left of y^* and half to its right. Recall from example 3.4 that y^* is the classical utilitarian solution. In fact, y^* is the Condorcet winner as well.

If we compare y^* to y on its left, $0 \leq y < y^*$, all voters in $[y^*, 1]$ prefer y^* to y, and so do those in $[(y + y^*)/2, y^*]$ because they are closer to y^* than to y. Thus the supporters of

---

4. All results are preserved if we deal with a small finite set of voters or if a positive fraction of the voters are piled up at certain locations.

y^* versus y form the proportion $1 - F((y + y^*)/2)$ of the population, and this constitutes a majority:

$$y < y^* \Rightarrow F\left(\frac{y + y^*}{2}\right) < F(y^*) = \frac{1}{2} \Rightarrow 1 - F\left(\frac{y + y^*}{2}\right) > \frac{1}{2}$$

A symmetrical argument applies when we compare y^* to y in $]y^*, \ 1]$: all voters living in $[0, (y + y^*)/2]$ prefer y^* to y and they form a majority because $F((y + y^*)/2) > F(y^*) = \frac{1}{2}$. This proves our claim that y^* is the majority winner. By similar arguments it is easy to show that the majority relation coincides with the preferences of an agent living at y^*. Location y is preferred by a majority to location y' if and only if y is closer to y', namely $|y - y^*| < |y' - y^*|$ (see exercise 4.6).

The remarkable coincidence of the Condorcet winner and the utilitarian optimum in example 4.6 depends on the particular assumption that the distance from the facility to one's home is the disutility function of each agent. An important observation is that the median of the distribution is still the Condorcet winner (if not the utilitarian optimum) for a much larger domain of individual preferences, called the *single-peaked* preferences.

Given an ordering of the set A from left to right (from 0 to 1 if outcomes in A are represented by real numbers as in the example above), we write $x < y$ when x is to the left of y and we say that z is "between" x and y if either $x \leq z \leq y$ or $y \leq z \leq x$. The preference relation R_i is *single peaked* (in the ordering of A) *with peak* x^i if x^i is the top outcome of R_i in A, and moreover for all outcome x, $x \neq x^i$, R_i prefers any outcome between x^i and x to x itself.

The simple geometric intuition for single-peaked preferences is shown on figure 4.1, where A is represented by an interval $[a, b]$. The preferences are increasing when x increases (moves right) from a to the peak x^i of R_i; they are decreasing when x increases from x^i to b. The important point is that the comparison of outcomes across the peak—say x to its left versus y to its right—are not restricted: see figure 4.1.

The assumption that all individual preferences are single-peaked is plausible in many problems where the outcomes are naturally arranged along a line. This is especially clear if we vote over the drinking age, or the tax rate, or the length of a patent. Another important example is the Downsian model of political competition, where A models the size of the defense budget, the funding of public education, and so on. Of course, a real assembly is rarely so simple as to be lined up from leftist to rightist on all issues, but on specific issues the assumption makes sense. A final example is product differentiation: the group of agents N must pick a software or a copier, or any item whose cost is equally split among all. There is a single dimension of "quality," ordered by price. The assumption that each user

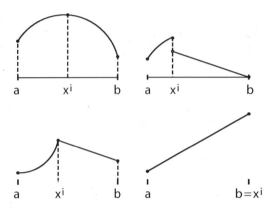

Figure 4.1
Single-peaked preferences

has single-peaked preferences over the different levels of quality amounts to the familiar convexity property.[5]

In example 4.6 the central argument is that the median y^* of the distribution of individual peaks x^i (where agent i lives) is the Condorcet winner. This argument is valid for any profile of single-peaked preferences. Consider an outcome x to the left of y^* ($x < y^*$) : all agents whose peak x^i is to the right of y^* or at y^* prefer y^* to x because y^* is between x and x^i. These agents form a majority by definition of the median; therefore y^* defeats x for the majority relation. A symmetrical argument shows that y^* defeats all outcomes to its right.

Another property of example 4.6 is preserved under any profile of single-peaked preferences: the majority relation is transitive, and is single peaked as well. Its peak is the median peak, and so is the Condorcet winner. Exercise 4.6 explains these facts.

The Condorcet winner is particularly easy to implement when preferences are single-peaked because each agent only needs to report her peak. The way she compares outcomes on the left of her peak to outcomes on its right, does not affect the Condorcet winner (although it does affect the majority relation over outcomes below the winner).

Moreover the definition of the feasible set A far away from the Condorcet winner does not matter either. If we extend A to the right or to the left by adding a few outcomes that stand no chance of being elected, the Condorcet winner does not change, another illustration of the property Independence of Irrelevant alternatives. Here is a simple example with seven agents with single-peaked preferences on [0, 100] and the following peaks:

$$x^1 = 35 \quad x^2 = 10 \quad x^3 = 22 \quad x^4 = 78 \quad x^5 = 92 \quad x^6 = 18 \quad x^7 = 50$$

5. If level x is preferred to level y, and x' is also preferred to y, then all levels in $[x, x']$ are preferred to y.

On $A = [0, 100]$ the median of these peaks is at $y^* = 35$, and this is true on the following smaller intervals:

$B = [20, 75]$:   peaks $x^1 = 35$, $\tilde{x}^2 = \tilde{x}^6 = 20$, $x^3 = 22$, $\tilde{x}^4 = \tilde{x}^5 = 75$, $x^7 = 50$

$C = [20, 40]$:   peaks $x^1 = 35$, $\tilde{x}^2 = \tilde{x}^6 = 20$, $x^3 = 22$, $\tilde{x}^4 = \tilde{x}^5 = \tilde{x}^7 = 40$

and on any interval containing 35.

By contrast, if one wishes to apply a scoring method in a problem like example 4.6, the entire preference relation of every voter matters, and so do the precise end points of the set A.

The last but not least desirable feature of the Condorcet method is *strategy-proofness:* a voter has no incentive to lie strategically when reporting the peak of his preferences. Even when a group of voters attempt to jointly misreport their peaks, they cannot find a move from which they all benefit.

We check this claim in example 4.6, where y^* is the median of the distribution of individual peaks x^i. In the argument below, it does not matter whether the set of agents is large (infinite, as in example 4.6) or small, finite, as in the numerical example three paragraphs above.

Denote by N_- the set of agents whose peak is (strictly) to the left of y^* on A ($x^i < y^*$), by N_+ the set of those whose peak is to its right ($y^* < x^i$), and by N_0 those with $x^i = y^*$. Suppose that the coalition T of voters agree to alter their reported peaks, from the true peak x^i to a fake $\tilde{x}^i$, while the rest of the agents report their peak truthfully as before. Denote by z^* the new median of the reported peaks: we show that either $z^* = y^*$ or at least one agent in T strictly prefers y^* to z^*. In the former case, the joint misreport is inconsequential; in the latter, it is not plausible because participation has to be voluntary.

The proof is by contradiction. Suppose that $z^* \neq y^*$ and that no i in T strictly prefers y^* to z^*. Say that z^* is to the right of y^* in A ($y^* < z^*$). Because preferences are single peaked, everyone in N_- and in N_0 strictly prefers y^* to z^*; therefore T is contained in N_+. By definition of the median, $N_- \cup N_0$ forms a strict majority, and we just proved that they all still report their true peak; therefore a majority prefers y^* to z^*, and z^* cannot be chosen when T misreports, contradiction. A symmetrical argument applies when z^* is to the left of y^*.

Strategy-proofness is the ultimate test of incentive-compatibility in mechanism design. In a strategy-proof allocation or voting mechanism, no participant has any incentive to report his own characteristics (preferences, endowment) strategically: the simple truth is always my best move, whether I have no information about other agents' messages, or full information, or anything in between. Two very important examples of strategy-proof mechanisms are majority voting over single-peaked preferences, and the competitive equilibrium when each market participant is negligible with respect to the total endowment of the economy (sections 6.3 and 7.1).

Note that all scoring rules fail to be strategy-proof, even when individual preferences are single peaked. An example with three outcomes a, b, c and nine voters illustrate the point. We have five voters with preferences $a \succ b \succ c$, and four voters with $b \succ a \succ c$; these preferences are single peaked for the ordering $a < b < c$. The Borda winner is a, but if the four "losing" voters report $b \succ c \succ a$, the winner is b and the misreport is thus profitable.

Majority voting à la Condorcet is thus a compelling voting method when the outcomes are arranged along a line and individual preferences are single-peaked. The assumption that the outcome set is a one-dimensional interval can be weakened to a tree pattern, but not to a one-dimensional "loop"; see exercises 4.8 and 4.9.

Real life voting rules, however, do not impose any restriction on the shape of individual preferences, and in this case incentive-compatibility becomes a thorny issue. A disappointing impossibility result, discovered in the early 1970s, eliminates any hope of a simple answer.

Any voting method defined for *all* rational preferences over a set A of three or more outcomes must *fail* the strategyproofness property: at some preference profile, some agent will be able to "rig" the election to his or her advantage (i.e., bring about the election of a better outcome) by reporting untruthfully his or her preferences. This important fact, known as the Gibbard-Satterthwaite theorem, is technically equivalent to Arrow's theorem discussed in section 4.6. It is formally stated in chapter 8.

4.5 Intermediate Preferences

We turn to the second configuration of preferences guaranteeing that the majority relation is transitive, hence a Condorcet winner exists. The property of *intermediate preferences* relies on an ordering of the agents, instead of an ordering of the outcomes in the case of single-peaked preferences. In example 4.8 below, the agents choose a taxation method and differ only by their pre-tax income (they are selfish, only interested in maximizing aftertax income): they are naturally ordered along the income scale.

We say that the profile has the intermediate preferences property if whenever two agents i, j agree to prefer outcome a to b, so do all agents "between" i and j. Say that the 100 agents are ordered as $N = \{1, 2, \ldots, 100\}$. Intermediate preferences imply that the set $N(a, b)$ of agents preferring a over b is an interval $[i_1, i_2]$, namely $N(a, b)$ consists of all agents i such that $i_1 \leq i \leq i_2$. The same observation applies to the set $N(b, a)$ of agents preferring b to a. Barring indifferences for simplicity, we see that $N(a, b)$ and $N(b, a)$ partition $[1, 100]$ in two disjoint intervals: thus $N(a, b)$ must be an interval of the type $[1, i^*]$ or $[j^*, 100]$.

We check that the majority relation is transitive. Pick three outcomes a, b, c such that $N(a, b)$ and $N(b, c)$ each contain 51 agents or more, so that the majority relation prefers a to b and b to c. If $N(a, b) = [1, i^*]$ and $N(b, c) = [1, j^*]$, with $i^*, j^* \geq 51$, then all agents in

[1, 51] prefer a to b and b to c, hence a to c, and the majority relation prefers a to c as claimed. A symmetrical argument applies if $N(a, b) = [i^*, 100]$ and $N(b, c) = [j^*, 100]$, with $i^*, j^* \leq 50$. Suppose next that $N(a, b) = [1, i^*]$ and $N(b, c) = [j^*, 100]$, with $i^* \geq 51$ and $j^* \leq 50$. Then agents 50 and 51 both belong to $N(a, b)$ and $N(b, c)$, hence to $N(a, c)$ as well. If $N(a, c)$ takes the form $[1, i]$, this implies $i \geq 51$ and if $N(a, c) = [j, 100]$, this implies $j \leq 50$: in both cases $N(a, c)$ is a strict majority and the claim is proved.

Example 4.7 Voting over Three Surplus-Sharing Methods   We consider first the three surplus-sharing methods in section 2.2, namely the proportional (PRO), equal surplus (ES), and uniform gains (UG) methods.

Given a particular profile of claims and amount of resources t to be divided, our agents vote to choose which method will be implemented. Agents are ranked by the size of their initial claims/investments. They compare the three methods exclusively by the size of their own share of total surplus, and the larger the better. Here is an example with 11 voters, total resources $t = 745$, and initial claims ranging from 10 to 120 and totalling 580. We compute the shares allocated by our three methods:

Agent	1	2	3	4	5	6	7	8	9	10	11
Claim	10	10	20	25	40	40	60	70	85	100	120
PRO	12.8	12.8	25.7	32.11	51.4	51.4	77.1	89.9	109.2	128.4	154.1
ES	25	25	35	40	55	55	75	85	100	115	135
UG	51.7	51.7	51.7	51.7	51.7	51.7	60	70	85	100	120

The four agents with the smallest claims rank the uniform method above equal surplus and the latter above proportional. The five agents with the largest claims have the exactly opposite preferences.[6] For the two middle agents with claim 40, the best method is equal surplus. Thus all preferences are single peaked with respect to the ordering {uniform, equal surplus, proportional} of the three outcomes. The median peak is 40 and "equal surplus" is the Condorcet winner at this profile.

Next we check the intermediate preferences property. It suffices to check that the sets $N(a, b)$ are intervals of the form $[1, i]$ or $[j, 11]$ for all a, b:

$$N(\text{UG}, \text{PRO}) = N(\text{ES}, \text{PRO}) = [1, 6]; \quad N(\text{ES}, \text{UG}) = [5, 11]$$

Assume that the commodity being distributed is a "bad," and that individual claims represent a liability. Now an agent prefers method m to another method m' if and only if his share under m is smaller than under m'. Observe that the new preferences are not single peaked

---

6. Recall from exercise 2.5 that the smallest claim and largest claim agents have these preferences for *all* surplus-sharing problems.

anymore, because each method is the worst outcome for some agents: PRO for agents [7, 11], ES for 5, 6, and UG for [1, 4]. On the other hand, the intermediate preferences property is preserved because the intervals $N(a, b)$ and $N(b, a)$ are simply exchanged:

$$N'(\text{UG}, \text{PRO}) = N'(\text{ES}, \text{PRO}) = [7, 11]; \quad N'(\text{ES}, \text{UG}) = [1, 4]$$

The proportional solution is the Condorcet winner; indeed, it is the best method for the six agents $1, 2, \ldots, 6$.

Exercise 4.13 shows that for all surplus-sharing problems of any size, the preferences over the three methods PRO, ES and UG have the intermediate preference property. Our next example shows that the same holds true when agents choose a rationing method within the one-parameter family uncovered in section 2.4.

Example 4.8 Voting over Tax Schedules The agents choose one of the equal sacrifice methods described at the end of section 2.4, namely they choose a common utility function u to measure sacrifice, and this function takes one of the following forms:

$$u_p(z) = -\frac{1}{z^p} \quad \text{for some positive parameter } p$$

$$u_0(z) = v_0(z) = \log z \tag{6}$$

$$v_q(z) = z^q \quad \text{for some positive parameter } q$$

Once their vote has elected one such utility function, taxes are computed by solving system (10) in chapter 2. Recall that the function $u_0 = v_0$ corresponds to the proportional method (flat tax), the function v_1 to uniform losses (head tax), and u_∞ to uniform gains (full redistribution).

Remarkably, the intermediate preferences property holds true for any number of taxpayers and any profile of taxable incomes, so that majority voting always delivers a Condorcet winner. Before explaining this result, we note that the pattern of preferences over this family of tax schedules is not in general single peaked for any ordering of the family.

Consider the profile of taxable incomes $x_1 = 20$, $x_2 = 80$, $x_3 = 100$, and total aftertax income $t = 120$ (i.e., total tax levied is 80). The three basic methods give the following aftertax incomes:

Agent	1	2	3
PRO	12	48	60
UG	20	50	50
UL	0	50	70

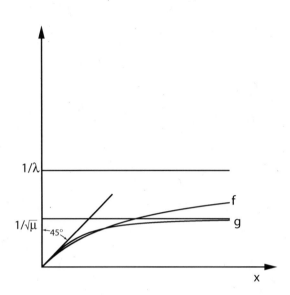

Figure 4.2a
Single crossing property in example 4.8

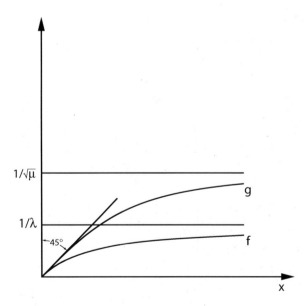

Figure 4.2b
Single crossing property in example 4.8

so that PRO is the worst method for agent 2, UG is the worst for agent 3, and UL is the worst for agent 1, which rules out single-peakedness for any ordering of the three methods.

We check now the intermediate preference property for the two methods u_1 and u_2.[7] Recall that the u_p methods are computed by solving the simpler system (9) in chapter 2. Fix the profile of taxable incomes x_i, the total aftertax income t, and denote by y_i, z_i the aftertax incomes under u_1 and u_2 respectively. System (9) tells us that there are two positive numbers λ, μ such that

$$\frac{1}{y_i} - \frac{1}{x_i} = \lambda \quad \text{and} \quad \frac{1}{z_i^2} - \frac{1}{x_i^2} = \mu \quad \text{for all } i$$

$$\Leftrightarrow y_i = \frac{x_i}{1 + \lambda x_i} \quad \text{and} \quad z_i = \frac{x_i}{\left(1 + \mu x_i^2\right)^{1/2}} \quad \text{for all } i$$

Compare the two concave functions $f(x) = x/(1 + \lambda x)$ and $\delta(x) = x/(1 + \mu x^2)^{1/2}$ for $x \geq 0$: they coincide at $x = 0$, where they both have a slope of 1, then they cross once at $x = 2\lambda/(\mu - \lambda^2)$ if $\mu > \lambda^2$, or not at all if $\mu \leq \lambda^2$. Figure 4.2 illustrate these two cases.

Therefore for any λ and μ, the set of agents i for whom $f(x_i) > g(x_i)$ is made either of all agents whose taxable income is below a certain level, or of all those with income above some level. This is exactly the intermediate preferences property when we order the agents according to their taxable incomes.

4.6   Preference Aggregation and Arrow's Theorem

As indicated in section 4.1, a social choice problem is made of three ingredients. The set A contains all the outcomes (states of the world) among which the set N of concerned agents—the "society"—must choose one. The choice of an outcome a in A affects the ordinal welfare of each concerned agent i: this is captured by a preference relation R_i on A, namely a complete and transitive binary relation.

The differences between individual preferences are resolved by the *aggregation* method F, associating to each profile of preferences $\tilde{R} = (R_i, i \in N)$, a collective—or social—preference relation $R^* = F(\tilde{R})$, interpreted as the ordinal collective welfare. The aggregation method plays exactly the same role, in the ordinal context, as the collective utility function in the cardinal context of the previous chapter.

---

7. The general argument is the subject of exercise 4.16.

Collective welfare is identified with a preference relation R^*, guiding the collective choice over any subset B of feasible outcomes: welfare is identical to choice. This construction is anthropomorphic, in the sense that the collective body is treated exactly like an individual agent. The mechanical computation of the collective relation R^* from the profile $\tilde{R}$ is social engineering at its best, or its worst, namely a controversial normative construction. It suggests one way of thinking about democratic institutions, but competing models offer alternative answers to this central question of political philosophy.

Recall from section 1.5 the basic tenet of the minimal state (libertarian) doctrine: collective decisions merely result from the interaction of free citizens exercising their political rights. This decision process may indeed yield a pattern of choices that can in no way be deciphered as rational, as maximizing some underlying collective preference. But this feature is by no means a subject of concern: collective choice is devoid of normative content, and any outcome of the free interplay of individual rights is as good as any other.

Social choice theory takes the diametrically opposed view that the process to reach a democratic compromise should rest on sound axiomatic foundations and allow positive predictions. For instance, cycles of the majority relation are deemed undesirable because they lead to the chronic formation of unstable coalitions and arbitrariness of the final decision which, ultimately, threatens the political legitimacy of the institutions for collective decision. The model of preference aggregation is the most general—the most ambitious—project of mechanism design in the microeconomic tradition. Its limited success, underlined by Arrow's impossibility theorem, can just as easily be viewed as a vindication of the minimal state doctrine—the search for rationality of collective choice is hopeless—or as the first step in a larger project of social engineering poised to discover specific allocation problems for which rational collective choice is within our reach.

The two voting methods proposed by Condorcet and Borda suggest two simple aggregation methods. Condorcet's argument is that for a given profile $\tilde{R}$ the majority relation is the correct expression of the general will (*volonté générale*). Formally this relation $R^m = F(\tilde{R})$ is defined as follows, for any pair of outcomes x, y:

$$x R^m y \Leftrightarrow |\{i \in N \mid x P_i y\}| \geq |\{i \in N \mid y P_i x\}| \tag{7}$$

namely the supporters of x against y are not outnumbered by their opponents.

We saw in the previous section that for some preference profiles $\tilde{R}$, the relation R^m is cyclic, hence violates the transitivity requirement for rational choice. In many collective decision problems, we can exclude a priori no preference relation on A. Voting over candidates to a political office is an obvious example, because of freedom of opinions. In this case the majority relation is not a valid aggregation method. On the other hand, the Borda scoring method provides an aggregation method for all preference profiles on any finite set A.

If p is the number of outcomes in A and R_i an arbitrary preference relation on A, we define the Borda scores $s(a, R_i)$ awarded by R_i. If R_i expresses strict preferences between any two outcomes (agent i is never indifferent between a and b), we set, as in section 4.2,

$$s(a, R_i) = p - k \quad \text{for the outcome ranked} \quad k\text{th in } A$$

(hence the top outcome gets $p - 1$ points and the bottom one gets 0 point). When R_i is indifferent between say a, b and c, these outcomes split equally the total scores they would fetch if preferences were strict and a, b, c were adjacent. To illustrate this straightforward construction, consider $p = 8$ and the following preference R_i:

$$\{a, b\} P_i c P_i \{d, e, f\} P_i g P_i h$$

where the brackets denote an indifference class; for example, R_i is indifferent toward d, e, and f. Outcomes a and b split the total score $7 + 6$, so they get 6.5 each; c gets 5; d, e, and f each get 3; g gets 1, and h gets 0.

The Borda aggregation method yields $R^b = F(\tilde{R})$ as follows for any pair of outcomes x, y:

$$x R^b y \Leftrightarrow \sum_{i \in N} s(x, R_i) \geq \sum_{i \in N} s(y, R_i) \tag{8}$$

The transitivity of the relation R^b follows at once from that of the inequality relation between scores.

Consider the profile (4) in example 4.3. We noted there that b, the Borda winner, owes its success over a to the relative position of c vis-à-vis b and a. By contrast, the majority relation (transitive in this example) puts a above b: if the issue is to choose between a and b, it compares the numbers of supporters of a versus b and b versus a, without paying any attention to c at all.

The property *independence of irrelevant alternatives* (IIA) requires that the collective preference R^* between any two outcomes x and y only depend upon individual preferences between any two outcomes. That is, if $\tilde{R}$ and $\tilde{R}'$ are two profiles of preferences that produce exactly the same sets of supporters of x versus y and y versus x:

$$\text{for all } i: \quad x P_i y \Leftrightarrow x P_i' y, \quad y P_i x \Leftrightarrow y P_i' x, \quad x I_i y \Leftrightarrow x I_i' y$$

then the collective preferences $R = F(\tilde{R})$ and $R' = F(\tilde{R}')$ compare x and y in precisely the same way:

$$x P y \Leftrightarrow x P' y, \quad y P x \Leftrightarrow y P' x, \quad x I y \Leftrightarrow x I' y$$

The majority aggregation method (7) meets the IIA property but does not always produce a rational collective preference. When it cycles, say $a P^m b$, $b P^m c$, and $c P^m a$, it is helpless to guide the choice among a, b, and c. Any method to break the cycle, for instance, at its weakest link (see example 4.4 and the discussion preceding it), leads to a violation of IIA: if we declare a the winner among a, b, c because the statement $cP^m a$ is the "weakest" (has the smallest number of supporters), then "a wins over b" depends on the individual preferences over a, b, and c, not just over a and b. Similarly, if the collective preference declares a, b, and c to be indifferent, then the mere knowledge of the supporters of a versus b and b versus a is not enough to determine the collective preference between a and b: it also matters whether a, b are part of some cycle of the majority relation (involving other outcomes) or not.

The Borda aggregation method (8) produces a rational collective preference for any profile $\tilde{R}$ but fails the IIA property. This means that the choice of the set A of outcomes/candidates on the ballot is of critical importance to the eventual outcome. Adding to $A = \{a, b\}$ a candidate c who stands no chance to win against either a or b (and will be ranked last by the collective preference) may turn around the choice between a and b, as in examples 4.2 and 4.3. Control of the "agenda," namely the set A of eligible candidates, is often tantamount to control of the election and of the collective preference. Thus the definition of A is controversial and may be the subject of a preliminary round of collective decision-making, the agenda of which is itself a matter of dispute, and so on ad infinitum.

Arrow's impossibility theorem explores the sharp trade-offs between the IAA property and the rationality of collective preferences, in the formal context of aggregation functions. In a nutshell, the theorem says that *any* aggregation function producing a rational collective preference and meeting IIA must be highly undesirable on account of its lack of efficiency or of fairness. A formal statement is given in chapter 8.

For instance, suppose that we want an efficient aggregation method, namely we insist that the collective preference R^* respects the unanimous preferences of the citizens. For any two outcomes x, y,

$$\{x P_i y \text{ for all } i \in N\} \Rightarrow x P^* y$$

Then the only rational aggregation methods meeting IIA are the *dictatorial* methods, where the collective preference relation R^* coincides with R_i^*, the preference relation of the dictator i^*. The point is that the dictator's preferences prevail irrespective of those of the rest of the agents, a state of affairs that we may call maximally unfair.

Suppose next that we restrict our attention to aggregation functions that are fair in the sense that all voters have equal influence a priori on the collective preference.[8] Some unpalatable rational aggregation methods meeting IIA are the "imposed" methods, always selecting the same collective preference R_o, irrespective of the preferences of our citizens. Such a method is fair, but it is pathetically inefficient: even when the citizens share a common

---

8. Formally, this means that the function F is symmetrical in its n variables R_i.

preference $R_i = R^o$ for all i, the collective preference ignores this fact entirely. It turns out that the only fair rational aggregation methods meeting IIA are imposed, except for at most two fixed outcomes a, b that can be compared, for instance, by the majority relation.

The proof of Arrow's theorem is beyond the scope of this book. The two "ways out" of the impossibility have been discussed earlier in this chapter. One way is to restrict the domain of admissible preference profiles, as with the single peaked (section 4.3) or intermediate (section 4.4) preferences. Another way is to weaken the rationality properties of the collective preference, by only requiring that its strict preferences do not cycle. This is the idea of qualified majorities briefly discussed at the end of section 4.3. The approach leads to indecisive collective preferences, however, with too many different outcomes declared winners.

4.7   Introduction to the Literature

The theory of rational choice and ordinal preferences, discussed in section 4.1, is the very foundation of microeconomic analysis. Textbook presentations are easy to find; a particularly good one is in Mas-Colell, Whinston, and Green (1995, ch. 1).

The original discussion of the optimal design of voting rules by Condorcet (dating back to 1785), is still extremely useful and accessible in the excellent English translation of McLean and Urken (1995). Our examples 4.1 to 4.3 are adapted from Condorcet's original examples.

The reunion paradox (example 4.4) is the basis of an important result due to Smith (1973) and Young (1974): the scoring methods are the only voting methods avoiding the reunion paradox and treating symmetrically both voters and candidates. Two excellent surveys on voting rules are Brams (1994) and Brams and Fishburn (2002); see also Ordershook (1986).

The central result underlying section 4.4 is due to Black (1948) and is formally described in exercise 4.6: the majority relation is a rational preference when individual preferences are single-peaked. The related property of strategyproofness has been studied extensively: Moulin (1980) uncovers the full family of strategy-proof voting rules on the single-peaked domain, a result later extended to multidimensional versions of this domain; see Sprumont (1995) and Barbera (2001) for a survey of this literature.

The seminal impossibility result on strategy-proof voting with unrestricted preferences is due to Gibbard (1973) and Satterthwaite (1975): it is briefly discussed at the end of section 4.4. Textbook presentations can be found in Moulin (1988, ch. 10) and Mas-Colell, Whinston, and Green (1995).

Grandmont (1978) introduced the notion of intermediate preferences, section 4.5, and Roberts (1977) noticed that preferences over tax schedules can be expected to fit this pattern.

Arrow's 1951 book, with the original proof of his theorem, is the unambiguous starting point of mathematical welfare economics, and in this sense its influence pervades the entire book. The formal statement and proof of the theorem is available in many books, among them Sen (1970), Kelly (1978), Moulin (1988), and Mas-Colell, Whinston, and Green (1995).

Peremans and Storcken (1996) introduce the concept of single-dipped preferences discussed in exercise 4.7.

Exercises to Chapter 4

Exercise 4.1 Two More Examples of Condorcet

a. In the following profile with 60 voters shows that the majority relation and the Borda scores yield the same ranking of the three outcomes. Compare it with the ranking of plurality voting.

Number of voters:	18	5	16	3	13	5
	a	*a*	*b*	*b*	*c*	*c*
	c	*b*	*c*	*a*	*b*	*a*
	b	*c*	*a*	*c*	*a*	*b*

b. In the next profile the majority relation has a cycle. What outcome wins if we use Condorcet's idea to break the cycle at its weakest link? What outcome (outcomes) is (are) elected by *some* scoring method?

Number of voters:	23	2	17	10	8
	a	*b*	*b*	*c*	*c*
	b	*a*	*c*	*a*	*b*
	c	*c*	*a*	*b*	*a*

Exercise 4.2 An Example due to Joe Malkovitch

We have 55 voters and five outcomes. The profile of preferences is as follows:

Number of voters:	18	12	10	9	4	2
	a	*b*	*c*	*d*	*e*	*e*
	e	*e*	*b*	*c*	*b*	*c*
	d	*d*	*e*	*e*	*d*	*d*
	c	*c*	*d*	*b*	*c*	*b*
	b	*a*	*a*	*a*	*a*	*a*

Check that the majority relation is transitive and orders the candidates exactly like the Borda scores. Compare with plurality voting.

Exercise 4.3 More on Profile (5)

Consider the preference profile (5) where the majority relation has a cycle: $n_i < n/2$ for $i = 1, 2, 3$. Check that the Borda winner corresponds to the index i maximizing $n_i - n_{i+1}$, where we set $n_{3+1} = n_1$. Check that the Condorcet solution (break the cycle at its weakest link) corresponds to i maximizing n_i.

Give an example where these two solutions are unique and different.

Exercise 4.4

Consider the profile with seven voters and four candidates:

Number of voters:	3	2	2
	c	b	a
	b	a	d
	a	d	c
	d	c	b

a. Compute the majority relation and show that it has several cycles. By "breaking" the two weakest majority preferences, check that the ordering $cPbPaPd$ obtains.

b. Compute the Borda ranking of our four candidates. Find an outcome x such that, upon removing x, the ranking of the other three candidates is completely reversed! The violation of which axiom does this illustrate?

Exercise 4.5 Location of a Noxious Facility (Example 3.5)

The public facility that must be located somewhere in $[0, 1]$ is undesirable (prison, waste disposal) and the distance from agent i's home x^i to the site y of the facility measures her utility $u_i(y) = |x^i - y|$. See example 3.5.

a. Show that the endpoint (0 or 1) farthest away from the median y^* of the distribution F of agents (see example 4.6) is the Condorcet winner. Recall from example 3.5 that the utilitarian optimum is the endpoint farthest away from the mean of F (the barycenter of all homes).

b. Show that the majority relation coincides with the preferences of the median agent living at y^*. Exercise 4.7 generalizes this property.

*Exercise 4.6 Majority Relation under Single-Peaked Preferences

a. In example 4.6, show that the majority relation strictly prefers y to y' if and only if $|y - y^*| < |y' - y^*|$.

b. In the rest of the exercise, we only assume that individual preferences are single-peaked on $[0, 1]$, as in the discussion following example 4.6. We denote by y^* the Condorcet winner.

Show that if $y < y' \leq y^*$, of $y^* \leq y' < y$, the majority relation R^m strictly prefers y' over y.

c. Check now that the majority relation is transitive *across its peak* y^*. Pick a, b, c such that $a < y^* < b < c$, and assume $a P^m b$. We know from question b that $b P^m c$. Show $a P^m c$. (*Hint:* An agent preferring a to b must have its peak to the left of b). Show similarly $a R^m b \Rightarrow a R^m c$.

Next pick a, b, c such that $b < a < y^* < c$, and assume $b P^m c$. Show $a P^m c$. (*Hint:* An agent preferring b to c must prefer a to c.) Conclude that the majority relation is single peaked, as claimed in section 4.4.

*Exercise 4.7 Majority Relation under Single-Dipped Preferences

We say that the preference relation R_i on $[0, 1]$ is *single dipped* if there is an outcome x^i, the *dip,* such that R^i decreases on $[0, x^i]$ and increases on $[x^i, 1]$. In other words, x^i is the worst outcome for R_i and for all x, $x \neq x^i$, R_i prefers x to any outcome between x and x^i.

We fix a profile of single-dipped preferences on $[0, 1]$, and we denote by y^* the median dip.

a. Show that the majority relation R^m is decreasing on $[0, y^*]$ and increasing on $[y^*, 1]$:

$$\{y < y' \leq y^* \text{ or } y^* \leq y' < y\} \Rightarrow y P^m y'$$

b. Show that R^m is transitive across its dip y^* (the argument is similar to that in question c of exercise 4.6.).

Exercise 4.8 Location of a Facility on a Network with a Loop

When the set of feasible locations of the facility is a one-dimensional network with a loop, the Condorcet winner often does not exist.

a. Consider the road network of example 3.8, depicted as figure 3.6. There are five agents living at A, B, C, D, and E respectively. If the "inner roads" to X are not feasible locations, it follows from example 4.6 that location C, the utilitarian optimum, is also the Condorcet winner. Assume now that the entire network on figure 3.6 is feasible to locate the facility.

Show that X, the utilitarian optimum is *not* a Condorcet winner, and neither is any other location.

b. Consider the road network of exercise 3.4, question a, depicted as figure 3.11. There are five agents living at A, B, C, D, and E respectively. Show similarly that no location of the facility is a Condorcet winner.

c. Consider the road network of exercise 3.4, question b, depicted as figure 3.12. There are nine agents, of whom two live at B, three at C, and four at D. Assume first that the direct road between C and B is closed. Show that A, the utilitarian optimum, is also the Condorcet winner.

Next show that when the road CB is open, the problem has no Condorcet winner.

*Exercise 4.9 Location of a Facility on a Star-Tree

The road network is a "star" as in exercise 3.6. Each outer location A_k is connected to the center O by a road of length d_k, and n_k agents live at A_k. See figure 3.13.

a. Assume that the facility is desirable, so an agent wants to minimize his travel cost to the facility. Show that the Condorcet winner coincides with the utilitarian optimum: it is the center O of the tree if none of the nodes A_k contains a strict majority of the total population; otherwise, it is this most populated location.

b. Now the facility is noxious and agents want it to be as far away as possible from where they live. Show that the Condorcet winner is A_{k^*}, the location farthest away from the center among those hosting a minority of the total population:

$$n_{k^*} < \frac{n}{2} \quad \text{and} \quad \left\{ \text{for all } k, \; n_k < \frac{n}{2} \Rightarrow d_{k^*} \geq d_k \right\}$$

(Note that the borderline case $n_1 = n_2 = n/2$ leads, as usual, to an "indecisive" majority relation.) Compare with the utilitarian optimum described in exercise 3.6.

Exercise 4.10 An Example with Intermediate Preferences

There are nine voters and three outcomes. Preferences are as follows:

Number of voters:	1	4	3	1
	b	a	b	a
	a	b	c	c
	c	c	a	b

a. Check that the Condorcet winner and Borda winners are different.

b. Show an ordering of the nine agents for which the profile has the intermediate preferences property.

Exercise 4.11 Voting over Surplus-Sharing and Taxation Methods

Using notations as in examples 4.7 and 4.8,

a. Give two examples of three person surplus-sharing problems with increasing claims $x_1 < x_2 < x_3$ and resources $t, t > x_1 + x_2 + x_3$, such that agent 2's shares are ordered respectively as follows:

$y_2(ES) > y_2(PRO) > y_2(UG)$

$y_2(ES) > y_2(UG) > y_2(PRO)$.

b. Give two examples of three-person taxation problems with increasing taxable incomes $x_1 < x_2 < x_3$ and total aftertax income $t, t < x_1 + x_2 + x_3$, such that agent 2's aftertax incomes are ordered respectively as follows:

$y_2(PRO) > y_2(UG) > y_2(UL)$

$y_2(PRO) > y_2(UL) > y_2(UG)$

Note that example 4.8 contains a three-person example where $y_2(PRO)$ is the smallest among these three shares.

Exercise 4.12 Voting over Taxation Methods

a. Consider the five voters profile of taxable incomes 10, 20, 50, 70, 80, and total aftertax income $t = 100$. Compute the aftertax distribution of incomes under the three basic methods PRO, UG, and UL and the majority relation.

b. Compute next the shares awarded by the Talmudic (T) and random priority (RP) methods defined in exercises 2.11 and 2.10 respectively. Check that the Talmudic method is the Condorcet winner and that RP is ranked third by the majority relation. Check that the Borda scores order the five methods in precisely the same way.

c. Consider the profile of taxable incomes 10, 15, 30, 40, 55, and aftertax income $t = 100$. Show that the Talmudic method is now the Condorcet loser as well as the Borda loser, with random priority ranked next to last in the majority and Borda relations.

*Exercise 4.13 Generalizing Example 4.7

We consider an arbitrary surplus-sharing problem with profile of claims x_i, $x_1 \leq x_2 \leq \cdots \leq x_n$ and resources $t, t \geq \sum_1^n x_i$.

a. Show that the profile of preferences over the three methods PRO, ES, and UG has the intermediate preferences property.

b. Show that the preferences of any agent over PRO, ES, UG are single-peaked when the three methods are so ordered.

Hint: By the inequalities proved in question a of exercise 2.5, it suffices to show that for any i, the inequalities $y_i(ES) < y_i(PRO)$, $y_i(ES) < y_i(UG)$, cannot both be true. Proceed by contradiction. The UG shares are $y_j(UG) = \max\{x_j, \lambda\}$; show that $\lambda \leq t/n$ and that agent i for whom both inequalities hold has $x_i \leq \lambda$.

Exercise 4.14 Voting over the Commons

In the model of the commons of chapter 6, three solutions are compared: CEEI (competitive equilibrium with equal incomes), VP (virtual price), and RP (random priority). The users of the commons are identified by their willingness to pay, providing a natural ordering of N. Using the formulas of section 6.6, show that the preferences of the users over the three methods have the intermediate preference property. Show that in general, there is no ordering of CEEI, VP, and RP in which these preferences are single peaked.

Exercise 4.15 Counting Preference Relations

a. Given an ordering of the choice set A with cardinality p, show that there are 2^{p-1} different preference relations that are single peaked in this ordering.

b. Given a preference profile with the intermediate preferences property (with respect to some ordering of N), show that there are at most $[p(p-1)/2] + 1$ different preference relations in this profile.

Exercise 4.16 Proving the Claim in Example 4.8

Consider an arbitrary profile x_i, $x_1 \leq x_2 \leq \cdots \leq x_n$, of taxable incomes and total aftertax income t, $t \leq \sum_1^n x_i$.

a. Show that the profile of preferences over the three methods PRO, UG, UL has the intermediate preferences property. *Hint:* Check successively the property for any two of the three methods, and for both orderings of the two methods in each case.

b. Show that the IP property is maintained if we add the Talmudic (T) and random priority (RP) methods defined in exercises 2.11 and 2.10.

c. The goal of this question is to prove the IP property when the choice set contains all equal sacrifice methods listed in formula (6). We prove a slightly more general result. Consider two increasing utility functions u, v and the associated equal sacrifice after tax incomes y_i, z_i.

For simplicity, we assume first that all y_i, z_i are positive—system (9) in chapter 2—so that there are two positive numbers λ, μ such that

$$u(x_i) - u(y_i) = \lambda, \quad v(x_i) - v(z_i) = \mu \qquad \text{for all } i$$
$$\Leftrightarrow y_i = u^{-1}(u(x_i) - \lambda), \quad z = v^{-1}(v(x_i) - \mu) \qquad \text{for all } i$$

The desired IP property amounts to the fact that the two increasing functions, $f(x) = u^{-1}(u(x) - \lambda)$ and $g(x) = v^{-1}(v(x) - \mu)$, have the *single-crossing* property over positive numbers x: the graphs of these two functions cross at most once.

We assume now that the function v is more concave than u, namely $v(x) = w(u(x))$, all $x \geq 0$, for some increasing and concave function w. Check that this implies the single-crossing property. Check that if v is more concave than u, the IP property over u, v holds even if some agents receive a zero share—system (10) instead of (9) in chapter 2. Check finally that for any two utility functions in the family (6), one of them is more concave than the other.

5 The Shapley Value

5.1 The Problem of the Commons and Two Examples

A commons is a technology used jointly by a given set of agents; the problem of the commons is to organize fairly and efficiently the exploitation of this technology. The microeconomic approach to distributive justice puts this problem at the top of its agenda: the Shapley value is an axiomatic solution to a simple model of the commons. Indeed, no systematic discussion of the commons problem was possible until the tools of (cooperative as well as noncooperative) game theory became available fifty years or so ago.

Joint ventures requiring coordinated action of partners with heterogeneous expertise are typical commons. The partners contribute their labor input and share the output (profit) generated by the enterprise. Examples include musical ensembles (example 2.4), law firms, and fishing or farming cooperatives.

The interesting question of distributive justice is to assess fairly the productive contributions from the various partners: recall the musical duo, example 2.4, where the two musicians are not equally famous. Similarly the fishermen may use various fishing techniques, with different impact on the future stock of fish; the partners in a law firm bring different kinds of expertise that are unequally scarce, and so on.

The sharing of joint costs falls squarely within the scope of the commons problem. In a cost-sharing model the agents demand certain services that are jointly produced by the technology (the commons), and they must share fairly the total cost of meeting these demands. A typical example (see example 5.6) is access to a network; each agent wants to be hooked to the central server but the connection cost is not uniform: some agents live near the server and need only a short cable, some agents are close to one another, another source of savings, and so on. This chapter and the next one are entirely devoted to cost-sharing problems like this one, and to the "dual" surplus-sharing problems where each agent contributes some productive input and the question is to share the resulting total output.

In terms of the general principles stated in section 2.1, the focus of this chapter is almost exclusively on the interpretation of reward: What is a fair assessment of individual responsibilities in the formation of total cost (or surplus)? Compensation is entirely absent from the discussion, and we always assume equal exogenous rights.[1] Fitness is not an issue in most of the chapter, where we assume inelastic demand of output or supply of input. That is to say, willingness to pay for the output or reservation values for providing the input play no role. The only exception is section 5.4, a prelude to the models of chapters 6 and 7. In the next chapter, by contrast, fitness is a paramount concern and the simultaneous pursuit of fitness and reward is the heart of the discussion.

---

1. Nevertheless, the axiomatic discussion of section 5.5 can be extended to accommodate asymmetric rights.

Example 5.1 Joint Venture: Example 2.4 Revisited   The formal model is identical to that of example 2.4, namely two agents must share a given amount of some divisible commodity, and the division takes only into account two individual characteristics. The interpretation is quite different: the goal is to share the cost of providing a certain service to our two agents, and the individual parameters are the stand-alone costs, namely the cost of providing service to one agent alone.

Teresa and David share an office space and need to connect their computer to the network. Teresa needs a small capacity link for which the company charges c_1, whereas David needs a larger one that costs c_2, $c_1 < c_2$. There is a single cable outlet in the office, and in order to connect both of them, the company must install an additional outlet at cost δ. Thus the total bill to equip both Teresa and David is $c_{12} = c_1 + c_2 + \delta$. We call c_i, $i = 1, 2$, the stand-alone costs of our two agents: if David is out of the picture, no extra outlet is needed and Teresa will pay c_1.

Formally we have a distribution problem as in section 2.2 where a bad (cost c_{12}) must be shared and total burden exceeds the sum of individual liabilities. Which one of our three basic solutions—proportional, equal benefits, and uniform gains—if any, should we use?

Suppose that the company is running a promotional campaign for the small capacity link that Teresa needs, so that her stand-alone cost is $c_1 = 0$. In this configuration the proportional solution is highly unappealing because it charges the entire cost $c_2 + \delta$ to David, when surely Teresa should bear a share of the mutual externality δ.

The uniform gains solution—which should be called uniform costs in the context of our example—is even worse in that it seeks to equalize cost shares irrespective of the difference in stand-alone costs. For instance, if $c_1 = 0$ as above, the solution charges $y_1 = \delta$ to Teresa and $y_2 = c_2$ to David as long as $\delta \leq c_2$; it charges $\frac{1}{2}(\delta + c_2)$ to both whenever $\delta \geq c_2$. The former is unpalatable because David contributes nothing to the cost δ of the mutual externality. The latter is too, because Teresa becomes responsible for half of David's stand-alone cost c_2.

The equal surplus solution is the only sensible way to share costs in this context, since c_i is clearly a separable cost. It simply splits equally the nonseparable cost δ, and charges $y_1 = c_1 + (\delta/2)$, $y_2 = c_2 + (\delta/2)$.

Now we change the story to one where the cost of connecting Teresa and David is smaller than the sum of their two stand-alone costs. This is called a deficit configuration in section 2.2, and a subadditive cost function in this chapter: $c_{12} < c_1 + c_2$. In the previous story the cost function is superadditive: $c_{12} > c_1 + c_2$; see section 5.3.

The company charges a fee δ_i to set up a link, and this fee increases with the capacity of the link. Here $\delta_1 < \delta_2$ as Teresa needs less capacity than David.

In addition the consumer must pay a flat fee δ for the technician's visit: this fee is the same no matter how many links the technician sets up in his visit. By joining their orders,

Teresa and David save one fixed fee. The stand-alone costs are $c_i = \delta_i + \delta$ for $i = 1, 2$, and the total cost is $c_{12} = \delta_1 + \delta_2 + \delta < c_1 + c_2$.

The uniform costs solution is as unappealing as above, for it ignores the difference between δ_1 and δ_2.[2] The proportional solution splits the cost-saving δ in proportion to the stand-alone costs $\delta_i + \delta$, which is an unpalatable compromise for exactly the same reasons as above. For instance, if δ_1 and δ are comparable, but δ_2 is much larger than both, Teresa gets essentially no rebate from her stand-alone costs.[3]

The uniform savings solution (i.e., the uniform losses solution of section 2.2) is the only sensible solution in the subadditive cost case. It splits the cost-savings δ equally between David and Teresa: $y_1 = \delta_1 + (\delta/2)$, $y_2 = \delta_2 + (\delta/2)$.

The discussion of example 5.1 suggests a general cost-sharing method, based on the computation of $n + 1$ numbers if the number of agents sharing the commons is n. Let c_i be agent i's stand-alone cost and c_N be the total cost of serving the whole population N. We compute individual cost shares by the equal surplus/uniform cost-saving methods of section 2.2. Thus, if the costs are superadditive, $c_N > \sum_j c_j$, each agent i pays her stand-alone cost c_i plus a surcharge equal to her fair share of the cost externality $c_N - \sum_j c_j$. If costs are subadditive, $c_N < \sum_j c_j$, everyone pays her stand-alone costs minus a common rebate, or pays nothing at all if this difference is negative:

$$c_N \geq \sum_j c_j \Rightarrow y_i = c_i + \frac{1}{n}\left(c_N - \sum_j c_j\right) \quad \text{for } i = 1, 2, \ldots, n$$

$$c_N \leq \sum_j c_j \Rightarrow y_i = (c_i - \mu)_+ \text{ where } \sum_j (c_j - \mu)_+ = c_N \quad \text{for } i = 1, \ldots, n \tag{1}$$

These cost shares are simple and intuitive, and in example 5.1 they deliver the correct solution. In the case of a two-person problem, the cost shares (1) take the simple form of an equal rebate for both users, provided that we make the reasonable assumption $c_i \leq c_{12}$ for $i = 1, 2$; namely serving both agents cannot be cheaper than serving only one. In the subadditive case, this assumption implies that the common rebate μ is below c_i for $i = 1, 2$. Therefore, in both cases—superadditive and subadditive—the cost shares are simply

$$y_1 = \tfrac{1}{2}(c_{12} + c_1 - c_2), \quad y_2 = \tfrac{1}{2}(c_{12} + c_2 - c_1) \tag{2}$$

2. This is provided that $\delta \geq \delta_2 - \delta_1$. When $\delta \leq \delta_2 - \delta_1$, the solution is even worse: it charges her stand-alone cost $\delta_1 + \delta$ to Teresa, and David gets the full saving of one fix fee—he pays δ_2.

3. Splitting the cost saving δ in proportion to the capacity costs δ_i would give essentially all the rebate to Teresa under the same premises, which is an equally unjustified outcome.

Figure 5.1
Mail distribution: Example 5.2

Our next example shows that things are not as simple when the cost must be shared among three or more users of the commons; in fact the cost shares (1) may be altogether unacceptable.

Example 5.2 Mail Distribution   Five villages share the cost of a daily mail distribution. The mail is dropped daily by an outside carrier in a certain location Ω. The villagers jointly hire a local distributor who picks the mail from Ω, delivers it to the five villages, where he picks the outgoing mail, and goes back to Ω. We neglect all sorting costs (the mail is dropped at Ω in five presorted packages). The local distributor's charge is proportional to the distance he must travel daily, and the price is $1 per kilometer.

The five villages are located along the single road starting at Ω and passing successively through A, B, D, E, and F. Distances, in kilometers, are indicated on figure 5.1. Thus the daily tour from Ω to F and back costs $110. The problem is to divide it fairly among our five customers.

The stand-alone costs—costs of delivering mail to agent i only—are as follows:

$$c_A = 20, \quad c_B = 30, \quad c_D = 90, \quad c_E = 100, \quad c_F = 110$$

Therefore the formula (1) gives $\mu = 63.\dot{3}$ and the following cost shares:

$$x_A = x_B = 0, \quad x_D = 26.7, \quad x_E = 36.7, \quad x_F = 46.7$$

This is obviously too soft on agents A and B who should bear a positive share of total cost!

We note that a division of the total cost 110 in proportion to the stand-alone costs above is plausible in this numerical example. However, in section 5.3 we show that the proportional solution may give unreasonable cost shares in a similar example with different distances; see example 5.4.

A simple separation argument leads to a genuine division of costs, which the Shapley value also recommends (as shown in the next section). The idea is to consider each interval such as BD separately and to split the corresponding fraction of total cost only among those agents who are responsible for it. For instance, the cost of covering the interval $[E, F]$ should be imputed to F alone. By the same token, the cost of $[D, E]$ should be split equally between E and F for this cost must be covered as soon as any of them receives mail, that of $[B, D]$ should be split three ways among D, E, and F, and so on. Hence we have the following cost shares:

$$x_A = \tfrac{1}{5}20 = 4, \quad x_B = x_A + \tfrac{1}{4}10 = 6.5, \quad x_D = x_B + \tfrac{1}{3}60 = 26.5$$

$$x_E = x_D + \tfrac{1}{2}10 = 31.5, \quad x_F = x_E + 10 = 41.5$$

The cost structure of example 5.2 appears in many contexts. The line may represent an irrigation ditch from the source O (river) to its end point E, and we must share the maintenance cost of the canal (taken to be proportional to its length) among the different farms, A, B, ... located along the canal.

More generally, consider the cost of building the capacity of a common facility. The length of a runway increases in the size of the planes that use it, the depth of a harbor increases in the size of ships, or the cost of a network increases with the bandwidth of a link. In each case agent i requires a capacity that costs c_i to build, and the stand-alone cost of building the capacity required by the set of agents S is

$$C(S) = \max_{i \in S} c_i \tag{3}$$

For the technology (3) the separation argument of example 5.2 is easily adapted. Order the agents by increasing capacities, say $c_1 \le c_2 \le \cdots \le c_n$. Note that the cost of serving S never exceeds c_{n-1} if S does not contain agent N, and always surpasses c_{n-1} by $c_n - c_{n-1}$ if S does contain this agent. Therefore assign the cost of increasing capacity from the level required by agent $n - 1$ to that required by agent n, to agent n only. Split similarly the cost $c_{n-1} - c_{n-2}$ of increasing capacity from level $n - 2$ to level $n - 1$, equally among agents $(n - 1)$ and n, and so on. The final cost shares are as follows:

$$x_1 = \frac{1}{n}c_1, \quad x_2 = x_1 + \frac{1}{n-1}(c_2 - c_1), \quad x_3 = x_2 + \frac{1}{n-2}(c_3 - c_2)$$

$$x_n = c_n - \left(\frac{1}{2}c_{n-1} + \frac{1}{6}c_{n-2} + \cdots + \frac{1}{n(n-1)}c_1 \right) \tag{4}$$

5.2   The Shapley Value: Definition

The basic model of the commons that is the subject of the current chapter was introduced more than fifty years ago in von Neumann and Morgenstern's *Theory of Games,* and is known in the jargon of that theory as the model of cooperative games with transferable utility. In the cost-sharing interpretation, the model specifies the set $N = \{1, 2, \ldots, n\}$ of agents who each want one unit of "service," and for each nonempty subset S of N (also called the coalition S of agents) a stand-alone cost $C(S)$ of serving the (agents in) coalition S.

For instance, in example 5.2, "service" is mail delivery and $C(S)$ is the cost of the smallest tour passing all i in S (ignoring the agents in $N \backslash S$ altogether). Thus the cost function C itself is the commons, the technology shared by all agents. The problem is to divide fairly the cost $C(N)$ of serving everyone when fairness is meant to reward the responsibility of the various agents in the total cost. Unlike formula (1), the Shapley value takes into account the stand-alone costs of all coalitions S containing more than one but fewer than n agents.

In the surplus-sharing interpretation, the number $C(S)$, often denoted $v(S)$, represents the efficient revenue (measured in money, or in some other numéraire) that the agents in S can generate by some unspecified manner of cooperation. The problem is to divide total revenue $v(N)$ by taking fairly into account the revenues $v(S)$ that various coalitions generate when standing alone. Two fundamental examples are the commons model of chapter 6, where $v(S)$ takes into account both the benefits and costs of production when the agents in S use the commons efficiently, and the exchange economy in chapter 7 where the agents are buyers or sellers and $v(S)$ is the total trading surplus of coalition S, meaning the net total benefit when the buyers and sellers in S trade optimally their own resources.

All examples in sections 5.1, 5.2, and 5.3 are cast in the cost-sharing framework. The examples in section 5.4 illustrate the (more subtle and more general) surplus-sharing model, as a prelude to its systematic application in chapters 6 and 7.

The Shapley value translates the Reward principle into an explicit division of $C(N)$ based on the $2^n - 1$ numbers $C(S)$, for all nonempty coalitions S. Formally this resembles the deficit or excess sharing problem of sections 2.2 through 2.4, where the division of t units of resources is based on the n numbers x_i (the claims, or demands). Yet the jump in mathematical complexity from $n + 1$ to $2^n - 1$ numbers is considerable, and the simple principles of proportionality, equal gains or losses cannot be generalized.

Example 5.3 Two Simple Three-Person Problems   Each of three agents Ann, Bob, and Dave want a "service," and we have determined the following seven stand-alone costs:

$$C(A, B, D) = 120, \quad C(i) = 60 \qquad \text{for } i = A, B, D \tag{5}$$

$$C(AB) = C(AD) = 120, \quad C(BD) = 60 \tag{6}$$

Notice that we write $C(i)$ for the stand-alone cost of agent i, whereas the notation c_i was used in examples 5.1 and 5.2. The new notation is heavier but more transparent once all stand-alone costs play a role. The cost-saving $3C(i) - C(ABD) = 60$ should not be divided evenly because the cost of serving each of the three pairs ij reveals more externalities between Bob and Dave than between Ann and either Bob or Dave.

Imagine that service consists of a cable connection to the source O. Ann lives 60 kilometers to the west of O, while Bob and Dave live in the same location, 60 kilometers to the east of O. Thus Bob and Dave can share the same cable. If the cost of cable is $1 per kilometer, the pattern of stand-alone costs is precisely (5). The separation argument in example 5.2 makes clear that Ann should pay her full stand-alone cost, whereas Bob and Dave split the cost-saving (they each pay 30).

The point of the Shapley value is that we can deduce exactly the same cost shares from the seven numbers, (5) and (6), without invoking a specific representation of the problem, geographic or otherwise. The argument is that the *marginal cost* of serving Ann is 60, no matter who among Bob and Dave is or is not served:

$$C(A) = C(AB) - C(B) = C(AD) - C(D) = C(ABD) - C(BD) = 60$$

From these equalities the Shapley value assigns the cost share 60 to Ann. Since they play symmetric roles in (5) and (6), Bob and Dave split equally the remaining cost of 60.

Now we introduce what seems like a small modification of the stand-alone costs of a two-person coalitions (other costs being unchanged):

$$C(AB) = 120, \quad C(AD) = C(BD) = 60 \qquad\qquad\qquad (7)$$

The coalitions $\{A, D\}$ and $\{B, D\}$ achieve a cost-saving of $60, whereas the coalition $\{A, B\}$ gets no saving whatsoever. Therefore Dave bears a larger share of responsibility for the overall saving $60. Should all this saving be passed to him, who would then pay nothing at all while Ann and Bob pay $60 each? That would be going too far, since Dave cannot get service for free when he stands alone. He needs Ann or Bob to bring about the saving, whence Ann and Bob must get some shares of it as well.

It is easy to represent the cost pattern (5) and (7) by a cable connection story. The three agents live in the same location, connected to the source O by a red cable and a blue cable. It costs $60 to rent either cable. Ann's machine (resp. Bob's) can only be connected via the blue cable (resp. the red cable). Dave's machine can use either cable, and two machines can use the same cable.

Yet the story of the red and blue cables does not help because Dave's responsibility in the cost of the red cable depends in some way of his cost share of the blue cable, and vice versa. There is no simple separation argument.

The Shapley value orders randomly Ann, Bob, and Dave, with equal probability on all six orderings, and assigns to an agent his *expected marginal cost*. For instance, the ordering B, A, D, yields the marginal costs

$$x_B = C(B) = 60, \quad x_A = C(AB) - C(B) = 60, \quad x_D = C(ABD) - C(AB) = 0$$

The six orderings and corresponding marginal costs are depicted in the following table:

Ordering	Marginal Cost shares		
	Ann	Bob	Dave
A, B, D	60	60	0
A, D, B	60	60	0
D, A, B	0	60	60
D, B, A	60	0	60
B, D, A	60	60	0
B, A, D	60	60	0
Shapley value	50	50	20

where the last row of cost shares is the arithmetic average of the six rows above. Thus Dave keeps $\frac{2}{3}$ of cost savings 60, while Bob and Ann gets $\frac{1}{6}$ each.

In general, for a given ordering of N, the marginal cost of serving agent i is $x_i = C(S \cup \{i\}) - C(S)$, where S is the set of agents preceding i in this ordering. The Shapley value imputes to agent i the (arithmetic) *average of her marginal costs over all orderings of N*. This share is her *expected marginal cost* when one of the $n!$ orderings of N is chosen at random (and with uniform probability over all orderings).

To write a precise formula for the Shapley value requires some combinatorial notations. Given $N = \{1, 2, \ldots, n\}$, we write $\mathcal{A}_i$ for the set of coalitions not containing agent i, and $\mathcal{A}_i(s)$ for the subset of $\mathcal{A}_i$ containing the coalitions of size s (where s is a number between 0 and $n - 1$); thus for $s = 0$, $\mathcal{A}_i$ is the empty set, and for $s = n - 1$ it contains the single coalition $N \backslash \{i\}$. The Shapley value charges the following cost share to agent i:

$$x_i = \sum_{s=0}^{n-1} \sum_{S \in \mathcal{A}_i(s)} \frac{s!(n - s - 1)!}{n!} \{C(S \cup \{i\}) - C(S)\} \tag{8}$$

In this summation the coefficient $s!(n - s - 1)!/n!$ is the probability that the coalition S (of cardinality s) contains precisely all the agents preceding i in a random ordering of N. For instance, this probability equals $1/n$ if S is empty (the probability that agent i comes first in the ordering), equals $1/n$ if $S = N \backslash \{i\}$ (the probability that i comes last), equals $1/n(n - 1)$ if $S = \{j\}$ (the probability that j comes first and i comes second), and so on.

The Shapley value formula is the single most influential contribution of the axiomatic approach to distributive justice. Its applications are diverse and numerous, as the examples in the next two sections and the discussion of chapters 6 and 7 demonstrate. Its normative justifications are very solid, as explained in section 5.5.

In a two-person problem, the Shapley value assigns the cost shares (2), as one sees at once by averaging marginal costs over the two orderings 1, 2 and 2, 1.

In a problem with three agents 1, 2, 3, formula (8) gives the following cost share for agent 1:

$$x_1 = \tfrac{1}{3}C(1) + \tfrac{1}{6}(C(12) - C(2)) + \tfrac{1}{6}(C(13) - C(3)) + \tfrac{1}{3}(C(123) - C(23))$$
$$= \tfrac{1}{3}C(123) + \tfrac{1}{6}(C(12) + C(13) - 2C(23)) + \tfrac{1}{6}(2C(1) - C(2) - C(3)) \tag{9}$$

Formula (9) also obtains by writing a table of marginal costs for the six ordering of 1, 2, 3 as we did in example 5.3, and averaging over the six rows.

We conclude this section by checking that in example 5.2, the Shapley value selects the very cost shares derived from the separation argument.

The cost function takes the form

$$C(S) = \max_{i \in S} c_i$$

and $c_A = 20, \quad c_B = 30, \quad c_D = 90, \quad c_E = 100, \quad c_F = 110$

Observe that in any ordering of $\{A, B, D, E, F\}$, the marginal cost of Ann is \$20 if she comes up first, and zero otherwise; that of Bob is decomposed in two parts: \$20 if he comes up first, plus \$10 if he is first among B, D, E, F (his marginal cost can be 30 or 10 or zero); that of Dave is \$20 if he is first in N plus \$10 if he is first among B, D, E, F, plus \$60 if he is first among D, E, F; and so on. Therefore the \$20 corresponding to the cost c_A are shared equally among all five agents; the next $\$10 = c_B - c_A$ are shared equally among B, D, E, F; the next $\$60 = c_D - c_B$ are shared equally among D, E, F, and so on, as in example 5.2. This argument generalizes to any cost function C taking the form (3), and gives the cost shares (4).

5.3   The Stand-alone Test and Stand-alone Core

A commons has *subadditive* costs if the production of the output (service to different agents) is cheaper for a group of agents than it is for each agent separately: the joint production brings positive externalities, cost savings that we must allocate among the participants. In the formal model $S \to C(S)$ introduced in the previous section, the subadditivity property says that for any two *disjoint* coalitions S, T, the stand-alone cost of $S \cup T$ is not higher than the sum of stand-alone costs of S and of T:

subadditivity: $C(S \cup T) \leq C(S) + C(T)$ when S and T are disjoint

Applying this property repeatedly yields an inequality that has already been discussed in examples 5.1 and 5.3: total cost is not larger than the sum of stand-alone costs:

$$C(N) \leq \sum_{i \in N} C(i)$$

Most examples discussed in this chapter involve subadditive costs (e.g., examples 5.2 through 5.8). However, the symmetric property of superadditive costs is also plausible. There the production of output involves negative externalities so that the stand alone cost of $S \cup T$ is greater (at least, not smaller) than the sum of the stand-alone costs of S and T:

superaddivity: $\quad C(S \cup T) \geq C(S) + C(T) \quad$ when S and T are disjoint

$$\Rightarrow C(N) \geq \sum_{i \in N} C(i)$$

Under superadditive costs, serving a group of agents is more expensive than serving each one separately.

Examples 5.1 offers a simple superadditive cost function. Many of the commons discussed in chapter 6 have superadditive costs. The typical example is a commons involving congestion, such as a pasture (example 6.2), a mine (example 6.6), or a queue (example 7.7). The entire discussion of chapter 6 is articulated around the two polar cases of increasing marginal costs (hence the superadditive cost function) and of decreasing marginal costs (hence the subadditive cost function): the two cases are important and interestingly different.

The stand-alone test is a simple fairness property directly inspired by the properties of sub- or superadditivity. It requires that everyone gets a share of the positive (resp. negative) externality created by a sub- (resp. super-) additive cost function.

Stand-alone Test

C subadditive $\Rightarrow x_i \leq C(i)$

C superadditive $\Rightarrow x_i \geq C(i)$

The test says that when the externality from joint production is of a constant sign, it should affect all the participating agents in the same direction.

Remarkably, the Shapley value meets the stand-alone test. To see this, recall the computation of the cost share x_i as the expected marginal cost $C(S \cup \{i\}) - C(S)$ of agent i, when S is the random set of agents preceding i in formula (8). Sub- (resp. super-) additivity of C gives

$$C(S \cup \{i\}) - C(S) \leq C(i), \qquad \text{resp.} \geq C(i)$$

hence the claim.

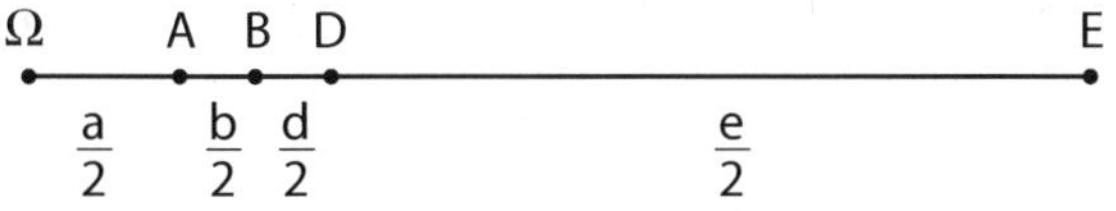

Figure 5.2
Mail distribution: Example 5.4

The stand-alone test is both compelling and easy to meet. Its generalization as the *stand-alone* core property is natural, but much more demanding.

Example 5.4 A Variant of Example 5.2   The five villages of example 5.2 are now four, and they are located along the single road starting at the source Ω and passing successively through A, B, D, and E. Distances $a/2, b/2, d/2, e/2$ correspond respectively to the intervals ΩA, AB, BD, and DE; see figure 5.2. The cost function $S \to C(S)$ is computed exactly as in example 5.2: the stand-alone cost $C(S)$ is the length of the shortest roundtrip starting at Ω and passing through all the locations in S. The Shapley division of total cost $C(N) = a + b + d + e$ is deduced from the separation argument leading to formula (4):

$$x_A = \frac{a}{4}, \quad x_B = \frac{a}{4} + \frac{b}{3}, \quad x_D = \frac{a}{4} + \frac{b}{3} + \frac{d}{2}, \quad x_E = \frac{a}{4} + \frac{b}{3} + \frac{d}{2} + e$$

Assigning cost shares in proportion to stand-alone costs is prima facie a reasonable solution:

$$x_A = \frac{a+b+d+e}{4a+3b+2d+e}a, \quad x_B = \frac{a+b+d+e}{4a+3b+2d+e}(a+b)$$

$$x_D = \frac{a+b+d+e}{4a+3b+2d+e}(a+b+d), \quad x_E = \frac{(a+b+d+e)^2}{4a+3b+2d+e}$$

The cost function is subadditive,[4] and the proportional solution obviously passes the stand-alone test because every cost share is but a fraction of one's stand-alone cost. On the other hand, some *coalition* of agents may end up paying more than stand-alone cost. For instance, if we choose $a = 10$, $b = d = 5$, $e = 50$, the proportional cost shares are computed as

$$x_A = 6.09, \quad x_B = 9.13, \quad x_D = 12.17, \quad x_E = 42.61$$

Thus $S = \{A, B, D\}$ end up paying 27.39 or 37 percent more than their stand-alone cost of 20. They are effectively subsidizing village E, which pays even less than the cost of the

---

4. The shortest trip stopping at every point of $S \cup T$ is shorter than any two round-trips serving all points in S and T respectively.

tour from D to E and back, for which E is solely responsible. Note that a similar argument applies to $S' = \{A, B\}$, which end up paying 15.22, or about 1.5 percent more than their stand-alone cost of 15.

The Shapley cost shares, on the other hand, never charge to a coalition S more than its stand-alone cost. This is clear from the formula above, because the agents in a coalition S pay only toward the cost of these segments that enter in the stand-alone cost of S.

The stand-alone core generalizes the stand-alone test to all coalitions of agents. Under subadditive costs, it views the stand-alone cost $C(S)$ as an upperbound on the total cost share of S; under superadditive costs, it takes this number as a lower bound on the cost imputed to S .

Stand-alone Core

$$C \text{ subadditive} \Rightarrow \sum_{i \in S} x_i \leq C(S) \qquad \text{for all } S \subseteq N$$

$$C \text{ superadditive} \Rightarrow \sum_{i \in S} x_i \geq C(S) \qquad \text{for all } S \subseteq N$$

The stand-alone core property is often interpreted as a bargaining argument (private contract) when the cost is subadditive. Suppose that any coalition S can form and use freely the technology C as it pleases (in particular, agents in $N \setminus S$ cannot object to, or block in any way, S's production plan). Because the cost function C is subadditive, it is always efficient to use a single copy of the technology C to serve everyone. However, coalition S can use its stand-alone options as a disagreement outcome (as in section 3.6), rejecting accordingly any profile of cost shares (x_i) where it is charged more than $C(S)$. This argument only applies to a subadditive cost function. Even then, it must be taken with a grain of salt because the core property may prove altogether impossible to meet (see example 5.8).

In the rest of this section we show that the bite of the stand-alone core property varies wildly from one specification of the cost function to the next. In examples 5.4 and 5.5 the property cuts a large set of acceptable cost shares, among which the Shapley value is normally to be found; in another case (example 5.6) the core property cuts a very small set (even a singleton, example 5.7) of cost shares, and in this case the Shapley value is typically not in the core. Finally the stand-alone core property may be altogether too demanding, despite the sub- or superadditivity of the cost function (example 5.8).

Example 5.5 Another Mail Distribution Problem The road network depicted on figure 5.3 shows the source (post office) at Ω and the three customers Ann, Bob, and Dave. The network is more complicated than in examples 5.2 and 5.4, but the problem is the same:

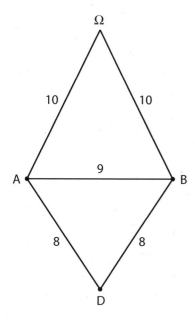

Figure 5.3
Mail distribution: Example 5.5

How should we divide the total cost of the daily tour between the three customers? The separability argument used in examples 5.2 and 5.4 does not apply here: we cannot allocate separately the cost of the various intervals of the network.

The shortest tour visiting A, B, and D goes from Ω successively to A, D, B, and back to Ω for a total cost

$$C(A, B, D) = 10 + 8 + 8 + 10 = 36$$

The stand-alone cost of A is 20 (going from Ω to A and back) as is that of B, whereas it takes a full \$36 to visit D:

$$C(A) = C(B) = 20, \quad C(D) = 36$$

Similar computations yield the stand-alone costs of two agents coalitions. For instance, the shortest tour passing through A and B costs $10 + 9 + 10 = 29$:

$$C(AB) = 29, \quad C(AD) = C(BD) = 36$$

The cost function C is subadditive as $C(ij) \leq C(i) + C(j)$ and $C(ABC) \leq C(i) + C(jk)$ for all combinations of $\{i, j, k\} = \{A, B, D\}$. The stand-alone core property places the following bounds on the cost shares x_A, x_B, x_C:

$$x_A, x_B \leq 20; \quad x_D \leq 36$$

$$x_A + x_B \leq 29; \quad x_A + x_D, x_B + x_D \leq 36$$

In view of the equality $x_A + x_B + x_D = 36$, these six inequalities can be written in a more compact way:

$$0 \leq x_A \leq 20, \quad 0 \leq x_B \leq 20, \quad 7 \leq x_D \leq 30$$

This system cuts a large subset of acceptable cost shares x, and falls very short of recommending a precise compromise between the share imputed to D, on one hand, and A, B, on the other hand.

If we respect the symmetry between A and B, we may at one extreme favor A, B against D as far as $x_A = x_B = 0$, $x_D = 36$; at the other extreme, $x_A = x_B = 14.5$, $x_D = 7$ is still in the stand-alone core. And we may also break the symmetry between A and B, for instance, $x_A = 0$, $x_B = 20$, $x_D = 16$.

Given the loose constraints imposed by the stand-alone core property, if is not surprising that the Shapley value passes this test. This solution is computed with the help of (9) as

$$x_A^* = x_B^* = 8.17, \quad x_D^* = 19.67$$

The next example starts from the same set of users on the same road network as example 5.5 but modifies the technology for providing service to these users. Instead of running a daily tour of all users, it is now necessary to run along the existing roads the shortest cable that will connect them to the source.

For the road network of example 5.2, depicted on figure 5.1, the length of the shortest cable joining the source Ω to the five locations A, B, D, E, F is exactly half that of a tour visiting them all; the same applies to any subset of locations. Thus the cost-sharing games "mail distribution" and "access to a network" are isomorphic (up to a factor of 2) for this road network.[5] By contrast in the case of the network of figure 5.3, the two technologies yield very different patterns of stand-alone costs; in the access problem, the stand-alone core shrinks to a small set.

Example 5.6 Access to a Network   The three customers Ann, Bob, and Dave need to be connected to a network with its source at Ω. In order to connect Ω to A, B, D—or to any subset of these three—the shortest feasible cable will be used along the links of the network of figure 5.3. The cost of a connection is the total length of the cable.

---

5. Exercise 5.7 generalizes this observation to all "tree" networks, meaning all networks without cycles.

Thus, in order to connect Ann alone, we need a cable between Ω and A for a stand-alone cost $C(A) = 10$. In order to connect Ann and Bob, we run a cable from Ω to A and from A to B (or from Ω to B and B to A) for a total cost $C(AB) = 19$. The shortest cable connecting A, B, and D uses three links ΩA, AD, and DB (or ΩB, BD, and DA), and so on. Hence we have the cost function

$$C(A) = C(B) = 10, \quad C(D) = 18$$

$$C(AB) = 19, \quad C(AD) = C(BD) = 18, \quad C(ABD) = 26$$

As in the previous example this cost function is subadditive. But unlike in that example, the stand-alone core property cuts a very small subset of cost shares:

$$x_A \leq 10 \quad \text{and} \quad \{x_B + x_D \leq 18 \Rightarrow x_A \geq 8\}$$

where the implication follows from the budget balance condition $x_A + x_B + x_D = 26$. Thus x_A and, by symmetry, x_B are between 8 and 10. Similarly

$$x_A + x_B \leq 19 \Rightarrow x_D \geq 7, \quad x_A, x_B \geq 8 \Rightarrow x_D \leq 10$$

To sum up, a triple of cost shares x_A, x_B, x_D is in the stand-alone core if (and only if) it meets the following system:

$$8 \leq x_A, x_B \leq 10, \quad 7 \leq x_D \leq 10, \quad x_A + x_B + x_D = 26$$

The cost-sharing most advantageous to Ann and Bob (and treating them equally) is $x_A = x_B = 8$, $x_D = 10$; the least advantageous is $x_A = x_B = 9.5$, $x_D = 7$. A good compromise is $x_A = x_B = 9$, $x_D = 8$.

The logic of the Shapley value solution is very different, and indeed the cost shares it recommends do not meet the stand-alone core property:

$$x_A^* = x_B^* = 7.5, \quad x_D^* = 11$$

In our next example the stand-alone core contains a single set of cost shares, yet this unique allocation is not convincing.

Example 5.7   Example 5.3 Continued   Consider the three-person cost-sharing example given by (5) and (7), which we repeat for convenience:

$$C(ABD) = 120, \quad C(i) = 60 \qquad \text{for } i = A, B, D$$

$$C(AB) = 120, \quad C(AD) = C(BD) = 60$$

These costs are subadditive. The Shapley value was computed as $x_A = x_B = 50$, $x_D = 20$. It fails the stand-alone core property by virtue of an objection of $S = \{A, D\}$ (or $\{B, D\}$): they can ignore Bob and split their own stand-alone cost of 60 as $x'_A = 45$, $x'_D = 15$, from which they both benefit. Now Bob can offer an even better deal to Dave, say $x''_B = 50$, $x''_D = 10$: this deal is feasible to Bob and Dave standing alone, and better for Bob than being left in the cold.

The bidding for Dave's cooperation does not stop here: Ann can offer an even better deal to Dave (e.g., $x'''_A = 55$, $x'''_D = 5$), and so on. The only resting point of the bidding war is when Dave has extracted the entire surplus: indeed, the unique vector of cost shares in the stand-alone core is $x_A = x_B = 60$, $x_D = 0$. This allocation may be plausible if Dave plays Ann against Bob, who never think of colluding against Dave. But it is not a plausibly fair division of the cooperative surplus, of which all the credit cannot go to Dave.

The next example is a subadditive cost function where the stand-alone core property is logically impossible. ·

Example 5.8 Buying a Software   Ann, Bob, and Dave want to purchase software to meet certain word-processing needs. There is no shortage of software on the market, but not all are compatible with either of their computers, nor do they fill all their needs.

After carefully studying the market, our partners have located four software products:

Software product	Satisfactory for	Cost
X	Ann, Dave	$800
Y	Bob, Dave	$900
Z	Ann, Bob	$1,000
E	Ann, Bob, Dave	$1,700

Every other software product is dominated by one of these four products. Software S is dominated by S' if S' is not more expensive than S, if it satisfies at least the same needs, and if at least one of these two comparisons is strict. The cheapest software meeting Ann's needs costs $800, which is Ann's stand-alone cost. Similarly $C(B) = 900$ and $C(D) = 800$.

Computing the Shapley value with the help of (9), we find that

$$x^*_A = 550, \quad x^*_B = 650, \quad x^*_D = 500$$

On the other hand, the stand-alone core property yields a logically impossible system of three inequalities and one equality:

$$x_A + x_B \leq 1,000, \quad x_A + x_D \leq 800, \quad x_B + x_D \leq 900$$

and

$$x_A + x_B + x_D = 1,700$$

Adding the three inequalities yields $x_A + x_B + x_D \leq 1,350$, a contradiction.

A natural solution in the spirit of these (out of reach) inequalities is this profile of cost shares where each inequality is violated by the same amount, namely

$$x_A + x_B - 1{,}000 = x_A + x_D - 800 = x_B + x_D - 900$$

This system—together with the constraint that total cost is \$1,700—yields the cost shares:

$$x_A = 567, \quad x_B = 667, \quad x_D = 467$$

which are not too different from the Shapley value, although the spread $x_B - x_D$ has increased to \$200.

In cooperative game theory the two ideas of the Shapley value and the stand-alone core have been studied for general cost or surplus functions $S \rightarrow C(S)$ (cooperative games with transferable utility). The feasibility of the stand-alone core property and the relation between the Shapley value and the stand-alone core have been investigated with full mathematical generality.

Finally, a couple of solutions selecting, for any cost function, a central point within the stand-alone core (or in the spirit of the stand-alone inequalities if the core is empty) have been constructed: example 5.8 provides an illustration.

Our last example is meant to remind us of one great advantage of the Shapley value, namely that it applies equally well to a cost function that is neither sub- nor superadditive. For such a cost function, even the stand-alone test ceases to make sense.

Example 5.9 Location of a Post Office   We modify example 5.2 by allowing the five agents to choose the location of the post office anywhere on the road network (as in examples 3.4 and 3.8) and the cost to be shared is that of the daily delivery tour starting from the post office and passing through all relevant customers.

Thus in the network of example 5.2 (figure 5.1) any location between A and F is efficient: the corresponding tour costs $C(ABDEF) = 90$. Similarly $C(ABDE) = 80$, $C(BE) = 70$, and so on. This cost function is neither sub- nor superadditive because

$$C(ABDE) = 80 > 10 + 10 = C(AB) + C(DE)$$

$$C(ABDE) = 80 < 70 + 70 = C(AD) + C(BE)$$

Thus the logic of the stand-alone core does not apply.

The Shapley value, on the other hand, suggests a judicious way to cut through the thorny pattern of externalities. Direct computation of this solution as the expected marginal cost is tedious—there are 120 orderings of five agents—but an argument based on the additivity property of the value (section 5.5) delivers the answer almost at once.

Consider the cost 60 of the interval BD (each interval is traveled on twice). In a random ordering of the five agents if will be imputed to one of A, B if (and only if) one of D, E, F is drawn first, and to one of D, E, F if (and only if) one of A, B is drawn first. As the agents A, B are equal in this subproblem (i.e., the costsharing of the interval BD), they receive an equal expected share, and D, E, F are treated equally as well. Thus the cost of interval BD is divided as

A, B each pay $\dfrac{1}{2} \cdot \dfrac{3}{5} \cdot 60 = \$18$

D, E, F each pay $\dfrac{1}{3} \cdot \dfrac{2}{5} \cdot 60 = \$8$

Similar computations for each of the four intervals give

Intervals	A	B	D	E	F	Total cost
AB	8	0.5	0.5	0.5	0.5	10
BD	18	18	8	8	8	60
DE	1.33	1.33	1.33	3	3	10
EF	0.5	0.5	0.5	0.5	8	10
Shapley value	27.83	20.33	10.33	12	19.5	90

Exercise 5.7 generalizes this decomposition argument.

5.4   Stand-alone Surplus

We illustrate the versatility of the surplus-sharing model, defined by a pair (N, v) where the function v associates to every coalition S in N a "surplus" $v(S)$. To interpret $v(S)$, we go through the Gedank experiment where the agents in S cooperate, and use efficiently the resources they control. This results in a net benefit $v(S)$, the stand-alone surplus of coalition S that can be distributed as easily as money among the members of S. An important assumption is that individual utilities are measured in a common numéraire (e.g., cash) that is freely transferable across agents, and moreover the marginal utility of the numéraire is constant (utility is linear in money).

The key to the construction above is to define what resources the agents in S control when they stand alone. Depending on the context this control is derived from "real" property rights or from "virtual" ones. The exchange of private goods under private ownership (discussed in sections 7.1 and 7.2) is a case where the property rights are real: agents in S are free to trade among themselves; the corresponding stand-alone core property is thus interpreted as a positive statement about the stability of private contracts. On the other hand, in most instances of the commons problems (chapter 6), the stand-alone surplus represents a virtual appropriation of the technology by a certain coalition: this surplus is nevertheless relevant to the normative discussion, and the application of a general solution like the Shapley value is vindicated. In the "mail distribution" stories (examples 5.2, 5.5, and 5.9) a coalition of agents is not legally able to dismiss the agents outside the coalition, but doing so as a thought experiment is a good way to untangle the web of mutual externalities. The public contract concerns all agents in N without dropping anyone, but it is fair by reference to what would happen if some agents were dropped. This interpretation pervades this chapter and the next one.

Example 5.10 Example 5.5 Revisited   As in example 5.5 the problem is to share the cost of mail delivery on the road network of figure 5.3. The difference is that we now take into account how much each agent is willing to pay for to receive mail everyday. Specifically we assume that

$$u_A = \$18, \quad u_B = \$11, \quad u_D = \$16$$

We compute the surplus function $S \to v(S)$ for each one of the seven coalitions in $\{A, B, D\}$. A single agent is not willing to pay for his own stand-alone cost ($u_A = 18 < 20 = C(A)$, etc.); therefore $v(i) = 0$ for $i = A, B, D$. Similarly any two agents' coalition is unable to achieve a positive surplus

$$u_A + u_B = 29 \leq 29 = C(AB)$$

$$u_A + u_D = 34 < 36 = C(AD)$$

$$u_B + u_D = 27 < 36 = C(BD)$$

therefore $v(ij) = 0$ for all two-person coalitions. Now efficiency commands to serve all three agents as $C(ABD) = 36 < 45 = u_A + u_B + u_D$; therefore $v(ABD) = 9$.

The surplus function is thus very simple: all three agents are equal hence the Shapley value (or any solution treating equals equally; see section 5.5) declares that each one should receive $3 of surplus, which amounts to the following cost shares:

$$x_A = 15, \quad x_B = 8, \quad x_D = 13$$

Compare these with the cost shares in example 5.5: now Ann is paying the biggest share, whereas Bob gets a rebate. Consideration of the net benefits turns the analysis on its head.

Notice that for some other choices of the willingness to pay, the surplus-sharing approach leads to virtually the same recommendation as in example 5.5: exercises 5.2 gives an example.

Our next example illustrates an important features of the stand-alone surplus computations: a coalition S standing alone may maximize its surplus by serving only a subset of S.

Example 5.11 Example 5.6 Revisited   The problem is to share the cost of a cable connecting A, B, and D to the source and following the links of the network of figure 5.3. We now assume the following willingness to pay for connection to the network:

$$u_A = \$12, \quad u_B = \$8, \quad u_D = \$12$$

Ann would pay for a connection if she was standing alone, and her net surplus would be $v(A) = 2$. Neither Bob nor Dave would buy a connection on their own: $v(B) = v(D) = 0$. Efficiency allows to connect only Ann and Dave, for a net surplus $12 + 12 - 18 = 6$ or all three agents for the same net surplus. Therefore

$$v(AD) = v(ABD) = 6$$

The coalition AB standing alone would not include Bob:

$$u_A + u_B - C(AB) = 1 < 2 = u_A - C(A)$$

hence

$$v(A) = v(AB) = 2$$

On the other hand, the coalition BD would gladly pay to connect both agents, for a surplus $v(BD) = 8 + 12 - 18 = 2$.

The surplus function v just computed is superadditive, as the reader can easily verify. The stand-alone property requires to deny any positive share of surplus to Bob:

$$\{y_A + y_D \geq 6 = y_A + y_B + y_D \quad \text{and} \quad y_B \geq 0\} \quad \text{imply} \quad y_B = 0$$

Ann and Dave share the surplus along the following guidelines:

$$2 \leq y_A \leq 4, \quad 2 \leq y_D \leq 4, \quad y_A + y_D = 6$$

The Shapley value takes a sharply different view point to distribute the six units of surplus. Bob is entitled to a positive share of surplus because he contributes a positive amount while working with Dave: $v(BD) > v(D)$. Therefore his marginal contribution is 2 whenever the ordering drawn is D, B, A. Compute the Shapley surplus shares with the help of formula (9), where cost is replaced by surplus

$$y_A = 3.33, \quad y_B = 0.33, \quad y_D = 2.33$$

If all three agents are connected, the cost shares are

$$x_A = 8.67, \quad x_B = 7.67, \quad x_D = 9.67$$

If only Ann and Dave are connected, Bob deserves a small cash compensation of 33cts for stepping aside and the other two agents pay:

$$x'_A = 8.67, \quad x'_D = 9.67$$

which covers the cost of connecting them, plus 33cts for Bob.

*5.5 Axiomatizations of the Shapley Value

The Shapley value has been axiomatically characterized in a number of ways, of which four are presented below.

A cost (or surplus) sharing problem is a pair (N, C) where N is a finite set of agents and C associates to each nonempty coalition S a real number $C(S)$. A solution associates to any such problem (N, C) a profile $x = \gamma(N, C)$ such that

$$x = (x_i)_{i \in N} \quad \text{and} \quad \sum_{i \in N} x_i = C(N)$$

The original characterization (due to Shapley) uses three axioms: *equal treatment of equals, dummy,* and *additivity.*

Equal treatment is the translation of equal exogenous rights (section 2.1) in the cost-sharing problem. We say that agents i and j are *equal* with respect to (N, C) if $C(S \cup \{i\}) = C(S \cup \{j\})$ for any set S in N containing neither i nor j (including the empty set).

Equal Treatment of Equals   If i, j are equal w.r.t. (N, C), then $\gamma_i(N, C) = \gamma_j(N, C)$.

The dummy axiom is normatively the most important of the three because no other axiom conveys the reward principle. Dummy does so in a fairly convincing way, by considering an agent for which the marginal cost of joining any coalition S is zero. Say that agent i is a *dummy* in problem (N, C) if we have

$$\partial_i C(S) = C(S \cup \{i\}) - C(S) = 0 \qquad \text{for all } S \subseteq N$$

Note that for a coalition S already containing agent i, the marginal cost $\partial_i C(S)$ is zero by definition; therefore the property above has bite only for the coalitions S in $\mathcal{A}_i$ (i.e., not containing i).

The **dummy** axiom requires that a dummy agent pays nothing:

$$\{\partial_i C(S) = 0 \text{ for all } S\} \Rightarrow \gamma_i(N, C) = 0$$

The third axiom, additivity, is the most mathematically demanding, and is motivated as a decentralization property. Consider a cost function C made up of two independent costs $C^i, i = 1, 2 : C(S) = C^1(S) + C^2(S)$ for all S. For instance, if the service provided to the agent is cable TV, C^1 may represent the (one-time) cost of installing the cable connection and C^2 the variable costs of the cable company (e.g., maintenance cost of the line). The **additivity** axiom requires the cost shares to depend additively on the cost function:

$$\gamma(N, C^1 + C^2) = \gamma(N, C^1) + \gamma(N, C^2)$$

Shapley's original characterization result says that the Shapley value is the only solution meeting the three axioms equal treatment of equals, dummy, and additivity. We provide the main idea of the proof by looking, once again, at example 5.2.

We define five subproblems, the sum of which is the initial cost-sharing problem:

$C^A(S) = 20$ for all $S \neq \emptyset$

$C^B(S) = 10$ for all S s.t. $S \cap \{B, D, E, F\} \neq \emptyset$; zero otherwise

$C^D(S) = 60$ for all S s.t. $S \cap \{D, E, F\} \neq \emptyset$; zero otherwise

$C^E(S) = 10$ for all S s.t. $S \cap \{E, F\} \neq \emptyset$; zero otherwise

$C^F(S) = 10$ for all S containing F; zero otherwise

Check first that the cost function C given by (3) is precisely $C = C^A + C^B + C^D + C^E + C^F$. Next consider one of the subproblems, say C^D. Here agents A and B are dummies, and moreover D, E, and F are equal with respect to C^D. Therefore equal treatment and dummy imply that A and B pay nothing and D, E, F share equally the cost $C^D(N) = 60$. Repeating this argument, we find that the cost of C^A is shared equally among all agents, that of C^B among B, D, E, F, and so on. In turn the additivity property yields the cost shares computed in examples 5.2.

The next characterization of the Shapley value replaces the dummy and additivity axiom by a single property called

Marginalism   For any two games (N, C^1), (N, C^2) and any agent i,

$$\{\partial_i C^1(S) = \partial_i C^2(S) \text{ for all } S\} \Rightarrow \{\gamma_i(N, C^1) = \gamma_i(N, C^2)\}$$

This says that agent i's cost share $\gamma_i(N, C)$ depends only on the list $\partial_i C(S)$ of his marginal contributions to all coalitions S.

It is easy to check that the only marginalist and symmetric solution for two-person problems is the Shapley value (8). Indeed, such a solution takes the form

$$y_1 = f(C(1), C(12) - C(2)), \quad y_2 = f(C(2), C(12) - C(1))$$

for some function f. The budget balance gives the following equation, upon using the letter variables x, y, z for $C(1), C(2), C(12)$:

$$f(x, z - y) + f(y, z - x) = z \text{ for all } x, y, z$$

It is a simple mathematical exercise to deduce that $f(x, x') = \frac{1}{2}(x + x')$ and the announced result for two-person problems.

To sum up, the Shapley value is the only solution for cooperative games satisfying {dummy, additivity, and equal treatment} or {marginalism and equal treatment}. All of the results discussed so far involve a fixed set N of agents, also called a *fixed population*. By contrast, the next two characterizations rely on *variable population* axioms. Given a game (N, C) we denote by $(N \backslash i, C^{-i})$ the restriction of this game to the subset $N \backslash i$, namely $C^{-i}(S) = C(S)$ for all S contained in $N \backslash i$.

Equal Impact   The impact of removing agent j on agent i's share is the same as that of removing agent i on agent j's share:

$$\gamma_i(N, C) - \gamma_i(N \backslash j, C^{-j}) = \gamma_j(N, C) - \gamma_j(N \backslash i, C^{-i})$$

Equal impact, unlike additivity, is a fairness statement. Additivity is a structural invariance property. Marginalism is somewhere in between.

Related to Equal Impact, we have the following axiom:

Potential   There exists a real-valued function $P(N, C)$, defined for all cooperative games (N, C), such that

$$\gamma_i(N, C) = P(N, C) - P(N \backslash i, C^{-i}) \qquad \text{for all } N, i, C$$

The Shapley value is the only solution satisfying potential; it is the only solution satisfying equal impact. Both results follow an easy induction argument on the size n of N: the statements are obvious for $n = 2$ once we note that $\gamma_i(\{i\}, C) = C(i)$ and posit $P(\emptyset, C) = 0$.

Thus the latter two results are closer to providing a constructive algorithm for deriving the Shapley value than a genuine axiomatization from first principles, like the two characterizations described earlier.

We note finally that the cost-sharing methodology leading to the Shapley value can take into account unequal exogenous rights.

If we remove the equal treatment requirement, the interesting class of *random order values* emerges. For each ordering σ of N, the σ marginal contribution solution γ^σ charges agent their marginal cost $\gamma_i^\sigma(N, C) = \partial_i C(S)$ where S is the set of agents preceding i in σ. For instance, if $\sigma = \{2, 4, 5, 1, 3\}$, we have $\gamma_4^\sigma(N, C) = C(42) - C(2)$; $\gamma_1^\sigma(N, C) = C(1245) - C(245)$; and so on. Each solution γ^σ meets dummy, additivity, and marginalism. The same holds true for any convex combination of these solutions provided that the coefficients of the combination are constant: these solutions are the random order values.

Each random order value computes cost shares by (1) drawing at random an ordering σ in a lottery over orderings that does not depend on the particular function C and (2) charging σ marginal contributions. The family of all the random order values is characterized by either dummy + additivity or, essentially, marginalism.

5.6   Introduction to the Literature

The normative analysis of a "value," which is a fair compromise in the kind of cost- or surplus-sharing problems discussed in this chapter, is one-half of the theory of cooperative games with transferable utility. The other half is the strategic analysis of coalition formation, and is not relevant to this book.

A number of textbook presentations of value theory are available: Owen (1982, chs. 10, 11), Moulin (1988, ch. 5), and Young (1994, ch. 5). The common theme, as in this chapter, is to contrast the additivity axiom leading to the Shapley value, with the stand-alone core requirement (interpreted as a normative principle of no subsidization). The latter leads to a value called the *nucleolus* (Schmeidler 1969), which is technically more complicated and normatively less compelling than the Shapley value; we only allude to the nucleolus, a central point in the stand-alone core, in example 5.8.

On the other hand, our choice of examples emphasizes the versatility of the cooperative game model, and in this respect it takes inspiration from an important methodological paper by Shubik (1962), and from a variety of applications to specific problems of joint costs, for instance, Thomas (1980). Example 5.2 originates in Littlechild and Owen (1973), who were the first to compute the Shapley value of the capacity cost function (3), in the problem of allocating airport landing fees. The subsequent literature on minimal cost spanning trees in networks can be viewed as a generalization of the airport game: it inspires our examples 5.5, 5.6, 5.9, and 5.11. Sharkey (1995) is an excellent survey of the relevant literature.

Many authors have contributed to the multiple axiomatic characterizations of the Shapley value reviewed in section 5.5. The seminal paper is Shapley (1953). The marginalist characterization is due to Loehman and Whinston (1974) and Young (1985); see also Chun (1989). The equal impact characterization is due to Myerson (1977), and that by the potential function to Hart and Mas-Colell (1989). The original characterization of random order values is due to Weber (1988), and the one based on marginalism to Khmelnitskaya (1999). The special relation between the Shapley value and the stand-alone core in concave cost-sharing games is due to Shapley (1971): see exercise 5.9.

Finally, a collection of essays is devoted exclusively to the Shapley value. Roth (1988) is still a useful introduction to the many applications and variants of this concept.

Exercises to Chapter 5

Exercise 5.1 Traveling Lecturer

A lecturer will visit Chicago, New York, and Washington from his home base in Boston. The cost of the round-trip of all six partial trips to a single city or a pair of cities is as follows:

Chicago	400	Chicago and New York	450
New York	300	Chicago and Washington	500
Washington	300	New York and Washington	300
Chicago, New York, and Washington	600		

a. Check that the cost function is subadditive.

b. How should the three sponsors of the trip, based in the three cities he will visit, split the total cost according to the Shapley value?

c. Show that the stand-alone core property is feasible in this example, and that the Shapley value does not meet this property.

d. We modify the cost function as follows:

Chicago and New York	400
Chicago and Washington	450
New York and Washington	300

Other stand-alone costs are unchanged. Check subadditivity, and show that now the stand-alone core is empty. Compute the Shapley value.

Exercise 5.2 Variant of Example 5.10

Assume a common willingness to pay of $18 for all three agents. Compute the stand-alone surplus function $S \to v(S)$ as in example 5.10. Check that v is superadditive and compute the division of $v(ABD)$ recommended by the Shapley value. Compare the corresponding cost shares with those found in example 5.5. Does the Shapley value surplus division meet the stand alone core property (for the superadditive function v)?

Exercise 5.3 Variant of Example 5.11

Assume a common willingness to pay $10. Answer the same questions as in the previous exercise (where the comparison is with the cost shares found in example 5.6).

Exercise 5.4 Surplus-Sharing Variant of Example 5.8

Each agent is willing to pay $700 for an adequate software.

Compute the superadditive surplus function $S \rightarrow v(S)$. Check, in particular, that the efficient production plan leaves Bob with no software.

Compute the Shapley value and show that it awards a cash transfer to Bob, as a compensation for stepping aside (as in example 5.11). Is the stand-alone core property (for the superadditive function v) feasible or not?

Exercise 5.5 Variant of Example 5.8

Four softwares a, b, c, d are available on the market, at a price of $100 each. Four agents want to combine their purchase of a couple of these softwares, so as to meet their specific needs.

Software a meets the needs of Ann and Bob; software b, that of Bob and Emily; software c, that of Ann and Dave; software d, that of Ann and Emily. Thus the cheapest way to meet all individual needs is to buy b and c for $200. The issue is to divide fairly this cost between the four agents.

a. Compute the stand-alone costs of all 14 coalitions and check the subadditivity property.

b. Compute the cost shares recommended by the Shapley value. Are they in the stand-alone core?

Exercise 5.6

Ann, Bob, and Dave share the cost of hooking up to a network. Their willingness to pay for this service is

Ann	Bob	Dave
60	50	40

The (stand-alone) costs of hooking the various subsets of agents are

$$C(A) = C(B) = 50, \quad C(D) = 60$$

$$C(AB) = C(AD) = 70, \quad C(BD) = 60$$

$$C(ABD) = 100$$

a. Ignoring first the willingness to pay, compute the cost shares recommended by Shapley value. Check that it is not in the stand-alone core. Show that the stand-alone core contains a unique set of cost shares and compute it.

b. From now on we take the willingness to pay into account. Compute the surplus function and show that efficiency requires serving all three agents.

c. Compute the Shapley value of the surplus function and compute the, again unique, allocation in the stand-alone core. Compare the cost shares proposed by these two solutions with the two found in question a by ignoring the willingness to pay.

Exercise 5.7 Tree Networks

A tree is a graph where all nodes are connected and there are no cycles. The agents live on certain nodes of the tree and to each edge (a link between two nodes) is attached a cost, building or maintenance cost. The tree on figure 5.4 has five agents living in different nodes and the source marked Ω. Example 5.2 is another example where the tree is a simple line.

a. Consider the mail distribution problem (as in examples 5.2 and 5.5) for the tree of figure 5.4. Check that the total cost of a tour serving all agents is twice the sum of the costs of all edges. Compute the cost shares recommended by the Shapley value, by mimicking the separability argument used in example 5.2.

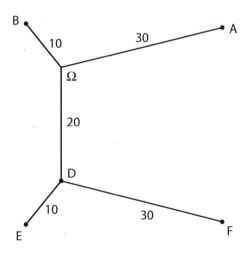

Figure 5.4
Network for exercise 5.7

b. Consider the problem "access to the network" as in example 5.6: the cost of serving a given coalition S is the total cost of the smallest subtree connecting the source to all agents in S. Check that the cost function to this problem is exactly one half of the cost function for the mail distribution problem so that the two problems are identical.

c. Suppose, as in example 5.9, that there is no assigned source and each coalition standing alone will locate the source so as to minimize the cost of a tour (or, equivalently, the cost of a subtree connecting everyone in the coalition to the source). Total cost is the same as in question a but some of the stand-alone costs are different. Compute the Shapley value, by mimicking the separability argument used in example 5.9.

*d. Generalize the computation of the Shapley value in questions a and c to an arbitrary tree where one or several agents can live on any one of the nodes.

Exercise 5.8

Consider the network depicted in figure 5.5, showing the three agents A, B, D, the source Ω and the cost of each edge.

a. Compute the subadditive cost function of the "mail distribution" problem with source Ω as in examples 5.2 and 5.5. Compute the Shapley value profile of cost shares. Does it meet the stand-alone core property?

b. Compute the subadditive cost function of the "access to the network" problem with source Ω as in example 5.6. Show that the stand-alone core is empty.

c. Now, as in example 5.9 and question c of exercise 5.7, the agents can locate a post office anywhere on the network of figure 5.5 so as to minimize the cost of delivering mail to all

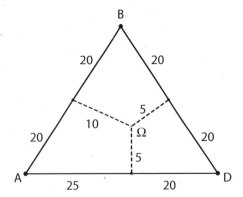

Figure 5.5
Network for exercise 5.8

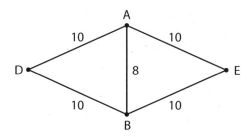

Figure 5.6
Network for exercise 5.9

of them. Note that the point Ω has no longer any special meaning, yet the inner network through Ω can be used to locate the post office. Compute the stand-alone cost function and check that it is not subadditive. Compute the Shapley value.

Exercise 5.9

Consider the four agents network depicted in figure 5.6.

a. Compute the cost function of the mail distribution problem when each coalition can choose freely the location of the source (as in example 5.9). Note that agents A, B play symmetric roles, as do D, E. Therefore one only needs to compute eight costs, corresponding to coalitions A, D, AB, DE, AD, ABD, ADE, and $ABDE$.

b. Compute the cost shares recommended by the Shapley value. (*Hint:* Use the symmetries of the problem.)

c. Consider the "access to a network" problem without a fixed source (as in example 5.9). Thus the cost of a given coalition S is that of the cheapest set of edges connecting all agents in S. Check that the cost function is not subadditive. Compute the Shapley value.

d. Now the source Ω is fixed midway on the edge joining Ann and Bob. Compute the cost functions in the "mail distribution" (example 5.5) and "access to a network" (example 5.6) versions. Compare with the functions computed in questions a and c above. Finally compute in both cases the Shapley value.

*Exercise 5.10 Concave Cost Functions

A cost function C is called *concave* if the marginal cost $C(S \cup i) - C(S)$ decreases as the coalition S enlarges. For all coalitions S, T,

$$S \subseteq T \Rightarrow C(S \cup i) - C(S) \geq C(T \cup i) - C(T)$$

a. For a three-person subadditive cost function, check that concavity is equivalent to three inequalities:

$$C(12) + C(23) \geq C(123) + C(2)$$

and two other inequalities by exchanging the role of the agents. Deduce that the cost function in example 5.5 is concave, but that in example 5.6 is not.

b. Show that the cost function in example 5.2 is concave. More generally, a cost function taking the form (3) is concave.

*c. Fix an arbitrary concave cost function C and an ordering of N, say $1, 2, \ldots, n$. Show that the corresponding profile of marginal costs

$$x_1 = C(1), \quad x_2 = C(12) - C(1), \quad x_3 = C(123) - C(12), \ldots, x_n = C(N) - C(N \setminus n)$$

meets the stand-alone core property. Deduce that the Shapley value meets this property as well.

The property above explains why the stand-alone core of a concave cost function is "large." It can be shown that the stand-alone core equals the set of all convex combinations of the marginal cost vectors.

6 Managing the Commons

6.1 The Tragedy of the Commons

This chapter focuses like the previous one, on the problem of the commons. Unlike in chapter 5, we focus on the efficiency-fitness consequences of the variable returns to scale of the production process. The tragedy of the commons, going back to Aristotle (*Politics*)[1] concerns the free access regime, where every agent uses independently and freely the common technology. This choice may be about driving one's own car in the morning traffic or riding the metro (example 6.3), waiting in line at the post office or walking (exercise 6.3), or sending one's cow to the village commons pasture (examples 6.2 and 6.5). Or it may be about buying a service of which the price depends on the number of buyers, as in the cost-sharing problems of chapter 4; also see examples 6.6 to 6.8.

The "tragedy" occurs when the result of uncoordinated selfish decisions by all agents (all potential users) is an inefficient (Pareto inferior; see section 3.1) outcome: the wasted welfare is the consequence of the distribution of property rights, namely the freedom to choose whether or not to participate in the production process and at what level.

The tragedy of the commons is illustrated in examples 6.1 to 6.3 below. The methodological importance of the tragedy is twofold. On the one hand, it embodies the simplest and most pervasive conflict between collective rationality (Pareto optimality) and strategic rationality (the free exercise of individual rights): the celebrated Prisoners' Dilemma belongs here; see example 6.1. The second interesting aspect of the tragedy is the question of fair compensation, a direct consequence of efficiency.

In the free access regime, the equilibrium outcome inefficiently overproduces (case of decreasing returns to scale; sections 6.3 and 6.4) or underproduces (case of increasing returns to scale; section 6.5). In the former case efficiency commands to reduce the production level by barring from the commons certain agents who wanted to use it under free access. It is fair to compensate these excluded agents: But who exactly should be compensated and by how much?

In the increasing returns case, efficiency requires to enroll in use of the commons new agents who wanted to stay out in the first place. These agents must be bribed to join, by a more advantageous deal: once again the issue is to define fair compensation.

We stress that the issue of fair compensation is logically independent from that of fair *reward* discussed in chapter 5. The central question of chapter 5 is the fair division of a joint cost when the various users are not equally responsible for the formation of these costs: for instance, connecting the users to a source when the users live at different distances from the source (examples 5.6 and 5.11). In this chapter, by contrast, the agents consume a

---

1. "What is common to the greater number has the least care bestowed upon it. Everyone thinks chiefly of his own, hardly at all of the common interest" (*Politics,* ii, 285).

homogeneous good (unlike the heterogeneous "connections" just mentioned); thus they are equally responsible for the total cost. On the other hand, they have different willingness to pay for service; hence efficiency requires one to serve certain agents and not some others (who could be among the efficient users in another configuration of users' willingness to pay). Compare this with most of chapter 5, where all users are always served and individual willingness to pay for service play no role[2] (they are taken to be very large—inelastic demand—and differences in these large numbers are irrelevant to the equity issue). The management of a technology in the common property regime is a very rich source of questions about distributive justice!

In the subsequent sections we propose three different answers to the question of fair compensation; we also address the implementation issue: what system of property rights over the commons delivers each one of these three solutions in equilibrium? The solutions are introduced and discussed in a series of examples, first with decreasing returns to scale (sections 6.3, 6.4), then with increasing returns (section 6.5). A general definition and systematic axiomatic discussion is the subject of section 6.6.

Example 6.1 Trash and Public Bad   Each agent chooses to leave his trash in the common area (cigarette butts in the street, oil refuse in the ocean) or to dispose of it in a proper dumping site. It costs $\$a, a > 0$, to use the dumping site: each trash bag left in the common area brings a net disutility of $b, b > 0$, to each agent and these losses add up linearly. We have n agents and we assume that

$$\frac{1}{n}a < b < a$$

If q among the other agents leave their trash in the common area, my net utility is $-bq - a$ if I use the dumping site, and $-b(q + 1)$ if I do not; therefore in the decentralized equilibrium, I do not as $b < a$.

This is an n-person example of the celebrated Prisoners' Dilemma. The selfish incentive to litter puts the entire trash in the street, and brings a disutility $-nb$ to every participant. But this outcome is Pareto inferior to the cooperative outcome where everyone picks her own trash, thus incurring a disutility $-a$ (no externality from other agents' trash); recall our assumption $-nb < -a$.

Example 6.1 is an example of a public good being produced by voluntary contribution: the cleanliness of the street is the public good (it is consumed by all agents without exception); a is the cost of providing one unit of public good and b is the corresponding per capita benefit.

---

2. With the exception of section 5.4.

Example 6.2 A Rural Commons   The commons is a pasture open to all villagers, covered
with 25,000 pounds of "grass." A cow can eat up to 250 pounds of grass, and transforms
grass into money at a one-to-one rate: 1 pound of grass gives 1 unit of meat with market price
$1. Each villager owns one cow and must choose between keeping it at home, where it will
get 100 pounds of grass (hence the revenue $100) or sending it to graze on the commons,
where it will eat its fair share of grass ($25,000/q$, where q is the number of cows on the
commons) or 250 pounds, whichever is less.

The efficient utilization of the commons is to send exactly 100 cows there, which will
each eat 250 units of grass, and keep all other cows at home. Each cow sent to the commons
brings a profit of $250 - 100 = 150$ above the home grazing option, and the efficient surplus
of $15,000 is thus extracted from the commons.

In the free access regime, however, we expect that the commons will be overgrazed
up to the point where the surplus is entirely dissipated. Note that with 100 cows on the
pasture, a farmer still benefits from sending an extra cow to the commons, where it will eat
$25,000/101$, much more than 100 pounds at home. When q cows are on the commons, there
is no incentive to send an extra cow if and only if $25,000/(q + 1) \leq 100$, and no incentive
to withdraw one cow if and only if $25,000/q \geq 100$. Thus in equilibrium we find 250 or
249 cows on the commons and the surplus is entirely dissipated! If $q = 250$, no villager is
better off than if the commons did not exist. If $q = 249$, the net surplus from the commons
is 100 units, or 40 cents per cow on the commons!

A simple solution to the tragedy is to limit access to 100 cows and select randomly
100 lucky villagers who are allowed to use the pasture. Ex ante each villager gets a fair
share $15,000/n$ of the efficient surplus. We will say more about random prioritizing in
section 6.4.

Example 6.2 exhibits a "full" tragedy of the commons, in the sense that at the free access
equilibrium outcome, the agents are no better off than if the commons did not exist. The
full tragedy always occur when the returns to scale decrease and the demand is perfectly
homogeneous: all agents have the same willingness to pay for "service" (case of a cost-
sharing problem) or the same opportunity cost for supplying one unit of input. When the
demand is heterogeneous, the free access outcome collects in general a substantial fraction
of the efficient surplus, as discussed in section 6.4.

In the last example about the tragedy, the agents choose between two technologies, each
one with variable returns. Depending on the nature of the returns (increasing or decreasing)
the tragedy does not occur or it takes a fairly mild form.

Example 6.3 Congestion Externalities   All players must use one of two technologies to
receive a certain service—getting no service is not an option: their willingness to pay is large

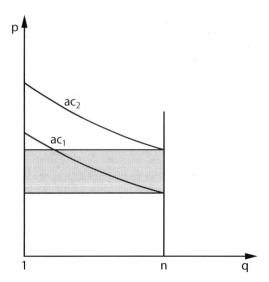

Figure 6.1
Surplus loss at bad equilibrium

enough to ensure this. There are n agents and the congestion cost from using technology i is $ac_i(q_i)$, where q_i is the number of users of technology i (so $q_1 + q_2 = n$). Note that ac stands for average cost.

For instance, all players must travel from A to B, and there are exactly two possible routes (technologies). Cost is travel time, and we assume that the common travel time $ac_i(q_i)$ of the players choosing route i, $i = 1, 2$, is strictly increasing in q_i: negative congestion externality. The equilibrium travel pattern is when both routes are (nearly) equally congested $ac_1(q_1) \simeq ac_2(q_2)$,[3] making every agent indifferent between the two possible choices. This outcome is clearly Pareto optimal because any situation q_1', q_2' with say $ac_1(q_1') > ac_2(q_2')$ has $ac_1(q_1') > ac_1(q_1)$ (exercise: Why?) so that users of route 1 are worse off than in equilibrium. Thus under negative congestion externalities there is no tragedy: free access to the commons yields an efficient outcome.

Suppose next that the congestion externalities are positive: $ac_i(q_i)$ decreases in q_i. Examples include the choice of a dress style among conformists, of a disco (the more crowded the merrier), of a PC versus a Mac (a machine compatible with a larger number of other users is more valuable). Now in the situation depicted in figure 6.1, technology 1 is cheaper (better) than technology 2 at every level: $ac_1(q) < ac_2(q)$ for all q, and yet there is a

---

3. More precisely $ac_i(q_i) \geq ac_j(q_j + 1)$ for $i, j = \{1, 2\}$.

noncooperative equilibrium where everybody is stuck with the inferior technology 2, namely $q_1 = 0, q_2 = n$.

Notice in figure 6.1 that $ac_1(1) > ac_2(n)$, so no one has an incentive to use the technology alone. The bad equilibrium $q_2 = n$ involves a loss of surplus $n \cdot (ac_2(n) - ac_1(n))$ which is the shaded area on figure 6.1. The tragedy is mitigated by the fact that we have *another* equilibrium where everyone uses the good technology 1, and this outcome is Pareto superior to the bad equilibrium outcome. Thus the solution of the tragedy in this example is a coordination device that the benevolent dictator provides (e.g., by encouraging the agents to use the good equilibrium). Once the equilibrium is reached, we do not need to restrict the agents's freedom of choice between the two technologies.

Exercise 6.2 proposes a variant of the traffic example (negative externalities from congestion) with a more complicated road network, where a tragedy occurs; namely the equilibrium outcome is inefficient.

6.2   Constant Returns to Scale

We consider the important benchmark case where the returns of the technology are constant (constant marginal cost). The free access equilibrium outcome is then efficient (no tragedy); we argue that this outcome is also fair in the sense of the Lockean theory of entitlements.

We use a cost-sharing model in the discussion, where each agent wants at most one unit of a certain good or service, and has a certain valuation/willingness to pay for this good. These valuations vary across agents.[4]

In classic microeconomic fashion the profile of these valuations is represented by a downward-sloping demand function d, where for every "price" p, $d(p)$ is the number of agents willing to pay p or more for service. We draw d as a continuous function, a convenient approximation of the real demand function with integer values. Naturally the value of $d(p)$ has to be large to vindicate the approximation.

We assume in this section that the marginal cost of producing one unit of service is constant and equal to γ, $\gamma > 0$. Thus $C(q) = \gamma q$ is the cost of producing q units for any level q.

There are no externalities in production: the cost of producing the unit I consume is not affected by how many other agents consume at the same time. Therefore free access to

---

4. The argument is identical in the output-sharing model where each agent may contribute at most one unit of productive input (e.g., labor) and has a certain opportunity cost/disutility for doing so. See examples 6.2 and 6.5, and exercise 6.9. In that model constant returns means that any unit of input increases the output by the same amount.

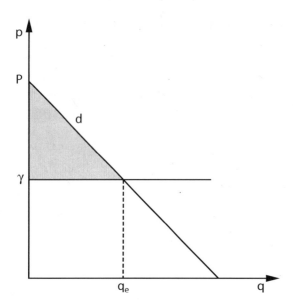

Figure 6.2
Constant returns to scale

the technology entails no inefficiency, no tragedy: every agent can buy service at price γ; those with valuation greater than γ do buy, and the others do not. An agent with valuation p ends up with a net surplus $(p - \gamma)_+ = \max\{p - \gamma, 0\}$. And $d(\gamma)$ units of the good are produced, which is the efficient production level. The efficient surplus σ_e is the shaded area on figure 6.2:

$$q_e = d(\gamma), \quad \sigma_e = \int_{\gamma}^{P} d(x)\,dx = \int_{0}^{q_e} (d^{-1}(y) - \gamma)\,dy$$

where P is the largest valuation in the demand profile, namely the lowest price at which the demand vanishes. The free access equilibrium is the compelling fair outcome of the constant returns economy. This is an important postulate on which rests Locke's argument of natural rights:

Though the earth and all inferior creatures be common to all men, yet every man has a property in his own person; this nobody has any right to but himself. The labour of his body and the work of his hands, we may say, are properly his. Whatsoever then he removes out of the state that nature hath provided and left it in, he hath mixed his labour with, and joined to it something that is his own, and thereby makes it his property. It being by him removed from the common state nature hath placed it in, it hath by this labour something annexed to it that excludes the common right of other men. For this labour being the unquestionable property of the labourer, no man but he can have a right to what that is once joined to, at least where there is enough and as good left in common for others.

Because returns are constant, after an agent uses the technology, he leaves "enough and as good in common for others"; therefore it is fair to let the agent "mix his labour" with the technology and "annex what he removes" from this usage. Put in different words, the cost function is additive; hence the cost share that should be imputed to one who receives q units of output is exactly $\gamma \cdot q$. Each agent is allowed to *stand alone* with the technology and derive whatever surplus he can by paying for his own demand; the resulting surplus shares exhaust the efficient surplus. We call this canonical outcome the stand-alone solution of the constant returns problem.

The stand-alone solution offers a convincing resolution of the "slavery of the talented" in example 3.9, once we normalize the input provided by agent i as $\tilde{x}_i = s_i x_i$, namely the product of his labor by his productivity. The technology is then $f(\tilde{x}_1, \tilde{x}_2) = \tilde{x}_1 + \tilde{x}_2$, and agent i's utility is $u_i = \min\{z_i, 20 - \tilde{x}_i/s_i\}$. The stand-alone solution eliminates the "talent externality" entirely.

The subject of this chapter is the management of a commons of which the marginal cost function is *not* constant. Then the Lockean argument collapses because an agent standing alone does not leave "enough and as good" for the other users.

All examples discussed below have returns to scale either decreasing at every level or increasing at every level. The three same solutions are discussed in both cases.

6.3   Fair Compensation: Three Interpretations

In our first example, the technology has increasing marginal costs of a very simple type: the marginal cost of the first 40 units is zero and that of any additional unit is infinite. In other words, we have 40 free goods and a demand for more than 40 goods. We provide three different answers to the question: What monetary compensation is fair for those who do not get a good?

Example 6.4 Free Goods   There are 100 agents each of whom wants at most one object, and their willingness to pay is uniformly spread between $0 and $100. So there are $d(p) = 100 - p$ agents who value the object at p or above.[5]

We must share 40 "free" objects among our 100 agents. The technology has zero marginal cost for the first 40 units and infinite (or at least greater than 100) marginal cost for any additional units.

---

5. The discrete version of the model has 100 agents with valuations $1, 2, \ldots, 100$, and a demand function shaped like a staircase; the continuous approximation makes all computations simpler without any loss of substance.

A simple example is the allocation of tickets for a popular sports event: 40 free tickets must be allocated among the 100 members of a club. Instead of distributing them randomly, one wishes to give them to the 40 agents with the highest valuation (those willing to pay $60 or more), provided that the other members are fairly compensated. Many other examples of rationing come to mind: seats in overbooked planes, license to broadcast in congested airwaves, repair services in limited supply, and so on.

Thus the problem is formally similar to the fair distribution question of section 2.2, where one has to divide resources in limited supply among agents with different "claims" over the resources. Here, however, the willingness to pay for an object is not interpreted as a claim: it is a measure of the surplus generated by giving an object to the agent in question. Efficiency alone says that if Ann's valuation/willingness to pay is higher than Bob's, she should receive an object before Bob gets one. Yet the claims of Ann and Bob over the resources are identical, which is why it is fair to compensate Bob when he gets no object.[6]

The first solution relies on the important test called no envy. Once objects are allocated and cash transfers are performed, the "lot" of an agent is either made of an object and a cash payment t or no object and a cash transfer t'. "No envy" says that no agent strictly prefers any other agent's lot to his own. The combination of efficiency and the no envy test determines the entire allocation. Indeed, all efficient agents above 60 must pay the same amount t (lest some of them be envious) and similarly all agents below 60 receive the same check for t'. Applying no envy between an efficient agent i just above 60 and an inefficient one j just below 60 gives[7]

i does not envy $j \Rightarrow 60 - t \geq t'$

j does not envy $i \Rightarrow t' \geq 60 - t$

hence $t + t' = 60$. Combined with budget balance, $40t = 60t'$, this gives $t' = 24$ and $t = 36$.

To interpret this solution, consider the competitive price $p_e = 60$ which must be charged for the demand to be equal to the supply (at 40 units). The competitive profit is $r = p_e \cdot q_e = 2,400$, and our solution divides r equally among all participants. Thus an agent below 60 gets a check for $r/100$, whereas one above 60 pays the competitive price p_e minus a rebate $r/100$, or $60 - 2,400/100 = 36$.

---

6. Despite the difference in interpretations, it is perfectly reasonable to apply formally the three basic solutions of chapter 2—the proportional, uniform gains, or uniform losses. It turns out that the first two solutions must be dismissed on normative grounds (explained in exercise 6.17), but the third, under the name of the virtual price solution, plays a central role below.

7. Here the continuous approximation is helpful to bring a unique solution. See exercise 6.4 for some examples with a finite set of agents.

The solution is called the *competitive equilibrium with equal incomes* (in short, CEEI). Its various generalizations, discussed below and in the next chapter, play a central role in the microeconomic analysis of fair division. Their common salient property is the no-envy test: once the lots are formed, no one can complain against her own lot because, according to her own preferences, she gets the best lot.

The CEEI solution treats the commons (the 40 objects) as a competitive firm and the agents as its stockholders, receiving equal shares of the profits when firm behaves competitively. An agent who has no interest in the goods being allocated (his valuation is zero) receives nevertheless a "rent," a positive share of the surplus created by the other agents. Thus a critical requirement to implement the CEEI is to monitor carefully who is entitled to the rent, as this entitlement is unrelated to the ability to derive some surplus from using the resources. The herb story in the next paragraph makes this point clear. We will see that the other two solutions, on the contrary, link the amount of my compensation to my own stand-alone benefit from the resources. Unlike CEEI, these solutions are compatible with an open membership policy.

Think of a rare herb growing only in the public land of a certain community and from which an effective drug against insomnia can be concocted. There is a limited supply of the herb so that we can only produce enough drug to treat 40 percent of the population. Everyone suffers from insomnia but to various degrees: agent p spends currently $\$p$ on alternative drugs with the same effect as one unit of the herb (assume there are 40 indivisible stems of herb). The CEEI solution gives the same \$24 dividend to all agents below 60, not distinguishing between those near 60 to whom it is barely inefficient to give the scarce drug and those near zero who have almost no use for the drug. To drive the point home, imagine that 40 agents do not suffer from insomnia while the 60 others have valuation uniformly spread between 40 and 100, so the demand function d is truncated below $p = 40$ as shown on figure 6.3b. The CEEI solution is not affected by the change, and the 40 agents who do not care for the herb at all get a "rent" that many would find objectionable, say if the herb cannot be sold for profit (it cannot be transported and must be consumed on the spot). On the other hand, if the explanation for a higher willingness to pay is the fact that agent p is a pharmacist who makes $\$p$ from selling one unit of herb, then the stockholder interpretation of the CEEI solution makes good sense. For comparison, citizens of an oil-rich country get a rent from the fact that some of them exploit the oil, and citizenship is an exogenous right independent of oil consumption. In section 6.6 we discuss two other undesirable features of the CEEI solution, namely failures of monotonicity when either the resources or the set of participants change.

The *virtual price solution* is defined by the property that every agent enjoys the same net surplus as if she was offered to buy an object at the common virtual price p_v. Thus agent p ends with the net surplus $(p - p_v)_+ = \max\{p - p_v, 0\}$. This price is $p = 20$ in our example

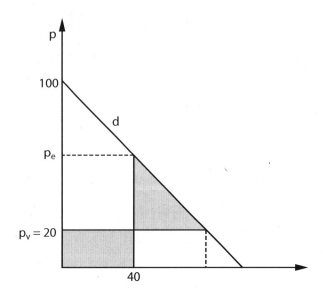

Figure 6.3a
Virtual price solution in example 6.4

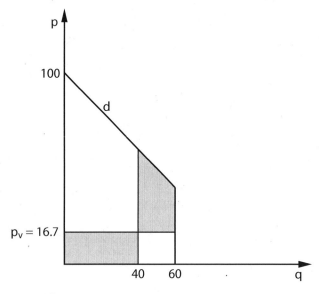

Figure 6.3b
Virtual price solution with truncated demand

(see below); hence only the agents willing to pay $20 or more get a positive benefit from the commons: the others are excluded entirely.

In order to compute p_v, we rely on the efficiency constraint, implying that the integral of $(p - p_v)_+$ over all agents equals the efficient surplus in the economy:

$$\int_0^{100} (y - p_v)_+ \, dy = \int_{p_v}^{100} (y - p_v) \, dx = 3{,}200$$

$$\Leftrightarrow \frac{(100 - p_v)^2}{2} = 3{,}200 \Leftrightarrow p_v = 20$$

See figure 6.3a. Notice the formal similarity with the uniform losses solution of section 2.2: everyone suffers the same loss from the utility level where the object is offered for free, except for the fact that no one suffers a net loss.

Thus the 40 efficient agents pay $20 each for their object (a 44 percent price cut from the CEEI solution), whereas the 40 agents between 20 and 60 are compensated by a personalized check for $(p - 20)$, ranging between $40 and zero. Agents below 20 receive nothing.

The VP solution interprets fairness as the option to either buy the object at the common price p_v or receive a check equivalent to this option. The virtual price is computed by a budget balance argument: the money collected by charging p_v to the 40 efficient agents pays exactly for compensating the inefficient agents above p_v. Thus $p_v = 20$ in our initial example, but with the truncated demand of figure 6.3b there are fewer inefficient agents above the virtual price. As a result the latter is smaller at $p'_v = 16.7$ (exercise: check this number).

Denying any share of the surplus to a low agent (one in [0, 20]) runs counter to the Lockean postulate that common ownership of the resources implies an equal right to consume them. Think of the default option where the 40 objects are randomly allocated among the 100 agents so each agent has a 40 percent chance of receiving an object. The surplus share $(0.4) \cdot p$ is agent p's "fair share" at the default option. To guarantee this share of surplus to every agent is to allow everyone to enforce the default option if he is not satisfied with the proposed solution.

The CEEI solution clearly guarantees his or her fair share to every agent, but the VP solution does not:

CEEI: $p \geq 60 \Rightarrow p - 36 \geq (0.4)p, \quad p \leq 60 \Rightarrow 24 \geq (0.4)p$

VP: $p \geq 33.3 \Rightarrow p - 20 \geq (0.4)p \quad$ but $\quad 33.3 > p > 0 \Rightarrow (p - 20)_+ < (0.4)p$

Our third solution is the Shapley value of the stand-alone game (section 5.4) associated with our production economy. This solution strikes a neat compromise between CEEI and

VP, a fact that remains true for all commons with decreasing returns.[8] The *Shapley solution* allocates a positive share of surplus to any agent with a positive valuation p, which is at least his fair share $(0.4)\,p$. However, this share goes to zero as p does, and an agent with zero valuation gets nothing.

Recall from chapter 5 that agent p's surplus share is her expected marginal surplus $v(S \cup \{p\}) - v(S)$, where v denotes the stand-alone surplus and S is the (random) coalition of agents preceding p, when each one of the 100! orderings of our agents is drawn with equal probability $1/100!$ Thanks to the law of large numbers, the computation of the Shapley shares is not difficult. We note first that $v(S \cup \{p\}) - v(S) = p$ whenever S contains less than 40 agents, which occurs with probability 40 percent. Therefore the Shapley solution guarantees her fair share $(0.4)p$ to agent p for all p. If S contains $100 \cdot \lambda$ agents, with $\lambda \geq 0.4$, its 40th highest agent has valuation $100 - (40/\lambda)$, because the agents in S are uniformly distributed between 0 and 100. Therefore the contribution of agent p to $v(S)$ is $(p - (100 - (40/\lambda))_+$. The fraction λ is uniformly distributed over $[0, 1]$, so agent p's expected surplus share is

$$\sigma_s(p) =$$

$$
\begin{cases}
(0.4)p + \displaystyle\int_{0.4}^{1} \left(p - 100 + \frac{40}{\lambda} \right) d\lambda = p - 23.35 & \text{if } 60 \leq p \leq 100 \\[4mm]
(0.4)p + \displaystyle\int_{0.4}^{40/(100-p)} \left(p - 100 + \frac{40}{\lambda} \right) d\lambda = 40 \log \left(\frac{100}{100 - p} \right) & \text{if } 0 \leq p \leq 60
\end{cases}
$$

Now the Shapley solution charges \$23.35 to an efficient agent (who gets a good) and gives a check (and no object) to an inefficient agent p. The check value increases with p, from 0 at $p = 0$ to \$36.65 at $p = 60$. Note that if p is close to zero, the check value is approximately $(0.4)p$, the fair share of surplus.

Figure 6.4 depicts the surplus function $\sigma(p)$ for the three solutions just discussed. It makes the general point that the Shapley solution is a compromise between CEEI and VP, both for low valuation and high valuation agents and for most agent in between.

Example 6.5 Example 6.2 Revisited   In example 6.2 the demand is homogeneous, meaning that all agents have the same valuation: hence fairness reduces to equal treatment of equals, and the \$15,000 of surplus should be split equally among all villagers (one hundred of them send their cow to the pasture for a fee, all others receiving an equal cash payment).

We consider now a heterogeneous population of 300 villagers, with different opportunity cost for sending their cows to the commons. An opportunity cost ρ means that a cow left at

8. See section 6.6.

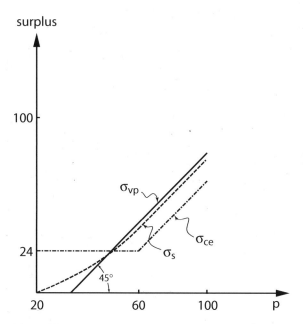

Figure 6.4
Surplus distribution of the three solutions

home would get ρ units of grass. We assume that ρ is uniformly spread between 0 and 300: there are $s(\rho) = \rho$ agents with opportunity cost at or below ρ for all ρ, $0 \leq \rho \leq 300$. Note that s is the familiar microeconomic supply function of the cow input. Figure 6.5 depicts the supply function along with the marginal return function, equal to 250 for the first 100 units and zero afterward.

Efficiency requires the villagers to send the 100 cows with the lowest opportunity cost to the commons while leaving the others at home, for a total surplus $\sigma_e = \$20{,}000$ (the area $Oabc$ on figure 6.5).

The CEEI solution hinges upon the "competitive" price $p_e = 150$, namely the price that must be charged in order to bring about the efficient supply of 100 cows: the return of each cow is $\rho_e = 250 - p_e = 100$, and there are exactly 100 villagers with opportunity cost at or below \$100. The competitive profit $r_e = p_e \cdot q_e = \$15{,}000$ is split equally among the 300 stockholders, who receive \$50 each: this is a rebate for the 100 efficient villagers, who end up paying \$100 each for using the commons and enjoying a return $250 - 100 = 150$; the remaining 200 inefficient users receive a check for \$50. Note that the 50 agents for whom the commons is useless no matter with whom they share it (those with opportunity cost between 250 and 300) get a rent from their share of ownership: applying the CEEI

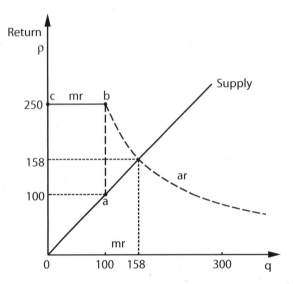

Figure 6.5
Cost and demand in example 6.5

solution requires the villagers to monitor membership carefully lest any number of illegal agents show up.

One strong point in favor of CEEI is its easy implementation when information about the supply (or demand) function is dispersed. Say that each villager knows his own valuation ρ but not (or not precisely) that of other villagers. The social planner ignores everything about the demand but knows the technology of the commons: she knows that 100 cows are enough to eat all the grass. To achieve the CEEI solution, she simply asks each agent to report/bid how much he is willing to pay for using the commons. The 100 highest bidders are allowed on the commons, and the 100th highest bid is denoted $\bar{b}$: the 100 winners pay $\overline{2b}/3$ each and the 200 losers receive a check for $\$(\bar{b}/3)$ each. A remarkable strategic property of this bidding game is in first approximation that the simple truthful bid is an equilibrium: an agent with opportunity cost ρ bids $b = 250 - \rho$.[9] We say that the CEEI solution is *strategy-proof*.

Before computing the virtual price solution, we compute the free access equilibrium. When q cows are grazing on the commons, each cow has a return of 250 if $q \leq 100$, and

---

9. Once each agent bids truthfully, the winning bid is $\bar{b} = 150$, and the first losing bid is 149. Thus a winner can only gain 67cts by bidding just above 149, which in first approximation is negligible. Alternatively, we may charge to each one of the 100 highest bidders only the 101th highest bid, which would eliminate completely their incentive to misreport, and preserve the profile of cash transfers of the CEEI in first-order approximation.

25,000/q if $q \geq 100$. For a return x, the supply (number of villagers willing to use the commons for this return) is x. Thus the free access equilibrium supply q_{fa} solves

$$\frac{25,000}{q} = q \Longleftrightarrow q_{fa} = 158$$

Here the commons is overcrowded by 58 percent, and the first 158 villagers get a return of 158 and a net surplus of $158 - \rho$. Others get nothing. Total surplus collected in the FA equilibrium is $\sigma_{fa} = q_{fa}^2/2 = 12,500$ or 61.25 percent of the efficient surplus $\sigma_e = 20,000$.

In the virtual price solution, each agent ends up *as if* the commons had a constant return equal to $250 - p_v$, where p_v is the virtual price. Thus the surplus share of agent ρ is $(250 - p_v - \rho)_+$ and the virtual price p_v is chosen so that these shares exhaust the efficient surplus $\sigma_e = 20,000$:

$$\int_0^{300} (250 - p_v - x)_+ \, dx = \sigma_e \Longleftrightarrow \frac{(250 - p_v)^2}{2} = 20,000 \Longleftrightarrow p_v = 50$$

An efficient agent ρ, $0 \leq \rho \leq 100$, gets a return of 200 for sending his cow to the commons; an agent ρ, $100 \leq \rho \leq 200$, gets a check for $200 - \rho$. Any agent above 200 gets no benefit at all from the commons.

The important and general fact is that at the VP solution and FA equilibrium the surplus distribution is *as if* the returns were constant and equal to, respectively, 200 for VP and 158 for FA. The VP solution is thus a straight Pareto improvement of the FA outcome: every agent active in the free access regime (every ρ below 158) gets a boost of \$42.

The VP solution gives no surplus whatsoever to an agent above 200, even though those between 200 and 250 can claim some share of surplus if their equal right to consume the resources is recognized. This Lockean argument was already introduced in example 6.4. Here the default option is to allow only 100 cows randomly selected on the commons, and a fair share of access is a 33.3 percent probability of getting a return of 250. The fair share of surplus for agent ρ is $(250 - \rho)_+/3$. The VP solution does not give that much to many inefficient agents:

$$(200 - \rho)_+ < \left(\frac{250 - \rho}{3} \right)_+ \Leftrightarrow 175 < \rho < 250$$

As in example 6.4, the Shapley solution strikes an appealing compromise between VP and CEEI. Recall that the surplus share of agent ρ is his expected marginal contribution to the stand-alone surplus of the set of agents preceding him. The trick to compute it is, again, the law of large numbers. Fix an agent ρ and let λ, $0 \leq \lambda \leq 1$, be the fraction of the total population of 300 villagers preceding this agent in the random order. By the law of large numbers, the distribution of opportunity costs within these $300 \cdot \lambda$ (random) villagers is a homothetic reduction of the initial distribution. Thus there are $s_\lambda(x) = \lambda x$ of them with opportunity cost below x.

Distinguish two cases. If $\lambda < 0.4$, fewer than 100 of the agents before ρ are using the commons, as $s_\lambda(250) < 100$. Therefore agent ρ's contribution to surplus is $(250 - \rho)_+$. If $\lambda \geq 0.4$, the commons are fully utilized before ρ and the highest opportunity cost of an active agent is $100/\lambda$, as $s_\lambda(100/\lambda) = 100$. In this case, agent ρ's contribution is therefore $((100/\lambda) - \rho)_+$. Our agent dislodges the marginally efficient agent $100/\lambda$ if his opportunity cost ρ is lower.

We compute agent ρ's surplus share, using the fact that λ is uniformly distributed on $[0, 1]$:

$$
\sigma_s(\rho)
$$
$$
= \begin{cases}
\displaystyle\int_0^{0.4} (250 - \rho)\, d\lambda + \int_{0.4}^1 \left(\frac{100}{\lambda} - \rho\right) = 191.6 - \rho & \text{if } 0 \leq \rho \leq 100 \\[2mm]
\displaystyle\int_0^{0.4} (250 - \rho)\, d\lambda + \int_{0.4}^{100/\rho} \left(\frac{100}{\lambda} - \rho\right) d\lambda = 100 \log\left(\frac{250}{\rho}\right) & \text{if } 100 \leq \rho \leq 250 \\[2mm]
0 & \text{if } 250 \leq \rho.
\end{cases}
$$

All inefficient agents who would use the commons if standing alone—meaning that $100 \leq \rho \leq 250$—receive a check that decreases from 91.6 to 0 as ρ raises from 100 to 250. This check is always bigger than their fair share $(250 - \rho)/3$.

All efficient agents get a return of 191.6—or equivalently they each pay \$58.4 to use the commons, slightly higher than \$50 at the VP solution but much lower than \$100 at the CEEI one. These comparisons are reversed for the completely inefficient agents $250 \leq \rho \leq 300$, who get a check of \$50 under CEEI, and nothing at VP or Shapley. Moreover one checks easily that all agents ρ, $152 \leq \rho \leq 250$, strictly prefer the CEEI check for \$50 to the Shapley check of $\$100 \log(250/\rho)$ and the latter to VP check of $(200 - \rho)_+$.

*6.4 Free Access versus Random Priority: Decreasing Returns

We noted in example 6.5 that the CEEI solution is strategy-proof. The bidding game described there is called the *revelation* game where everyone reports his or her willingness to pay for using the common and the allocation is the CEEI solution at the reported demand function. This game is incentive compatible; that is to say, no one is tempted to misreport his valuation or opportunity cost. This is true as a first-order approximation when the number of participants is large. It holds true for any technology, with increasing or decreasing returns, and for any demand function.

On the other hand, neither the revelation game of the VP solution nor that of the Shapley solution are incentive compatible. Consider example 6.5. Under VP, an inefficient agent ρ receives a check $200 - \rho$, or no check if $\rho \geq 200$. Clearly, it pays to underreport one's opportunity cost. An agent above 200 can report an opportunity cost just above 100 and get a check for almost \$100 instead of no check. All inefficient agents have the same incentive, so the reported demand function ends up with all inefficient agents lumped just above 100 and the virtual price climbs to $\bar{p}_v = 100$, namely the solution of

$$\int_0^{100} (250 - \bar{p} - x)\, dx + 200(250 - \bar{p} - 100) = \sigma_e = 20,000$$

The VP outcome after strategic manipulation is exactly the CEEI outcome for the true demand function: each efficient agent pays \$100 to use the commons and all others receive a check of $250 - p_v - \bar{\rho} = \$50$ as an inefficient agent reports $\bar{\rho} = 100$!

The direct revelation game of the Shapley solution brings about precisely the same incentives: every inefficient agent pretends to be barely inefficient; others can't manipulate further. The resulting outcome is, again, the CEEI solution of the true demand game.

If the VP solution can't be implemented as a direct revelation game, it is nevertheless "subimplemented" by the free access game. The surplus of agent ρ in the equilibrium of the FA game is $(158 - \rho)_+$, versus $(200 - \rho)_+$ in the virtual price solution. Thus the VP solution is a straight Pareto improvement above the FA equilibrium. In this example the FA equilibrium allocation implies a surplus loss of 38.75 percent, but we give other examples below where the surplus loss is much smaller: examples 6.6 and 6.8.

The free access game is simple to play and its equilibrium easy to predict. It automatically eliminates the agents who have little or no use for the commons: participation in the FA game can be "open," because only the agents most interested in using the commons will show up. Compared with the CEEI bidding/revelation game, where being allowed to participate implies a rent (case of decreasing returns) or a tax (case of increasing returns: section 6.5), irrespective of one's willingness to use the commons, it is either a windfall or a burden. In both cases the set of legal participants must be set exogenously and carefully monitored.

The *random priority* game is another simple mechanism to manage the commons. The agents are ordered randomly (with uniform probability on all orderings) and offered successively to use the commons at the current marginal cost (or return). The lucky agents (those who are drawn early) face a low marginal cost (or a high marginal return), but the deal offered to successive agents becomes less and less attractive as more and more agents accept the offer.

We observed earlier that in the pasture story of example 6.2 with homogeneous demand (all agents have the same valuation) the free access equilibrium dissipates the entire surplus, whereas the random priority equilibrium is first best efficient: 100 villagers chosen at random are offered a return of 250, which they all accept, and no further access is allowed (i.e., the next agents are offered a marginal return of zero). This obervation generalizes to any decreasing returns commons where all agents are identical (same willingness to pay or same opportunity cost). The FA equilibrium brings zero surplus, whereas the RP equilibrium captures the efficient surplus.

As a strategic game, random priority is as simple to play as the free access game: an agent can't affect the price he is offered (that price is determined by how many other agents accepted their offer earlier), and he accepts it if and only if this deal is advantageous for him. Hence the equilibrium prediction of RP as compelling as that of FA, or of the CEEI bidding game. From the welfare point of view, the key property of the RP game is to subimplement the Shapley solution in the same sense as we speak of the FA game subimplementing the VP solution.

We compute the equilibrium outcome of the random priority game in example 6.5. The 300 agents are randomly ordered, and the first ones are offered a return 250 for their cow until 100 agents accept, after which the return falls to zero. Obviously the 50 agents between 250 and 300 always refuse and the others always accept. In this way the efficient quantity 100 is produced. Moreover agent ρ, $0 \leq \rho \leq 250$, gets the surplus $250 - \rho$ with probability $100/250 = 40$ percent, so his expected share is $100 - (0.4)\rho$. Total surplus collected is:

$$\sigma_{rp} = \int_0^{250} (100 - (0.4)x)\, dx = 12{,}500$$

Although this surplus is the same as that collected at the FA equilibrium,[10] its distribution is much different. As in the Shapley solution, all "active" agents who benefit from the commons when standing alone (all ρ, $0 \leq \rho \leq 250$) receive a positive share of surplus.

In order to prove our claim that the Shapley solution is Pareto superior to the random priority outcome, we can check directly the inequalities:

$$100 - (0.4)\rho \leq 191.6 - \rho \qquad \text{for } 0 \leq \rho \leq 100$$

$$100 - (0.4)\rho \leq 100 \cdot \log \frac{250}{\rho} \qquad \text{for } 100 \leq \rho \leq 250$$

Alternatively, we can fix an arbitrary ordering where S is the set of agents preceding agent ρ, and check that ρ's marginal contribution $v(S \cup \{\rho\}) - v(S)$ is not smaller than his net surplus when all agents in S have been offered a slot before him.

---

10. The property is preserved when we retain the asssumptions of a linear supply function and a constant return up to the capacity; see exercise 6.9.

Our next example is a canonical cost-sharing problem with linearly increasing marginal cost and linearly decreasing demand. We compute and compare the two pairs FA equilibrium/VP solution, and RP equilibrium/Shapley solution.

Example 6.6 Mining Nuggets   We have 100 agents, each of whom wants at most one nugget of gold. The number of agents willing to pay p or more is $d(p) = 100 - p$. So the demand is the same as in example 6.4; that is, the individual valuations are spread uniformly between 0 and 100.

The marginal cost increases linearly with the quantity produced: $mc(q) = 2q/3$. For example, the 30th unit costs $20. Thus total cost of producing q units is $q^2/3$, and the average cost is $ac(q) = q/3$.

The mineral nuggets are buried at various depths. The cost of digging a nugget at depth q increases linearly with q, and we assume that the number of nuggets at depth q is independent of q. Hence we have the cost function above.

The efficient amount of digging is $q_e = 60$, since at the price $p = mc(60) = 40$, the demand is $d(p) = 60$. The efficient surplus is $\sigma_e = \$3,000$: this is the area OAB on figure 6.6.

Our two mechanisms FA and RP correspond to two natural regimes of property rights. In the free access regime the mine is exploited by a central (not for profit) agency that takes the orders of its members (each member can only order one nugget or nothing at all) and splits the cost equally among all buyers.

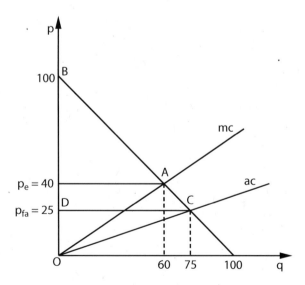

Figure 6.6
Cost and demand in example 6.6

The random priority regime allocates the property rights on a "first come first serve" basis: the first agent to "discover" the mine can dig the easiest and obtain a nugget at marginal cost $mc(1)$, the next agent can get a nugget with the next cheapest effort at $mc(2)$, or $mc(1)$ if the first agent decided not to dig, and so on. The exploitation of the commons under RP requires a lighter monitoring structure than under FA: the agency simply draws a random ordering and enforces the corresponding priority.[11] No collection of costs are involved for the active participants.

In the free access equilibrium an agent seeking one nugget pays the average cost $ac(q)$, where q is the total demand. Thus the equilibrium quantity is found at the intersection of the demand and average cost functions: the quantity produced is $q_{fa} = 75$, since $ac(75) = 25$ and $d(25) = 75$. Relative overproduction in the free access regime is 25 percent. The surplus collected in the FA outcome is the area BCD on figure 6.6:

$$\sigma_{fa} = \int_0^{75} ((100 - y) - 25)\, dy = 2,812$$

or a modest 6.25 percent relative surplus loss.

We compute next the VP solution. The virtual price p_v is defined by the property that giving $(p - p_v)_+$ units of surplus to agent p, for all p, exhausts the efficient surplus:

$$\int_{p_v}^{100} (p - p_v)\, dp = 3,000 \iff \frac{(100 - p_v)^2}{2} = 3,000 \iff p_v = 22.5$$

At the VP outcome, all efficient agents (above 40) get an object and pay 22.5. An agent p, $22.5 \leq p \leq 40$, receives a check for $\$(p - 22.5)$, and agents below 22.5 get not surplus at all. Thus the gain from the FA outcome to the VP solution is \$2.5 for all agents active at the FA equilibrium.

Given that the relative surplus loss by the FA outcome is only 6.25 percent, we conclude that the FA mechanism implements the VP solution at a small and uniform cost for every agent.

We turn to the RP equilibrium where the agents are randomly ordered and agent p is offered to buy a nugget at a price $mc(q)$, with q being the number of agents ranked before p who accepted their (better) offer. The computation relies, as usual, on the law of large numbers.

Consider the first $100 \cdot \lambda$ agents randomly drawn. Their valuations are uniformly spread between 0 and 100. In other words, their demand function is $d_\lambda(p) = \lambda.d(p) = \lambda.(100 - p)$. Let $q(\lambda)$ be the expected number of agents who have accepted their offer among the 100λ

---

11. In addition to this normative interpretation, the RP mechanism can also be viewed as a stylized rendering of the race for preferential access to the commons where success in the race bears no statistical relation to willingness to pay. If it did, this would make the outcome closer to efficiency.

first agents. The next $100 \cdot \varepsilon$ agents drawn get an offer $mc(q(\lambda)) = 2q(\lambda)/3$ (as ε is very small, we can neglect the small increase of $q(\lambda)$). The fraction of those who accept is $d(2q(\lambda)/3)/100$, since the demand of the remaining $100 \cdot (1 - \lambda)$ agents is just $(1 - \lambda)d$. Therefore the variation of $q(\lambda)$ is governed by the equation

$$dq(\lambda) = \left(100 - \tfrac{2}{3}q(\lambda)\right) d\lambda \qquad \text{and } q(0) = 0$$

The solution of this differential equation is

$$q(\lambda) = 150.(1 - e^{-2\lambda/3}) \qquad \text{for } 0 \leq \lambda \leq 1$$

so that the RP equilibrium output is $q_{rp} = q(1) = 73.0$.

Thus in the RP regime, the relative overproduction is only 21.6 percent over the efficient level. On the other hand, the computations below show that the surplus collected at the RP equilibrium is $\sigma_{rp} = 2,761$ or 8 percent of relative surplus loss, slightly bigger than in the FA regime.

We compute the surplus $\sigma_{rp}(p)$ accruing to agent p. If agent p is drawn after a fraction λ of the initial population, she will buy the good if $p \geq mc(q(\lambda))$ and decline otherwise, so that her expected surplus is

$$\sigma_{rp}(p) = \int_0^1 (p - mc(q(\lambda)))_+ \, d\lambda = \int_0^1 (p - 100(1 - e^{-2\lambda/3}))_+ \, d\lambda$$

$$\Longleftrightarrow \sigma_{rp}(p) = p - 27.0 \qquad \quad \text{if } \frac{2}{3}q_{rp} = 48.7 \leq p \leq 100 \tag{1}$$

$$\sigma_{rp}(p) = \frac{3}{2}p + \frac{3}{2}(p - 100) \log \frac{100}{100 - p} \quad \text{if } 0 \leq p \leq 48.7$$

Finally we compute the Shapley solution and compare it to the RP equilibrium outcome. In the Shapley solution, agent p receives his expected marginal contribution to the stand-alone surplus of the agents preceding him in a random ordering of the initial population of 100 agents. Suppose that a fraction λ of the population precedes agent p. By the law of large numbers, the demand of these $100 \cdot \lambda$ agents is $d_\lambda(p) = \lambda \cdot (100 - p)$; hence their efficient output level (when standing alone) q_λ is as follows:

$$\lambda \left(100 - \frac{2}{3}q_\lambda\right) = q_\lambda \Longleftrightarrow q_\lambda = 100\frac{\lambda}{1 + 2\lambda/3}$$

Agent p's contribution to this coalition is $(p - 2q_\lambda/3)_+$: he replaces a marginally efficient agent if his valuation is above $2q_\lambda/3$; otherwise, he adds no extra surplus. Because the fraction λ is uniformly distributed over $[0, 1]$, we deduce agent p's surplus $\sigma_s(p)$ under the Shapley solution:

$$\sigma_s(p) = \int_0^1 \left(p - 100 \frac{2\lambda/3}{1 + 2\lambda/3} \right)_+ d\lambda$$

$$\iff \sigma_s(p) = p - 23.4 \qquad \text{if } 40 \le p \le 100 \, (p \text{ is efficient}) \tag{2}$$

$$\sigma_s(p) = 150 \log \frac{100}{100 - p} - \frac{3}{2}p \quad \text{if } 0 \le p \le 40$$

Comparing formulas (1) and (2), one can check directly that the Shapley solution is Pareto superior to the RP equilibrium. A general argument is sketched in section 6.6.

The third solution, CEEI, is much easier to compute. Recall that it is defined by the property of no envy combined with efficiency. All efficient agents pay the same price $\bar{p}$ and all inefficient agents receive the same cash compensation $\bar{t}$.

We start by charging the efficient price $p_e = 40$ to all efficient agents and giving no money to the inefficient agents. There is no envy because everybody who wants the good at that price gets it and no one else does. The money collected exceeds the cost of producing q_e units; the difference is the competitive profit:

$$r = p_e q_e - C(q_e) = 40 \cdot 60 - 1{,}200 = \$1{,}200$$

It is split equally among all agents. Therefore $\bar{p} = 28$ and $\bar{t} = 12$. The surplus function σ_{ce} is

$$\sigma_{ce}(p) = p - 28 \quad \text{if } 40 \le p \le 100$$

$$\sigma_{ce}(p) = 12 \qquad \text{if } 0 \le p \le 40 \tag{3}$$

Upon comparing formulas (2), (3) and $p_v = 22.5$, we can check a general feature of commons with decreasing returns: CEEI is best for low, inefficient agents and worst for efficient agents; VP is best for efficient agents and worst for low inefficient ones; and the Shapley solution strikes a compromise between VP and CEEI at both ends of the demand function. See section 6.6 for a general statement. In example 6.6, as in example 6.5 above, efficient agents even prefer either one of the FA or RP equilibrium outcome to the CEEI solution. This is not a general property as discussed in exercise 6.15.

6.5   Increasing Returns

When marginal costs decrease (or marginal returns increase) the problem of the commons runs into new difficulties. One aspect, discussed in the next paragraphs, is the relative fragility of the random priority mechanism relative to the free access mechanism. Another

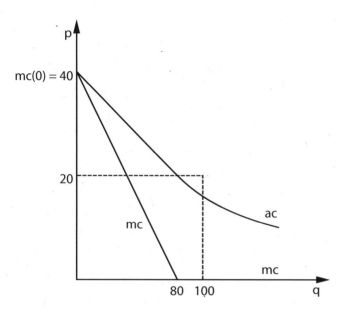

Figure 6.7
Increasing returns and homogeneous demand

aspect is the new interpretation of our three efficient solutions, illustrated in examples 6.7 and 6.8.

Consider the simple case of a homogeneous demand of output (or supply of input). This cost-sharing problem has, for instance, each one of the 100 agents willing to pay the same amount \$20 for service. In figure 6.7 are drawn a decreasing marginal cost function, and the associated average cost function. The important facts are $ac(100) < 20$ and $mc(0) = ac(0) > 20$. Because of the former inequality, it is efficient to serve all agents (with total surplus $2{,}000 - C(100)$). Because of the latter inequality, the random priority mechanism never takes off, as no one accepts to buy the first unit at the initial marginal cost.

The free access game, on the other hand, has two equilibrium outcomes. In the bad equilibrium noone demands the good; if an agent changes his mind, he must pay $ac(1)$, greater than his valuation. In the good equilibrium, everyone gets the good and pays $ac(100)$: this is both efficient and fair. The good equilibrium is uniformly preferred to the bad equilibrium, and will occur if the agents are able to coordinate their actions: the suggestion "do buy because everyone is doing so" will be followed if one believes that others are following it; hence the good outcome is self-enforcing.

Recall that in the case of increasing marginal costs, if the demand is homogeneous (as in example 6.2), the RP equilibrium is *the* fair and efficient outcome, whereas the FA equilibrium overproduces to the point of dissipating the whole surplus. Now the picture is completely reversed, and the random priority regime is totally ineffective because no agent is willing to pay the high marginal cost $mc(0)$. The same problem arises in our next example where no agent alone can afford to pay the initial fixed cost.

However, if the high valuation agent is ready to pay for the highest marginal cost, the efficiency losses of our two mechanisms are not too different: for instance, with a homogeneous demand, both RP and FA yield the fair and efficient outcome. Another instance is example 6.8 below, where both equilibrium outcomes lose only 4 to 5 percentage points of the efficient surplus.

Example 6.7 Fixed Cost Commons with decreasing marginal costs are often called natural monopolies because efficiency commands to operate only one production process, in contrast with the case of increasing marginal costs where one should use as many copies of the technologies as are available. Every technology requiring to pay a large fixed cost before it can be operated is of the decreasing marginal cost type—at least for low levels of output. An example is the production of most technologically advanced commodities: software, new drugs, and a bus system require a large development cost followed by low variable costs of usage.

Our numerical example is a technology with a fixed cost of $1,800. This cost must be paid before any production takes place, and a marginal cost of $10 per unit:

$$C(q) = 1,800 + 10q \qquad \text{for any } q > 0$$

As in examples 6.4 and 6.6 there is one hundred potential users, and their willingness to pay is uniformly spread between 0 and 100. So the demand function is $d(p) = 100 - p$. Efficiency commands them to serve the 90 agents above 10 (as usual we identify an agent and his willingness to pay), because the surplus from the constant returns exceeds the fixed cost:

$$\int_{10}^{100} (100 - x)\, dx = 4,050 > 1,800 \iff \sigma_e = 2,250$$

The CEEI solution is especially simple in this example. It charges $10 for service, hence collecting $900 from the 90 efficient agents; then the fixed cost is equally split among *all* potential users, efficient or not. Thus each agent above 10 ends up paying $28 for service, and the 10 agents below 10 pay a *tax* of $18 and receive no service.

The CEEI is strategy-proof precisely because the tax is blind. An efficient agent who pretends that he is inefficient (i.e., below 10) still pays $18 and gets no service; an inefficient agent p pretending he is efficient does not reduce his own tax. As in the decreasing returns case, the CEEI solution is characterized by the no-envy property *plus* efficiency: ignoring the $18 tax, which does not create envy because it is uniform, everyone faces the same offer to buy service for $10.

The CEEI solution forces the inefficient agents to pay a tax for which they get nothing in return. Therefore an open membership policy would kill it: all agents below 28 would quietly disappear, forcing the solution to charge $35 to each one of the 72 agents above 28 (total cost being $1,800 + 720$), which in turns drives away 7 more agents and raises the price to $37.7, and so on, until the free access equilibrium is reached with the 60 agents above 40 paying $40 each (more below on the FA equilibrium).

Monitoring the membership of the commons is as crucial for the CEEI solution under increasing returns as it was under decreasing returns, but for symmetric reasons. The potential users must be forced to stay and pay their share of tax in the former case, and to keep outsiders from showing up to get a piece of subsidy in the latter case.

Financing the fixed cost of a bus or subway system from the general tax budget, while asking its users to pay marginal cost, is routinely taken to be the correct fiscal policy. It is fully efficient and arguably fair as a tool for macroeconomic redistribution, since obviously a public transportation system creates positive externalities on all residents, whether or not they use it. The argument is weaker for subsidies to an opera house or a sports arena; hence the CEEI solution is much less compelling in that case. A solution offering a net welfare loss to some of the participants is outright unacceptable for the microproblems of distributive justice that are the focus of this book. Voluntary participation is the most important feature of the contractarian approach (sections 1.5), whether we view it as a positive property (no one will sign a private contract that amounts to a surplus loss) or a normative one (no public contract should exploit a citizen to the advantage of others).

The free access and random priority games guarantee voluntary participation because everyone has the option to "stay out." In the presence of a fixed cost, the RP mechanism is utterly ineffective, as no single agent is willing to pay the entire fixed cost (one order of magnitude above any individual valuation), so nothing is every produced. The FA mechanism, on the other hand, has a bad (Pareto inferior) equilibrium where no one buys service, and a good equilibrium where the 60 highest agents buy service at the average cost $ac(60) = 40$. Figure 6.8 depicts the two intersections of the demand and average cost curves (the graphs of d and of ac) at $q = 30$ or $q = 60$. Notice that $q = 30$ is not a FA equilibrium because a small deviation, by a single agent or a few agents, precipitates an irreversible shift away from the initial allocation. By contrast, $q = 60$ or $q = 0$ is robust to small deviations increasing or decreasing the number of buyers.[12]

---

12. Starting from the allocation where the 30 highest agents buy and pay $ac(30) = 70$, suppose that agent 30—who is indifferent between buying or not—drops out. Now $ac(29) > 71$, so the agent 71 wishes to drop out too, and so on. Symmetrically, if we add agent 31 to the buyers, the new price is $ac(31) = 68$, and buyer 32 wishes to join as $ac(32) = 66.25 < 68$, and so on. By contrast, it is easy to check that a small deviation away from the $q = 60$ equilibrium is not destabilizing.

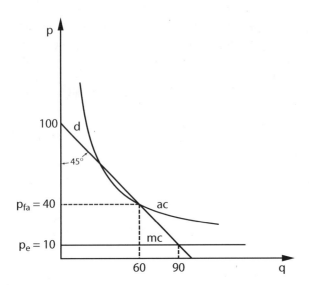

Figure 6.8
Cost and demand in example 6.7

The good FA equilibrium underproduces by 33 percent, as $q_{fa} = 60$ and $q_e = 90$. Underproduction is a general feature of the FA mechanism under increasing returns.[13] For efficiency we would like more users to join, but by voluntary participation, we cannot charge the same price $ac(90) = 30$ to all 90 efficient users. The FA surplus is $\sigma_{fa} = \int_{40}^{100} (100 - x)\, dx = 1,800$, hence a relative efficiency loss of 20 percent.

In any efficient allocation where participation is voluntary, the inefficient agents don't pay anything, nor do they deserve to be paid since their contribution to the total surplus, and to the stand-alone surplus of any coalition, is nil. On the other hand, the barely efficient agents, between 10 and 30, can't pay their share $ac(90)$ of total cost, so they must get service at a discount rate.

The virtual price solution does this, but it denies any share of surplus to the agents who get a discount rate. Compute the virtual price p_v in the usual fashion: agent p gets a surplus share $(p - p_v)_+$, as if she were offered to buy service at price p_v. Efficiency of the surplus distribution gives p_v as the solution of

$$\int_{p_v}^{100} (100 - x)\, dx = \sigma_e \Leftrightarrow \frac{(100 - p_v)^2}{2} = 2,250 \Leftrightarrow p_v = 32.9$$

---

13. The same is true of the RP equilibrium whenever this game entails positive production, as in our next example.

Thus p_v is smaller than the FA equilibrium price $ac(q_{fa}) = 40$, and as usual, the VP solution is a Pareto improvement of the FA equilibrium. Among the 30 agents (between 10 and 40) that become active when we go from the FA to the VP outcome, more than three-quarters (between 10 and 32.9) do not get any positive share of surplus: these agents pay their full willingness to pay for service. In the VP solution, getting service at a discount rate is no reason to rejoice!

The VP solution is hard on the barely efficient agents. One could argue normatively that it is hard to deny them any share of the surplus, since they pay more than the marginal cost of \$10 by which other agents benefit from their presence (they pay a fraction of the fixed cost). In a positive vein, we predict that securing the participation of a marginally efficient agent is difficult: he can bring a loss of surplus upon others at no cost to himself, a credible threat that he may use to his advantage.

The Shapley solution is, once again, the more reasonable of the three, as it gives a positive share of surplus to every efficient agent, and none to every inefficient one.

An inefficient agent gets no surplus because, as noted earlier, he is a dummy: the stand-alone surplus of any coalition is the same with or without our inefficient agent.[14] It turns out that an efficient agent p gets a share of surplus proportional to $p - 10$. To check this, let $\lambda, 0 \le \lambda \le 1$, be the fraction of the population preceding agent p in a random ordering. As usual, the law of large numbers says that the demand function of these 100λ agents is λd. The stand-alone surplus of these agents is zero if and only if

$$\int_{10}^{100} \lambda(100 - x)\, dx < 1,800 \Leftrightarrow \lambda < \frac{4}{9}$$

In this case the single agent p cannot reverse the sign of the inequality, because his own contribution $(10 - p)$ to the fixed cost is negligible with respect to the remaining deficit. So the stand-alone surplus remains zero after he joins.

For $\lambda \ge 4/9$, the agents preceding p have already paid for the fixed cost; hence p's marginal contribution is $p - 10$. We conclude that the Shapley share of surplus is $\sigma_s(p) = (5/9)(p - 10)$.

Figure 6.9 illustrates the distributions of surplus proposed by our three solutions. Notice that the Shapley solution is no longer a compromise between VP and CEEI for the extreme values of p. For any p above 74, the Shapley solution is the least favorable of the three, and for $10 \le p \le 63$ it is the most favorable. The bias of the Shapley solution is toward a more egalitarian distribution of surplus. See section 6.6 for a general statement.

---

14. This property always holds under increasing returns.

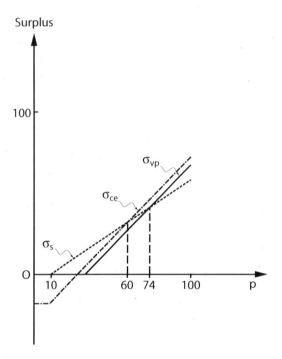

Surplus

100

σ_{vp}

σ_{ce}

σ_s

O

10   60 74   100   p

Figure 6.9
Surplus distribution in example 6.7

The random priority mechanism fails to collect any surplus in this example, whereas the free access equilibrium subimplements the virtual price solution with a 33 percent efficiency loss.

In fact a fairly modest increase of the fixed cost, from $1,800 to $2,100, makes the FA mechanism as ineffective as that of the RP. To illustrate, an FA equilibrium with a positive output level q is found at the intersection of the graphs of the demand and average cost functions:

$$d(ac(q)) = q \Leftrightarrow 100 - \left(\frac{2,100}{q} + 10 \right) = q$$

but the right-hand side equation has no solution. Clearly, the only FA equilibrium is $q = 0$, where no one buys anything.

The key advantage of the RP and FA mechanisms is decentralized strategic behavior of the participants: every potential user chooses to buy service or not without any knowledge of the particular valuations of their fellow agents. In the FA game, all I need to know to make my decision is the current average cost of production (or average return), namely a one-parameter index of the profile of individual valuations (the demand function). In the RP game, I do not need to know even that, because the price I am offered when my turn comes is a one-time offer that I can't influence. Therefore I can instruct a machine (or a central agency overseeing the game) to accept an offer below p and reject one above p; my best choice is to set p equal to my valuation (my best strategy is to reveal truthfully my preferences) regardless of the rest of the demand function.

When truly decentralized games such as FA or RP fail, the only recourse of the mechanism designer is to set up a game in which the agents have a strong incentive to discover the particular demand profile in which they are living, and use this information strategically. Such mechanisms can be constructed to implement practically any efficient solution one can think of. They are realistic only among a small number of potential users who know each other well, much less so in problems involving dozens of agents or more. Exercise 6.16 proposes one such game to implement the virtual price solution. An even more complicated mechanism is required to implement the Shapley solution.

Our last example is the counterpart of the "linear" example 6.6 for the increasing returns economy: here the marginal and demand functions cost decrease linearly. It turns out that both the FA and RP equilibrium outcomes perform very well in this problem.

Example 6.8 Airwave Interferences   In a residence with 100 apartments, each resident may or may not buy a device to eliminate the interferences on his wireless phone. Once a unit is equipped with the device, its own emissions cease to affect the other residents, thus reducing the cost of the device they need to buy. If q residents have already bought the device, the cost of the device meeting the needs of the next one is

$$mc(q) = 40 - \frac{q}{3} \qquad \text{for all } q, \ 0 \le q \le 100$$

thus decreasing linearly from \$40 for the first customer to \$7 for the last one.

The demand function, as in examples 6.4, 6.6, and 6.7, is $d(p) = 100 - p$: for every $p = 1, \ldots, 100$ there is exactly one agent willing to pay \$$p$ for a line free of interferences; see figure 6.10.

The implementation of the free access mechanism is the same as in example 6.6: the agency collects orders and splits the cost among the subscribers. That of the random priority mechanism requires an agency endowed with more coercive power than under increasing returns. In addition to drawing a random ordering of the potential users, the agency must also prevent the agents from declining to buy in the first rounds but reentering later

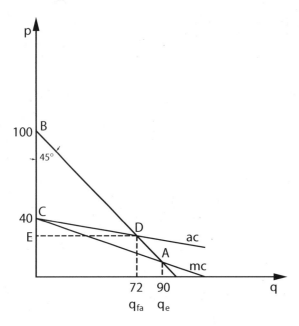

Figure 6.10
Cost and demand in example 6.8

when the marginal cost has dropped. The offer made to any one agent must be credibly final.

The free access equilibrium is computed at the intersection of the demand and average cost functions:

$$d(ac(q)) = q, \qquad \text{where } ac(q) = 40 - \frac{q}{6} \Rightarrow q_{fa} = 72$$

Here the FA equilibrium is unique: the zero output is not an equilibrium because a number of agents want to buy at the highest price of $40.

The welfare performance of the FA equilibrium is visualized by figure 6.10, showing the efficient output level $q_e = 90$ (point A) and the efficient surplus $\sigma_e = \$2,700$ (area ABC). The FA equilibrium produces 20 percent under the efficient level, but collects $\sigma_{fa} = \$2,592$ (area BDE), an efficiency loss of only 4 percent.

In order to compute the RP equilibrium, we proceed as in example 6.6. The key is the number $q(\lambda)$ of agents who have accepted their offer among the first 100λ agents. The agents drawn immediately after these are offered the price $mc(q(\lambda))$; hence they will accept with probability $d(mc(q(\lambda)))/100$, and the equation governing $q(\lambda)$ is

$$dq\,(\lambda) \;=\; \left(60 + \frac{q(\lambda)}{3}\right)d\lambda \quad \text{and} \quad q(0) = 0$$

$$\Rightarrow q(\lambda) = 180(1 - e^{\lambda/3}), \qquad 0 \le \lambda \le 1 \Rightarrow q(1) = q_{rp} = 71.2$$

The output level under RP is within 1 percent of that under FA.

The RP surplus is computed as follows: if y units have been sold so far (thus $100\,q^{-1}(y)$ agents have been drawn), the next unit is allocated with uniform probability among all agents above $mc(y)$. Thus the average surplus generated by this unit is

$$\int_0^{d(mc(y))} (d^{-1}(z) - mc(y))\,dz \;=\; \frac{\int_{mc(y)}^{100} d(x)\,dx}{d(mc(y))} \;=\; \frac{1}{2}\left(60 + \frac{y}{3}\right)$$

$$\Rightarrow \sigma_{rp} = \int_0^{q_{rp}} \frac{1}{2}\left(60 + \frac{y}{3}\right)dy = 2{,}559$$

The RP surplus is lower than that of the FA, but by less than 1.5 percent, and its loss, relative to the efficient surplus, is only 5.2 percent. We conclude that the welfare performances of our two mechanisms are excellent and practically identical.

Exercise 6.11 computes the surplus distribution of these two equilibrium outcomes, and of the three canonical solutions, VP, Shapley, and CEEI.

*6.6   Axiomatic Comparison of the Three Solutions

In this final section we compare the CEEI, VP, and Shapley solutions by means of three simple axioms of equity. The fair share axiom imposes a bound of individual surplus; the population and resource monotonicity[15] properties speak about two simple changes in the parameters of the problem.

We derive first the general formulas for the surplus distribution recommended by our three solutions.

Computing and Comparing the Solutions

We start with a general commons with an increasing marginal cost function mc and a decreasing demand function d as in figure 6.11a, where the competitive profit $r = p_e q_e - C(q_e)$ is the shaded area. All three solutions charge the competitive price p_e to each efficient

---

15. Resource monotonicity was discussed earlier in example 2.9 and section 3.5.

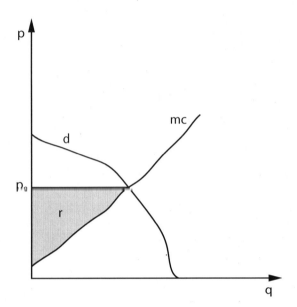

Figure 6.11a
Efficient production: Increasing marginal costs

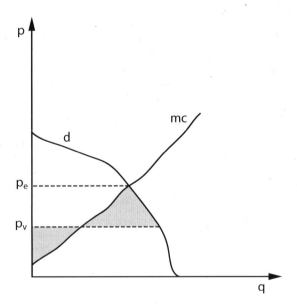

Figure 6.11b
Virtual price solution

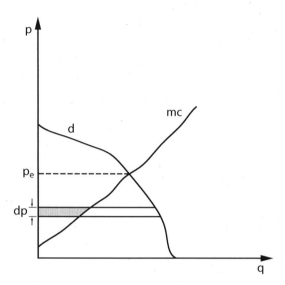

Figure 6.11c
Computing the Shapley solution

user, then use the budget surplus r to give a rebate to efficient users and a cash compensation to some inefficient users.

The CEEI solution divides r equally among all $d(0)$ legal beneficiaries of the commons, including those below $mc(0)$. The rebate of an efficient user equals the check received by all inefficient ones.

The VP solution cuts through r as shown on figure 6.11b so as to give an actual rebate $p_e - p_v$ to each efficient user, and a smaller check $p - p_v$ to the inefficient users above p_v. The virtual price p_v is the solution of

$$\int_{p_v}^{p_e} d(x)\, dx = r$$

Denoting by p_{fa} the average cost at the FA equilibrium—at the intersection of the demand and average cost—the following inequalities bound the virtual price p_v:

$$ac(q_e) < p_v < p_{fa} < p_e$$

The proof is left as an exercise for the reader.

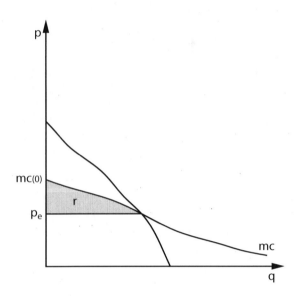

Figure 6.12a
Efficient production: Decreasing marginal costs

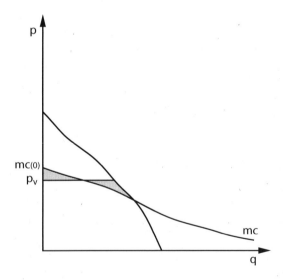

Figure 6.12b
Virtual price solution

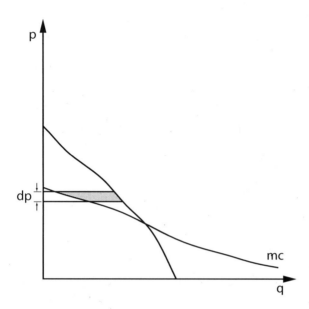

Figure 6.12c
Computing the Shapley solution

The Shapley solution divides the "slice" of r at level p equally among all agents above p; see figure 6.11c. Thus the rebate of agent p is as follows:

efficient agent, $p \geq p_e$:   rebate $\displaystyle\int_{mc(0)}^{p_e} \frac{mc^{-1}}{d}(x)\,dx$

$$(4)$$

inefficient agent, $p_e \geq p \geq mc(0)$:   cash $\displaystyle\int_{mc(0)}^{p} \frac{mc^{-1}}{d}(x)\,dx$

The rebates awarded to the efficient agents are ranked as follows:

$$\frac{r}{d(0)} < \int_{mc(0)}^{p_e} \frac{mc^{-1}}{d}(x) < p_e - p_v \tag{5}$$

so that an efficient agent always prefers VP over Shapley and the latter over CEEI; see exercise 6.14 for a proof of (4) and (5). On the other hand, it is easy to see that an agent just above $mc(0)$ prefers CEEI over Shapley over VP.

The case of decreasing marginal costs depicted on figure 6.12 yields similar computations. The competitive deficit $r = C(q_e) - p_e q_e$ is depicted on figure 6.12a.

The CEEI solution splits r equally among the $d(0)$ participants: the surcharge $r/d(0)$ paid by every efficient agent equals the tax on every inefficient one.

The virtual price p_v cuts through r as shown on figure 6.12b:

$$\int_{p_e}^{p_v} d(x)\,dx = r$$

An efficient agent above p_v pays a surcharge $p_v - p_e$ above p_e, efficient agents between p_v and p_e pay exactly their valuation for the good, and inefficient agents get no transfer. As in the decreasing returns case, the virtual price is bounded between the efficient average cost and the FA equilibrium price:

$$p_e < ac(q_e) < p_v < p_{fa}$$

Finally the Shapley solution divides the p–slice of r equally among all agents above p; see figure 6.12c. Thus the price paid by an efficient agent between p_e and $mc(0)$ increases with p. Their surcharge above p_e is computed as follows:

$$p \geq mc(0): \quad \text{surcharge} \int_{p_e}^{mc(0)} \frac{mc^{-1}}{d}(x)\,dx$$

$$mc(0) \geq p \geq p_e: \quad \text{surcharge} \int_{p_e}^{p} \frac{mc^{-1}}{d}(x)\,dx \tag{6}$$

Inefficient agents get no transfer whatsoever.

The comparison of the surcharges to the efficient agents yields only two systematic comparisons:

$$\frac{r}{d(0)} < p_v - p_e, \quad \frac{r}{d(0)} < \int_{p_e}^{mc(0)} \frac{mc^{-1}}{d}(x)\,dx \tag{7}$$

Efficient agents prefer CEEI to both VP and Shapley but their preferences over the latter two can go either way. On the other hand, barely efficient agents (just above p_e) always prefer Shapley over VP and the latter over CEEI; see exercise 6.14.

Fair Share

The concept of *fair share* for a potential user of the commons was introduced in examples 6.4 and 6.5. Its general formulation is as follows: say an agent p is one among n potential users of the commons. Imagine a homogeneous demand where *all* n agents have valuation p, and compute the corresponding surplus σ: agent p's fair share is precisely σ/n.

The fair share is what an agent receives in a hypothetical profile where everyone else shares this agent's preference. In a commons with *decreasing* returns (e.g., examples 6.4, 6.5, and 6.6) it is feasible and normatively appealing to use agent p's fair share as a *lower bound* on her actual share of surplus. The argument is as follows: if every other person entitled to the commons were identical to me (i.e., had the same preferences), I would receive my fair share of surplus (by equal treatment of equals and by efficiency). The difference between my actual share and my fair share is therefore caused by the heterogeneity of our preferences. If this heterogeneity affects me negatively and someone else positively—in the sense that I get less than my fair share whereas he gets more than his fair share—the situation is discriminating against my preferences, which is unfair.

The requirement that his fair share of surplus be guaranteed to each potential user of a decreasing returns commons is the main critique of the virtual price solution. On the other hand, both the CEEI and Shapley solutions guarantee every agent's fair share. This point was already made in examples 6.4 and 6.5; exercise 6.13 provides a general argument.

We turn to an increasing returns common, where the fair share of agent p is similarly defined as the per capita surplus in the hypothetical economy made up of n clones of agent p.

Consider example 6.7. With 100 agents willing to pay p for their good, the efficient outcome consists of producing 100 units if the benefit $100(p - 10)$ exceeds the fixed cost 1,800, namely if $p \geq 28$, and of not producing at all otherwise. Hence agent p's fair share of surplus is $fs(p) = (p - 28)_+$. But this time it is *not* feasible to guarantee the surplus share $fs(p)$ to every agent p. To see this, we compare the surplus σ_{vp} in the VP solution to the fair share:

$$\sigma_{vp}(p) = (p - 32.9)_+ < (p - 28)_+ = fs(p) \quad \text{if } 28 < p \leq 100$$

$$\sigma_{vp}(p) = 0 = fs(p) \qquad\qquad\qquad\quad \text{if } 0 < p \leq 28.$$

The VP solution is efficient; hence our claim that guaranteeing $fs(p)$ to every agent p is not feasible. This computation reveals an important and systematic difference between the cases of increasing and decreasing returns to scale: in the latter the heterogeneity of individual preferences is a source of mutual benefits; in the former it forces a loss of surplus. Formally, the surplus distribution $fs(p)$ is feasible under decreasing returns and unfeasible under increasing returns. In the latter case a sensible normative requirement is to use the fair share $fs(p)$ as an *upper* bound on agent p's net surplus: every agent must bear a share of the negative externality created by the heterogeneity of preferences.

In example 6.7 this upper bound rules out a positive surplus share for all agents below 28, a property met by the VP and CEEI solutions but not by Shapley. When we combine the fair share upper bound with voluntary participation, ruling out a negative surplus share for any agent, we find that inefficient agents must get no cash transfer, and that all efficient agents between 10 and 28 must pay their full valuation p: thus these two axioms point very clearly toward the VP solution.

The fact that VP and CEEI meet the fair share upperbound and Shapley does not, holds true for any d and any decreasing mc: exercise 6.13.

Population and Resource Monotonicity

The property of population monotonicity is closely related to the stand-alone test of section 4.4. Consider, to fix ideas, a commons in the costsharing format (as in examples 6.4, 6.6 to 6.8). The stand-alone surplus is a subadditive function when marginal costs increase, and a superadditive function when marginal costs decrease. This follows easily from the fact that the cost function is superadditive in the former case, and subadditive in the latter.[16] Therefore the stand-alone test applied to any coalition S requires that the total surplus allocated to S be no larger (resp. no smaller) than its stand-alone surplus when marginal costs increase (resp. decrease).

Our first observation is that the CEEI solution violates the stand-alone test in both cases. In the superadditive case, it gives a rent to some agents with low valuation who are unable to extract any surplus when standing alone to use the commons. See the discussion of examples 6.4 and 6.5.

Symmetrically, in the subadditive case, the CEEI solution levies a tax on all inefficient agents, of whom the stand-alone surplus is zero. This violates the stand-alone test which is equivalent to voluntary participation for these agents; see example 6.7.

The VP and Shapley solution, on the other hand, meet the stand-alone test. They even satisfy a more demanding property called *population monotonicity*. In the superadditive case, one more agent to share the commons is bad news: by consuming the good, she raises the average cost of serving the others. Symmetrically one more agent is good news in the subadditive case because she will lower the average cost (e.g., in example 6.4 she can bear a share of the fixed cost). This suggests the following normative requirement, where we denote by $\sigma(p, N)$ the surplus share of agent p under a certain solution σ when N is the set of potential users of the commons:

superadditive cost/increasing marginal cost case:

$$N \subseteq N' \Rightarrow \sigma(p, N) \geq \sigma(p, N')$$

subadditive cost/decreasing marginal cost case:

$$N \subseteq N' \Rightarrow \sigma(p, N) \leq \sigma(p, N')$$

---

16. Superadditivity is the property $C(q_1 + q_2) \geq C(q_1) + C(q_2)$ and subadditivity is the opposite inequality.

It is clear that population monotonicity implies the stand-alone test (in both cases). Fix a coalition S in N and sum up the inequalities $\sigma(p, N) \geq \sigma(p, S)$ over all p in S. By efficiency of σ, the right-hand sum is the stand-alone surplus of S.

The virtual price and Shapley solutions are both population monotonic. This is easy to check for the VP solution, for any demand and marginal cost function.

In the superadditive case, the virtual price p_v is smaller than the efficient price $p_e = mc(q_e)$.[17] Moreover the contribution of a new agent p to the efficient surplus is approximately $(p - p_e)_+$, where p_e is the efficient price of the initial population N. If the virtual price remains the same or decreases as a result of the new entry, the surplus distributed by the VP solution will increase by at least $(p - p_v)_+$, contradiction. The argument is similar in the subadditive case. The proof that the Shapley solution is population monotonic is more involved.[18]

Finally we discuss *resource monotonicity*. It requires every agent to benefit (or at least not to suffer) where the commons improve in the sense that the marginal cost function decreases or stays put (at every level of output). Technological progress that reduces some marginal costs can only increase the efficient surplus, and resource monotonicity says that every individual agent gets a share of this bounty.

Somewhat surprisingly, the CEEI solution is not resource monotonic. In example 6.4 we distribute 40 free goods among 100 agents and every inefficient agent receives a check for \$24, or one-hundredth of the competitive profit $p_e \cdot q_e = 60 \cdot 40$. When the number of free goods doubles to 80, the competitive surplus decreases to $20 \cdot 80 = \$1,600$, and so does the check of the 20 agents below 20.

The violation of resource monotonicity is equally easy to demonstrate in the increasing returns case. Consider example 6.7 where the CEEI solution imposes a tax of \$18 on every inefficient agent (below 10). When the fixed cost increases above \$4,050 (or when the marginal cost increases above 40), it becomes inefficient to produce anything, and no one is taxed anymore, which is good news for these 10 agents.

The VP solution is resource monotonic. When the resources increase, the efficient surplus increases as well. Hence the virtual price must decrease, and the surplus $(p - p_v)_+$ of any given agent p increases or stays put.

The Shapley value is resource monotonic as well. Let S be the coalition of agents preceding a certain agent p in a random ordering of N, and let p_0 be the efficient price for coalition S standing alone. Then agent p's marginal contribution to S is $(p - p_0)_+$. When

17. Exercise: Why?

18. It is a consequence of the property of super- or submodularity of the stand-alone surplus game; see chapter 7 in Moulin (1995).

the marginal cost function decreases, the efficient price of S standing alone decreases (or stay put). Hence agent p's marginal contribution to S can only go up or remain constant.

The following table summarizes the axiomatic discussion:

	CEII	Virtual price	Shapley
Decreasing returns			
Fair share guarantee	Yes	No	Yes
Population monotonicity	No	Yes	Yes
Resource monotonicity	No	Yes	Yes
Strategy-proofness	Yes	No	No
Open membership	No	Yes	Yes
Increasing returns			
Fair share upper bound	Yes	Yes	No
Population monotonicity	No	Yes	Yes
Resource monotonicity	No	Yes	Yes
Strategy-proofness	Yes	No	No
Open membership	No	Yes	Yes

6.7   Introduction to the Literature

The tragedy of the commons goes back to Aristotle and Adam Smith. Its modern formulation—and its name—is due to Hardin (1968).

The literature is split by the distinction between decreasing and increasing returns. On the former, the discussion centers on the overexploitation of exhaustible resources—Dasgupta and Heal (1979) and Ostrom (1991)—and on the management of congestion externalities. On the latter, the central notion is that of a natural monopoly. The efficient organization of production requires to run a single copy of the technology, and the issue is to distribute the cooperative surplus efficiently and fairly. Two basic references are Baumol, Panzar, and Willig (1982) and Sharkey (1982).

The Locke quote at the end of section 6.2 is in Locke (1690).

Sections 6.4 and 6.5 offer a brief discussion of the main themes of mechanism design in the context of our problem. A general reference on implementation theory is Moore (1993). Three recent papers address the implementation of the Shapley value, hence are potentially relevant to the discussion preceding example 6.8: Gul (1989), Hart and Mas-Colell (1996), and Perez-Castillo and Wettstein (2001). The random priority mechanism is introduced by Crès and Moulin (1998).

The axiomatic discussion of section 6.6 is developed with more details in Moulin (2001c).

Exercises to Chapter 6

Exercise 6.1 Restaurant Bill

This restaurant offers three dinner combinations: economy for $10, standard for $15, and deluxe for $25. Everyone orders individually, but the total bill of the party is equally divided among all patrons. The goal of the exercise is to determine whether splitting the bill equally generates a tragedy of the commons. If it does, one wishes to compute the relative efficiency loss. The answer depends on individual preferences = willingness to pay for the different meals, and the number of patrons in the party.

a. A party of 3 identical patrons with the following willingness to pay: economy 16, standard 20, deluxe 29

b. A party of 3 identical patrons with the following preferences: economy 15, standard 20, deluxe 32

c. A party of 4, with preferences as in question a (two patrons) or as in question b (two patrons).

Exercise 6.2 The Traffic Paradox

a. There are two routes between A and B, one through C and one through D; see figure 6.13a. Travel time on the four segments increases with congestion. Let x_k be the number of users of segment k. The corresponding travel time is

$10x_k$ if k is AD or CB

$50 + x_k$ if k is AC or DB

Six commuters must go from A to B and can choose either one of the two roads. A player's only concern is to minimize total travel time. Show that the equilibrium outcome has three agents on each road, and that this outcome is efficient (no tragedy). *Hint:* You can use example 6.3.

b. A road between C and D is now open on which travel time is $10 + x_k$; see figure 6.13b. Show that in the new (unique) equilibrium outcome, two agents follow ADB, two agents follow ACB, and two follow $ADCB$. Show that travel time has strictly increased for everyone! What is the efficiency loss of this "tragedy"?

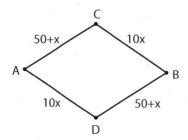

Figure 6.13a
Road network in exercise 6.2a

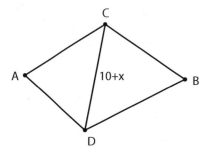

Figure 6.13b
Road network in exercise 6.2b

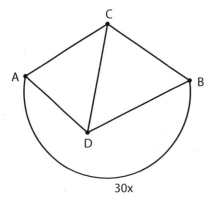

Figure 6.13c
Road network in exercise 6.2c

c. A direct road between A and B is opened on which travel time is $30x_k$; see figure 6.13c. Compute the new unique equilibrium outcome. Do we have a "tragedy"?

*Exercise 6.3 Queuing

A server processes one agent per unit of time (think of queuing at the post office). Each potential user wants one unit of service but dislikes waiting. If he waits for t periods before being served his net utility is $p - t$. Thus he loses one "util" per unit of time in the queue and is willing to wait at most p periods. Agents must choose at time $t = 0$ whether to stay in the queue or not.

a. If q agents choose to stay, the server at each period picks one of the remaining agents at random, and without bias, until the queue is empty. Assume that each agent maximizes her expected utility. Show that the strategic situation is the free access game to a commons with marginal cost $mc(q) = q$ for all $q \geq 0$. Show, in particular, that if an agent's optimal decision is to stay for one period, then she will stay until she gets service: staying in the queue for a few periods and "balking" before receiving service can't be optimal.

b. Now the server draws a random priority ordering of all agents at time $t = 0$ (with uniform probability on all orderings) and serves agents in that order. Each participant decides to stay or balk at time $t = 0$. Show that the strategic situation is the random priority game of section 6.4.

c. Suppose that a large number of agents are willing to wait at most 20 periods for service: each individual valuation p is between 20 and 21. Show that in the free access regime (queuing protocol of question a), the surplus (measured in time savings) is at most 39, whereas the efficient surplus is at least 190.

Give a general formula for a large number of users, each willing to wait the same number of k of periods.

Exercise 6.4 Discrete Variant of Example 6.4

We have five agents with the following willingness to pay for one object:

Ann and Bob: $80

Chris and Dave: $60

Erwin: $10

a. Suppose that three free objects are available. Efficiency commands to give them to Ann, Bob, and either Chris or Dave—say, Chris to fix ideas. Compute the pattern of monetary compensations recommended by our three solutions CEEI, VP, and Shapley.

b. Drop Ann and compute the new set of transfers; check that the CEEI solution is not population monotonic (in some CEEI allocation, Erwin is worse off).

c. Go back to the five agents population of question a, and compute the three solutions when there is exactly one object and when there are five objects; check that the CEEI solution is not resource monotonic.

*Exercise 6.5 Generalizing Example 6.4

Consider first the model of example 6.4 with a continuum of agents. The n agents' willingness to pay are uniformly spread between $\bar{p}$ and 0, so the demand function is $d(p) = n(1 - (p/\bar{p}))$. There are k free objects, $k \leq n$, and we set $k = \lambda n$, so λ is the proportion of agents who can get an object.

a. Show that the efficient agents are those above $(1 - \lambda)\bar{p}$ and that the CEEI solution

charges for an object $\$(1 - \lambda)^2 \bar{p}$ to agent p if $p \geq (1 - \lambda)\bar{p}$

gives $\$\lambda(1 - \lambda)\bar{p}$ to agent p if $p \leq (1 - \lambda)\bar{p}$

Check that this solution fails to be either resource or population monotonic; check that it gives his fair share to every agent.

b. Show that the virtual price p_v is equal to

$$p_v = \frac{(1 - \lambda)^2}{1 + \sqrt{2\lambda - \lambda^2}}\bar{p}$$

Check that the VP solution gives his fair share to every efficient agent but fails to do so for some inefficient ones.

c. Show that the Shapley solution

charges for an object $\$(1 - (1 - \log \lambda)\lambda)\bar{p}$ to agent p if $p \geq (1 - \lambda)\bar{p}$

gives $\$ - \lambda\bar{p}\log(1 - \frac{p}{\bar{p}})$ to agent p if $p \leq (1 - \lambda)\bar{p}$

d. Draw the surplus functions of all three solutions and comment on their distributive consequences.

Exercise 6.6 A Discrete Example with Quadratic Cost

The technology has quadratic costs namely $mc(q) = q$ and total cost $C(q) = 1 + 2 + \cdots + q = q(q + 1)/2$. The queuing model of exercise 6.3 is an example.

We have 25 agents with the following willingness to pay u_i for service:

$u_i = 1.5$ for $i = 1, \ldots, 10$

$u_i = 2.5$ for $i = 11, \ldots, 20$

$u_i = 5.5$ for $i = 21, \ldots, 25$

a. Show that the efficient output is $q = 5$ and that the free access equilibrium is the efficient outcome.

b. By contrast, the random priority equilibrium inefficiently serves some of the 20 inefficient agents with positive probability. To compute exactly the expected quantity produced by, and surplus collected at, the RP equilibrium is not easy. General formulas show that the expected output is $q_{rp} = 7.7$ and that the relative surplus loss is 38 percent.

Show by simple computations that the relative surplus loss under RP is at least 25 percent and the expected output is at least 7.

c. Compute the allocations selected by the CEEI solution. By question a, the VP solution charges \$3 for an object to each efficient agent and ignores the inefficient agents. Show that the Shapley solution is the following allocation:

pay 2 cts to agent i, $i = 1, \ldots, 10$

pay 12 cts to agents i, $i = 11, \ldots, 20$

charge for an object \$3.28 to agents $i = 21, \ldots, 25$

Hint: An agent $p = 1.5$ gets 50 cts of surplus if he is drawn first; otherwise, he gets nothing. An agent $p = 2.5$ gets \$1.00 if he is first among all 25 agents, and an additional 50 cts if he is first among the 15 agents not smaller than 2.5.

Exercise 6.7 Another Discrete Example with Quadratic Cost   Marginal cost is $mc(q) = q$ as in the previous exercise. We have 12 agents and the following profile of valuations for an object:

10, 8, 8, 6, 6, 6, 5, 5, 4, 4, 2, 1

a. Find the efficient output quantity q_e and the efficient surplus σ_e. Note that there are two efficient output levels.

b. Define the CEEI Solution by the properties of efficiency and no envy. Show that there is a *range* of allocations meeting these two properties. Find the one most advantageous to the efficient agents, and the one least advantageous to them.

c. Show that the virtual price p_v is \$3.9.

d. Show that the Shapley solution distributes the surplus as follows:

Valuation	10	8	6	5	4	2	1
Surplus	$5.92	$3.92	$1.92	$1.09	49 cts	9 cts	0

Hint: An agent with valuation 4 gets $1 if he is first among the eleven highest agents *plus* $1 if he is first or second among the ten highest agents, *plus* $1 if he is first, second or third among the same ten agents.

Compare this distribution of surplus to the two distributions under CEEI and VP, and to the profile of fair shares.

Exercise 6.8 A Discrete Example with Decreasing Marginal Costs In each one of the following problems, you must compute the efficient output and surplus, the free access, and random priority equilibrium allocations, as well as the three solutions CEEI, VP, and Shapley.

a. Four agents with valuations 60, 50, 30, and 10. The first k units of the good cost $40, the next units are free. Answer for $k = 1, 2$, or 3. Discuss resource monotonicity.

b. The same technology as in question a, but the valuations of the four agents are now 90, 30, 30, and 10.

c. Eleven agents with valuations $u_1 = 10$ and $u_i = 2$ for $2 \leq i \leq 11$. The first unit of the good costs a, and the rest are free. Discuss according to a.

d. This is a surplus-sharing model where ten agents may or may not supply an output and have the following opportunity cost of doing so:

$$u_i = 3 \text{ for } i = 1, 2, 3, 4$$
$$u_i = 6 \text{ for } i = 5, 6, 7, 8, 9, 10$$

The marginal returns are

$$mr(q) = 0 \qquad \text{for } q = 1, \ldots, k$$
$$mr(q) = 10 \qquad \text{for } q = k + 1, \ldots, 10$$

where k is a fixed parameter. Discuss for $k = 1$, $k = 3$, or $k = 5$. *Hint for Shapley:* Use the slicing technique alluded to in exercises 6.6 and 6.7 and captured by formula (6) when the number of agents is large. Observe that if an interval of prices $[p, p + \delta]$ contains no valuation u_i and no marginal cost $mc(q)$, the slice of surplus $\delta(d(p) - mc^{-1}(p))$ is equally divided among all agents in $d(p)$. Then divide the range of prices relevant to the efficient surplus σ_e in a sequence of such intervals.

Exercise 6.9 Generalization of Example 6.5   The marginal return of the technology is constant and equal to r for the first $\bar{q}$ units of input, and drops to zero afterward.

Each agent can supply one or zero unit of input. There are $s(\rho) = a\rho$ agents with opportunity cost at or below ρ: these agents are glad to work if they are paid more than ρ.

Notice that if $ar \leq \bar{q}$, the problem is essentially one with constant returns as in section 6.2, so that the canonical stand-alone solution is optimal. From now on, assume $\bar{q} < ar$.

a. Compute the free access and random priority equilibrium outcomes. Show that the surpluses σ_{fa} and σ_{rp} are equal and independent of a, and that the relative surplus is at least 50 percent.

b. Compute the three solutions CEEI, VP, and Shapley and draw the corresponding surplus functions.

Exercise 6.10 Generalizing Example 6.7   The cost function $C(q) = \gamma + cq$, for all $q > 0$, has a fixed cost γ and constant marginal cost c. The n agents are uniformly spread between 0 and $\bar{p}$. Hence the demand function $d(p) = n(1 - (p/\bar{p}))$. We assume $\bar{p} \geq c$.

a. Show that the efficient surplus in the absence of any fixed cost ($\gamma = 0$, i.e., constant returns technology) is

$$\sigma_0 = \frac{1}{2}\, n\, \frac{(\bar{p} - c)^2}{\bar{p}}$$

b. Assume $\sigma_0/2 < \gamma < \sigma_0$. Show that the only free access equilibrium is the "zero" outcome, whereas the efficient output is $q_e = d(c)$.

c. Assume $0 \leq \gamma \leq \sigma_0/2$. Show that the Pareto superior free access equilibrium underproduces by 50 percent and loses no more than 50 percent of the efficient surplus:

$$q_{fa} = \frac{1}{2} q_e, \quad \sigma_{fa} \geq \frac{1}{2} \sigma_e$$

Exercise 6.11 Computations for Example 6.8

a. Show that the CEEI solution makes every efficient agent pay $23.50; it also levies a tax of $13.50 on an inefficient agent.

b. Show that the virtual price is $p_v = \$26.50$.

c. Show that the Shapley solution charges $27.00 to every agent above 40. Compute the price it charges to an agent p, $10 \leq p \leq 40$.

Hint: Apply the formulas in section 6.6.

*Exercise 6.12 Improving upon the FA Equilibrium

Consider an arbitrary commons (d, mc) with increasing marginal cost as in section 6.6, depicted in figure 6.11.

The free access equilibrium is p_{fa}, q_{fa} at the intersection of the demand and average cost curves (e.g., point C in figure 6.6). The goal of the exercise is to show a simple Pareto improving move from the FA equilibrium to an efficient outcome.

Starting from the FA outcome, the agents in $[p_e, \; p_a]$ are bribed out of the commons by a payment of $\$(p_e - p_{fa})$ each. This payment is financed equally by all efficient agents, who end up paying

$$p = ac(q_e) + (p_e - p_{fa})\frac{q_{fa} - q_e}{q_e}$$

Show that $p < p_{fa}$ so that every agent active at the FA equilibrium prefers the new outcome (and others see no change). Note that the proposed outcome is easy to implement if we can discriminate between efficient and inefficient agents. However, an agent just below p_e has an incentive to pretend being efficient (just above p_e).

Hint: Show that the above inequality is equivalent to $p_e(q_{fa} - q_e) < C(q_{fa}) - C(q_e)$, and use figure 6.6 to conclude.

*Exercise 6.13 Fair Share Guarantee and Fair Share Upperbound

Fix an arbitrary commons (d, mc) with increasing marginal cost as in section 6.6. Agent p's fair share is the per capita surplus in an economy made of $d(0) = n$ identical clones of agent p:

$$fs(p) = \frac{1}{n} \max_{0 \le q \le n} \{pq - C(q)\} = \frac{1}{n}\{pmc^{-1}(p) - C(mc^{-1}(p))\}$$

a. With the data of example 6.6 compute the fair share function $fs(p)$ and check that it is a lowerbound of the surplus awarded by the CEEI and Shapley solutions. Check that this is not true of the VP solution.

b. Using the formulas in section 6.6, show that the CEEI and Shapley solutions guarantee a fair share of surplus to every agent.

In the decreasing marginal cost case, the definition of the fair share is identical but its computation is different:

$$fs(p) = \frac{1}{n} \max_{0 \le q \le n} \{pq - C(q)\} = (p - ac(n))_+$$

c. With the data of example 6.8, compute the fair share function, and check that it is an upperbound of the surplus awarded under VP and CEEI. This is not true of the Shapley solution.

d. Using the formulas in section 6.6, show that the VP and CEEI solution never give more than a fair share to any agent.

*Exercise 6.14 Proof of Properties (4), (5), (6), and (7)

a. To prove formula (4) for an arbitrary problem (d, mc) where mc increases, we define an auxiliary function g and its inverse f:

$$g(x) = \frac{mc^{-1}(x)}{d(x)} = \lambda \Leftrightarrow x = f(\lambda)$$

When the fraction λ, $0 \le \lambda \le 1$, of the potential users is drawn, the resulting demand is λd, by the law of large numbers, and $x = f(\lambda)$ is the corresponding efficient price. Therefore the surplus distribution of the Shapley value is

$$\sigma_s(p) = \int_0^1 (p - f(\lambda))_+ \, d\lambda = \int_0^{\min\{g(p),1\}} (p - f(\lambda)) \, d\lambda \qquad \text{for } p \ge mc(0)$$

$$= 0 \qquad \text{for } p \le mc(0)$$

Use the change of variable $\lambda \to x = f(\lambda)$ to derive formula (4).

b. To prove inequalities (5), the only difficult part is the right-hand side inequality. Prove first the following inequality and equality:

$$\int_{mc(0)}^{p_v} \frac{mc^{-1}}{d}(x) \, dx \le \frac{1}{d(p_v)} \int_0^{p_v} mc^{-1}(x) \, dx = \frac{1}{d(p_v)} \int_{p_v}^{p_e} (d - mc^{-1})(x) \, dx$$

c. Prove (6) and (7) by similar arguments.

*Exercise 6.15 Comparing the CEEI and FA Outcomes

In an arbitrary commons (d, mc) with increasing marginal cost (section 6.6), prove the following inequality:

$$p_e - \frac{r}{q_{fa}} < p_{fa}$$

Deduce that, depending on the number of inactive agents at the FA equilibrium (i.e., agents below p_{fa}), the efficient agents may prefer their CEEI allocation to their FA allocation, and vice versa.

Next assume that our commons has decreasing marginal costs and prove the inequality

$$p_e + \frac{r}{q_e} < p_{fa}.$$

Deduce that all efficient agents prefer the CEEI solution to the FA allocation.

Exercise 6.16 Implementing the FA Solution

Consider a commons (d, mc), as in section 6.6. It does not matter whether marginal costs increase, decrease, or are arbitrary.

The following mechanism is played in two successive rounds. In the first round each agent independently bids, that is, announces a price Π. One of the lowest bidders is declared winner (it does not matter how the winner is selected in case of ties; for instance one can use a lottery).

In the second round, each nonwinner agent must choose one of two possible allocations: buy one unit of service at price Π^* (where Π^* was the lowest bid in round 1) or get no service and pay nothing. It does not matter in what order the nonwinners make their decisions.

Finally, the winner settles all accounts; namely he chooses whether or not to get one unit of service and pays the (positive or negative) balance generated by his and the other players' decisions. If q nonwinners choose to buy, he must pay $C(q) - \Pi^* q$ or $C(q + 1) - \Pi^* q$ depending on whether or not he himself gets service.

Show that in the equilibrium of this game among agents who know the demand function, every agent bids p_{fa} in the first round and the FA solution is implemented.

*Exercise 6.17 Uniform Gain and Proportional Solutions

In a general cost-sharing problem (d, mc), the proportional solution divides the efficient surplus σ_e in proportion to individual willingness to pay. The uniform gain solution gives a common share of surplus λ or his own valuation for the good, whichever is less, to every agent. These solutions are defined in section 2.2.

a. Show that the surplus functions σ_{pr} and σ_{ug} of these two solutions are as follows:

$$\sigma_{pr}(p) = \mu \cdot p$$

where $\mu = \sigma_e / D(0)$ and $D(0) = \int_0^P d(x)\, dx$,

$$\sigma_{ug}(p) = \min\{\lambda, p\}$$

where $\int_0^\lambda d(x)\, dx = \sigma_e$.

b. Show that neither of these two solutions equals the canonical stand-alone solution in the benchmark case with constant marginal cost.

c. Compute these two solutions in examples 6.4 and 6.6, and compare them to our three main solutions. Check that in example 6.6, the uniform gains solution does not guarantee the fair share of every efficient agent. Construct an example (d, mc) with increasing marginal cost, where the proportional solution also fails to guarantee the fair share of some efficient agents.

d. Under decreasing marginal costs, show that neither the proportional solution nor the uniform gains solution gives his stand-alone surplus to all agents. Use example 6.8.

e. Show that both solutions are resource monotonic.

7 Fair Trade and Fair Division

7.1 Private Ownership and Competitive Trade

The subject of this final chapter is the exchange and distribution of heterogeneous private goods. Some of the solutions discussed below (e.g., the competitive equilibrium with equal incomes) were introduced in chapter 6. There we had a technology producing homogeneous private goods, here there is no production but several heterogeneous commodities. The differences in individual preferences over these private goods create opportunities to trade when the goods are privately owned, and this compels us to distribute unequal individual shares in the fair division problem.

We address successively two central microeconomic questions: Will private ownership of the resources result in a fair and efficient trade? When the resources are the common property of a given community, what does it mean to allocate them fairly and efficiently?

The two questions are clearly related. Indeed, the economist's pet fair division method (answering the latter question in the previous paragraph) simply transforms common ownership into equal privately owned shares, and turns the fair division issue into a special case of the former question.

The central concept is *competitive trade,* namely the decentralized organization of exchange by means of a common signal called the *competitive price* vector. Remarkably the competitive equilibrium allocation is, at the same time, the positive prediction of the outcome of strategic trading under private ownership, and a normative definition of fairness for the allocation resulting from exchange. The positive statement relies on the analysis of the core-stability, to which the sections 7.1 to 7.3 are devoted. The normative interpretation of fairness is the no-envy property introduced in chapter 6, and systematically discussed in sections 7.4 to 7.6.

We take an ordinal viewpoint throughout the chapter. As in chapter 4 the relevant description of individual welfare is an ordinal preference relation comparing bundles of commodities. Any cardinal measurement of utility (chapter 3) is deemed irrelevant and hence omitted from the model. However, the model is not a welfarist one as in chapter 4, because the physical description of individual shares is crucial to the definition of competitive trade, as well as to the normative tests of no envy and egalitarian equivalence.

In terms of the four principles of justice of section 2.1, compensation is entirely absent, since every agent is deemed responsible for his or her preference ordering over the commodities and no one can ask for a larger share on account of a disadvantageous welfare. Reward is similarly irrelevant because the commodities to be exchanged or divided are given as manna form heaven, and individual participants in the trade or division problem are not related to the production of these resources. The two principles at work are thus fitness (in the sense of efficiency) and exogenous rights, the latter taking the form of the private property rights when we discuss trade in the first three sections, or of the less precise notion of common property when the problem is fair division in the last three sections.

We turn to competitive trade. Our first two examples explain the positive and normative interpretations of the competitive exchange allocation: it is a resting point of private contracting given the property rights (core-stability property); competitive trade is fair because no one prefers someone else's net trade to her own (no-envy property).

Example 7.1 Swapping Time Slots   One of the n physicians in this community must be "on call" for each one of the next n weekends. Each doctor will be on call exactly one weekend. Until last year the slots were centrally allocated by the hospital on which they all depend, with doctor i allocated to slot $i, i = 1, 2, \ldots, n$. Swapping was not allowed. This year the hospital manager, after taking a microeconomics class, has decided to allow mutually beneficial swaps; each doctor is entitled to his previous slot but voluntary exchanges involving any number of physicians are now possible.

Consider the following example:

$$\begin{array}{llllllll} \text{Agent} & 1 & 2 & 3 & 4 & 5 & 6 \\ \text{Top choice} & 1 & 1 & 5 & 6 & 3 & 4 \end{array} \tag{1}$$

Note that agents $3, 5$ have a perfect trade, as each owns the slot that the other covets. Similarly agents $4, 6$ have a perfect trade. Finally agent 1 does not want to exchange his slot for any other slot; so agent 2 is unable to improve upon his initial situation and the unique core allocation is

$$\begin{array}{lllllll} \text{Slot} & 1 & 2 & 3 & 4 & 5 & 6 \\ \text{Agent} & 1 & 2 & 5 & 6 & 3 & 4 \end{array}$$

Consider the price of $10 for each one of the slots $1, 3, 4, 5, 6$ and $5 for slot 2. Agent 3 can "buy" slot 5 after selling his own slot (because these two slots have the same price): this is called a competitive trade, because it is of zero net value at the competitive price. Clearly, it is the best competitive trade for agent 3. Conversely, agent 5's optimal trade is to buy slot 3 in exchange of slot 5. Therefore the swap between 3 and 5 is a competitive one. The optimal trades by agents 4 and 6 has them similarly swapping. Agent 1's best competitive trade is to keep his slot. Finally agent 2 cannot exchange her cheap slot for any of the five expensive slots; hence her only competitive trade is no trade.

The money in which we measure prices $10 and $5 is what economists call fiat money, namely a coupon that can be redeemed for a slot of equal or lower value but is otherwise useless (i.e., this coupon cannot be used to buy any other valuable commodity). The only role of prices in this example is to block agent 2 from buying another slot than her own. Any price vector p_i, $i = 1, \ldots, 6$ such that

$$p_3 = p_5, \quad p_4 = p_6, \quad p_2 < p_i, \qquad i = 1, 3, 4, 5, 6$$

leads to the same competitive trade.

Consider next the following pattern of preferences by our six agents over the six slots:

Agent	1	2	3	4	5	6
1st choice	3	3	3	2	1	2
2nd	2	5	1	5	3	4
3rd	4	6	...	6	2	5
4th	1	...		4	...	6
...		...		...		

$$\tag{2}$$

where at most the top four choices of each individual preference matters.

The *top trading cycle* algorithm identifying the unique core-stable allocation works as follows in this example. Draw an arrow from each agent i to the agent denoted $\tau(i)$ who owns agent $i's$ first choice slot:

$$\tau(1) = \tau(2) = \tau(3) = 3, \quad \tau(4) = \tau(6) = 2, \quad \tau(5) = 1$$

Look for a cycle of the mapping τ, namely a subset of agents S such that τ permutes[1] the elements of S. Core-stability requires that the agents in such a cycle swap their slots according to τ. They all end up with their first choice, and the corresponding private contract relies exclusively on their own property rights. In example (2) the only cycle is $\{3\}$, which means that 3 keeps his slot. In example (1), the mapping τ had three cycles, $\{3, 5\}$, $\{4, 6\}$, and $\{1\}$.

Back to example (2), we put aside agent 3 and his slot, and construct the mapping τ anew on the reduced problem (with five agents and five slots):

$$\tau'(1) = \tau'(4) = \tau'(6) = 2, \quad \tau'(2) = 5, \quad \tau'(5) = 1$$

Now the unique cycle is $\{1, 2, 5\}$. Therefore these three agents swap their slots according to τ'. This is, again, a consequence or core-stability. The swapping contract relies on their property rights only, and gives them their best slot, given that slot 3 is not available.

We are left with two agents 4, 6 and their two slots. Both prefer to swap rather than keep their initial slot: $\tau''(4) = 6$ and $\tau''(6) = 4$. This is the third and final cycle, and the

---

1. Namely τ is a bijection of S into itself.

corestable assignment is now entirely determined:

Agent 1 2 3 4 5 6
Slot   2 5 3 6 1 4

To interpret this trade as competitive, we can use any price vector where slot 3 is the most expensive, slots $\{1, 2, 5\}$ share a middle price, and slots $\{4, 6\}$ are the cheapest:

$$p_3 > p_1 = p_2 = p_5 > p_4 = p_6$$

Agent 1 cannot afford to buy slot 3 after selling her own at p_1; her best buy is slot 2. Similarly agent 2's competitive trade is to sell his slot to buy slot 5. And so on it goes.

Exercise 7.2 discusses two more examples of the slot-swapping problem and computes its unique competitive trade by the top trading cycle algorithm.

Our second example is closely related to the model of the commons under increasing marginal costs (chapter 6). The key feature is that the market consists of a large number of small participants, where an agent is small if he or she owns an insignificant fraction of total resources in the market. Under this negligibility assumption, the competitive trade enjoys no less than three additional equivalent definitions: it is the unique corestable allocation; the unique efficient allocation passing the no-envy test; it is also the Shapley value of the stand-alone surplus game (section 5.4).

Example 7.2 Market for a Homogeneous Good   We have 40 "sellers" who each own one unit of a homogeneous "service" and 100 "buyers" who each want at most one unit of service. Each seller can provide the service at no cost: think of a piece of software that can easily be copied. The buyers differ in their willingness to pay for the service: one of them wants to pay, up to $100, the next one $99, and so on. Thus, as in examples 6.4 and 6.6, there are $d(p) = 100 - p$ agents who would make a positive profit by paying $$p$ for the service. As in example 6.4, there are 40 "free" units of the commodity, yet they are not the common property of the buyers as in chapter 6. Each seller owns a specific piece of the technology, and expects to make some profit. The efficient surplus $3,200 is achieved when the 40 most eager buyers—those willing to pay more than $60—are served: How should we divide this surplus between buyers and sellers?

The competitive price $p_e = 60$ is the compelling answer: this is the price at which the supply of 40 units equals the demand. By trading at this price, the 40 sellers receive the surplus share $2,400, whereas the remaining $800 are split unevenly between the 40 buyers with buyer p getting $$(p - 60)$.

The most important difference between this competitive outcome and the three solutions discussed in chapter 6 is that the inefficient buyers (those willing to pay less than $60) receive no share of the surplus. We justify this from three different angles. The simplest explanation is that the competitive allocation treats everyone fairly because it offers the same deal to everyone, buyer or seller: one unit of service can be bought or sold for $60. Thus $p = 60$ plays the role of the virtual price of the last chapter except that it is now a very real price. We say that the overall transaction generates *no envy* either among buyers or among sellers.

A second, and quite subtle, justification of the competitive allocation relies on the Shapley value of the cooperative game involving now 140 players. As in section 5.4 and chapter 6, the stand-alone surplus of a given coalition of sellers and buyers measures the gains from trade within this coalition. For instance, a coalition with no sellers or with no buyers has a zero stand-alone surplus.

We compute the Shapley value of the stand-alone game. If a certain inefficient buyer, say $p = 20$, is drawn second, and the first draw is a seller, our buyer receives his marginal contribution to surplus, $20. The probability of this or any other ordering of the 140 agents where our inefficient buyer receives $20 is, however, very small. By applying the law of large numbers (e.g., as in examples 6.4 and 6.6), we check that the marginal contribution of an inefficient agent is vanishingly small.

When agent p is drawn after a fraction λ of the 140 participants, the 140λ agents preceding him contain, with probability of almost one, 40λ sellers and 100λ buyers, the latter with a demand $d(p) = \lambda(100 - p)$. Therefore in the λ-reduced economy the efficient price is $60, irrespective of λ. Now agent $p's$ contribution to the surplus is $(p - 60)_+ = \max\{p - 60, 0\}$, and we conclude that inefficient agents are not contributing any surplus.

The two arguments above in support of the competitive allocation are normative. The third argument, core-stability, is positive: it relies on the availability of private contracts among any subset of sellers and buyers. An allocation is *stable in the sense of the core* if no subset (coalition) of players has a private contract, involving only the resources owned by the agents in the coalition, that all members of the coalition prefer to the proposed allocation. Among the coalitions considered in the definition above is the *grand* coalition comprising all agents, therefore core-stability requires Pareto optimality. The appeal of the concept is that the threat of partial contracts singles out a small subset of efficient outcomes, in some cases a unique allocation as in the current example.

Consider an efficient and core-stable allocation. By efficiency, the 40 top buyers, and only these buyers, are served. We check that all buyers pay the same price p for their object. If this was not the case, let buyer 1 pay the largest price p_1: total revenue of the sellers is strictly less than $40p_1$. Thus there exists a seller who receives strictly less than p_1, say q. This seller and buyer 1 have a better deal, namely trade at a price below p_1 and above q; hence the allocation in question is not core-stable. A symmetrical argument establishes that all sellers are paid the same amount p for their object.

We show now that the common price p must be 60. As the trade is voluntary, the price cannot exceed 60—or one of the buyers would prefer not to trade. If p was below 60, say

55, then one of the inefficient buyers, say $p' = 58$, could offer a better deal to one of the sellers. For instance, he would offer to buy an object for $57, which violates core-stability.

Having shown that a corestable outcome must be the competitive outcome, it is now easy to check that this outcome is indeed core-stable. If a coalition finds a better private contract involving the exchange of k objects, it must contain k sellers who each receive more than $60. Hence one of the buyers pays more than $60 for his object and cannot be better off in the new contract.

The discussion of example 7.2 generalizes to any market for a homogeneous good where each agent wants at most one unit of the indivisible good and owns at most one unit. The agents who initially own a unit (sellers) are arranged by increasing reservation price so as to construct the *supply function* $s(p)$: $s(p)$ is the number of agents who are willing to sell their object at price p (equivalently, who are willing to pay less than p for an object). The supply function is increasing in p; see figure 7.1. The agents who initially own only cash (buyers) are arranged by decreasing willingness to pay so that the *demand function* $d(p)$ is the number of buyers willing to buy when the price is p. The competitive price is at the intersection of the demand and supply functions; see figure 7.1.

Formally, the model is identical to the commons problem in chapter 6 when we identify the supply function with an *increasing* marginal cost function; see section 6.3. The

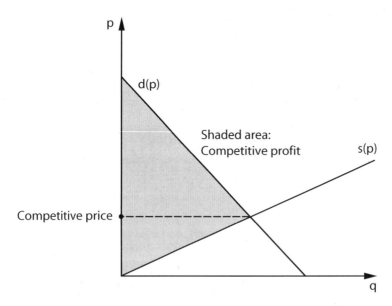

Figure 7.1

main difference is that we split the efficient surplus between buyers and sellers. The three normative solutions in chapter 6—CEEI, virtual price, and Shapley—differ in the way they distribute the competitive profit $r = p_e q_e - C(q_e)$. This is the area below the competitive price and above the supply function in figure 7.1. Here the competitive profit goes unambiguously to the sellers, and the competitive allocation is the uniquely compelling solution.

As in example 7.2, the latter claim rests on three arguments. The competitive allocation is the unique core-stable trade, it is the Shapley value of the stand-alone cooperative game, and it is the only efficient allocation without envy on net trades. Finally, the mechanism eliciting their willingness to pay (resp. reservation price) from every buyer (resp. seller) is strategy-proof, for exactly the same reasons making the CEEI solution strategy-proof in the commons problem; see the discussion at the beginning of section 6.4.

The proof of the first two claims is given above in the case of example 7.2. Its straight-forward generalization to the general demand and supply functions of figure 7.1 is left as an exercise to the reader. We prove the third claim of no envy. In an efficient allocation, an efficient buyer (resp. seller) acquires one object and pays some money (resp. gives up an object and receives some money). By no envy on net trades, all efficient buyers pay the same amount p and all efficient sellers receive the same amount p'. Similarly all inefficient agents (potential buyers or sellers) get the same (positive or negative) cash transfer t.

Consider an efficient buyer Ann just above p_e and an inefficient buyer Bob just below p_e. No envy on net trades between these two yields

Ann not envious: $p_e - p \geq t$

Bob not envious: $t \geq p_e - p$

so that $p_e - p = t$. A similar argument involving a barely efficient and a barely inefficient sellers gives $p' - p_e = t$. Finally, budget balance requires $q_e p = q_e p' + kt$, where k is the number of inefficient agents. The first two equalities imply $2t = p' - p$, and the latter becomes $q_e(p - p') = k(p' - p)/2$, from which $t = 0$, $p = p' = p_e$ immediately follow.

An important special case of the bilateral market for homogeneous indivisible goods is often called the *gloves market* (this terminology is explained below). There are n identical buyers willing to pay p_1, for the good, and m identical sellers with the reservation value p_2 for their unit. Moreover $p_1 > p_2$, so the efficient trade yields a surplus $\sigma = \min\{n, m\}(p_1 - p_2)$.

Assume $n > m$, meaning that the sellers are the short side of the market. Then the competitive price is p_1: at any lower price, the demand n exceeds the supply (at most m); at any higher price the demand vanishes but the supply is n; at price p, each buyer is indifferent between buying or not buying. Thus any demand between 0 and n is competitive, whereas the competitive supply is m.

A symmetrical argument shows that the competitive price is p_2 when $m > n$, that is, when the buyers are the short side of the market. Thus the short side of the market captures the entire surplus: each agent on the short side nets $(p_1 - p_2)$, whereas each agent on the long side breaks even (does not benefit from trade, or does not trade).

A familiar interpretation of this market is that one side of the market is made of agents who each own a right-hand glove, whereas each agent on the other side owns a left-hand glove. A pair (one right-hand and one left-hand glove) is worth \$1, but a single glove is worthless. Call, arbitrarily, the right-hand glove owners the "buyers," and the left-hand glove owners the "sellers," and we get the economy described in the previous paragraph with $p_1 = 1$ and $p_2 = 0$.

The point of the gloves market example is that competitive trade leaves no room for compromise: its interpretation of fairness is questionable because the long side of the market, as a whole, ought to be rewarded for its contribution to the efficient surplus. Moreover the competitive surplus distribution changes discontinually with the parameters of the economy, as a tiny change of n, m resulting in a switch from $n < m$ to $m > n$ implies a massive transfer of the entire surplus from one side of the market to the other.

7.2   Imperfect Competition

In the economy of example 7.2, each agent owns, sells, and buys at most one unit. Hence each participant has a negligible fraction of *market power*. Removing any one agent does not affect noticeably the competitive equilibrium allocation. For instance, we can use the law of large numbers to compute the Shapley value because each agent has a negligible impact on the overall demand and supply.

One reason the negligibility assumption fails is increasing returns in the production of the good (or goods) traded in a given market. When the cost function is subadditive (positive externalities in production), efficiency commands the agents to run only one production process, even if many potential sellers/firms own a copy of the technology. The presence of these potential firms cancels the profit of the chosen firm, a clear manifestation of competition in the sense of core-stability. But the notion of competitive price collapses.

Our next example illustrates this important fact in the simplest case of a subadditive cost function, namely one with a fixed cost to start production and constant marginal cost once the fixed cost is paid.

Example 7.3 Competition under Decreasing Average Costs   The economy is as in example 6.7 with, as usual, a demand function $d(p) = 100 - p$, and a technology involving a fixed cost \$1,800 and a marginal cost \$10 for each unit produced:

$$C(q) = 1,800 + 10q \qquad \text{for } q = 1, 2, \ldots, C(0) = 0$$

The difference from example 6.7 is that two or more firms own a copy of the technology.

1. We start with the benchmark case with no fixed cost so that the good is produced at constant unit cost \$10. An efficient allocation serves the 90 agents willing to pay 10 or more, and the efficient surplus is $\sigma_0 = \int_{10}^{100}(100 - p)\,dp = 4,050$. The competitive price is $p_e = 10$. In the competitive allocation each efficient buyer pays \$10 for his unit; the two firms split arbitrarily the production of the 90 units and break even by selling at unit cost, thus making no profit whatsoever.

As in example 7.2, this competitive allocation is characterized by the property of core-stability. To check this claim, note that the total surplus is not diminished if one of the firms goes away, since one copy of the technology is enough to bring about the entire surplus σ_0. Therefore the surplus share of each firm is zero, and σ_0 is shared among the buyers. Furthermore, a two-agent coalition made of one firm and buyer p, brings the stand-alone surplus $(p - 10)_+$, so every efficient buyer p receives at least $p - 10$. By definition of σ_0, these inequalities must all be equalities, and the claim is proved.

In exercise 7.3 we observe that the competitive allocation can also be characterized by no envy and efficiency, provided that we add voluntary participation (no one suffers a net loss of welfare from the initial situation before any production takes place) to these two requirements. We also note there that the Shapley value is *different* from the competitive trade if there is only a small number of potential firms. The two concepts lead to the same allocation only when the number of potential firms is large.

2. Now we take into account the fixed cost of \$1,800. It is efficient to produce 90 units to serve the 90 agents willing to pay 10 or more, but the corresponding surplus drops to $\sigma = 4,050 - 1,800 = 2,250$. Efficiency requires to run a single copy of the technology so as to pay the fixed cost only once. Because we have two or more firms, it is still possible to generate the whole surplus when we drop any one firm. Therefore in any corestable allocation, each firm receives zero surplus! The same applies to any inefficient buyer, whose departure does not affect the available surplus σ.

To sum up, one firm produces 90 units and breaks even (its revenue is \$2,700), and all other firms shut down. Every inefficient buyer ($p \leq 10$) is inactive, and every efficient buyer ($p \geq 10$) is active. We cannot implement such an allocation by quoting a single price $\bar{p}$ to which every agent will react competitively. At price $\bar{p} = 10$ the correct (efficient) agents buy, but the revenue does not cover the fixed cost. When the price signal is set at the *monopoly* level[2] $\bar{p} = 55$, the firm sells 45 units and makes a profit of \$225, but the efficient buyers between 10 and 55 are not served. The resulting inefficiency is the loss of surplus:

$$\int_{45}^{90} (100 - q - 10)\, dq = 1,012.5$$

Upon dropping the competitive approach, we have no alternative "positive" approach to select a particular allocation in the core: there is no simple strategic equilibrium story involving the firms and buyers (active as well as inactive) to do so. On the other hand, the normative concepts of chapter 6 apply if we simply ignore the firm (who gets no surplus share) and view the model as a commons problem, as we did in example 6.7. Recall from that example that the Shapley value distributes the \$2,250 of surplus in proportion to $(p - 10)$ among all efficient buyers, whereas the virtual price solution charges \$32.9 for service to all agents p, $p \geq 32.9$, and charges p to each agent p, $10 \leq p \leq 32.9$. It is easy to check that both allocations are in the core. On the other hand, the CEEI solution levies an \$18 tax from every inefficient buyer. Hence it fails the test of voluntary participation and, a fortiori, core-stability.

An alternative normative route to distribute the surplus between the buyers and the potential firms relies on the familiar stand alone cooperative game involving 100 buyers and k firms. We simply use the Shapley value of this game. This solution gives a positive share of surplus to the firms. Therefore it is not core-stable when $k \geq 2$. The total share of the k firms decreases to zero as k grows large, and in the limit the solution coincides with the Shapley value of the commons problem. Exercise 7.3 gives more details.

The critical negligibility assumption fails when one of the market participants controls one side of the market, either because she owns all of the tradable commodities, or the unique copy of the technology required to produce them, or because she is the sole buyer of these commodities. We speak of a monopoly or a monopsony situation respectively.

In our next example a monopoly owns a technology with increasing marginal costs and the following general facts are illustrated. The competitive equilibrium is well-defined, and it is core-stable as well. There are, however, many other distributions of the surplus compatible with core-stability, including the one where the monopolist keeps the entire surplus, but excluding the Shapley value distribution.

Example 7.4 Monopoly in the Market for Homogeneous Goods   We modify the economy of example 7.2, by assuming that Ann, the monopolist, owns all 40 units of the homogeneous good, which she can produce at no cost.

---

2. The firms's profit when potential buyers react competitively to the price p is $(100 - p)(p - 10) - 1,800$. This profit is maximal when $\bar{p} = 55$.

In the competitive allocation the monopolist sells them to the top 40 buyers at $60 per unit, and her profit is $2,400. This allocation is corestable, and it is, in fact, the best core allocation from the buyer's point of view. To check these claims, we use the important fact that in any core allocation, agent i's share of total surplus $v(N)$ cannot exceed his marginal contribution to surplus, namely $v(N) - v(N \setminus i)$ (in the notation of section 5.5). This follows, as usual, from the fact that the coalition $N \setminus i$ gets at least $v(N \setminus i)$ by core-stability.

For buyer i willing to pay (at most) p for the good, the marginal contribution is $v(N) - v(N \setminus i) = (p - 60)_+ = \max\{p - 60, 0\}$, which is his share of surplus at the competitive allocation. Conversely, we check that the competitive allocation is core-stable. A coalition not containing Ann is powerless; one not containing Ann must offer her more than $2,400 to induce her participation, and change an average price below 60 to induce the participation of the buyers. This is clearly impossible.

Thus the seller's competitive surplus depicted on figure 7.1 is the lowest possible surplus share in the core for Ann, the monopolist. Her highest possible share is $3,200, which is the full surplus. Indeed, a coalition of buyers is powerless, and a coalition including Ann cannot generate more than $3,200. To garner her largest profit, the monopolist must charge a different price to each one of the 40 efficient buyer, just below p to buyer p. To collect the smallest profit compatible with core-stability, she charges uniformly the competitive price $60.

We turn to the Shapley value of the stand-alone game involving Ann and 100 potential buyers. Unlike in example 7.2, this solutions moves away not only from the competitive allocation but also from core-stability. In fact the Shapley value gives a positive share of surplus to *all* buyers, even the inefficient ones. If an agent willing to pay $30 is drawn among the first 40 buyers and after Ann, his marginal contribution to surplus is $30; this event has positive probability (i.e., 0.08), hence the claim.

We compute Ann's surplus share. In a random ordering of the 100 buyers plus Ann, we let λ to be the fraction of buyers preceding her. Thus λ is uniformly distributed over $[0, 1]$. By the law of large numbers, the λ buyers are uniformly spread between 0 and 100 and generate the demand $d_\lambda(p) = \lambda(100 - p)$. The total surplus available to be shared by λ buyers and Ann is her marginal contribution, and this is computed as follows:

$$y_{i_0} = 5{,}000\,\lambda \qquad\qquad \text{if } 0 \le \lambda \le \frac{2}{5}$$

$$y_{i_0} = 20 \cdot \left(200 - \frac{40}{\lambda}\right) \quad \text{if } \frac{2}{5} \le \lambda \le 1$$

Ann's Shapley share is the expected value of this quantity or

$$x_{i_0} = E y_{i_0} = 2{,}800 - 800 \log\left(\frac{5}{2}\right) = 2{,}067 < 2{,}400$$

She gets less than her competitive share of surplus. Similar computations (explained in exercise 7.4) give the shares of the various buyers:

$$\sigma(p) = \frac{8p}{100 - p} \quad \text{if } 0 \le p \le 60$$

$$\sigma(p) = \frac{1}{2}p - 18 \quad \text{if } 60 \le p \le 100$$

The highest buyers, or $84 \le p \le 100$, actually get a better surplus share at the competitive allocation. All others prefer their Shapley share to the competitive one.

Comparing examples 7.2 and 7.4, we see that the Shapley value penalizes the sellers for merging into a monopoly, a counterintuitive feature from the positive standpoint, and a fairly puzzling one from the normative standpoint. In what interpretation of fair trade do we want to reduce the surplus share of sellers (or buyers) upon consolidation? The core concept, on the other hand, conveys the right intuition about merging, despite the fact that core-stability cuts a fairly large set of surplus distributions. That is, the monopolist (the merged sellers) secure at least the surplus share assigned to the sellers before merging (their competitive surplus share).

In between the configurations of examples 7.2 and 7.4, with forty small sellers and one monopolist (forty merged into one) respectively, we find the *oligopoly* situation where a few sellers each own a significant fraction of the resources: we say that each seller has "market power."

In the market of example 7.4, suppose that the sellers are arranged in two "firms," owning respectively 30 units and 10 units. Then the competitive allocation is, once again, the only core-stable allocation! In other words, *two is enough for perfect competition*. It makes no difference whether we have a large number of small sellers or a handful of large oligopolists: in both cases the core-stability and competitive equilibrium analysis offer exactly the same distribution of surplus between the buyers and the sellers. This remarkable property is independent of the size of our two firms, or of their numbers, provided that there are at least two of them: the crucial feature is the homogeneity of the goods provided by the oligopolists. Its proof is the subject of exercise 7.5. The property holds true as well when costs are subadditive, as demonstrated in example 7.3 above.

7.3   Destructive Competition

In some allocation problems a core-stable outcome cannot be found because the distribution of property rights is too generous to coalitions excluding some agents. The emptiness of the core means that the logic of private contracting finds no resting point. In turn, this raises two types of problems:

• *Instability.* The never-ending formation and dissolution of alliances is a source of unbounded transaction costs. Moreover it eliminates our ability to predict which private contracts will be signed and between which players. The resulting indeterminacy is not necessarily destroying any cooperative surplus, but it does make the outcome of the game arbitrary in a deeper sense than when we say that the selection of one among many corestable outcomes is arbitrary. Under core-instability it is vain to bring normative properties of fairness—or any other axiomatic property—to the negotiation table in the hope of reducing the set of admissible agreements: a "rational" agreement cannot be reached.

• *Inefficiency.* In the process of forming and dissolving private contracts, that the transient outcomes resulting from these temporary agreements may well be inefficient.

Our first example of an empty core does not involve trade; it is a "pure externality" game, and a striking illustration of the difficulties generated by the individual right to freely dispose of one's trash.

Example 7.5 The Garbage Game Every player holds one bag of trash and lives on a different lot. Each player can choose to drop his bag in any lot (dumping is free and unrestricted). The returns to scale of the garbage externality increase: if k bags are on player i's lot, his disutility is k^2, and this number is interpreted as his willingness to pay to have the trash removed. A player does not suffer any loss from trash not sitting on his lot. All participants have symmetric roles—equal preferences, endowment of trash, and choice of possible actions—therefore equal treatment of equals requires that they end up with the same disutility.

Because the externality caused by garbage has increasing returns, efficiency commands to keep one bag of trash per lot (no dumping), for a disutility of -1 per agent. This is the only fair and efficient outcome. However, $(n-1)$ players can sign a private contract to dump all their trash on an outcast player, and to share the cost of the trash that this player will no doubt dump in retaliation. Hence the $(n-1)$ players in the coalition end up with a small cost of $1/(n-1)$, whereas the outcast's disutility is $(n-1)^2$. The net efficiency loss is

$$(n-1)^2 + 1 - n = n^2 - 3n + 1$$

Note that a coalition of size $(n-1)$ is the most likely to form because it minimizes the net cost to each of its members. On the other hand, the outcome above is not core-stable because the outcast can offer to $(n-2)$ other players an alternative coalition where he (the former outcast) would bear all the cost of the new outcast's trash. This kind of deal is always profitable to all parties; hence the core is empty.

Our next example is a trade game that has received much attention by economists: it shows that the competition between firms with U-shaped averages costs can easily result in an empty core.

Example 7.6 Taxis   Three taxis compete for seven customers. All customers want to do the same trip (airport to downtown) and each is willing to pay $7 for it.

Each taxi holds up to three passengers and the cost of a trip is $6, irrespective of the number of passengers transported. Thus the marginal cost of successive units of service for one given taxi are $(6, 0, 0, +\infty)$.

Efficiency requires that three taxis transport all seven passengers for a total surplus $\sigma = 7.7 - 3.6 = \$31$. Note that one taxi may be running with a single passenger, which is still a cost-effective trip.

The three taxi drivers may wish to charge each customer a uniform price p and to split equally the revenue: in this way the taxi that ends up with a single customer is not penalized. They could charge $p = 5$, say, and distribute a profit of $7.5 - 3.6 = 17$, hence obtain $5.7 per taxi. However, one taxi would make a bigger profit by charging $4.50 and luring away three customers, as $3 \cdot (4.5) - 6 = \$7.50$. It can be shown that *any* three-way split of the total surplus of $31 among the three taxis—even an unequal split—is similarly vulnerable to "cream-skimming" as above.

The simplest way to check that no allocation is core-stable is to compute the upperbound $v(N) - v(N \backslash i)$ for each one of the ten agents. Upon removing one customer *or* one taxi, efficiency consists of running two taxis with three passengers each, for a total surplus $6.7 - 2.6 = \$30$. Therefore $v(N) - v(N \backslash i) = 1$ for any one of the ten agents. Thus a core allocation cannot distribute more than $10 of surplus, in contradiction of efficiency.

There is no competitive price either, as the supply is 9 whenever the price exceeds 2 but the demand is only 7 for any price smaller than 7.

When the core is empty, no competitive equilibrium exists either: this general fact admits no exception. The only remedy to an empty core configuration is to limit the contracting opportunities of some coalitions, which effectively alters the distribution of individual rights. In the taxi example, destructive competition is avoided by preventing scouting and enforcing a uniform pricing policy, a common practice in airports. In industries with fixed costs and excess capacities (shipping, oil exploration), the instability resulting from an empty core is to be expected and its remedy is the formation of a tight cartel limiting cut-throat competition.

Core-instability uncovers a fundamental difficulty of private contracting under certain distributions of individual property rights. It forces one to alter the right of free association and to find other routes to define what constitutes a fair trade: this could take the form of a mechanical formula like the Shapley value or be derived as the equilibrium of a new set of individual rights. This is a critique of libertarian ideology, which is poised to rely exclusively on private contracts (section 1.5): the choice of the mechanical formula in question, or of new individual rights, is the object of a public contract requiring a normative justification and enforced by the public authority.

7.4   No Envy and the Assignment Problem

The rest of this chapter is devoted to fair division, namely the equitable distribution of commodities that are the common property of a given set of microeconomic agents. Each agent evaluates his share of free goods by means of ordinal preferences for which he or she is fully responsible. No consideration of needs or desire should influence the final distribution. In the terminology of chapter 2, compensation and reward are irrelevant, we are only interested in efficiency and exogeneous rights: that is, we wish to distribute the resources efficiently while at the same time respecting the equality of the participants rights.

Think of dividing a cake in which various flavors are unevenly distributed. One child would like a slice with a cherry, another is partial to chocolate, and so on. Or consider two countries dividing a geographically diverse piece of land, over which their interests are different: one who wishes an access to the sea very badly will be ready to concede a larger area to the other, and so on. These two examples show that fair division problems range from the most trivial contracts to the most dramatic ones—recall the division of the Indian subcontinent between India and Pakistan. Splitting an estate in a bankruptcy, inheritance, or divorce situation provides other examples.

Achieving efficiency while respecting the equality of the agents' rights is not difficult when all agents have identical preferences over the objects. As discussed in section 3.3., the compelling fair division of the resources aims at awarding "equal" shares—shares that all participants find equivalent with respect to the common preference ordering—and there is generally a unique way to do so efficiently. For instance, if the goods are divisible (as in the examples of the next section), simply giving $1/n$th of the total resources to each participant is generally efficient.[3] With indivisible goods, we look for a division of the resources maximizing the leximin ordering; see section 3.3.

With heterogeneous individual preferences, efficiency typically rules out giving identical shares to everyone, thus the interpretation of "equal rights" is not straightforward. The test of no envy, introduced in chapter 6, offers an extremely appealing answer. This concept is a major contribution of microeconomic theory to the modern thinking of distributive justice, one nearly as important as the Shapley value.

3. The only exception is when some individual preferences fail the convexity property.

A distribution of the resources is nonenvious, or it passes the no-envy test, if every agent prefers (weakly) his or her share to that of any other agent: I cannot complain about my share because no one else has a share that I would exchange for mine. A nonenvious distribution that is also efficient is one coherent answer to the fair division puzzle.

The no-envy test is especially successful in an *assignment problem.* There are n agents, n indivisible objects, and cash transfers are feasible. Each agent wants at most one object, and his preferences are represented by his willingness to pay for the different objects. An allocation consists of n lots (n is the number of agents), where a lot is made of one object and a (positive or negative) price tag. The sum of all price tags is zero. A nonenvious assignment is one where each agent gets his favorite lot. It can be shown that no matter how the n^2 willingness to pay of each agent for each object are chosen, we can always find price tags achieving a nonenvious assignment. Moreover a nonenvious assignment is automatically efficient! See exercise 7.10 for a proof.

Some of the commons problems in chapter 6 can be interpreted as assignment problems. In example 6.4 we have 100 agents with willingness to pay uniformly spread between 0 and 100, and 40 free objects to be assigned. Add 60 *null* objects, corresponding to no object, to have an assignment problem where agent p is willing to pay $\$p$ for a (real) object and 0 for a null object. The CEEI solution is reinterpreted as the following nonenvious assignment. Each real object bears the price $36 and each null object has a negative price –$24 (a net payment). The top 40 agents (with valuation between 60 and 100) pick a real object, and the other 60 agents pick a null object (as usual, we neglect to specify on which side falls the agent willing to pay exactly $60).

In our next assignment problem, each object is different. Once again the no-envy criterion points to the efficient assignment of objects and to a unique system of cash transfers. Note that the uniqueness property follows from the fact that we have a continuum (a large number) of agents. In a general assignment problem with a finite number of participants, the no-envy test does not capture a unique set of cash transfers; see exercise 7.9 for examples.

Example 7.7 Scheduling   One hundred agents need one unit of service each. The server processes one agent per hour. All agents dislike waiting, but their disutilities per hour of wait vary. Agent p suffers a net loss of $\$p$ per unit of time he has to wait; his *dis*utility for being scheduled at time t (i.e., waiting for t hours) is $p \cdot t$. The disutility is measured in dollars, and represents the cost to this agent of waiting t hours.

The parameters p are spread uniformly between 1 and 100, so we have exactly p agents with a marginal disutility not larger than p. The random scheduling solution is a useful benchmark: it orders the agents randomly, with uniform probability on all orderings. Thus the expected wait of any agent is 50, and the expected total waiting cost is $\int_0^{100} 50p\,dp =$ 250,000.

Random scheduling pays no attention to the differences in waiting costs across agents, and is therefore inefficient. To minimize total disutility of waiting, the scheduling order must be by decreasing marginal disutility; if agents p, p' with $p < p'$ wait, respectively, t and t' hours, with $t < t'$, total waiting cost decreases when they swap slots: $p't + pt' < pt + p't'$.

Thus the efficient scheduling assigns agent p to slot $100 - p$, and the total waiting cost is $\int_0^{100} p \cdot (100 - p)\, dp = 166{,}667$, which is a 33 percent gain over the random scheduling benchmark.

We compute now the profile of monetary compensations dictated by the no-envy test. A price $\pi(p)$ is attached to the slot $100 - p$, and this price can be positive or negative. The test requires that agent p prefer her lot $(100 - p, \pi(p))$ to any other lot $(100 - p', \pi(p'))$:

$$p(100 - p) + \pi(p) \leq p(100 - p') + \pi(p')$$

$$\Leftrightarrow p^2 - \pi(p) \geq pp' - \pi(p') \text{ for } p, p', 0 \leq p, p' \leq 100 \qquad (3)$$

The system of inequalities (3) determines the function $\pi(p)$ entirely provided that we regard as usual 100 as a large number, and use calculus. Fix p, and note that the function $p' \to pp' - \pi(p')$ reaches its maximum at $p' = p$. Thus its derivative is zero at p, namely $p = \dot{\pi}(p)$ where $\dot{\pi}$ denotes the derivative of the π function. The only function π such that $\dot{\pi}(p) = p$ and $\int_0^{100} \pi(p)\, dp = 0$ is $\pi(p) = p^2/2 - 1{,}667$.

Therefore the "patient" agents from 0 to 58 are compensated for being served last ($\pi(p)$ is negative iff $p \leq 58.4$), whereas the impatient agents from 59 to 100 must pay for early service (the largest out of pocket payment is 3,333, twice the largest compensation). The net disutility of agent p is always smaller than his benchmark disutility under random scheduling, with a net gain of at least \$417:

$$p(100 - p) + \pi(p) = -\frac{p^2}{2} + 100p - 1{,}667 \leq 50p - 417 \qquad \text{for all } p$$

An important property of the nonenvious assignment is strategyproofness: in the direct revelation game where agents report their marginal waiting cost, after which the allocation just described is implemented, it is a dominant strategy for each agent to report truthfully his or her type p. This follows at once from system (3) and the negligibility assumption: when a single agent reports p' instead of p, the function π is not altered; therefore the right-hand term of the first inequality in (3) is agent $p's$ disutility after misreporting.

The CEEI solution in the commons problems of chapter 6 is also characterized by the no-envy test and efficiency (under the negligibility assumption), and it is also strategyproof (see sections 6.3 and 6.5, in particular example 6.5). This is not a coincidence: in the assignment problem the efficient and nonenvious assignments can always be interpreted as competitive equilibria with equal incomes. This property does not require the negligibility assumption; see exercise 7.10.

When cash is not available, another way to achieve equity in assignment is a lottery. Consider the assignment of time slots in example 7.1. We start from an arbitrary initial assignment, the initial distribution of property rights. From there the equilibrium of private contracting—the unique corestable assignment computed by the top trading cycles algorithm—leads us to a new assignment where all opportunities to trade have been exhausted. The point of example 7.1 is that this assignment is unique, for any distribution of property rights and any profile of preferences. The corresponding trade is unambiguously fair, given the property rights.

Now suppose that we allocate property rights randomly and without bias (every assignment of property rights is equally probable) and perform the corresponding fair trade. The resulting (random) assignment is intuitively fair, because, ex ante, all agents get equal random property rights.

Example 7.8 Time-Sharing   Three fitness addicts are sharing three treadmills during a one hour period. The three machines have different features, and our three agents have the following preferences:

agent 1: $a \succ b \succ c$

agent 2: $a \succ c \succ b$

agent 3: $b \succ c \succ a$

They decide to time-share the machines in a fair and efficient way. Note the analogy with example 3.6 where the problem was to time-share a public good (music), whereas here the three objects are consumed privately over a certain period of time.

Time-sharing is formally equivalent to a random assignment of the machines to our three customers: to give machine a to agent 2 with probability $1/3$ is to let her use this machine for 20 minutes out of an hour. Thus we may randomly assign property rights to the machines, and use the top trading cycles algorithm of example 7.1 to compute the resulting core allocation.

There are six possible assignments of property rights and the corresponding corestable outcomes are as follows

$1 : a, 2 : b, 3 : c \rightarrow 1 : a, 2 : c, 3 : b$

$1 : a, 2 : c, 3 : b \rightarrow 1 : a, 2 : c, 3 : b$ no trade

$1 : b, 2 : a, 3 : c \rightarrow 1 : b, 2 : a, 3 : c$ no trade

$1 : b, 2 : c, 3 : a \rightarrow 1 : a, 2 : c, 3 : b$

$1 : c, 2 : a, 3 : b \rightarrow 1 : c, 2 : a, 3 : b$ no trade

$1 : c, 2 : b, 3 : a \rightarrow 1 : c, 2 : a, 3 : b$

The resulting random allocations of our three agents are summarized in the following matrix, where the entry (i, x) tells us the probability that agent i receives object x:

	a	b	c
1	$\frac{1}{2}$	$\frac{1}{6}$	$\frac{1}{3}$
2	$\frac{1}{2}$	0	$\frac{1}{2}$
3	0	$\frac{5}{6}$	$\frac{1}{6}$

Thus agent 1 gets his favorite machine for 30 seconds, his second best choice for 10 and his worst one for 20 seconds, and so on. This is the fair compromise obtained by an unbiased randomization of the property rights and by implementing the corresponding optimal trade. It is a solution in the spirit of the competitive equilibrium with equal incomes discussed in chapter 6 and in the next section.

In the example above the solution is an efficient compromise. However there are some configurations of individual preferences for which the idea of randomizing property rights yields a serious inefficiency. Here is an example with four agents and four objects:

1   $a \succ b \succ c \succ d$
2   $a \succ b \succ c \succ d$
3   $b \succ a \succ d \succ c$
4   $b \succ a \succ d \succ c$

All agents agree that a, b are better than c, d, but 1, 2 and 3, 4 have opposite preferences on a versus b and on c versus d. Consider agent 1. If he receives object a (in the random assignment of property rights), he will not exchange it. If he receives object b, he will exchange it with either agents 3 or 4 if a goes to one of them, yet he will keep object b if a goes to agent 2. If he receives c or d, he will not be able to trade it for a or b. Thus the probability that agent 1 ends up with a is $\frac{1}{4} + \frac{1}{4} \cdot \frac{2}{3} = \frac{5}{12}$ and the probability that he ends up with b is $\frac{1}{4} \cdot \frac{1}{3} = \frac{1}{12}$. Similar computations yield the overall assignment matrix:

	a	b	c	d
1	$\frac{5}{12}$	$\frac{1}{12}$	$\frac{5}{12}$	$\frac{1}{12}$
2	$\frac{5}{12}$	$\frac{1}{12}$	$\frac{5}{12}$	$\frac{1}{12}$
3	$\frac{1}{12}$	$\frac{5}{12}$	$\frac{1}{12}$	$\frac{5}{12}$
4	$\frac{1}{12}$	$\frac{5}{12}$	$\frac{1}{12}$	$\frac{5}{12}$

This random assignment is surely fair, but it is plainly inefficient. The following matrix makes everyone better off while preserving fairness:

	a	b	c	d
1	$\frac{1}{2}$	0	$\frac{1}{2}$	0
2	$\frac{1}{2}$	0	$\frac{1}{2}$	0
3	0	$\frac{1}{2}$	0	$\frac{1}{2}$
4	0	$\frac{1}{2}$	0	$\frac{1}{2}$

This assignment obtains by drawing with equal probability one of the two priority orderings $1, 3, 2, 4$ and $4, 2, 3, 1$.

7.5 The CEEI and Egalitarian Equivalent Solutions

The fair division problems discussed in this and the next section involve several divisible commodities, none of which is singled out as the numéraire (money) with respect to which we measure (as willingness to pay) the allocation of other commodities.

The no-envy test no longer implies efficiency as it did in the assignment problem of the last section. For instance, a division of the resources in equal shares for all participants is certainly nonenvious, yet it is generally inefficient. Even the combination of no envy and efficiency may allow very different allocations, as illustrated in our next example.

The competitive equilibrium with equal incomes (CEEI) systematically selects a specific efficient and nonenvious distribution of the resources. As discussed in chapter 6, the CEEI interpretation of common property is to give equal shares of private property to all participants, by splitting the resources equally among all, and to reach efficiency from there by fair competitive trade.

Example 7.9 Sharing Capacity A network (roads, cable connections, etc.) consists of two links, one from A to B and one from B to C. There is no direct link from A to C. Each one of the two links has a capacity of 100.

There are three types of users. Some users of the network pass some traffic between A and B, and only on this link; their set is denoted N^{AB}. The users in the set N^{BC} use similarly only the link BC. Finally there is a set N^0 of agents passing traffic from A to C, via B: these users create congestion on both links.

If z_i^{AB} and z_i^{BC} are the shares of capacity on the two links allocated to an agent i in N^0, his net utility is the amount of traffic he can carry, which is $u_i = \min\{z_i^{AB}, z_i^{BC}\}$. The utility of an agent i in N^{AB} is simply $u_i = z_i^{AB}$, namely his share of capacity on link AB; similarly $u_i = z_i^{BC}$ for i in N^{BC}.

We assume in this example a total population of 100 users, 40 of them in N^{AB}, 30 in N^{BC}, and 30 in N^0. All agents have identical exogenous rights on the network, and we wish to divide capacity fairly between them. Cash transfers are ruled out. The users in N^0 are more demanding than the other users, and this suggests that they should receive a lower share of capacity. The question is to attach a specific number to this intuition.

Efficiency and the basic equal treatment of equals go a long way toward determining the allocation of the 100 units of capacity to each type. It would be inefficient to give to an agent in N^0 different amounts of the two goods. By equal treatment, two agents of the same type receive identical allocations:

All i in N^0 get z units of capacity on each link

All i in N^{AB} get x units of capacity on AB

All i in N^{BC} get y units of capacity on BC

$$x = \frac{100 - 30z}{40}, \quad y = \frac{100 - 30z}{30} \tag{4}$$

The no-envy property implies equal treatment of equals (exercise: Why?) and not much more. Under efficiency (4), no envy amounts to $x \geq z$ and $y \geq z$, meaning that a type AB agent does not envy an agent of type O and neither does a type BC agent. There is no envy between a type AB and a type BC, or from a type O toward a type AB or BC. In view of (4) this amounts to $z \leq 10/7$.

Another simple test of equity is the fair share guarantee, introduced in chapter 6 (examples 6.4 and 6.5; see the systematic discussion in section 6.6). Here each agent can claim a 1/100th share of both capacities, or one unit of each, so that $x, y, z \geq 1$. We can easily check that the two inequalities $x, y \geq 1$ follow from $z \leq 10/7$, given (4). Thus the combination of no envy, fair share, and efficiency leaves us with the bounds:

$$1 \leq z \leq \frac{10}{7} \tag{5}$$

The CEEI solution selects relative prices of the two capacities and endows each agent with $100/n$ units of each good: the prices are chosen in such a way that the demand and supply of each good are exactly balanced. AB-agents exchange their share of BC-capacity for more AB-capacity and vice versa. On the other hand, agents in N^0 cannot buy more of *each* commodity, so they do not take part in the exchange. The relative prices equilibrating demand and supply are $p_{AB} = \frac{4}{7}$, $p_{BC} = \frac{3}{7}$. The resulting competitive demands are

All i in N^{AB} sell 1 unit of BC, buy 3/4 unit of $AB \Rightarrow x = 1.75$

All i in N^{BC} sell 1 unit of AB, buy 4/3 unit of $BC \Rightarrow y = 2.33$

All i in N^0 do not trade $\Rightarrow z = 1$

The N^0 agents get exactly their fair share utility (i.e., the utility from consuming one unit of each good), whereas the other agents get, respectively, a 75 and 133 percent increase over their fair share utility.

The second general fair *division method* is directly inspired by the relative egalitarian (KS) solution of section 3.6. The *egalitarian equivalent* solution (EE for short) equalizes across agents the utilities measured along the "numéraire" of the commodity bundle to be divided. In other words, this solution gives to each participant an allocation that he or she views as equivalent (with his or her own preferences) to the same share of the pie, where the "pie" stands for the resources to be divided and a share is a homothetic reduction of the pie—this is the same fraction of the total available amount of each commodity.

In our example the utility functions used above are already calibrated in this fashion; that is to say, the utility from the bundle (z, z) is precisely z (for each type of agent). Therefore the EE solution simply equalizes these utilities. However, system (4) is incompatible with the equality $x = y = z$. Hence we must invoke the leximin ordering of section 3.3 to combine the egalitarian objective with efficiency. This yields the following allocation:

$$x = z = \frac{10}{7} = 1.43, \quad y = \frac{40}{21} = 1.90 \tag{6}$$

Agents in N^{AB} and N^0 get a 43 percent increase over their fair share utility, and those in N^{BC} get a 90 percent increase. The EE solution gives to N^0 agents their best envy-free allocation—see (5)—whereas the CEEI solution merely gives them their fair shares.

A remarkable and surprising property links the CEEI solution and the Nash bargaining solution of sections 3.4 and 3.6. This property helps us in the next two examples and many more to compute the CEEI solution and the competitive prices.

We say that the utility function $u_i(z_i)$ defined for the vector of commodities z_i is *homogeneous* if for every positive number λ, we have $u_i(\lambda \cdot z_i) = \lambda \cdot u_i(z_i)$. Examples include the additive utility functions in the next two examples, as well as the utility function $u_i(z_i^1, z_i^2) = \min\{z_i^1, z_i^2\}$ in example 7.9.[4]

---

4. Not every preference ordering can be represented by a homogeneous utility function. A necessary condition is that its indifference curves must be homothetic, meaning that they can all be deduced from one of them by the transformation $z \rightarrow \lambda z$.

When all agents have homogeneous utility functions, the CEEI solution picks precisely the same allocation of resources as the Nash solution. This is the allocation maximizing the product of these utility functions. In example 7.9 the Nash collective utility at an efficient allocation given in (4) is $x^{40} \cdot y^{30} \cdot z^{30}$, and the claim is easily checked.

The EE solution, on the other hand, is nothing other than the KS solution. In other words, the efficient allocation of the resources equalizing across all agents the relative increase over their fair share utility, namely the ratios $u_i(z_i)/u_i(\omega)$. It uses the leximin ordering to resolve any efficiency/equality trade-off, as in example 7.9.

Example 7.10 Sharing Capacity Revisited   Now the network consists of two different links (A-link and B-link) between the same two points. The A users can only use the A-link, the B users can only use the B-link, and the O users can use either link. The number of these three types of users are 40, 30, and 30 respectively. We have 100 units of capacity on each link.

Using the same notation as in example 7.9, our three utility functions are $u_i = z_i^A$, $u_i = z_i^B$, and $u_i = z_i^A + z_i^B$, respectively, for users of types A, B, and O. Efficiency and equal treatment of equals together mean that each A agent gets the same amount x of A capacity (and none of B capacity), each B agent gets y units of B capacity, and the O agents each get the $1/30$ share of what is left:

$$z^A = \frac{100 - 40x}{30}, \quad z^B = \frac{100 - 30y}{30} \tag{7}$$

Observe that (7) leaves two degrees of freedom, as opposed to only one in the case of system (4) in example 7.9. The CEEI solution obtains by maximizing the Nash collective utility function over these allocations:

$$\text{maximize} \quad x^{40} y^{30} \left(\frac{100 - 40x}{30} + \frac{100 - 30y}{30} \right)^{30}$$

$$\text{over} \quad x, y: \quad 0 \le x \le \frac{100}{40} = 2.5, \, 0 \le y \le \frac{100}{30} = 3.33$$

Compute the first-order optimality conditions for an interior solution, namely a solution where none of the inequality constraints is an equality:

$$\frac{40}{x} = \frac{30.40}{\delta}, \quad \frac{30}{y} = \frac{30.30}{\delta}, \quad \text{where } \delta = 200 - 40x - 30y$$

$$\Leftrightarrow x = y = 2 \quad \text{and} \quad z^A = \frac{2}{3}, \quad z^B = \frac{4}{3}$$

Thus all agents receive the same total share of capacity, $x = y = z^A + z^B = 2$. For an O agent, this is precisely her fair share of total resources, but for an A agent or a B agent, this is twice as much: one unit of both goods is worth no more than one unit of the good they like. The competitive prices are simply $p^A = p^B$ so that each A agent (resp. B agent) can trade one-for-one his fair share of B capacity (resp. A agent). The O agents absorb the imbalance, as for them the two goods are identical.

In example 7.9 it made sense that the O types should get no more than their fair share, as they were unable to trade any of it with the other users. But in the current example, an O agent has "flexible" preferences allowing to trade both with A agents and B agents. Yet in the CEEI outcome the O agents do trade, but they get no benefit from the trade. The CEEI allocation ends up equalizing the utilities $u_i(z_i)$ across all agents of all types, which seems to be harsh on the O agents.

Contrast this with the EE solution equalizing across all agents $u_i(z_i)/u_i(100, 100)$. If i is an A agent or a B agent, $u_i(100, 100) = 100$, whereas $u_i(100, 100) = 200$ for an O agent. Therefore, if i, j, k are an A, B, and O agent, respectively,

$$u_i(z_i) = u_j(z_j) = \tfrac{1}{2}u_k(z_k)$$

We can restrict attention to efficient allocations treating equals equally, and described by formula (7):

$$x = y = \frac{1}{2}\left(\frac{100 - 40x}{30} + \frac{100 - 30y}{30}\right) \Rightarrow x = y = \frac{20}{13} = 1.54$$

$$z_i^A = 1.28, \quad z_i^B = 1.79$$

As in example 7.9, the EE solution is much more generous than CEEI to the O agents. Unlike in example 7.9, it goes beyond the bounds of the no-envy test: an O agent ends up with more B capacity than a B agent, hence is envied by this agent. This is going too far in rewarding the accommodating preferences of the O types. Each user has identical exogenous rights to the resources, which do not appear to be respected by a solution allocating to this agent a strictly larger share of every commodity than to that agent. Recall that the differences in individual preferences reflects different tastes not different needs; these differences call for unequal shares (if we want efficiency) but can hardly justify a systematic advantage in every commodity. We must dismiss the egalitarian equivalent solution in example 7.10.

Exercise 7.11 and 7.12 generalize examples 7.9 and 7.10, respectively, to arbitrary sizes of the three types of users. The comparison of the two solutions remains qualitatively identical.

Our next example involves two agents between whom we must divide a handful of commodities. Because we have only two agents, the EE solution does not exhibit the damning inequity uncovered in example 7.10. It provides a legitimate interpretation of fairness that we contrast with the competitive interpretation of the CEEI solution.

Example 7.11a Sharing Five Studios   An estate consists of five studios located in the same city, and it must be divided between the two heirs, Joan and Peter. The apartments cannot be sold: our two heirs can only time-share the five units, for instance, a share of 2/3 in one unit means access during 8 months of the year. A possible story is that the heirs inherit the right to use the studios (they both have many children) at a low, controlled rent, not the ownership of the studios. John and Peter are both short of cash, so monetary transactions between them are ruled out.

The five studios are different, and the two heirs have different preferences. A simple and practical method to share these five divisible goods consists of giving 100 points to Joan and 100 points to Peter, asking them to distribute these points among the five studios, with the understanding that the score of a studio reflects one's utility for this particular item. Suppose that Joan and Peter have distributed their points as follows:

Studio	A	B	C	D	E	
Joan	20	10	15	35	20	(8)
Peter	10	25	20	10	35	

We view these numbers as defining a separably additive utility function over the five items. For instance, if Joan gets studios A, C in full, a 30 percent share of B and 50 percent of E, her utility is taken to be $20 + 15 + (0.3) \cdot 5 + (0.5) \cdot 20$. What matters in allocating the points are the relative scores of the different items. The total number of points allotted to each participant is irrelevant.

Under the assumption of separably additive utilities, the description of efficient allocations is very simple. Consider the two items A and B. Joan would not trade one unit of A for less than 4 units of B, but Peter would give away one unit of A for 0.4 units of B. Therefore an allocation where Joan receives a positive share of B, while Peter gets a positive share of A cannot be efficient: they would easily find a Pareto-improving trade, such as at the rate 1 : 1 between A and B. The same principle applies to any pair of items. For instance, consider items C, E: as $15/20 > 20/35$, efficiency rules out giving a positive share of E to Joan and a positive share of C to Peter.

Now we reorder the items in (8) by means of the ratio of their scores from Joan versus Peter:

Studio	D	A	C	E	B
Joan	35	20	15	20	10
Peter	10	10	20	35	25

In this new setup, whenever item X is to the left of item Y, we have

$$\frac{\text{score}(X, \text{Joan})}{\text{score}(X, \text{Peter})} > \frac{\text{score}(Y, \text{Joan})}{\text{score}(Y, \text{Peter})} \Leftrightarrow \frac{\text{score}(X, \text{Joan})}{\text{score}(Y, \text{Joan})} > \frac{\text{score}(X, \text{Peter})}{\text{score}(Y, \text{Peter})} \tag{9}$$

In an efficient allocation of the five items, if Joan gets a positive share of item Y, she must receive any item X to the left of Y in full: if Peter gets a positive share of X, we derive a contradiction via (9). Thus we see that the set of efficient allocations is made of five successive "segments," where k is one of 0, 1, 2, 3, 4, Joan gets the k left items, Peter gets the $4 - k$ right items, and they split the item left in the middle.

The fair share of an agent is worth 50 points (i.e., the utility for a 50 percent share in each item) therefore in an efficient allocation where Joan and Peter get their fair share, Joan gets 100 percent of D (and at least 50 percent of A), whereas Peter gets B (and at least 5/7 of E). This leaves only three types of allocations:

	D	A	C	E	B	
J	1	x	0	0	0	with $\frac{1}{2} \le x \le 1$
P	0	1 − x	1	1	1	
J	1	1	x	0	0	with $0 \le x \le 1$
P	0	0	1 − x	1	1	
J	1	1	1	x	0	with $0 \le x \le \frac{2}{7}$
P	0	0	0	1 − x	1	

Note that the no-envy test is equivalent in this example to the fair share test: this follows easily from the fact that utilities are linear with respect to the vector of shares allocated to an agent, and we have only two agents.[5]

We are now ready to compute the CEEI and EE solutions. For the former, we maximize the Nash product over the three efficient segments just described, keeping in mind that the maximum is achieved at a unique allocation.

On the middle segment where Joan gets D, A and Peter gets E, B, the Nash product is

$$(35 + 20 + 15x)(20(1 - x) + 35 + 25)$$

of which the maximum obtains at $x = \frac{1}{6}$. Because this is an interior solution, we need to look no further: the maximum of the Nash product in the top segment is at $x = 1$, and it is at $x = 0$ in the bottom segment. Note that if we started in the top segment, the maximum of the Nash product would be at $x = 1$; in the bottom segment it would be at $x = 0$.

---

5. As an exercise, prove this claim.

The price system supporting the Nash optimum allocation as a competitive price with equal incomes is easy to compute. An agent maximizing his linear utility over a given budget constraint will choose to buy positive amounts of several goods only if the relative prices of these goods coincide with the ratio of his own marginal utilities. Therefore, setting for convenience $p_C = 1$, we find the competitive price as follows:

$$\frac{p_D}{1} = \frac{35}{15}; \quad \frac{p_A}{1} = \frac{20}{15} \quad \text{from Joan's competitive demand}$$

$$\frac{p_E}{1} = \frac{35}{20}; \quad \frac{p_B}{1} = \frac{25}{20} \quad \text{from Peter's competitive demand}$$

At those prices, the value of Joan's allocation equals that of Peter's allocation: $p_D + p_A + \frac{1}{6} p_C = \frac{5}{6} p_C + p_E + p_B$.

The EE solution is simply the equal utility efficient allocation, because the utility of any agent for the entire "pie" is conventionally taken to be 100. In general, the EE allocation could occur on a different segment than that of Nash (exercise 7.13 gives an example), but in this particular example it doesn't.

$$35 + 20 + 15x = 20(1 - x) + 35 + 25 \Rightarrow x = \frac{5}{7}$$

An important feature of the CEEI solution in example 7.11a is that it often picks a corner solution, namely an allocation between two consecutive efficient segments where no item is shared (each item goes 100 percent to Joan or to Peter). This property, which the EE solution does not share, is helpful in practice where division of an item entails some additional monitoring costs, as in our story where a commodity is access to a studio.

Example 7.11b Numerical Variant
By fair share, Joan gets at least D and Peter gets at least E, B:

	D	A	C	E	B
Joan	40	25	20	10	5
Peter	10	20	25	20	25

Maximizing the Nash product over the interval where Joan gets D and a fraction x of A amounts to

maximize $(40 + 25x)(20(1 - x) + 25 + 20 + 25)$ over $0 \leq x \leq 1$

with solution $x = 1$. When Joan gets D, A, and x of C, we get

maximize $(40 + 25 + 20x)(25(1 - x) + 20 + 25)$ over $0 \leq x \leq 1$

with solution $x = 0$.

We conclude that the Nash optimum is to give D, A to Joan and C, E, B to Peter. This is supported as a competitive equilibrium by prices such that

$$p_A = \frac{8}{5}p_B, \quad p_B \leq \frac{5}{4}p_C \qquad \text{from Joan's competitive demand}$$

$$p_D = \frac{4}{5}p_C, \quad p_E = p_C, \quad p_C \leq \frac{5}{4}p_B \qquad \text{from Peter's competitive demand}$$

$$p_A + p_B = p_C + p_D + p_E \qquad \text{equal incomes of Joan and Peter}$$

Hence the price system takes the form

	A	B	C	D	E
Price	112	70	65	52	65

Compute finally the EE solution, that gives a positive piece x of item C to Joan:

$$40 + 25 + 20x = 25(1 - x) + 20 + 25 \Rightarrow x = \frac{1}{9}$$

*7.6 Axiomatics of Fair Division

The two equity tests fair share guarantee and no envy lead the preceding discussion.[6]

The *fair share* of a certain agent when dividing a certain bundle of commodities among n agents is computed from the hypothetical profile where all n agents have precisely the same preferences as the agent in question. In examples 7.9 to 7.11, the "pie" consists of a bundle $\omega = (\omega_1, \ldots, \omega_K)$ of divisible commodities, and when all participants have identical preferences, the unambiguously fair division is to give an equal share ω/n to each person. Similarly in the time-sharing example 7.8, the fair share is an equal probability $1/3$ to be assigned to each machine. The fair share guarantee axiom states that in the actual profile of (different) individual preferences, an agent should not strictly prefer the fair share ω/n to his actual allocation z_i.

---

6. Both properties are important in the commons problem (chapter 6), where no envy pinpoints to the CEEI solution and fair share brings a critique of the virtual price and Shapley solution under decreasing and increasing returns respectively (section 6.6).

The no-envy property is the second key equity test. It states that agent i's share z_i of the resources cannot be inferior, in this agent's preferences, to the share z_j of another agent. The no-envy test applies ex post to the actual distribution of shares, just like fair share guarantee is an ex ante lower bound on individual welfares, in the sense that fair share does not depend on the preferences of agents other than j. No envy has an appealing interpretation in terms of incentive compatibility: once the arbitrator has laid out on the table the n shares $z_i, i = 1, \ldots, n$, the assignment of these particular shares to the n participants (one share per participant) is entirely nonconflictual. The share earmarked for j is precisely the one agent j likes best. Hence, if the n agents queue to help themselves to this "buffet," the correct assignment will emerge irrespective of the ordering in the queue.

The fair share guarantee and no-envy tests are logically unrelated, that is to say neither property implies the other.[7] The normative appeal of the CEEI solution rests on the fact that it is an efficient allocation of the resources meeting both equity tests. In the assignment problems of example 7.7, as well as in the economies of chapter 6, the CEEI solution is the *only* efficient allocation passing the no-envy test. In the case of the assignment problem (example 7.7 and exercise 7.9) the no-envy test even implies efficiency (exercise 7.10). On the other hand, in the fair division problems of the previous section, the CEEI solution is a single-valued selection among a multitude of efficient and nonenvious allocations.

Recall from example 7.10 that the EE solution violates the no-envy test in the especially strong sense that an agent may end up with a strictly larger amount of every good than another agent. Similar configurations occur in exercises 7.12 and 7.14.

We conclude with a discussion of the two monotonicity properties already prominent in the commons problem.

Resource monotonicity states that an increase of the "pie," that is, the resources to be divided, should never result in a loss of welfare for any participant: agent i does not strictly prefer his initial share to his share after the resources have increased.

Population monotonicity considers similarly the departure of one of the agents among whom the resources must be shared; the same resources feed now a smaller number of mouths. The axiom rules out a loss of welfare for any of the remaining participants.

The interpretation of these two properties in section 6.6 applies identically in the present context (see also sections 2.5 and 3.5). Now population monotonicity provides a counter argument in support of the EE solution against the CEEI one.

As already noted in exercise 6.4, the CEEI solution violates population monotonicity. The same holds true when the resources consist of divisible commodities as in this chapter. However, the EE solution always is population monotonic. This is because it equalizes the

---

7. An exception is when all utility functions are linear, as in examples 7.10 and 7.11, as well as exercises 7.12 through 7.15. Then fair share guarantee is a consequence of no envy, but the converse implication does not hold.

utility functions (normalized by taking the vector of resources as the numéraire) so the arguments of section 2.5 apply here.

Turning finally to resource monotonicity, we note first that *neither* the CEEI *nor* the EE solution is resource monotonic. An example for CEEI was already offered in exercise 6.4. As for EE, observe that when the resources change, the scale of individual utilities change as well; hence the general fact that an egalitarian solution is resource monotonic (section 2.5) does not apply. A three-person example where the EE solution fails resource monotonicity is the subject of exercise 7.15.

The following table summarizes the axiomatic discussion:

	Fair share guarantee	No envy	Population monotonicity	Resource monotonicity
CEEI	Yes	Yes	No	No
EE	Yes	No	Yes	No

Our last example uncovers a puzzling incompatibility between fair share guarantee and resource monotonicity, and casts serious doubts on the usefulness of the latter axiom in the fair division of heterogeneous commodities.

Example 7.12 Example 3.7 Continued   Suppose that we know a solution φ for selecting in the two-person economy of example 3.7 an efficient allocation of resources between Jones and Smith for every amount of resources in goods A and B. Assume that this solution is resource monotonic and always guarantees a fair share to both Jones and Smith. Here we derive a logical contradiction.

Consider the resources to be $\omega = (24, 12)$, meaning 24 units of A and 12 units of B. The fair share $\omega/2$ yields the utility $u_2(12, 6) = 12$ to Smith. In *any* allocation where Smith gets at least 12 utils, he must receive at least 12 units of A and 6 of B. Thus, because our solution meets the fair share test, Jones's utility when the resources are $(12, 12)$ is at most $u_1(12, 6) = 6$.

Invoke now resource monotonicity to deduce that when the resources are $\omega_0 = (12, 12)$, Jones's utility is at most 6. By considering the resources $\omega' = (12, 24)$ and exchanging the roles of Smith and Jones, we deduce similarly that Smith's utility is at most 6 when we divide $\omega_0 = (12, 12)$. But notice that Jones and Smith can get 8 utils each by dividing ω_0 as $(a_1, b_1) = (4, 8)$ (Jones) and $(a_2, b_2) = (8, 4)$ (Smith), and we have reached a contradiction of efficiency.

An easy way to construct an efficient and resource monotonic fair division method is to select one commodity, say good A, and to equalize all utilities measured along this numéraire. That is, agent i's utility for the allocation z_i is the amount u_i of good A that makes her indifferent between z_i and u_i units of A. Because this calibration is independent of the pie ω, resource monotonicity follows. But this solution unjustifiably penalizes an agent who dislikes good A, relative to the other goods. In other words, this solution has a strong normative bias in favor of good A. Consider Mary and Paul with the following linear utilities over goods A and B:

$$u_M(a_1, b_1) = a_1 + 4b_1, \quad u_P(a_2, b_2) = 4a_2 + b_2$$

The resources are 100 units of A and the same amount of B. Using good A as numéraire, the following allocation brings equal utilities to Mary and Paul:

$$z_M = (a_1^*, b_1^*) = (0, 29.4), \quad z_P = (a_2^*, b_2^*) = (100, 70.6)$$

Indeed, Mary is indifferent between z_M and 117.6 units of good A, and so is Paul![8] The overwhelming advantage of Paul follows from the asymmetric treatment of the goods.

7.7   Introduction to the Literature

We start with the material of sections 7.1 to 7.3.

The equivalence of the competitive equilibrium and the core of an exchange economy was first proved by Debreu and Scarf (1963) in a model involving replication of a given exchange economy, and subsequently generalized to economies with a continuum of agents. Textbook presentations are provided in Hildenbrand and Kirman (1974) as well as Mas-Colell, Whinston, and Green (1995).

When goods are indivisible and agents consume at most one unit, the equivalence is much easier to prove, as noted by Shapley and Scarf (1974), and discussed in example 7.1.

The model with indivisible goods is especially well suited for examining the limits of core-stability and competitive analysis under nonconvex preferences and nonmonotonic returns to scale. See the detailed treatment in Telser (1988), which inspired the discussion of section 7.3, and in particular, example 7.6.

The variant of the Debreu-Scarf theorem for the assignment problem (exercise 7.10) is discussed in chapter 3 of Moulin (1995).

Two general references for sections 7.4 and 7.5 are Young (1994) and Moulin (1995). The latter also covers the axiomatic discussion of section 7.6.

The article by Alkan, Demange, and Gale (1991) inspired the recent literature on assignment, and in particular, the discussion in section 7.4. Example 7.8 and the (unnumbered)

---

8. The exact values are $b_1^* = 500/17$, $b_2^* = 1,200/17$.

example concluding section 7.5 are adapted from Abdulkadiroglu and Sönmez (1998) and Bogomolnaia and Moulin (2000).

Of the two solutions discussed in section 7.5, the CEEI is the oldest one, going back to Kolm (1972) and Varian (1974). The egalitarian equivalent solution was proposed by Pazner and Schmeidler (1978). Brams and Taylor (1999) discuss several applications of the egalitarian equivalent solution to conflict resolution, much in the spirit of example 7.11. The equality of the CEEI and Nash solutions when utility functions are homogeneous follows from a general result on aggregation of competitive demands attributed to Eisenberg, Chipman, and Moore (1976). See, for example, theorem 3 in chapter 14 of Arrow and Intriligator (1982).

More details on the axiomatic discussion in section 7.6 can be found in Thomson and Varian (1985) and in chapter 4 in Moulin (1995). Finally, two recent books on cake-cutting methods propose simple algorithms to achieve fair division when utilities are linear over the "cake": Brams and Taylor (1996), Robertson and Webb (1998).

Exercises to Chapter 7

Exercise 7.1 The Three Arabs (from the sixteenth-century story by Chevalier de Meriziac in *Problèmes plaisants et délectables*)

Two arabs were about to have dinner. One had five dishes, the other had three, and all dishes were of equal value. A third arab showed up and proposed to share these dishes with them. He promised to pay his share of the meal, which he did by giving 8 deniers. How must the other two arabs share those 8 deniers?

Model this problem as one of fair trade and find the correct solution, which is *not* 5 deniers for the first and 3 deniers for the second.

Exercise 7.2 Variants of Example 7.1

a. We have seven physicians. Initially each physician i owns slot i. Their preferences over slots are described in the table below, except for the irrelevant information about slots that a physician sees as inferior to his own:

Agent	1	2	3	4	5	6	7
Top slot	x_3	x_3	x_4	x_5	x_4	x_1	x_1
	x_2	x_1	x_5	x_4	x_1	x_7	x_2
	x_1	x_2	x_2		x_2	x_3	x_5
			x_3		x_5	x_2	x_6
						x_6	x_7

Perform the top trading cycle algorithm and find the corestable assignment of slots. Find a set of competitive prices—as in (2)—for which supply and demand coincide.

b. We have three slots and three agents, with the following preferences:

Agent	1	2	3
Top	x_3	x_1	x_1
	x_1	x_3	x_2
	x_2	x_2	x_3

Compute the unique corestable outcome and a set of competitive prices.

Next assume that agents 1 and 2 exchange their slots prior to the opening of the barter algorithm. Check that agent 2 is made better off while 1 receives the same slot as before.

*Can you find an example with four players and houses where a reallocation prior to barter within a coalition of three agents is strictly profitable to two of them and leaves the third one with the same slot?

Exercise 7.3 More on Example 7.3

a. In this question and the next, the cost function is $C(q) = 10q$ (no fixed cost) and the demand function is the usual $d(p) = 100 - p$. We have one or more firms, each owning a copy of the technology. Show that the competitive allocation is the *unique* efficient allocation meeting no envy (applied only between firms or between buyers) and voluntary participation (nonnegative surplus share for everyone).

b. Compute the Shapley value of the stand-alone surplus game in the case of a monopoly (thus with $100 + 1$ agents) and in the case with two potential firms (duopoly; 102 agents in total).

c. Now there is an $1,800 fixed cost to produce any positive amount of output. In the monopoly case, show that the Shapley value of the stand-alone surplus game with 101 agents awards $625 to the firm, and compute the surplus shares of the efficient buyers. Compute similarly the Shapley value with two potential firms (102 agents in the game). Show that as the number of firms grows, the total surplus share awarded by the Shapley value to the firms goes down. With an arbitrary large number of firms, we find the Shapley value of the commons problem, as in example 6.7.

Exercise 7.4 Shapley Value in Example 7.4

Notation as in example 7.4. Consider first a buyer $p, 0 \le p \le 60$, and let λ be the fraction of *buyers* preceding him in the random ordering. Conditional on this, the probability that the monopolist precedes our buyer is λ.

Distinguish two cases. If $0 \leq \lambda \leq 2/5$, check that our buyer receives the surplus share p if the monopolist precedes him. If $2/5 \leq \lambda \leq 40/(100 - p)$, check that this share is $p - 100 + 40/\lambda$. Finally, if $40/(100 - p) \leq \lambda \leq 1$, this share is zero.

Combine the three cases above to derive the expected surplus share of our buyer p, $0 \leq p \leq 60$. Describe similar computations for the case of a buyer p, $60 \leq p \leq 100$. Note that the only critical value of λ is $2/5$ in this case.

Exercise 7.5 Two Is Enough for Competition

Notation as in example 7.4. Seller 1 owns 30 units, and seller 2 owns 10 units. Demand is $d(p) = 100 - p$; hence total surplus is 3,200.

We consider distributions of surplus where seller i's share is x_i, $i = 1, 2$, and buyer p's share is y_p. The goal is to show that the unique corestable distribution is the competitive one.

a. Show that $x_1 = 1,200$, $x_2 = 400$, and $y_p = \max\{p - 40, 0\}$ is the unique competitive allocation, and that it is corestable as well.

b. Show that core-stability implies that $y_p = 0$ for any inefficient buyer, namely $p < 60$.

c. For any coalition S of buyers, core-stability implies that

$$|S| \leq 30 \Rightarrow x_1 + \sum_{p \in S} y_p \geq \sum_{p \in S} p$$

$$|S| \leq 10 \Rightarrow x_2 + \sum_{p \in S} y_p \geq \sum_{p \in S} p$$

Show that if S is made of efficient buyers only, these inequalities are equalities.

d. Deduce from question c:

$$\frac{x_1}{30} = \frac{x_2}{10} = p - y_p \qquad \text{for all } p, 60 \leq p \leq 100$$

Conclude that (x_1, x_2, y_p) is the surplus distribution of the competitive allocation.

Exercise 7.6 Variants of Example 7.6

a. Suppose that there are only two taxis instead of three in example 7.6. With seven customers, each willing to pay \$7, it is no longer feasible to transport all customers. Show that there is a unique corestable allocation of surplus in which the two taxis share the efficient surplus equally and customers get nothing.

b. Suppose that we have two taxis and only four customers (with the same cost or willingness to pay as above). Show that the core is empty. *Hint:* If the core is nonempty, it contains a symmetric surplus distribution where the two taxis (and the four customers) get identical shares.

c. With two taxis and five customers, show that the core is empty.

d. Now we have two taxis and a limo. The limo seats up to six passengers and it costs $14 to run, irrespective of the number of passengers (at most six). Show that the core is empty if we have eight customers.

Hint: If the core is nonempty, it contains a surplus distribution where all customers get the same share x, each taxi gets y, and the limo gets z. Write the core constraints for the coalitions containing one taxi and three customers, or the limo and six customers.

Is or is not the core empty if we have ten customers? six customers?

Exercise 7.7 A Variant of Example 6.4

a. We have 40 objects of high quality (A-objects) and 60 objects of low quality (B-objects). There are 100 agents, and agent p, $0 \le p \le 100$, is willing to pay p for an A-object and $p/2$ for a B-object.

Show that efficiency requires to give an A-object to each one of the top 40 agents.

Agent p gets a (positive or negative) cash transfer $x(p)$, and the sum of all transfers is zero. Show that the unique set of transfers, ensuring that no agent is envious, is as follows:

$$x(p) = -18 \quad \text{for } 60 \le p \le 100$$

$$x(p) = +12 \quad \text{for } 0 \le p \le 60$$

b. Suppose now we have 30 A-objects and 40 B-objects. Thus in any assignment, 30 agents end up with no objects. Compute the efficient allocation of objects and the unique set of cash transfers satisfying the no-envy test.

Exercise 7.8 Another Solution in Example 7.7

This solution splits equally the cost savings from (expected waiting cost under) random scheduling. Check that agent p's waiting cost (disutility) is then $v(p) = 50p - 833$, and compute the price tag attached with the slot p, $0 \le p \le 100$.

Show that this solution is not strategy-proof, specifically which agents p want to report a higher marginal cost and which ones want to report a lower marginal cost?

*Exercise 7.9 Job Assignment

Three partners, Ann, Bob, and Charles, have been awarded three jobs. Each partner can only do one job, and each job can be done by any partner. They are free to assign the three jobs as they please.

a. Each job pays $1,000, but the costs to each agent of performing each job vary as follows:

	Ann	Bob	Charles
Job 1	800	500	400
Job 2	900	700	400
Job 3	1100	700	500

Check that we have two efficient (cost-minimizing) assignments of the jobs to the three partners. Compute the unique set of cash transfers achieving the no-envy test.

b. Consider the following cost structure:

	Ann	Bob	Charles
Job 1	800	500	700
Job 2	900	700	800
Job 3	600	400	500

Check that we have two efficient assignments. Yet there is a range of cash transfers achieving the no-envy test. Show that this range is a one-dimensional interval, in the sense that the transfer to Bob, say, can be chosen in an interval, and this determines the other two transfers to Ann and Charles. Compute the interval in question.

c. Now the cost structure is as follows:

	Ann	Bob	Charles
Job 1	800	500	700
Job 2	900	700	800
Job 3	700	400	500

Here there is a unique efficient assignment. Show that the set of cash transfers achieving no envy is now a two-dimensional triangle. Describe the corresponding set of transfer profiles to a given pair of agents, say, Ann and Bob.

*Exercise 7.10 No Envy and the CEEI in the Assignment Problem

a. In this question we show that no envy implies efficiency.

The n agents are labeled $1, 2, \ldots, n$, and we have n objects $a, b, c, \ldots$. Consider an assignment where agent i gets object a_i, and a cash transfer t_i (so that $\sum_i t_i = 0$). We assume that this assignment meets no envy and show that there is no other assignment of objects to agents producing a higher surplus than $i \rightarrow a_i$.

If $i \rightarrow b_i$ is another assignment of objects to our agents, let $j(i)$ be the agent such that $a_{j(i)} = b_i$. No envy implies for all agent i that

$$u_i(a_i) + t_i \geq u_i(b_i) + t_{j(i)}$$

Show that these inequalities imply $\sum_i u_i(a_i) \geq \sum_i u_i(b_i)$ as desired.

b. Given the nonenvious and efficient assignment of question a, we choose a number r large enough so that $r \geq t_i$ for all i and define a profile of prices p by $p_{a_i} = r - t_i$ for $i = 1, \ldots, n$. Show that our assignment is the competitive equilibrium allocation corresponding to prices p and the income r for each agent.

Exercise 7.11 Generalization of Example 7.9

There are now n_1 agents in N^{AB}, n_2 agents in N^{BC}, and n_0 agents in N^0. All others assumptions in example 7.9 are preserved.

a. Generalize the formula (4) describing the efficient allocations treating equals equally. Show that an allocation guarantees fair shares and is nonenvious if and only if

$$\frac{100}{n} \leq z \leq \frac{100}{n_0 + \max\{n_1, n_2\}}$$

where $n = n_0 + n_1 + n_2$.

b. Show that the CEEI solution is given by

$$z = \frac{100}{n}, \quad x = \frac{n_1 + n_2}{n_1} \frac{100}{n}, \quad y = \frac{n_1 + n_2}{n_2} \frac{100}{n}$$

c. Assume $n_1 \geq n_2$, without loss of generality, and compute the EE solution:

$$z = x = \frac{100}{n_0 + n_1}, \quad y = \frac{n_1}{n_2} \frac{100}{n_0 + n_1}$$

*Exercise 7.12 Generalization of Example 7.10

· Using the same notations and assumptions as in the example 7.10, we have n_1 A agents, n_2 B agents, and n_0 zero agents who use two links.

a. Generalize the description of the efficient allocations treating equals equally, in particular formula (7).

b. Compute the CEEI solution by distinguishing two cases. If $|n_1 - n_2| \le n_0$, show that

$$x = y = z^A + z^B = \frac{200}{n}$$

$$z^A = \left(1 + \frac{n_2 - n_1}{n_0}\right) \frac{100}{n}, \quad z^B = \left(1 + \frac{n_1 - n_2}{n_0}\right) \frac{100}{n}$$

where $n = n_1 + n_2 + n_0$ is the total number of users. If $n_1 > n_2 + n_0$, show that

$$x = \frac{100}{n_1}$$

$$y = z^B = \frac{100}{n_0 + n_2}, \quad z^A = 0$$

Check that a O agent gets strictly more than his fair share in the latter case.

c. Compute the EE solution by distinguishing two cases $|n_1 - n_2| \le 2n_0$ and $|n_1 - n_2| > 2n_0$. Show, in particular, that

$$|n_1 - n_2| \le 2n_0 \Rightarrow x = y = \frac{200}{n + n_0}$$

$$z^A + z^B = \frac{400}{n + n_0}$$

Give the exact values of z^A, z^B, and check that if $n_1 > n_2$ (resp. $n_2 > n_1$) an O agent receives more of good B (resp. A) than a B agent (resp. A agent).

Exercise 7.13 Variants of Example 7.11

a. Consider the following distribution of points among four items:

	A	B	C	D
Joan	25	40	10	25
Peter	30	20	30	20

Show that the CEEI solution gives items B, D to Joan and items A, C to Peter. Show that the EE solution gives object B and $\frac{8}{9}$th of D to Joan and the rest to Peter.

b. Compute similarly our two solutions for the following distribution of points among six objects:

	A	B	C	D	E	F
Joan	50	10	10	10	10	10
Peter	15	15	15	15	20	20

Exercise 7.14 Linear Utilities

We assume throughout that individual preferences are represented by linear utilities over two goods A and B. If agent i gets a_i units of good A and b_i of good B, his utility is $u_i = \alpha a_i + \beta b_i$ for some fixed parameters α, β. Naturally only the ratio α/β matters.

a. In this chocolate-vanilla cake the chocolate part amounts to $\frac{1}{3}$ and vanilla to $\frac{2}{3}$. Ann likes vanilla twice as much as chocolate, and Bob likes vanilla just as much as chocolate. What division of the cake is recommended by the egalitarian equivalent solution? by the CEEI solution?

b. Answer the same questions when Charles shows up to share the cake with Ann and Bob, and Charles likes chocolate twice as much as vanilla.

c. In this question we must share 100 units of good A and 100 units of good B among three agents. The profile of parameters α, β is as follows:

	A	B
John	8	1
Mary	8	3
Paul	3	2

Show that the CEEI solution gives to John and Mary 50 units of good A each, and all 100 units of good B to Paul. What is the competitive price vector? Show that the EE solution gives only 45 units of good A to John, and 55 units to Mary, while Paul keeps all of good B. Comment on the difference between these two solutions.

b. We now have 90 units of each good, and 10 agents with the following preferences:

$$u_1(a_1, b_1) = a_1 + 9b_1$$

$$u_i(a_i, b_i) = 9a_i + b_i, \qquad i = 2, \ldots, 10$$

Show that the efficient allocations treating equals equally are of the following form:

	A	B
Agent 1	x'	90
Agents 2, ..., 10	x	0

	A	B
Agent 1	0	x'
Agents 2, ..., 10	10	x

where $x' = 90 - 9x$.

Compute the CEEI solution. Check that the "mainstream" agents get a little less than a 9 percent increase above their fair share utility, whereas the eccentric agent gets an 80 percent increase.

Show that in the EE solution all agents get about 9.75 percent increase above the fair share utility. Compare agent 1's share in the two solutions.

*Exercise 7.15 Resource Monotonicity and the EE Solution

We have four goods A, B, C, and D. Three agents have the following linear preferences over the four goods, where the table indicates the marginal utility of each agent i for each good X:

	A	B	C	D
John	12	3	3	1
Mary	3	12	3	27
Paul	3	3	12	27

a. Assume first that the pie consists of one unit of goods A, B, C and no good D. Show that the EE solution (and the CEEI solution as well) give all of good A to John, all of B to Mary, and all of C to Paul.

b. Assume now that the pie grows by the addition of one unit of good D. Show that the EE solution is now

John: 0.90 units of good A

Mary: 0.05 of good A, 1 unit of B, 0.5 unit of D

Paul: 0.05 of good A, 1 unit of C, 0.5 unit of D

Deduce a violation of resource monotonicity.

c. What is the CEEI solution in the situation of question b?

8 A Glossary of Definitions and Results

Chapter 2

1. (Section 2.2) A deficit-sharing (also called rationing) problem consists of a set N of agents, a claim x_i, $x_i \geq 0$ for each agent $i \in N$, and the amount t, $t \geq 0$, of (homogeneous) resource such that $t < x_N = \sum_i x_i$.

   An excess-sharing (also called surplus-sharing) problem consists of N, x_i, t as above, such that $x_N < t$. A solution (also called method) associates to each deficit (resp. excess) problem (N, x, t) a share y_i for each $i \in N$, such that

   $y_N = t$ and for all $i, 0 \leq y_i \leq x_i$ (*deficit*); or $x_i \leq y_i$ (*excess*)

2. The proportional solution is given by the same formula in the deficit and excess cases:

$$y_i = \frac{x_i}{\sum_N x_j} t$$

   It is invariant to the merging, splitting, or transfer of claims among the participants. The former two properties are explained immediately after example 2.4. The latter properties consider two profiles of claims x and x' that only differ in their i and j coordinates:

$$\{x_k = x'_k \text{ if } k \neq i, j; \ x_i + x_j = x'_i + x'_j\} \Rightarrow y_i + y_j = y'_i + y'_j$$

   where y and y' are, respectively, the solutions for (N, x, t) and (N, x', t).

   In rationing problems the proportional method is characterized by either one of the three properties above (invariance to merging of claims; to splitting of claims; to transfer of claims).

3. The uniform gains solution is defined as follows, respectively for the deficit and the excess case:

deficit: $\displaystyle\sum_N \min\{\lambda, x_i\} = t \Rightarrow y_i = \min\{\lambda, x_i\}$

excess: $\displaystyle\sum_N \max\{\lambda, x_i\} = t \Rightarrow y_i = \max\{\lambda, x_i\}$

   Two different sets of algorithms to compute the solution in both cases are proposed immediately after example 2.5 and in exercise 2.6. The uniform gains solution guarantees to agent i a share y_i not smaller than $\min\{x_i, t/n\}$; exercise 2.8.

   In the deficit case, the uniform gains solution meets independence of higher claims:

for all i, j: $\ x_i \leq x_j < x'_j \Rightarrow y_i = y'_i$

where x and x' only differ in their jth coordinate, and y, y' are the corresponding solutions. See example 2.6, and the discussion following it. In combination with equal treatment of equals (for all $i, j : x_i = x_j \Rightarrow y_i = y_j$), the independence of higher claims property characterizes the uniform gains solution. See exercise 2.3.

In the excess case, the uniform gains solution meets independence of lower claims:

$$\text{for all } i, j: \quad x'_j < x_j \leq x_i \Rightarrow y_i = y'_i$$

In combination with equal treatment of equals, this property characterizes the uniform gains solution.

4. The uniform losses solution for deficit problems is defined as follows:

$$\sum_N \max\{x_i - \mu, 0\} = t \Rightarrow y_i = \max\{x_i - \mu, 0\}$$

The equal surplus solution for surplus (excess) sharing problems is

$$y_i = x_i + \frac{1}{n}\left(t - \sum_N x_j\right)$$

Two sets of algorithms to compute these two solutions are proposed immediately after example 2.5 and in exercise 2.6. The uniform losses solution (deficit case) places the cap $\max\{x_i - (x_N - t)/n, 0\}$ on agent i's share; exercise 2.8.

5. (Section 2.3) The contested garment method is defined for deficit problems involving only *two* agents.

Contested garment shares

$$y_1 = \frac{1}{2}(t + \min\{x_1, t\} - \min\{x_2, t\})$$

$$y_2 = \frac{1}{2}(t - \min\{x_1, t\} + \min\{x_2, t\})$$

It satisfies the two properties of truncation and concession:

Truncation. Given the profile of claims x and resources t, define x' by $x'_i = \min\{x_i, t\}$ for all i; then $y = y'$, which means that the profile of shares is the same under x or x'.

Concession. Given x, t and i, set $c_i = \max\{t - x_{N\setminus i}, 0\}$, $t' = t - c_i$ and define x' by $x'_i = x_i - c_i$ and $x'_j = x_j$ for all j, $j \neq i$. Then the solution y' of the problem (x', t') is $y'_i = y_i - c_i$ and $y'_j = y_j$ for all j, $j \neq i$.

The contested garment solution is characterized by the combination of equal treatment of equals, truncation, and concession.

There are two generalizations of the contested garment method to any number of agents. The run to the bank presented in exercise 2.10 is an application of the Shapley value. The Talmudic solution in exercise 2.11 combines the uniform gains and uniform losses solution. Both methods meet truncation and concession.

6. *Duality.* To a solution $(N, t, x) \rightarrow r(N, t, x) = y$ of all deficit problems, we associate its dual solution r^* which is defined as follows:

$$r^*(N, t, x) = x - r(N, x_N - t, x)$$

The dual r^* of the solution r divides the deficit $x_N - t$ exactly as r divides the resources t. The uniform gains and uniform losses solutions are dual solutions; the proportional and contested garment solutions (as well as both generalizations of the latter) are self-dual.

7. (Section 2.4) A deficit problem (N, t, x) can always be interpreted as a taxation problem, where x_i is agent i's taxable income, y_i his income net of tax, and $x_N - t$ is the total tax to be levied. Thus a solution $(N, t, x) \rightarrow r(N, t, x)$ is interpreted as a tax schedule.

The fair ranking property is compelling in this interpretation:

$$x_i \leq x_j \implies y_i \leq y_j \quad \text{and} \quad x_i - y_i \leq x_j - y_j$$

Tax schedules can be progressive or regressive:

$$\text{progressivity:} \quad x_i \leq x_j \Rightarrow \frac{x_i - y_i}{x_i} \leq \frac{x_j - y_j}{x_j}$$

$$\text{regressivity:} \quad x_i \leq x_j \Rightarrow \frac{x_i - y_i}{x_i} \geq \frac{x_j - y_j}{x_j}$$

Uniform gains is the most progressive tax schedule meeting fair ranking; uniform losses is similarly the most regressive tax schedule; exercise 2.7.

An equal sacrifice method is defined by fixing a concave reference utility function u, which is increasing and continuous. The corresponding taxation method is defined by

$$\text{for all } i: \quad y_i > 0 \Rightarrow u(x_i) - u(y_i) = \max_j \{u(x_j) - u(y_j)\}$$

It is progressive if and only if u is more concave than the log function $u(z) = a(\log z)$, where a is concave and increasing. If $u(z) = b(\log z)$, where b is convex and increasing, the equal sacrifice method is regressive.

A solution $(N, t, x) \rightarrow r(N, t, x)$ is scale invariant if $r(N, \lambda t, \lambda x) = \lambda r(N, t, x)$ for any problem (N, t, x) and positive factor λ. The scale-invariant equal sacrifice methods correspond to the following two families of reference utility functions:

$u_p(z) = -1/z^p$ for some $p, 0 < p < +\infty$; all corresponding methods are progressive

$u^q(z) = z^q$ for some $q, 0 < q < 1$; all corresponding methods are regressive

The u_p method converges to uniform gains as p becomes arbitrarily large; it converges to the proportional method as p goes to zero. The u^q method converges to the proportional one as q goes to zero, and to uniform losses as q goes to one. See exercise 2.14.

8. (Section 2.5) The utilitarian model of resource allocation specifies for each agent $i, i \in N$, a utility function u_i that is increasing and continuous. The problem is to divide t units of resources when the share y_i produces the utility $u_i(y_i)$ for agent i.

Two simple solutions are compared:

Utilitarian (classical).   Find $y_i \geq 0$ maximizing $\sum_i u_i(y_i)$ under $y_N = t$.

Egalitarian*.   Find $y_i \geq 0$ such that $y_N = t$ and for all i, $y_i > 0 \Rightarrow u_i(y_i) = \min_j u_j(y_j)$.

Three axiomatic properties are examined:

Resource monotonicity.   For N and $u_i, i \in N$, fixed, the share y_i is nondecreasing in t for all i.

Population monotonicity.   For $N, u_i, i \in N$, and t fixed, and all $j \in N$,

$$r_i(N, t, u) \leq r_i(N \backslash j, t, u_{-j}) \qquad \text{for all } i, i \neq j$$

where u_{-j} stands for the profile of utility functions of $N \backslash j$.

Continuity in the utility functions.   A small change in one utility function u_i, ceteris paribus, results in a small change of the profile of shares $y_j, j \in N$.

The egalitarian solution always meets all three properties, for any choice of the increasing and continuous functions u_i; exercise 2.15.

The utilitarian solution may fail all three properties; example 2.9. However, if each utility function u_i is concave, the utilitarian solution coincides with the egalitarian solution for the utility functions $v_i = -u_i'$. Therefore in this case the utilitarian solution meets all three properties as well.

Chapter 3

1. An individual utility function $\tilde{u}_i$ associates to every outcome ("state of the world") x a number $\tilde{u}_i(x)$ measuring agent i's welfare at x.

Given a profile of utility functions $\tilde{u}_i$, $i \in N$, the Pareto relation is the following transitive (but typically not complete) relation among outcomes: y is Pareto superior to x iff $\tilde{u}_i(y) \geq \tilde{u}_i(x)$ for all $i \in N$, and $\tilde{u}_i(y) > \tilde{u}_i(x)$ for at least one $i \in N$. The outcome x is called Pareto optimal, or efficient, if no outcome y is Pareto superior to x.

2. A social welfare ordering is a binary relation $\succsim$ over utility profiles $u = (u_i)_{i \in N}$, meaning over vectors in $\mathbb{R}^N$. The SWO is, by definition, complete and transitive (it is a rational preference over $\mathbb{R}^N$). Moreover it is monotonic (i.e., compatible with the Pareto relation) and symmetric:

Monotonicity. $\{u_i \geq v_i$ for all $i \in N$ and $u_i > v_i$ for some $i\} \Rightarrow u \succ v$.

Symmetry. If u obtains from v by permuting the coordinates, then $u \sim v$ where $\succ$ is the strict component of $\succsim$, and $\sim$ its indifference relation.

A collective utility function $W(u)$ is defined over utility profiles, is strictly increasing in each coordinate, and is a symmetric function of its coordinates u_i. A CUF W defines a SWO as follows: $u \succsim v \Leftrightarrow W(u) \geq W(v)$, but not all SWOs obtain in this way. A prominent example is the leximin SWO defined below.

3. (Section 3.2) The SWO $\succsim$ is independent of unconcerned agents if the comparison between any two profiles u, v does not depend on the welfare of those agents i such that $u_i = v_i$. Formally, for all utility profiles u, v, u', v', we have

$$\{u_i = v_i \Rightarrow u'_i = v'_i; u_i \neq v_i \Rightarrow u'_i = u_i, \ v'_i = v_i \text{ for all } i\} \Rightarrow \{u \succsim v \Leftrightarrow u' \succsim v'\}$$

(this is the same statement as property (1) in section 3.2).

The SWO $\succsim$ is continuous if for all u, the sets $\{v \mid v \succsim u\}$ and $\{v \mid u \succsim v\}$, called, respectively, the upper and lower contour sets of u, are topologically closed.

An important theorem. The SWO $\succsim$ is continuous and independent of unconcerned agents if and only if it is represented by an additive CUF, namely $W(u) = \sum_i g(u_i)$, where g is an increasing and continuous function.

Given a utility profile u and two agents i, j such that $u_i \neq u_j$, a shift from (u_i, u_j) to (u'_i, u'_j) such that $u_i + u_j = u'_i + u'_j$ and $|u'_i - u'_j| < |u_i - u_j|$ is called a Pigou-Dalton transfer. The SWO $\succsim$ meets the Pigou-Dalton transfer principle if it does not decrease through such transfers: $u' \succsim u$, where $u'_k = u_k$ for all $k \neq i, j$. In this case we also say that $\succsim$ is averse to inequality.

The (SWO represented by an) additive CUF $W(u) = \sum_i g(u_i)$ is averse to inequality if and only if g is concave.

4. In this subsection we restrict attention to positive utility profiles: $u_i > 0$ for all i. The SWO $\succsim$ is independent of the common utility scale if we have

$$u \succsim u' \Leftrightarrow \lambda u \succsim \lambda u' \qquad \text{for all } u, u' \text{ and all } \lambda > 0$$

The additive CUF W represents a SWO independent of the common utility scale if and only if it takes one of the following three forms:

$$W_p(u) = \sum_i u_i^p, \qquad \text{with } p > 0 \text{ and fixed}$$

$$W_o(u) = \sum_i \log u_i$$

$$W^q(u) = -\sum_i \frac{1}{u_i^q} \qquad \text{with } q > 0 \text{ and fixed}$$

Thus the family above describes all continuous SWOs independent of unconcerned agents and of the common utility scale. They are all averse to inequality, except for W_p when $p > 1$.

The SWO represented by W_1 is called classical utilitarianism, that represented by W_o, or equivalently by the Nash CUF $W_N(u) = \Pi_i u_i$, is called the Nash SWO. It is the limit of the SWO represented by W_p as p goes to zero, or by W^q as q goes to zero.

5. (Section 3.3) When q becomes arbitrarily large, the SWO represented by W^q converges to the leximin SWO defined as follows. Denote by Lex the lexicographic ordering of $\mathbb{R}^n$:

$(a_1, \ldots, a_n)\mathrm{Lex}(b_1, \ldots, b_n)$

  $\Leftrightarrow \{\text{for some } k, 0 \le k \le n, \ a_i = b_i, \ \text{for } i \le k \text{ and } a_{k+1} > b_{k+1}\}$

For any utility profile $u \in \mathbb{R}^n$, write u^* for the vector in $\mathbb{R}^n$ obtained by rearranging increasingly the coordinates of u. The leximin ordering is defined by $u \succsim v \Leftrightarrow u^* \text{ Lex } v^*$. This SWO is independent of unconcerned agents and is the most averse to inequality among all SWOs described in the previous section. It is not continuous, however. It is only partially represented by the egalitarian CUF W_e, $W_e(u) = \min_i u_i$, in the sense that $W_e(u) > W_e(v) \Rightarrow u \succ v$ but the converse statement does not hold.

The leximin SWO meets the following Independent of the common utility pace property. For any increasing bijection f from $\mathbb{R}$ into itself, and any utility profile $u \in \mathbb{R}^N$, write $f(u)$ for the profile $(f(u_i))_{i \in N}$. Then we have

$$u \succsim v \Leftrightarrow f(u) \succsim f(v) \qquad \text{for all } u, v$$

The leximin SWO is characterized by the combination of inequality aversion and the above independence property.

6. (Section 3.4) The classical utilitarian SWO is independent of individual zeros of utilities: the comparison of u and v does not change if agent i's utility u_i, v_i is replaced by $u_i + \delta$,

$v_i + \delta$ respectively, ceteris paribus. Formally, this amounts to the property

$$u \succsim v \Leftrightarrow u + w \succsim v + w \qquad \text{for all } u, v, w \in \mathbb{R}^N$$

This property single-handedly characterizes the classical utilitarian SWO.

The Nash SWO, defined only over positive utility profiles, is independent of individual scales of utilities: the comparison of u and v does not change if agent i's utility u_i, v_i is replaced by $\lambda u_i, \lambda v_i$ respectively, ceteris paribus. Formally,

$$u \succsim v \Leftrightarrow w \cdot u \succsim w \cdot v \qquad \text{for all } u, v, w \in \mathbb{R}_+^N$$

where we use the notation $a \cdot b = (a_i b_i)_{i \in N}$. The Nash SWO is single-handedly characterized by this property.

7. (Section 3.6) A bargaining problem among the agents of N is a pair (B, u^d), where B is the set of feasible utility profiles (a subset of $\mathbb{R}^N$) and u^d is a particular point in $\mathbb{R}^N$ called the disagreement utility profile. A bargaining solution selects for each problem (B, u^d) a utility profile in B that is Pareto optimal and bounded below by u^d. Of course, we must chose B and u^d in such a way that the set of such profiles is nonempty.

Define the maximal feasible utility for a given agent, compatible with guaranteeing the disagreement utility to every other agent:

$$u_i^{\max} = \max u_i \quad \text{over all } u \quad \text{s.t.} \quad u \in B \quad \text{and} \quad u \geq u^d$$

The Nash solution of the bargaining problem (B, u^d) is the utility profile u maximizing $\Pi_i (u_i - u_i^d)$ over the feasible set B. This solution is uniquely defined if B is convex and topologically closed, and if u^d feasible in B. The Kalai-Smorodinsky solution is the Pareto optimal utility profile in B equalizing the relative gains from u^d to $u^{\max}$:

$$\frac{u_i - u_i^d}{u_i^{\max} - u_i^d} = \frac{u_j - u_j^d}{u_j^{\max} - u_j^d} \qquad \text{for all } i, j$$

If the set B is convex and topologically closed, and u^d is feasible in B the KS solution is typically well defined. If it is not, we can refine the definition as follows: use the leximin SWO to compare the profiles $(u_i - u_i^d)/(u_i^{\max} - u_i^d)$. The unique maximum gives the KS solution.

Both the Nash and KS solution are independent of individual utility scales. Both guarantee to each participant his or her disagreement utility plus $1/n$th of the maximal feasible gain above that level:

$$u_i \geq u_i^d + \frac{1}{n} \left(u_i^{\max} - u_i^d \right)$$

One property drawing a wedge between the two solutions is related to the rationality of choices discussed in chapter 4 (section 4.1). Suppose that a bargaining solution picks u in the bargaining problem (B, u^d), and consider a problem (B', u^d) such that $B' \subseteq B$ and $u \in B'$. In B' we have fewer options, but the "optimal" profile u is still available. Then the solution should select u in the bargaining problem (B', u^d).

The property above is satisfied by the Nash bargaining solution. In combination with the independence of individual utility scales, it characterizes this solution. By contrast, the KS solution violates the rationality property; example 3.12.

Chapter 4

1. (Section 4.1) The set of outcomes (states of the world) is denoted A. Agent i's preference ordering R_i is a binary relation on A, that is,

Complete.   For all $x, y \in A$, at least one of $x R_i y$ or $y R_i x$ holds.

Transitive.   For all $x, y, z \in A$, $\{x R y$ and $y R z\} \Rightarrow x R z$.

A collective choice problem is a triple $(A, N, \tilde{R})$, where $\tilde{R} = (R_i)_{i \in N}$ is a preference profile specifying a preference ordering for each agent $i \in N$. A voting rule associates to every problem $(A, N, \tilde{R})$ an outcome $x = f(A, N, \tilde{R})$ called the winner, or a subset of tied winners.

A preference aggregation method associates to every problem $(A, N, \tilde{R})$ a preference ordering $R = F(\tilde{R})$ interpreted as the collective preference over A. It is an ordinal analogue of the collective utility function of chapter 3, associating a collective utility to every profile of cardinal individual utilities.

2. (Section 4.2) Given the set A of p outcomes, a set of scores is a sequence of numbers $s_k, k = 1, \ldots, p$ such that $s_k \geq s_{k+1}$ for $k = 1, \ldots, p-1$, and $s_1 > s_p$. If R_i is a strict preference relation on A (i.e., two distinct outcomes are never equivalent), the score of outcome a under R_i is $s(a, R_i) = s_k$, where k is the rank of a in R_i (the top outcome gets the score s_1, the next one gets s_2, etc.). If R_i allows indifferences, the score of outcome a is $s(a, R_i) = (s_k + s_{k+1} + \cdots + s_{k+m})/(m+1)$ if $(k-1)$ outcomes are strictly preferred to a and m other outcomes are equivalent to a.

Given a collective choice problem (A, N, R), each outcome receives a score $s(a, \tilde{R}) = \sum_i s(a, R_i)$. The scoring voting rule elects the set of outcomes with the highest score. The scoring aggregation method compares the outcomes by means of their scores; $R^b = F(\tilde{R})$ is defined as follows:

$$x R^b y \Leftrightarrow s(x; \tilde{R}) \geq s(y; \tilde{R})$$

The plurality voting (or aggregation) rule corresponds to the choices of scores $s = 1$, $s_k = 0$ for $k = 2, \ldots, p$. Borda proposed instead the scores $s_k = p - k$, for $k = 1, \ldots, p$ and argued that his method selects a more accurate compromise between individual opinions.

A property shared by all scoring methods is "reunion consistency" (example 4.4). Consider two choice problems $(A, N_1, \widetilde{R^1})$ and $(A, N_2, \widetilde{R^2})$ with the same set of outcomes and disjoint set of voters N_1 and N_2. We set $B_i = f(A, N_i, \widetilde{R^i})$ for $i = 1, 2$, and we require that

$$B_1 \cap B_2 \neq \emptyset \Rightarrow f(A, N_1 \cup N_2, \widetilde{R^1} \cup \widetilde{R^2}) = B_1 \cap B_2$$

The reunion consistency property is the basis of a characterization of scoring methods.

Given a collective choice problem $(A, N, \tilde{R})$, the majority relation $R^m = F(\tilde{R})$ is defined on each pair x, y by giving the advantage to this outcome preferred by a majority of voters:

$$x R^m y \Leftrightarrow |\{i \in N \mid x R_i y\}| \geq |\{i \in N \mid y R_i x\}|$$

The majority relation R^m is complete, but it may not be transitive, as shown on the canonical profile of preferences over three outcomes discussed after example 4.3. If the majority relation happens to be transitive, it defines a bona fide aggregation method. A maximal element of the majority relation is called a Condorcet winner, after the mathematician contemporary of Borda who proposed it first. This is simply an outcome a such that $a R_m b$ for all $b \in A$. The set of Condorcet winners may be empty, as shown by the canonical profile just mentioned.

A voting rule is called Condorcet consistent if it selects the set of Condorcet winners whenever this set is nonempty. Any Condorcet consistent voting rule is vulnerable to the reunion paradox of example 4.4.

3. (Section 4.3) When A is the set of allocations of a certain bundle of private goods, and each voter cares only about his or her own share, the majority relation normally fails to be transitive, and its cycles are pervasive; example 4.5.

4. (Section 4.4) When the (finite or infinite) set A of outcomes is arranged along the real line, we can speak of an outcomes x being to the left—or to the right—of another outcome y, of x being between y and z and, so on.

Let R_i be an individual preference relation on A with strict component denoted P_i : $x P_i y$ means $x R_i y$ and not $y R_i x$. We call R_i single peaked on A if the following two properties hold:

R_i has a unique maximal element x^i called its "peak": $x^i P_i x$ for all $x \neq x^i$.

For all x, y and all z between x and y, $x P_i y \Rightarrow z P_i y$.

When all individual preferences are single peaked, the majority relation is transitive. It is also single peaked and its peak—the Condorcet winner—is the median of individual peaks; exercise 4.6.

5. (Section 4.5) When the set of voters is arranged along the real line, we can speak of agent i being between agents j and k. We say that the preference profile $\tilde{R}$ has the intermediate preference property if for any three agents i, j, k, and any two outcomes x, y we have

$$\{i \text{ is between } j \text{ and } k; \ x R_j y; x R_k y\} \Rightarrow \{x R_i y\}$$

When this property holds, the majority relation is transitive; hence there exists a Condorcet winner.

6. (Section 4.6) Arrow's theorem. For an aggregation method F, the independence of irrelevant alternatives property is defined precisely in section 4.6, so we do not repeat this definition here. No scoring aggregation method meets the IIA property, whereas the majority aggregation method satisfies this property.

Fix N, A and assume that A contains three or more outcomes. Let F be an aggregation method defining a rational collective preference $R = F(\tilde{R})$ for every collective choice problem $(A, N, \tilde{R})$. Suppose that F meets the IIA property, and also respects the unanimous preferences of the voters, in the following sense:

$$\{x P_i y \text{ for all } i \in N\} \Rightarrow \{x P y\} \qquad \text{for all } x, y \text{ and } \tilde{R}$$

where P_i, P are the strict component of R_i, R. Then F must be a dictatorial aggregation method, namely there is an agent i^*, the dictator, such that the collective strict preference always agree with the dictator's strict preferences:

$$\{x P_{i^*} y \Rightarrow x P y\} \qquad \text{for all } x, y \text{ and } \tilde{R}$$

In the statement of Arrow's theorem, it is crucial to allow for any set of rational preferences over A. If all individual preferences are restricted to be single-peaked as in section 4.4., or if the preference profile meets the intermediate preference property of section 4.5, then the majority relation is a fair aggregation method meeting the IIA and unanimity properties just described.

7. (Section 4.4) Strategy-proofness.

Fix A and N and consider a single-valued voting rule f: for each problem $(A, N, \tilde{R})$, it selects a unique outcome $x = f(A, N, \tilde{R})$. Suppose that agent i, instead of reporting his true preferences R_i, reports R_i' instead, and denote the new profile $\tilde{R}' = (\tilde{R} \mid^i R_i')$ and $y = f(A, N, \tilde{R}')$ the new outcome of the election. We say that the misreport R_i' by agent i is a successful manipulation at $\tilde{R}$, if this agent strictly prefers the new outcome: $y P_i x$, where P_i is the strict component of his true preference.

We call the voting rule strategy-proof if for all problems $(A, N, \tilde{R})$, no agent has a successful manipulation at $\tilde{R}$. If all individual preferences are restricted to be single-peaked as in section 4.5, and if a misreport must be single-peaked as well, then the Condorcet winner defines a strategy-proof voting rule; see Black (1948). However, if all rational preferences over A are permitted, and A contains three or more outcomes, a strategy-proof voting rule must be dictatorial, in the sense that the best outcome for the dictator i^* is always elected:

$$x P_{i^*} y \quad \text{for all } y \neq x \Rightarrow f(N, A, \tilde{R}) = x, \qquad \text{for all } x \text{ and } \tilde{R}$$

The Gibbard-Satterthwaite theorem is technically equivalent to Arrow's theorem.

Chapter 5

1. (Sections 5.1, 5.2) A cost-sharing game—also called a cooperative game with transferable utility—is a pair (N, C), where N is the set of agents and the cost function C specifies for each coalition (subset of N, including N itself) its stand-alone cost $C(S)$. The interpretation is that $C(S)$ is the cheapest cost incurred in order to provide "service" to all agents in S, independently of the set $N \backslash S$ of agents outside coalition S.

The question is to divide $C(N)$ among the agents in N, in a way that rewards fairly their respective contributions to total cost. The problem is that the cost function C does not provide a clear separation of individual contributions.

The Shapley value charges to each agent his expected marginal cost, when the agents are randomly ordered and each agent pays the increment of the stand-alone cost after he is added to the agents preceding him. The mathematical formula is

$$x_i = \sum_{s=0}^{n-1} \sum_{S \in \mathcal{A}_i(s)} \frac{s!(n-s-1)!}{n!} \{C(S \cup \{i\}) - C(S)\}$$

where $\mathcal{A}_i(s)$ denotes the set of coalitions of size s not containing i.

In a two-person game $N = \{1, 2\}$, this gives the following share:

$$x_1 = \tfrac{1}{2}(C(12) + C(1) - C(2))$$

In a three-person game, this gives similarly

$$x_1 = \tfrac{1}{3}C(1) + \tfrac{1}{6}(C(12) - C(2)) + \tfrac{1}{6}(C(13) - C(3)) + \tfrac{1}{3}(C(123) - C(23))$$
$$= \tfrac{1}{3}C(123) + \tfrac{1}{6}(C(12) + C(13) - 2C(23)) + \tfrac{1}{6}(2C(1) - C(2) - C(3))$$

In the capacity game where each agent has a capacity c_i and the cost function is $C(S) = \max_{i \in S} c_i$, the Shapley shares are

$$x_1 = \frac{1}{n}c_1, \quad x_2 = x_1 + \frac{1}{n-1}(c_2 - c_1), \quad x_3 = x_2 + \frac{1}{n-2}(c_3 - c_2)$$

$$x_n = c_n - \left(\frac{1}{2}c_{n-1} + \frac{1}{6}c_{n-2} + \cdots + \frac{1}{n(n-1)}c_1\right)$$

(where we assume $c_1 \leq c_2 \leq \ldots \leq c_n$).

2. (Section 5.3) The cost function C is subadditive if for any two disjoint coalitions S, T, we have $C(S \cup T) \leq C(S) + C(T)$. It is superadditive if, under the same premises, the opposite inequality holds true.

Some natural stand-alone cost functions are neither sub- nor superadditive; see example 5.9. For these cost functions the stand-alone test is not defined.

The stand-alone test requires $x_i \leq C(i)$ when C is subadditive (no one pays more than her own stand-alone cost), and $x_i \geq C(i)$ when C is superadditive. The Shapley value meets the stand-alone test.

The stand-alone core strengthens the stand-alone test by requiring that the cost share $\sum_s x_i$ of any coalition S be not larger (resp. not smaller) than the stand-alone cost $C(S)$ when C is subadditive (resp. superadditive).

For a subadditive (or superadditive) cost-sharing game, the stand-alone core may well be empty. Example 5.8 and exercise 5.8 illustrate this important fact.

When the stand-alone core is non empty, it may not contain the Shapley value: examples 5.6, 5.7, as well as exercises 5.5, 5.6, illustrate this fact.

On the other hand, in two important classes of cost-sharing games, the Shapley value occupies a central position in the stand-alone core. These are the concave and the convex cost functions.

For a concave cost function,

for all S, T: $\quad S \subseteq T \Rightarrow C(S \cup \{i\}) - C(S) \geq C(T \cup \{i\}) - C(T)$

the inequality is reversed for a convex cost function. The cost function C is concave in example 5.2, and more generally, in the capacity game $C(S) = \max_S c_i$. The cost function is concave in examples 5.5 and 5.6, and more generally, in the games constructed from a tree network and described in exercise 5.7.

Exercise 5.10 explains why the Shapley value lies squarely in the stand alone core when the cost function is concave. The argument for a convex function is identical.

3. (Section 5.4) When we take into account, in addition to the stand-alone costs of all coalitions, the willingness to pay for service of each potential user, the question of how to

divide the cooperative surplus between the the participants can be answered with the same methodology. Once must compute the stand-alone surplus $v(S)$ of each coalition:

$$v(S) = \max_{T \subseteq S} \left(\sum_{i \in T} u_i \right) - C(T)$$

This definition reflects the fact that it may not be efficient to serve all users in S, given the pattern of costs and willingness to pay. The entire discussion of the Shapley value and the stand-alone core can now be revisited.

4. (Section 5.5) Among all the conceivable methods to share total cost $C(N)$ among N while taking into account the entire list of stand-alone costs $C(S)$, the Shapley value stands out for the large number and diversity of its axiomatic characterizations. The four main characterizations are presented in section 5.5 with full mathematical precision; therefore this discussion is not repeated here.

Chapter 7

1. (Sections 7.1 through 7.3) In an exchange economy among N, each agent $i \in N$ is endowed with rational preferences $\succsim_i$ over the consumption of private commodities, and owns a bundle of commodities ω_i. The model also specifies the feasible trades, namely the feasible reallocation of the resources among the participants resulting in an allocation $z = (z_i)_{i \in N}$, where z_i is agent i's after-trade consumption.

An allocation z is blocked by coalition S, $S \subseteq N$, if the agents in S can trade among themselves their initial endowments, and reach an allocation z' such that $z'_i \succsim_i z_i$ for all $i \in S$ and $z'_i \succsim_i z_i$ for at least one $i \in S$. An allocation z is in the core of the exchange economy if it is not blocked by any coalition. Note that a core allocation is, in particular, Pareto optimal.

A feasible allocation z is a competitive equilibrium if there exists a price vector p (one price for each tradable commodity) such that for all $i \in N$, z_i is agent i's competitive demand at price p: $z_i \succsim_i y_i$ for all y_i such that $p \cdot y_i \leq p \cdot \omega_i$.

The link between the core allocation and competitive allocations is an important discovery of modern mathematical economics. The central result, known as the Debreu-Scarf theorem, says that if each market participant has negligible market power—in the sense that her initial endowment is a negligible fraction of total resources in the economy—the two concepts are equivalent: an allocation is competitive if and only if it is in the core of the economy. See Mas-Colell, Whinston, and Green (1995, ch. 18) or Moulin (1995) for a textbook exposition of this result.

Examples 7.1 and 7.2 in section 7.1 are two exchange economies with a unique competitive allocation that is also the unique core allocation. In example 7.2 monetary transfers are feasible and the competitive allocation is also the Shapley value of the stand-alone cooperative game.

In example 7.4 (section 7.2) one market participant is a monopoly (he owns the entire supply of a commodity on which all opportunities to trade depend); hence the negligibility assumption fails. The competitive allocation is only one among many core allocations: it is the core allocation least advantageous to the monopolist.

In example 7.3 the firms have decreasing average costs; hence efficiency of trade requires that only one firm operate. As a result the competitive analysis breaks down: there is no price vector at which the market clears. The core analysis gives useful guidelines on the distribution of surplus among the market participants.

Finally in example 7.6 (section 7.3) both approaches break down, as a result of the U-shaped average costs of the firms (sellers). There are no competitive equilibrium and no core allocation. This means that private contracting under private ownership cannot deliver a convincing distribution of surplus; hence normative solutions, such as the Shapley value of the stand-alone game, are called for.

2. (Sections 7.4 and 7.5) The no-envy test is an equity property defined for a broad range of fair division problems. Say that the bundle of resources ω is divided among N as $z = (z_i)_{i \in N}$. The no-envy test requires that $z_i \succsim_i z_j$ for all i, j: no agent would prefer to exchange his share for the share of another participant.

A competitive equilibrium with equal incomes specifies an allocation z and a price vector such that for all i, z_i is agent i's competitive demand at price p when his endowment is ω/n, or equivalently his income is $1/n$th of the worth $p \cdot \omega$ of the resources. A competitive equilibrium with equal incomes meets the no-envy test, and it is also Pareto optimal.

In the assignment problem of example 7.7, as well as in the general assignment model of exercise 7.10, every Pareto optimal allocation meeting no envy is also a CEEI solution for an appropriate set of prices. In general, the CEEI solution is only one among a large set of Pareto optimal allocations meeting no envy; see examples 7.9, 7.10, and 7.11.

An egalitarian equivalent allocation is a Pareto optimal allocation z such that there exists a positive number λ for which $z_i \sim_i \lambda \cdot \omega$ for all i: everyone is indifferent between receiving z_i or a fraction λ of total resources. Note that λ is necessarily between $1/n$ and 1.

For an important class of fair division problems, the two solutions CEEI and EE correspond precisely to the two bargaining solutions of chapter 3 (section 3.6). This is when each preference relation $\succsim_i$ can be represented by a homogeneous utility function $\tilde{u}_i$: $\tilde{u}_i(\lambda z_i) = \lambda \tilde{u}_i(z_i)$ for all z_i, and all $\lambda > 0$.

For such utility functions we define a bargaining problem as follows:

$B = \{u = (u_i) \mid u_i = \tilde{u}_i(z_i) \text{ for all } i, \text{ for some feasible allocation } z \text{ of } \omega\}$

$u_i^d = \tilde{u}_i(0) = 0$

Then every CEEI allocation z yields the same utility profile $u = \tilde{u}_i(z_i)$, and u is the Nash solution of the bargaining problem (B, u^d). Furthermore every EE allocation yields the same utility profile, namely the Kalai-Smorodinsky solution of the bargaining problem (B, u^d).

Note that the result holds true only when the commodities are divisible and utility functions are monotonic and continuous. Examples 7.10 and 7.11, where all utilities are linear, and example 7.9 illustrate this result.

3. Section 7.6 pursues the critical comparison of the two fair division methods CEEI and EE at the axiomatic level. The two properties of resource monotonicity and population monotonicity are discussed in section 2.5 for the problem of dividing fairly a single divisible commodity. Here resource monotonicity turns out to be overly demanding; example 7.12. Population monotonicity, on the other hand, drives a wedge between our two solutions: the EE solution meets this property, but the CEEI solution does not; exercise 6.4.

References

Abdulkadiroglu, A., and T. Sönmez. 1998. Random serial dictatorship and the core from random endowments in house allocation problems. *Econometrica* 66: 689–701.

Alkan, A., G. Demange, and D. Gale. 1991. Fair allocation of indivisible goods and criteria of justice. *Econometrica* 59: 1023–39.

Arrow, K. 1963. Rational choice functions and orderings. *Social Choice and Individual Values,* 2nd ed., 1st ed. 1951. New York: Wiley.

Arrow, K., and M. Intriligator, eds. 1982. *Handbook of Mathematical Economics,* vol. 2. Amsterdam: North-Holland.

Aumann, R. J. 1987. Game theory. In J. Eatwell, M. Milgate, and P. Newman, eds., *The New Palgrave,* vol. 2, London: Macmillan, pp. 460–82.

Aumann, R. J., and M. Maschler. 1985. Game theoretic analysis of a bankruptcy problem from the Talmud. *Journal of Economic Theory* 36: 195–213.

Axelrod, R. 1984. *The Evolution of Cooperation.* New York: Basic Books.

Banker, R. 1981. Equity consideration in traditional full cost allocation practices: An axiomatic perspective. In S. Moriarty, ed., *Joint Cost Allocations.* Norman: University of Oklahoma.

Barbera, S. 2001. An introduction to strategyproof social choice functions. *Social Choice and Welfare* 18(4): 619–53.

Baumol, W., J. Panzar, and R. Willig. 1982. *Contestable Markets and the Theory of Industry Structure.* New York: Harcourt, Brace, Jovanovitch.

Binmore, K. 1994. *Game Theory and the Social Contract,* vol. 1. Cambridge: MIT Press.

Black, D. 1948. On the rationale of group decision making. *Journal of Political Economy* 56: 23–34.

Black, D. 1958. *The Theory of Committes and Elections.* Cambridge: Cambridge University Press.

Blackorby, C., D. Primont, and R. Russell. 1978. *Duality, Separability and Functional Structure.* Amsterdam: North-Holland.

Bogomolnaia, A., and H. Moulin. 2001. A new solution to the random assignment problem. *Journal of Economic Theory* 100: 295–328.

Bossert, W., and J. Weymark. 1996. Utility in social choice. In S. Barbera, P. Hammond, and C. Seidl, eds., *Handbook of Utility Theory.* Dordrecht: Kluwer.

Brams, S. 1993. Voting procedures. In R. J. Aumann and S. Hart, eds., *The Handbook of Game Theory with Economic Applications,* vol. 2. Amsterdam: North-Holland.

Brams, S., and P. Fishburn. 2000. Fair division of indivisible items between two people with identical preferences. *Social Choice and Welfare* 17: 247–67.

Brams, S., and P. Fishburn. 2002. Voting procedures. In K. Arrow, A. Sen, and K. Suzumura, eds., *Handbook of Social Choice and Welfare,* vol. 1. Amsterdam: North-Holland.

Brams, S., and A. Taylor. 1996. *Fair Division.* Cambridge: Cambridge University Press.

Brams, S., and A. Taylor. 1999. *The Win–Win Solution.* New York: Norton.

Buchanan, J., and G. Tullock. 1962. *The Calculus of Consent.* Ann Arbor: University of Michigan Press.

Chun, Y. 1989. A new axiomatization of the Shapley value. *Games and Economic Behavior* 1: 119–30.

Cohen, G. A. 1995. *Self-ownership, Freedom and Equality.* Cambridge: Cambridge University Press.

Cook, K., and K. Hegtvedt. 1983. Distribution justice, equity and equality. *Annual Reviews of Sociology* 9: 217–41.

Crès, H., and H. Moulin. 1998. Commons with increasing marginal costs: Random priority versus average cost. *International Economic Review,* forthcoming.

Dasgupta, P., and G. Heal. 1979. *Economic Theory and Exhaustible Resources.* Cambridge: Cambridge University Press.

D'Aspremont, C., and L. Gevers. 1977. Equity and the informational basis of collective choice. *Review of Economic Studies* 44(2): 199–209.

Debreu, G. 1960. Topological methods in cardinal utility theory. In K. Arrow, S. Karlin, and P. Suppes, eds., *Mathematical Methods in the Social Sciences*. Stanford: Stanford University Press.

Debreu, G., and H. Scarf. 1963. A limit theorem on the core of the economy. *International Economic Review* 4: 235–46.

Demers, A., S. Keshav, and S. Shenker. 1990. Analysis and simulation of a fair queuing algorithm. *Internet-Working: Research and Experience* 1: 3–26.

Deutsch, M. 1975. Equity, equality and need: What determines which value will be used as the basis of distributive justice? *Journal of Social Issues* 3(31): 137–49.

Dworkin, R. 1981. What is equality? Part 2: Equality of resources. *Philosophy and Public Affairs* 10: 283–345.

Elster, J. 1992. *Local Justice*. New York: Russell Sage.

Felsenthal, D. S., and M. Machover. 1998. *The Measurement of Voting Power*. London: Edwar Elgar.

Fleurbaey, M. 1996. *Théories économiques de la justice*. Paris: Economica.

Foley, D. 1967. Resource allocation and the public sector. *Yale Economic Essays* 7(1): 45–98.

Gibbard, A. 1973. Manipulation of voting schemes: A general result. *Econometrica* 45: 665–82.

Gorman, W. M. 1968. The structure of utility functions. *Review of Economic Studies* 35: 367–90.

Grandmont, J. M. 1978. Intermediate preferences and the majority rule. *Econometrica* 46: 317–30.

Gul, F. 1989. Bargaining foundations of the Shapley value. *Econometrica* 57: 81–95.

Hardin, G. 1968. The tragedy of the commons. *Science* 162: 1243–48.

Harsanyi, J. C. 1955. Cardinal welfare, individualistic ethics, and interpersonal comparisons of utility. *Journal of Political Economy* 63: 309–21.

Hart, S., and A. Mas-Collel. 1989. Potential, value and consistency. *Econometrica* 57(3): 589–614.

Hart, S., and A. Mas-Collel. 1996. Bargaining and value. *Econometrica* 64: 357–80.

Hayek, F. A. 1976. *The Mirage of Social Justice*. London: Routledge and Kegan Paul.

Herrero, C., and A. Villar. 2001. The three musketeers: From classical solutions to bankruptcy problems. *Mathematical Social Sciences* 42(3): 307–28.

Hildebrand, W., and A. Kirman. 1974. *Introduction to Equilibrium Analysis*. Amsterdam: North-Holland.

Kalai, E. 1977. Proportional solutions to bargaining solutions: Interpersonal utility comparisons. *Econometrica* 45(77): 1623–30.

Kalai, E., and M. Smorodinsky. 1975. Other solutions to Nash's bargaining problem. *Econometrica* 43(3): 513–18.

Kaminski, M. 2000. Hydraulic rationing. *Mathematical Social Sciences* 40: 131–55.

Kelly, J. S. 1978. *Arrow Impossibility Theorems*. New York: Academic Press.

Khmelnitskaya, A. 1999. Marginalist and efficient values for TU games. *Mathematical Social Sciences* 38(1): 45–54.

Kolm, S. C. 1972. *Justice et equité*. Paris: CNRS.

Kolm, S. C. 1996. *Modern Theories of Justice*. Cambridge: MIT Press.

Littlechild, S. C., and G. Owen. 1973. A simple expression for the Shapley value in a special case. *Management Science* 20: 370–72.

Locke, J. [1690] 1960. *Second Treatise of Government*. Cambridge: Cambridge University Press.

Loehman, E., and A. Whinston. 1974. An axiomatic approach to cost allocation for public investment. *Public Finance Quarterly* 2: 236–51.

McLean, I., and A. Urken. 1995. *Classics of Social Choice*. Ann Arbor: University of Michigan Press.

Mas-Collel, A., M. Whinston, and J. Green. 1995. *Microeconomic Theory*. New York: Oxford University Press.

Mirlees, J. 1974. Notes on welfare economics, information and uncertainty. In T. Balch, D. McFadden, and S. Wu, eds., *Essays on Economic Behavior under Uncertainty*. Amsterdam: North-Holland.

Moore, J. 1993. Implementation in environments with complete information. In J.-J. Laffont, ed., *Advances in Economic Theory*. Cambridge: Cambridge University Press.

Moulin, H. 1980. On strategy-proofness and single peakedness. *Public Choice* 35: 437–55.

Moulin, H. 1987. Equal or proportional division of a surplus, and other methods. *International Journal of Game Theory* 16(3): 161–86.

Moulin, H. 1988. *Axioms of Cooperative Decision Making*. Cambridge: Cambridge University Press.

Moulin, H. 1995. *Cooperative Micro-economics: A Game Theoretic Introduction*. Princeton: Princeton University Press.

Moulin, H. 2002. Axiomatic cost and surplus sharing. In K. Arrow, A. Sen, and K. Suzumura, eds., *Handbook of Social Choice and Welfare*. Amsterdam: Elsevier, ch. 6.

Moulin, H. 2001b. Normative microeconomics and the social contract. Third Taesung Kim Memorial Lecture. University of Seoul, South Korea.

Moulin, H. 2001c. Three solutions to a simple commons problem. *Journal of Economics,* Seoul, forthcoming.

Myerson, R. B. 1977. Graphs and cooperation in games. *Mathematics of Operations Research* 2: 225–29.

Nash, J. 1950. The bargaining problem. *Econometrica* 28: 155–62.

Nozick, R. 1974. *Anarchy, State and Utopia*. New York: Basic Books.

Ordershook, P. C. 1986. *Game Theory and Political Theory*. Cambridge: Cambridge University Press.

O'Neill, B. 1982. A problem of rights arbitration in the Talmud. *Mathematical Social Sciences* 2: 345–71.

Ostrom, E. 1991. *Governing the Commons*. Cambridge: Cambridge University Press.

Owen, G. 1982. *Game Theory,* 2nd ed. New York: Academic Press.

Pazner, E., and D. Schmeidler. 1978. Egalitarian-equivalent allocations: A new concept of economic equity. *Quarterly Journal of Economics* 92: 671–87.

Peremans, W., and T. Storken. 1996. Strategyproof locations of public bads. Mimeo. Limburg University.

Perez-Castrillo, D., and D. Wettstein. 2001. Bidding for the surplus: An non-cooperative approach to the Shapley value. *Journal of Economic Theory,* forthcoming.

Peters, H. 1992. *Axiomatic Bargaining Game Theory*. Dordrecht: Kluwer Academic.

Rabinovitch, N. 1973. *Probability and Statistical Inference in Medieval Jewish Literature*. Toronto: University of Toronto Press.

Rawls, J. 1971. *A Theory of Justice*. Cambridge: Harvard University Press.

Rawls, J. 1988. Social unity and primary goods. In A. Sen and B. Williams, eds., *Utilitarianism and Beyond*. Cambridge: Cambridge University Press.

Rescher, N. 1966. *Distributive Justice*. Indianapolis: Bobbs-Merill.

Roberts, K. 1977. Voting over income tax schedules. *Journal of Public Economics* 8: 329–40.

Roberts, K. 1980a. Possibility theorems with interpersonal comparable welfare levels. *Review of Economic Studies* 47: 409–20.

Roberts, K. 1980b. Interpersonal comparability and social choice theory. *Review of Economic Studies* 47: 421–39.

Robertson, J., and W. Webb. 1998. *Cake-Cutting Algorithms*. Natick, MA: AK Peters.

Roemer, J. 1996. *Theories of Distributive Justice*. Cambridge: Harvard University Press.

Roemer, J. 1998. *Equality of Opportunity*. Cambridge: Harvard University Press.

Roth, A. 1979. *Axiomatic Models of Bargaining*. Berlin: Springer.

Roth, A., ed. 1988. *The Shapley Value: Essays in Honor of Lloyd Shapley*. New York: Cambridge University Press, 1988.

Samuelson, P. 1947. *Foundations of Economic Analysis*. Cambridge: Harvard University Press.

Satterthwaite, M. 1975. Strategyproofness and Arrow's conditions: Existence and correspondence theorems for voting procedures and social choice functions. *Journal of Economic Theory* 10: 187–217.

Schmeidler, D. 1969. The nucleolus of a characteristic function game. *SIAM Journal of Applied Mathematics* 17: 1163–70.

Sen, A. K. 1970. *Collective Choice and Social Welfare*. San Francisco: Holden Day.

Sen, A. K. 1977. On weights and measures: Informational constraints in social welfare analysis. *Econometrica* 45(7): 1539–72.

Sen, A. K. 1985. *Commodities and Capabilities*. Amsterdam: North-Holland.

Shapley, L. S. 1953. A value for *N*-person games. In H. W. Kuhn and W. Tucker, eds., *Contributions to the Theory of Games II*. Princeton: Princeton University Press.

Shapley, L. S. 1971. Cores of convex games. *International Journal of Game Theory* 1: 11–26.

Shapley, L. S., and H. Scarf. 1974. On cores and indivisibility. *Journal of Mathematical Economics* 1: 23–28.

Sharkey, W. 1982. *The Theory of Natural Monopoly*. Cambridge: Cambridge University Press.

Sharkey, W. 1995. Networks models in economics. In M. O. Ball et al., eds., *Network Routing*. Amsterdam: Elsevier.

Shenker, S. 1995. Making greed work in networks: A game theoretic analysis of switch service disciplines. *Transactions on Networking* 3: 819–31.

Shubik, M. 1962. Incentives, decentralized controls, the assignment of joint costs and internal pricing. *Management Science* 8(3): 325–43.

Smith, J. 1973. Aggregation of preferences with variable electorate. *Econometrica* 41(6): 1027–41.

Sprumont, Y. 1991. The division problem with single-peaked preferences: A characterization of the uniform allocation rule. *Econometrica* 59(2): 509–20.

Sprumont, Y. 1995. Strategyproof collective choice in economic and political environments. *Canadian Journal of Economics* 28: 68–107.

Straffin, P. D. 1980. *Topics in the Theory of Voting*. Boston: Birkhaüser.

Telser, L. G. 1988. *Theories of Competition*. Amsterdam: North-Holland.

Thomas, A. 1980. *A Behavioral Analysis of Joint Cost Allocation and Transfer Pricing*. Champaign, IL: Stipes Publishing.

Thomson, W. 1999. *Bargaining Theory: The Axiomatic Approach*. New York: Academic Press.

Thomson, W., and H. Varian. 1985. Theories of justice based on symmetry. In L. Hurwicz, D. Schmeidler, and H. Sonnenschein, eds., *Social Goals and Social Organization*. Cambridge: Cambridge University Press.

Varian, H. 1974. Equity, envy and efficiency. *Journal of Economic Theory* 29(2): 217–44.

Weber, R. J. 1988. Probabilistic values for games. In A. Roth, ed., *The Shapley Value*. Cambridge: Cambridge University Press.

Winslow, G. 1982. *Triage and Justice*. Berkeley: University of California Press.

Yaari, M., and M. Bar-Hillel. 1984. On dividing justly. *Social Choice and Welfare* 1: 1–24.

Young, H. P. 1974. An axiomatization of Borda's rule. *Journal of Economic Theory* 9: 43–52.

Young, H. P. 1985. Monotonic solutions of cooperative games. *International Journal of Game Theory* 14(2): 65–72.

Young, H. P. 1987. On dividing an amount according to individual claims or liabilities. *Mathematics of Operations Research* 12: 397–414.

Young, H. P. 1990. Progressive taxation and equal sacrifice. *American Economic Review* 80(1): 253–66.

Young, H. P. 1994. *Equity, in Theory and Practice*. Princeton: Princeton University Press.

Index